The Longman Companion to

The Middle East since 1914

Longman Companions to History

General Editors: Chris Cook and John Stevenson

Now available:

The Longman Companion to

The Middle East
since 1914
Second edition

Ritchie Ovendale

Longman
London and New York

Addison Wesley Longman Limited
Edinburgh Gate,
Harlow, Essex CM20 2JE, England
and Associated Companies throughout the world.

*Published in the United States of America
by Longman Publishing, New York*

First Published 1992
Second edition 1998

0582 31555 7 PPR

Visit Addison Wesley Longman on the world wide web at http://www.awl-he.com

British Library Cataloguing in Publication Data
A catalogue record for this book is
available from the British Library

Library of Congress Cataloging in Publication Data

Ovendale, Ritchie.
   The Longman companion to the Middle East since 1914 / Ritchie
Ovendale. – 2nd ed.
     p.   cm. – (Longman companions to history)
     Includes bibliographical references (p.   ) and index.
     ISBN 0-582-31555-7 (pbk.)
     1. Middle East–History–20th century–Handbooks, manuals, etc.
I. Title. II. Series.
DS62.4.094   1998
956.04–dc21   98-14432
                                                                    CIP

Set by 7

Produced through Longman Malaysia, VVP

Contents

List of maps

Acknowledgements

I should like to thank my former colleagues Jane Davis, Clive Jones, Roland Maddock, and James Piscatori for guiding me to sources and loaning me material. Mrs Chris. Chadwick of the Hugh Owen Library, University College of Wales, Aberystwyth, gave me an hour of her expertise and made the whole project seem feasible. I am grateful to the staff of the Hugh Owen Library, including Mr A.M.E. Davies, Mrs Elizabeth Howells, Peter James and Ron Job, for their cheerful assistance. Moorhead Wright, Lincoln Ball, Julian Eastwood and Alisdair MacKenzie helped me to operate a computer. Ian Tompkins offered advice on religions and sects.

The publishers would like to thank the following for permission to reproduce copyright material: the British Petroleum Company Plc for tables 1, 2, 3 and 4 from *BP Statistical Review of World Energy* (1997); Keesing's Worldwide Ltd for table 6 from *Keesing's Record of World Events* (Keesing's Worldwide LLC), Vol. 42, 1996, pp. R156, R159.

Preface

I have used *The Concise Oxford Dictionary of Current English*, 8th edition (1990), as a guide to the form of Arab words incorporated into English. In its form of transliteration the *Concise Oxford* omits diacritical marks (those marks used to indicate different sounds or values of a letter). The following are examples of the forms I have chosen to use: Alawites, Ali, Bahais, Bedouin, Druze, fedayeen, Hadith, hajj, hegira, intifada, Ismailis, jihad, Kaaba, Koran, *mujtahids, peshmerga, riba, Salat,* Sanussis, *Sayyids, Shahada,* shariah, Sherifs, Shiite (Shias), Sunna, ulema, Wahhabis, Zeidis. To make an Arabic noun plural I have added an 's' to the singular form. The common spellings of place names have been used. Examples are: Bahrain, Bekaa, Hejaz, Jedda, Kuwait, Mecca, Nejd, Sharm el-Sheikh, Shatila, Shtaura (not Bahrayn, Biqa (Beka'a), Hedjaz, Jeddah, Kuwayt, Mekka, Najd, Sharm al-Sheikh, Chatila, Shtoura). I have also followed the convention of assigning a geographic connotation only to the lands occupied by Israel after the Six Day War: 'Gaza Strip' and 'occupied territories'.

In transliterating Arab names I have retained the definite article ('al-', 'el-', or 'Al') where appropriate. Usually the form 'al-' is used. In the case of Saudi Arabia and the Gulf states, however, I have observed the convention of using the form 'Al' to denote the ruling dynasty. Also where an Arab author has written in English I have adopted his or her own spellings of the name (for example Anwar el-Sadat not Anwar al-Sadat). The elision system has been avoided as it requires some knowledge of Arabic to make sense of it. Some examples are: Jabir al-Ahmad Al Sabah, Nuri al-Said, Abdullah Al Thani, (not Jabir al-Ahmad as-Sabah, Nuri as-Said, Abdullah ath-Thani). Common practice in Arabic names is to use 'ibn' (or 'bin') to denote 'son of'. In the interests of consistency I have used 'ibn' in this text. 'Abu' indicates 'father of'. Titles generally have been omitted from the lists of rulers, Prime Ministers and Foreign Ministers. Where titles appear in the text 'sherif' and '*sayyid*' are used to designate descendants of the Prophet. Among the titles for religious officials in the Shiite tradition 'Ayatollah' means 'sign of

Allah' and represents the highest officials. 'Pasha' was the title placed after the name of a Turkish officer of high rank in the Ottoman empire; it remained in use in Egypt.

Chronologies

1. The emergence of modern nation states in the Middle East

1820 Britain concludes a General Treaty of Peace for suppressing piracy and slave traffic with the Arab tribes of the Persian Gulf. The signatories include the sheikhs of Ras al-Khaimah, Sharjah, Umm al-Qaiwain, Ajman and Fujairah. Bahrain admitted to treaty a month later. Treaty follows attacks by seafaring Arab tribes on British-flagged ships, British expeditions against pirates in 1806, 1809, and British attacks on the pirate headquarters at Ras al-Khaimah in 1818. First of series of treaties that elaborates the relationship between Britain and the sheikhdoms over the next hundred years. A British squadron is stationed at Ras al-Khaimah.

1839 Captain Stafford Haines of the Indian Navy captures Aden on 16 January. This follows the plunder in 1837 of an Indian ship, flying the British flag, wrecked near Aden. Under the subsequent peace treaty the Sultan of Lahej, in return for an annual payment, agrees to Aden becoming part of the British Empire administered from Bombay. Aden's strategic importance increases later, with the opening of the Suez Canal, and again when oil replaces coal as the major fuel in the 20th century. Aden is also important as a fuelling station, as well as being a source of fresh water.

1850s–1860s Growing Arab national consciousness. With a literary revival in Syria, newly established local societies begin to study Arab history, literature and culture of the golden age of the Arab Empire which is identified with the Abbasid dynasty and lasted for about five hundred years from around 750 until the sack of Baghdad by a Mongol general in 1258. This has political overtones. With a meeting of the Syrian Scientific Society the Arab national movement possibly uttered its first cry: a poem was read praising the achievements of the Arab race, the splendours of Arab literature and inciting the Arabs to go to their own past for inspiration.

1860 Civil war in the area of Mount Lebanon between Druze landlords and Maronite Catholic tenants. Massacre of thousands of Maronites leads to persecution in other parts of Syria, where the

Ottomans had ended Egyptian rule in 1840. A conference of European powers meeting in Beirut decides to create the autonomous province (*sanjak*) of Mount Lebanon, to be ruled by a Christian governor chosen by the Turkish Sultan from outside Lebanon and a Maronite-dominated council formed on a religious (confessional) basis. Mount Lebanon to be protected by Britain, France, Russia, Prussia, Austria and Italy. France becomes the main patron of Catholics in the Arab Levant.

1861 Following political claims by Iran (Persia) and Turkey to Bahrain, a group of islands in the Persian Gulf, the Sheikh of Bahrain undertakes not to prosecute war, piracy and slavery by sea in return for British support against aggression.

1866 Syrian Protestant College founded, under American auspices (later American University of Beirut), and helps to stimulate Arab nationalist sentiment by training new Arab élites.

1869 Suez Canal opened. The ruler of Egypt, Said, had granted a concession to a French engineer, Ferdinand de Lesseps, to build the canal in 1854, and work on it had started in 1859.

1880, 1892 Britain assumes responsibility for Bahrain's external affairs; Bahrain becomes seat of British Resident in Gulf.

1881 Against the background of the rise of a nationalist outlook in Egypt, particularly among the young officers in the army who resent the Turkish overlordship, along with liberal reformers, a group of Egyptian army officers led by Arabi Pasha forces the Khedive, Tawfiq, (the title 'Khedive' for the viceroy of Egypt had been given to Ismail Pasha by the Turkish government in 1867 and lasted until 1914) to form a new ministry. Britain and France send a joint note proclaiming their resolve to maintain the Khedive.

1882 After the appointment of Arabi as Minister of War, Britain and France send naval squadrons to Alexandria in May. Egyptian opinion inflamed and Europeans killed in riots in Alexandria in June. Germany and Turkey refuse to send expeditionary force and French Chamber of Deputies disallows French intervention. The French fleet withdrawn in July after a British ultimatum to Arabi to stop building fortifications at Alexandria. After British bombardment Arabi withdraws forces from Alexandria and the Khedive places himself under British protection. A British expeditionary force lands and on 22 September routs Arabi's troops at Tel el-Kebir. British troops occupy Cairo and the Khedive's authority is restored.

4

1883 Unable to incorporate Egypt into the British Empire lest that result in a European war, a revolt in the Sudan and the hostility of France makes a withdrawal of British troops impossible, so British policy becomes based on the report of Lord Dufferin: the Egyptians have to be persuaded that Britain wants to help them to govern themselves 'under the uncompromising aegis of British friendship'. This relationship is managed by Evelyn Baring (later Lord Cromer) who arrives with the title of British Agent and Consul-General in Egypt and stays until 1907.

c. **1889** Dissatisfaction with despotism of the Turkish Sultan Abdul Hamid II, who set back the educational, political and economic reforms instituted by his predecessors earlier in the century, increases Arab national awareness. Young Turk movement formed. This movement, the successor to the Young Ottomans (a revolutionary secret society formed in 1865 and inspired by a literary revival), spreads rapidly among the students in law, medical and military colleges in Istanbul and the provinces of the Ottoman Empire.

1892 Rulers of emirates along the Trucial Coast in Central and Southern Arabia start to conduct all external affairs through the British government.

1895 Group of Young Turks found a secret society called the Committee of Union and Progress which emphasizes the ideal of unity and equality of all races and creeds within the Ottoman Empire. Contacts made with Turkish exiles in Paris; Committee also attracts support of Freemasons and Jews.

1898 Anglo–Egyptian condominium (joint control) established over Sudan after defeat of the Mahdi's successor, the Caliph Abdallahi. (Mahdi: meaning 'the guided one'. The Mahdi had led the Sudanese forces, largely made up of national-religious tribesmen against the Egyptians and the British.)

1899 Treaty signed between Mubarak, the Sheikh of Kuwait, and Britain, recognizes Kuwait as an independent state under British protection. Sheikh wants British protection as he fears a Turkish occupation. Britain wants to thwart German plan to extend Berlin–Istanbul–Baghdad railway to Kuwait. Mubarak agrees not to cede, mortgage or otherwise dispose of his territories to anyone except the British government, nor to enter into any relationship with a foreign government other than the British without British consent.

1903 Germany secures concession for building of Berlin–Istanbul–Baghdad Railway.

1904 April: Britain agrees to recognize the pre-eminence of French interests in Morocco in return for a reciprocal recognition of British interests in Egypt.

1907 Britain and Russia divide Persia (Iran) into spheres of influence.

1908 Shocked by Abd al-Hamid II's mismanagement of Macedonia, the last large Ottoman province in Europe, and alarmed by reports that Edward VII of Britain and Tsar Nicholas of Russia were planning to partition Turkey, important army officers including Mustafa Kemal (later Atatürk) join the Young Turks and bring with them units of the Macedonian army. They start a rebellion in Salonika, the Macedonian capital, and it spreads quickly. Abd al-Hamid II restores constitutional rule and parliamentary government. The Young Turks proclaim the new order: 'There are no longer Bulgars, Greeks, Romanians, Jews, Muslims; under the same sky we are all equal, we glory in being Ottomans.' The Arabs hope that this means the end of Turkish domination. But Arab expectations of autonomous provinces enabling development of Arab culture are frustrated. Electoral system means Turks are dominant in parliament, though Arabic-speaking Ottoman citizens outnumber Turks in Ottoman Empire.

1909 Abdul Hamid II abdicates after Young Turks send troops to Istanbul to restore order following mutiny of Istanbul garrison.

1911 Italy starts a war against Turkey and secures Libya and the Dodecanese islands.

1912 Greece, Serbia and Bulgaria, fearing Young Turks might try to recover Balkans, form a secret alliance and in October launch a war against Turkey, capturing Salonika and Western Thrace by December.

1913 February: after French decision to consolidate its influence in Syria and Lebanon, Quai d'Orsay decides to lay groundwork for this through the Berlin–Istanbul–Baghdad railway negotiations and makes provision for additional French investment in railway and harbour developments in Syria and the expansion of other enterprises. Syrian Arabs disliked the French presence and they had already formed a Reform Committee for Beirut, unfriendly to the

French, and determined to press for decentralization of the Ottoman Empire.

March: conscious of Arab grievances through information from its agents in Cairo, Beirut, and Damascus, French government allows Maronite literary figure, Shukri Ghanim, to arrange the First Arab National Congress in Paris. Ghanim loses control to Nadra Mutran who was thought to oppose the idea of a French protectorate over Syria. French lose control of conference but hope to persuade delegates to 'abandon the chimerical dream of Arab autonomy'.

21 June: Arab National Congress forwards resolution to Sir Edward Grey, the British Foreign Secretary, demanding that the Arabs should be able to exercise their political rights and play an effective role in the administration of the Ottoman Empire; decentralized governments should be established in the Arab provinces.

1914 July: Kaiser of Germany prepares for war and subversion against Britain in the Middle East: assures ruler of Afghanistan of his desire for the Muslim nations to be independent, and of the continuation of the common interests of Germany and the Muslims after the war; General Liman von Sanders, the inspector-general of the Ottoman army and a German is commanded to stay on in Constantinople to promote feeling against Britain; a team is formed under Max von Oppenheim to arrange subversion in Muslim countries and it works in close alliance with German Zionists.

5 November: after commandeering two Turkish battleships in British shipyards, Britain blockades the Dardanelles, and demands that Turkey affirms its neutrality by expelling the German mission, and following British shelling of Turkish ports at entrance to Dardanelles on 3 November, Turkey declares war on the Allies.

Germany makes contact with Hussein, the Sherif of Mecca, who as custodian of the holy places and a lineal descendant of Muhammad is thought to have great influence. Hussein agrees to aid German propaganda, and also to other unspecified operations in the area he controls and is paid by the Germans until at least June 1915. As a reinsurance policy the Germans also contact Ibn Saud, who had recaptured the Saudi capital Riyadh in 1902 and after his conquests of the Nejd and eastern Arabia had been recognized by Britain as 'Sultan of Nejd and its Dependencies', but could not expand further there as the Persian Gulf coast was under British exclusive influence.

An Ottoman–British agreement defines the borders between Kuwait, Nejd and Iraq. Britain had appointed a political agent to

Kuwait in 1904 and after negotiations with Turkey starting in 1909 Britain, in effect, secured the autonomy of Kuwait. By 1914 Kuwait is referred to as being 'under British protection' in communications with the Ottoman Empire.

18 December: Egypt, nominally a province of the Ottoman Empire, is declared a British protectorate. Since the British occupation of 1882, Egypt had become a vital link in Britain's imperial network and could not be abandoned. Britain assumes responsibility for the defence of the Suez Canal. A combination of British and Egyptian officials continues to administer Sudan.

1915 Ibn Saud – who rules over al-Hasa, the coastal region lying beneath Kuwait on the Persian Gulf, and most of the Nejd, the large area in the centre of the Arabian peninsula – concludes an anti-Turkish treaty with Britain through the Viceroy of India.

8 April: H.H. Asquith, the British Prime Minister, sets up an interdepartmental committee, the Committee on Asiatic Turkey, chaired by Sir Maurice de Bunsen, to discuss British desiderata. One member, Mark Sykes, devises a scheme of devolution, dividing the Ottoman Empire into five provinces with Britain able to secure influence in the Asian ones. Committee finally recommends this scheme on 30 June: British desiderata include the fulfilment of the pledges already given to the Gulf and the Arab sheikhs, and generally, of the assurances to the Sherif of Mecca and the Arabs. Palestine is considered a special case which could eventually be settled with the other powers: a self-determining Palestinian people could prove to be a neutral guardian of the holy places in Jerusalem.

14 July: Hussein, Sherif of Mecca, sends message to Britain explaining that the Arabs have decided to regain their freedom and hope for British assistance. Emphasizing the identity of British and Arab interests, the Sherif proposes defensive and conditionally offensive alliance. Terms included British 'recognition' or 'acknowledgement' (depending on translation) of the independence of the Arab countries from Mersina and along the latitude of 37 degrees to the Persian frontier in the north, in the east by the Gulf of Basra, on the south by the Indian Ocean with the exception of Aden, and on the west by the Red Sea and the Mediterranean up to Mersina.

24 October: McMahon (High Commissioner of Egypt), in a cautious and perhaps deliberately obscure letter, informs Hussein that the two districts of Mersina and Alexandretta, and portions of Syria to the west of the districts of Damascus, Homs, Hama and Aleppo could not be said to be purely Arab and should not be prejudiced, and should therefore be excluded. Britain's existing treaties with

Arab chiefs could not be prejudiced, and Britain was not free to act in those areas which would harm the interests of its ally, France. The Arabs should recognize Britain's established position in the *vilayets* (provinces) of Baghdad and Basra which necessitated special administrative arrangements. It is understood that the Arabs would employ only British advisers.

5 November: Hussein accepts British proposals with regard to Mersina and Alexandretta, but argues about Beirut and Aleppo, as well as Baghdad and Basra.

13 December: McMahon writes to Hussein that as French interests involved, reservations about Aleppo and Beirut require further consideration.

21 December: French willing to accommodate Arabs in case they go over to enemy. Propose that the envisaged Arab 'confederation' be divided into British and French commercial spheres of influence.

1916 18 February: Hussein notes that required understanding and intimacy has been attained.

26 April: agreement between Britain, France and Russia about the partition of Asiatic Turkey. In an independent Arab 'confederation', Britain to have a sphere of influence in Mesopotamia, and in Syria the ports of Haifa and Acre. France to have a sphere of influence over the coastal strip of Syria, the Adana *vilayet*, Cilicia and Southern Kurdistan, with Kharput. Russia to acquire Armenia and part of Kurdistan and northern Anatolia.

9 May: Sykes–Picot agreement between Britain and France. Details of agreement kept secret and not divulged to the Arabs. Plan envisaged an Arab confederation in which France would have economic priority in the north and Britain in the south. France, in an area along the Syrian coast, and Britain at the head of the Persian Gulf, could establish such direct or indirect administrations as they desired. Britain took the ports of Haifa and Acre in Palestine, and Mosul fell within the French region of economic priority as did Homs, Hama, Aleppo and Damascus.

June: Hussein raises the Arab revolt to enable Arabs to regain their freedom from their Turkish rulers. By the end of September forces of Arab tribesmen have captured Mecca, Jedda and Taif, but Medina remains in Turkish control. The momentum of the revolt seems uncertain.

1916–17 Campaign in Arabia led by General Edmund Allenby, in which Arab army participates and T.E. Lawrence becomes a legend, culminates in Allenby's entry into Jerusalem on 11 December 1917.

9

1916: Abdullah ibn Qasim Al Thani, *de facto* ruler of Qatar on the Persian Gulf, signs an agreement with Britain for British protection and Britain taking over responsibility for Qatar's external affairs.

1917 2 November: Balfour Declaration which takes the form of a letter from Arthur James Balfour, the Secretary of State for Foreign Affairs, to Lord Rothschild who is regarded as the head of the Jewish community in Britain. Letter says that Britain favours establishment in Palestine of a national home for the Jewish people, on the understanding that nothing should be done to prejudice the civil and religious rights of existing non-Jewish communities in Palestine. Balfour Declaration reflects the new status Zionism has achieved in British political thinking: not only is Palestine necessary for the security of empire, but it is thought that Zionist sympathies for the Allied cause could help the war effort.

November: Bolshevik government in Russia publicizes Sykes–Picot agreement and increases Arab alarm.

1918 8 January: Woodrow Wilson's Fourteen Points outlined to Congress. In making this speech Wilson outlined his vision of the postwar world. In particular the president shaped it as a reply to demands from the Russian leader, Vladimir Lenin, for revolution and an end to the war without territorial annexations on either side. Wilson's speech reflected liberal ideas of self-determination and nationality. The twelfth point states that the Turkish portions of the Ottoman Empire needed sovereignty, but the other nationalities in the Ottoman Empire 'should be assured an undoubted security of life and an unmolested opportunity of autonomous development'.

October: Allied forces take Damascus, Beirut and Aleppo from the Turks.

30 October: Turkey capitulates and signs Mudros armistice.

November–December: Allenby allows the troops led by Feisal, the commander of the Arab forces and the third son of the Sherif of Mecca, to take over administration in captured cities. After objections from France, Feisal's flag is lowered in Beirut. Iraq (Mesopotamia) becomes an Anglo–Indian administrative unit. Rest divided between France and Britain: France administers Syria (though for a while the main Syrian towns of the interior are under Feisal's authority and dependent for administration on an attachment of British officers, the British Occupied Enemy Territory Administration East) and the Lebanon coastal area from Tyre to Cilicia; Britain the territory that later forms the Palestine mandate. In the rest of

Arabia Ibn Saud, 'Sultan of Nejd and its Dependencies', attempts to extend his influence.

1919 6 February: Feisal pleads for the independence of all the Arab countries to the Council of Ten, the body made up of the leaders of the ten principal Allied governments, meeting in Paris to establish the terms for the peace at the end of the First World War.

David Lloyd George, the British Prime Minister, following disagreements with the French, decides that as France is not going to send commissioners to the Middle East to determine the wishes of the inhabitants as to a mandatory power, Britain cannot do so either. So two American commissioners, Charles R. Crane and H.C. King, go on their own. King–Crane commission finds opposition in Syria to any separation of Syria and Palestine, a preference for an American mandate and failing that a British one, but under no circumstances would Syrians peaceably accept France as the mandatory power.

An Anglo–Persian agreement is instigated by Lord Curzon, the British Secretary of State for Foreign Affairs, which while reaffirming Persia's (Iran's) independence and territorial integrity, provides for the appointment of British military and civil advisers. Iranian parliament, the Majlis, refuses to ratify the agreement and British advisers are sent home.

1920 March: an elected assembly in Damascus proclaims Feisal king of the sovereign independent state of Syria, which includes Palestine, Lebanon and Transjordan.

April: San Remo Conference. Leading allied powers decide the future of the Middle East. Form of mandates to be decided by Britain and France and then submitted to the League of Nations. The mandates for Syria and Lebanon are allotted to France, and those for Palestine and Mesopotamia to Britain.

Feisal urged by Arabs in Syria to declare war on French. Feisal allows attacks on French positions on the Lebanon border. On 14 July ultimatum from French Commander-in-Chief that French forces be allowed to occupy Aleppo, Homs, Hama and the Bekaa plain, which Feisal accepts. But France has already decided to seize Syria, and with 90,000 troops – mainly North African Arabs and black Senegalese – it takes Damascus on 25 July.

Agreement of Seeb between Sultan Taimur and 'the people of Oman': authority of sultan restored over both tribal interior and trading communities of coast, Muscat and Sohar. This settles

11

insurrection against Sultan of Oman, which followed the election in 1913 of a new Imam in the tribal interior.

June: after destruction of the Arab dream of a free Arab confederacy under Feisal with the announcement of the mandate system, a rebellion breaks out in Iraq. British authority there breaks down. Quelling the rebellion costs £40 million and 2,000 casualties. A.T. Wilson, head of civil administration, recommends that Feisal should head an Arab administration in Iraq.

1921 26 February: Soviet–Persian treaty signed by which the Soviet government remits Persian debts and gives up extra-territorial privileges for Russian nationals. Despite clause authorizing the sending of Russian troops into Persia if it were judged that Persia had become a base for military action against Russia, the Majlis ratifies treaty.

March: conference of British administrators and military officers in Middle East held at Cairo. Conference expresses unanimous view in favour of persuading Feisal to head a civilian administration in Iraq.

August: after referendum, Feisal confirmed as King of Iraq.

1922 16 September: League of Nations receives a British memorandum that the provisions of the mandate pertaining to Zionism (i.e. the mandate for Palestine) would not be applicable to Transjordan. This follows introduction of Article 25 into the terms of the League of Nations mandate for Palestine, which entitles Britain to 'postpone or withhold' application of certain unsuitable provisions, and to provide local administration for Transjordan. Zionist leaders had been informed of this on 25 April and had accepted the distinction between Palestine and Transjordan without comment. The British memorandum defines Transjordan as consisting of all territory lying to the east of a line drawn from a point 2 miles (3 km) west of Aqaba up the centre of the Wadi Araba, Dead Sea and Jordan river to its junction with the River Yarmuk, and thence up the centre of that river to the Syrian frontier. Council of League of Nations endorses the British memorandum.

December: Britain recognizes the independent constitutional government in Transjordan under the Emir Abdullah.

Britain pledges itself to intervene in the affairs of Egypt only if the imperial interest or that of foreign communities necessitate it. Egypt could conduct its own foreign policy provided it did not clash with Britain's international interests.

1923 Republic of Turkey proclaimed after Turkish War of Independence led by Mustafa Kemal Atatürk, in which Turkey drove Greece out of those areas – Thrace, Izmir and parts of the Aegean – which Greece had seized between 1918 and 1922.

1924 After murder in a Cairo street of Sir Lee Stack, the Governor-General of the Sudan and Commander-in-Chief (Sirdar) of the Egyptian army, Britain forces the evacuation of the Egyptian army from the Sudan, and establishes a new Sudan force under British control in 1925. Britain becomes predominant power in Sudan, which is in effect governed by a British civil service.

Ibn Saud and his Wahhabi tribesmen warriors invade the Hejaz and capture Mecca. This follows unsuccessful attempts by Britain to reconcile Ibn Saud with his rival and enemy, Hussein, the Sherif of Mecca. After the Turkish republic abolished the Islamic caliphate, Hussein declared his assumption of the title of 'Prince of the Faithful and Successor of the Prophet'. The Wahhabis were enraged and invaded the Hejaz. Hussein persuaded by the people of the Hejaz to abdicate in favour of his eldest son, Ali. Hussein went into exile to Cyprus. Ali held out in Jedda for a year but abdicates in December 1924. Ibn Saud becomes ruler of most of the Hejaz.

1925 Reza Khan, the former commander of the Persian Cossack brigade, establishes himself as Reza Shah in Iran (Persia). In October a new constituent assembly in Iran (Persia) vests the crown of the country in Reza Shah, whose heirs have the right of succession. Reza Khan takes the name Pahlavi for his dynasty and starts enforcing authority of central government.

French had divided their mandated area into four distinct units: a much enlarged Lebanon including Beirut and Tripoli; a Syrian republic; and the districts of Latakia and Jebel Druze. French could only hope for support from Christian Maronites. Syrian leaders had increasingly encouraged Muslims in Lebanon to ask for their attachment to Syria. With the arrest by the French of Druze notables protesting that a native governor be appointed, in July, a rebellion is declared by Sultan al-Atrash, a young notable who has close ties with Syrian nationalists in Damascus. On 23 August al-Atrash makes a proclamation in his capacity as 'president of the provisional national government', demanding complete independence for Syria, the evacuation of foreign forces and the establishment of a united Syrian Arab state 'from coast to the interior'. French bombard Damascus in October, and again in May 1926.

1926 A constitution drafted in Paris is imposed on Lebanon. It establishes the principle that seats in parliament and the Cabinet should be divided between the Christians and the Muslims, effectively giving the Christians a working majority. The offices of President and Prime Minister are also allocated on religious grounds.

8 January: after surrender of Medina and Jedda, Ibn Saud becomes King of Hejaz and Nejd, in effect most of the Arabian peninsula. This is acknowledged by Britain in the Treaty of Jedda in 1927.

1928 Britain signs a treaty with Transjordan under which a British Resident appointed by the High Commissioner for Palestine is to guide the Emir Abdullah on foreign relations, jurisdiction over foreigners, finance and related matters. Britain also provides advisers and a subsidy to Jordan.

1930 22 May: Constitution establishes a parliamentary republic in Syria. France retains control over foreign affairs and security. Constitution suspended between 1932 and 1937.

30 June: Anglo–Iraqi treaty formally confers independence on Iraq but binds Iraq to have 'full and frank consultations with Great Britain in all matters of foreign policy'.

1931 Captain John Bagot Glubb (Glubb Pasha) establishes Desert Patrol as a section of the army in Transjordan (the Arab Legion) to keep order in the desert. Using tribesmen to maintain security, Glubb wins their confidence and many later serve in regular forces of Transjordan.

1932 22 September: Ibn Saud takes title of King of Saudi Arabia.

3 October: under British sponsorship Iraq becomes a member of the League of Nations.

1933 8 September: death of King Feisal of Iraq. Heir, Ghazi, encourages factionalism. Some politicians later organize a tribal uprising which proves difficult to control, against their rivals who make up the government. Political parties do not develop and elections are controlled. Parliamentary democracy is not established and Iraq is increasingly ruled by incompetent and authoritarian cabinets.

1934 Independence of Yemen is confirmed by boundary settlements with Saudi Arabia at Taif, and with the British who controlled Aden.

1936 Anglo–Egyptian treaty negotiated between Sir Miles Lampson and Nahas Pasha, the Prime Minister of Egypt. In effect the treaty did not lessen Britain's power or prestige in Egypt. Although British occupation formally came to an end, British troops remained in the country, though provision was made for their gradual withdrawal to the Suez Canal Zone and Sinai, and a limit of 10,000 land forces and 400 air personnel. In the event of war Britain had the right of re-occupation and the unrestricted use of Egyptian roads, ports and airports. The Condominium Agreement of 1899 was reaffirmed, but Britain remained the predominant power with Egypt having only a share in the higher administrative and judicial posts of the Sudan government.

21 March: the official name of Persia becomes Iran.

9 September: treaty of friendship and alliance signed between France and Syria (ratified 26 December). French mandate to end within three years. Syria to be admitted to the League of Nations. Jebel Druze, Jebel Alawi, and Alexandretta to be included in the state with special status. Lebanon to maintain its individuality.

13 November: Franco–Lebanese treaty gives Lebanon considerable autonomy.

1937 British support ensures that the question of navigation rights on the Shatt al-Arab river between Iraq and Iran goes in Iraq's favour.

1938 Group of officers known as 'The Seven' secure power in Iraq for Nuri al-Said, Feisal's former chief of staff. Nuri, a pro-British civilian, dominates Iraq for twenty years.

1939 July: against background of publication of May 1939 White Paper limiting Jewish immigration into Palestine, Britain moves Middle East Reserve Brigade from Palestine to the Canal Zone.

September: on outbreak of war against Germany, Iraq breaks off relations with Germany. Turkey is neutral. Those areas of the former Ottoman Empire under British or French control are nonbelligerent but within the war zone. The Suez Canal and retention of India is of strategic and political importance to Britain. Protection of oil supplies from Iraq is also important. Egypt is Britain's Mediterranean base. The Allies regard the Middle East as secure.

1940 With fall of France, Syria and Lebanon come under control of Vichy government. Britain announces that it will not allow a German occupation of the two countries but the Vichy government orders the High Commission in Beirut to collaborate with the Axis powers.

1941 May: Germans capture Crete and British position in Mediterranean undermined. Pro-Axis Rashid Ali government in Iraq, which

15

had seized power in March against the background of German victories in France, crushed by Anglo–Indian troops. An armistice between the rival factions achieved under British supervision and Iraq works with Allies for rest of war.

June: Italy enters war on Germany's side. Britain fights Italian forces in Eritrea with British troops from the Sudan, and in Libya with British troops from Egypt.

8 June: Free French forces under General Charles de Gaulle and British troops launch a three-pronged invasion of Syria and Lebanon from Palestine after German aircraft sent to help Rashid Ali had been allowed to use Syrian airfields. Following six weeks fighting, armistice signed, and Vichy troops given choice of repatriation to Vichy France or joining Free French forces.

Following entry of Soviet Union into war, it is sensitive to activities of Nazi agents in Iran. When Iran refuses an Anglo–Soviet request to allow arms supplies to be sent across Iran to the Soviet Union, British and Soviet troops invade Iran on 25 August. Iranian troops can do little, and on 16 September Reza Shah abdicates and is succeeded by his son, Muhammad Reza Pahlavi.

16 September: Free French leaders approve proclamation of Syria as independent nation. Britain had agreed to help de Gaulle oust the Vichy regimes in the Levant on the understanding that France would recognize the independence of Syria and Lebanon. De Gaulle, however, is reluctant to give up the liberated countries and wants treaties based on the 1936 agreements with France which do not go as far as independence.

26 November: Lebanese government proclaims Lebanon as independent sovereign state.

1942 Nuri al-Said and Abdullah develop ideas of 'Greater Syria', i.e. the union of Transjordan, Syria, and Palestine, into the unification of the 'Fertile Crescent' which would be formed by the union of Transjordan, Palestine, Lebanon and Syria, and to include in the end Iraq and Saudi Arabia.

29 January: Britain and Soviet Union sign a treaty guaranteeing the independence of Iran.

4 February: in Egypt Sir Miles Lampson, the British Ambassador, surrounds King Farouk's palace with British tanks and forces him to appoint Nahas Pasha of the Wafd as leader. Farouk, surrounded by Italians and advised by his Prime Minister, Ali Maher, who had pro-Axis sympathies, had favoured a more neutral policy in Egypt as an insurance against an Axis victory. Lampson had secured the replacement of Maher. The Wafd had favoured co-operation with Britain at a time when Fascist influence was evident in Egypt with the Greenshirt organization, and the Muslim Brotherhood, a puritanical religious group, was threatening the authorities.

1943 Britain's position in Middle East enhanced with Italy's surrender. German threat of invasion of Middle East recedes. Those in Middle East who had hoped that an Axis victory would ensure the fulfilment of demands for independence disappointed. Most Middle Easterners still want to remove European domination and suzerainty.

In Lebanon major political factions, both Christian and Muslim, agree to a National Pact. Using the 1932 census, power is distributed along sectarian lines and ensures a Maronite presidency, a Sunni Muslim premiership, a speaker of the House (parliament) as a Shiite Muslim, and parliamentary seats divided between Christians and Muslims in a 6-to-5 ratio.

November: Lebanese government passes legislation which removes from the constitution all provisions considered to be inconsistent with the independence of Lebanon. French Delegate General arrests President and suspends constitution. Britain, the United States and the other Arab states support Lebanese demands.

22 December: France transfers all powers exercised under the terms of the mandate to the Lebanese and Syrian governments.

1945 February: Turkey declares war on Germany and Japan and joins United Nations.

26 February: Syria joins the United Nations.

March: the League of Arab States (Arab League) set up by Egypt, Lebanon, Iraq, Syria, Transjordan, Yemen and Saudi Arabia to encourage Arab unity and co-operation.

May–June: when France sends troops into Syria and Lebanon, those countries respond by breaking relations with France. Rioting follows and French shell Damascus. Churchill demands a French cease-fire in Syria and Lebanon from de Gaulle.

23 September: Egypt demands revision of Anglo–Egyptian treaty of 1936. Requests termination of British military occupation and the transfer of Sudan to Egyptian control.

13 December: France and Britain agree to evacuate troops from Syria. Evacuation completed by 15 April 1946.

1945–6 British and United States forces leave Iran, but Soviet Union attempts to establish client states in Azerbaijan and Kurdistan. After United Nations resolutions in March 1946, Soviet Union evacuates northern regions of Iran.

1946 10 March: Britain and France agree to evacuate Lebanon. Evacuation completed by 31 August.

22 March: Britain recognizes independence of Transjordan and enters into an alliance with the new state.

9 May: after discussions between Lord Stansgate, the British Minister for Air, and Ismail Sidki, the Egyptian Prime Minister, Britain announces that it is willing to withdraw its military forces from Egypt.

25 May: Emir Abdullah proclaimed King of Transjordan. Transjordan's admission to the United Nations vetoed by the Soviet Union.

1947 25 January: Britain informs Egypt that Sudan is to be prepared for self-government.

26 January: following breakdown of negotiations over the revision of Anglo–Egyptian treaty of 1936 on the issue of Sudan, Egypt refers the question to the United Nations. Laid before the Security Council on 5 August but no decision taken.

12 March: President Truman announces a programme of American economic and military aid to Turkey.

14 April: treaty of alliance signed between Iraq and Transjordan.

November: following terrorist outrages in the Palestine mandate, disillusionment with an American Palestine policy dictated by domestic politics that was leading to the deaths of British soldiers in the mandate, the British decide to refer the matter to the United Nations. The subsequent report of the United Nations Special Commission on Palestine leads to United Nations decision to partition Palestine into separate Arab and Zionist states.

1948 15 January: Treaty of Portsmouth signed between Britain and an Iraqi delegation. This followed informal and secret talks with the regent and government of Iraq about the revision of the Anglo–Iraqi treaty of alliance of 1930. To avoid demands for the evacuation of two British air bases in Iraq, Britain negotiated on the principle of sharing the bases, and a Joint Defence Board to co-ordinate defence plans. With the news of the treaty there was a political outburst in Iraq, and the regent had to repudiate the treaty within a week of its being signed.

15 March: new Anglo–Jordanian treaty is signed which gives appearance of an arrangement between equals. A joint defence board is established, responsible for external and strategic planning.

14 May: David Ben-Gurion proclaims the establishment of a Jewish state in Palestine, to be called Israel. Despite American pressure,

Britain had refused to stay on in the mandate. London had told the American Secretary of State, George Marshall, that there was overwhelming popular demand in Britain to get the boys back home from Palestine: the long experience of being shot at by both sides and being vilified by Zionists and by some countries had 'so calloused that British conscience that it is insensate on this particular subject'.

15 May: various Arab armies enter Palestine: the Arab Legion goes into the area allocated to the Arabs in Judea and Samaria; the Egyptian army moves through Gaza and Beersheba; the Lebanese go into Arab Galilee; the Iraqis eventually go alongside the Arab Legion; the Syrians held near the border.

1 December: on day of cease-fire arranged between Israelis and commander of Arab Legion in Jerusalem, Abdullah, to the fury of Egypt and other Arab states, organizes a ceremonial conference in Jericho where Palestinian and Transjordanian delegates favoured the joining of Palestine and Transjordan as an indivisible Hashemite Kingdom of Jordan.

1949 24 February: armistice signed at Rhodes between the Egyptians and Israelis. Further agreements soon signed with Lebanon and Jordan, and finally with Syria. By these Israel gained 21 per cent more land than it had under the 1947 partition plan; indeed it covered almost 80 per cent of the area of the Palestine mandate.

30 March: first of series of coups and counter-coups in Syria, largely brought about by the humiliating defeat at the hands of Israel. In effect Syria ruled by Colonel Adib Shishakli between 1950 and 1954. Baath Party grows in strength, particularly after uniting with Akram Hourani's Socialist Party in 1952.

2 June: Transjordan renamed 'The Hashemite Kingdom of Jordan'.

1950 24 April: Arab Palestine finally incorporated into Jordan. Most Arab League members, apart from the fellow Hashemite Kingdom of Iraq, object. Abdullah's expansionist ideas for a Greater Syria and Fertile Crescent are regarded with suspicion. Egypt leads Arab opposition.

25 May: Tripartite Declaration made by Britain, the United States and France. Acknowledges that the Arab states and Israel needed to maintain a certain level of armed forces for the purposes of legitimate self-defence of the area as a whole. The three powers agree to consider all applications for arms or war materials by the countries of the Middle East in the light of these principles.

27 November: Nuri al-Said, the Prime Minister of Iraq, declares that his country's alliance with Britain had become obsolete.

1951 Mossadeq becomes Prime Minister of Iran and nationalizes Anglo–Iranian Oil Company.

20 July: Abdullah assassinated by a Palestinian youth in al-Aqsa Mosque in Jerusalem. Evidence given at subsequent trial suggests that assassination a protest against Greater Syria policy of Abdullah. Egypt refuses to extradite some of those convicted. Jordanian throne passes to a mentally unstable son, and in 1952 to the British-educated King Hussein, then only seventeen. Arab refugees from Palestine make up one-third of the population of Jordan, and although given citizenship they remain a discontented element.

27 October: Egypt abrogates the 1936 Anglo–Egyptian treaty and the Condominium agreement over the Sudan. The Prime Minister, Nahas Pasha, hopes that this will help him to secure the support of Farouk, who is proclaimed 'King of Egypt and Sudan', and the people. Egypt rejects the idea of a Middle East Command, a defence arrangement in which it would participate alongside other countries including Britain, France, Turkey and the United States. After this Egyptians use terrorism and economic sanctions to undermine British position in Suez Canal Zone.

24 December: Libya declared an independent United Kingdom headed by King Muhammad al-Idris, under the auspices of the United Nations. The provinces Tripolitania and Cyrenaica had been under British administration and Fezzan under the French following Italy's defeat in 1942.

1952 July: Free officers, nominally led by General Muhammad Neguib, including Gamal Abdul Nasser and Anwar el-Sadat, seize power in Egypt, deposing King Farouk.

Turkey joins North Atlantic Treaty Organization.

Britain assists forces of Sultan of Oman to re-establish control over part of Buraimi area (disputed with Saudi Arabia even before the discovery of oil), which had been taken over by forces from Saudi Arabia.

1953 19 August: Mossadeq deposed in Iran. Rift had developed between him and Shah against background of worsening economic position of Iran and Anglo–American proposals for a settlement of the dispute over oil rights. Shah, who had fled to Rome during disturbances, returns to Iran on 22 August.

Trucial Oman Scouts, a military force under the patronage of the

British Political Resident in the Gulf, established to intervene in inter-state disputes among emirates along Gulf.

1954 January: Sudan achieves internal self-government.

19 October: in a treaty with Egypt, Britain agrees to give up its rights to the Suez base and to evacuate the Canal Zone within twenty months.

1955 Sultan of Oman, in an attempt to recover power over the interior, occupies Nizwa and Ibri where oil exploration taking place. Tribes of interior resist, and under Ghalib ibn Ali, who had been elected Imam by Hinawi tribe, an unsuccessful attempt is made to establish an independent Imamate. Ghalib's brother Talib ibn Ali flees to Saudi Arabia and then Egypt.

Nasser, who had replaced Neguib as head of state in 1954, asks for aid for proposed Aswan High Dam from Britain, United States and World Bank.

Baghdad Pact formed. Initially a defence treaty signed on 24 February between Iraq and Turkey. Britain, Pakistan and Iran join later in 1955.

1956 2 March: in Jordan King Hussein dismisses the British commander of the Arab Legion, Glubb Pasha. Glubb is replaced as Commander-in-Chief of Jordan's armed forces by Major-General Radi Annab. Glubb's dismissal followed demonstrations in Amman against Jordan joining the Baghdad Pact, and the visit of the new Prime Minister, Samir Rifai, to Syria, Lebanon, Iraq, Egypt and Saudi Arabia.

Nasser nationalizes Suez Canal Company. Anglo–French invasion of the Canal Zone. (See chronology 7: The Suez Crisis of 1956.)

1957 January: Eisenhower Doctrine for the Middle East outlined: economic strength for nations of Middle East; flexibility of President to use funds; provision to use armed forces of the United States. Seen as an attempt to fill the vacuum left by Britain and France in the Middle East and to act as a stop sign to the Russians.

Talib ibn Ali leads force trained in Saudi Arabia against Sultan of Oman. British and Trucial Oman Scouts repel forces into Jebel al-Akhdar where they hold out for two years.

Jordan abrogates 1948 treaty with Britain on 13 March. British subsidy to be replaced by support from Saudi Arabia, Egypt and Syria. Suleiman Nabulsi resigns as Prime Minister on 10 April after differences with Hussein over closer connections with the Soviet

Union. Hussein assisted in this by Americans under the Eisenhower Doctrine.

1958 February: Egyptian and Syrian Presidents jointly announce the complete merger of their two states into a United Arab Republic. Initiative comes from Syria. Nasser initially hesitant as he felt Syrians were unprepared. Egyptians dominate bureaucracy of the new republic.

Merger between Jordan and Iraq for two weeks; broken up by revolution in Iraq.

14 July: *Coup d'état* starts in Iraq. King Feisal and Nuri al-Said had increasingly lacked a popular base in Iraq and were resented by many army officers. Brigadier Abd al-Karim Kassem had formed an organization similar to the group that had overthrown the monarchy in Egypt. Feisal and Nuri assassinated. Kassem becomes Prime Minister. Iraq aligns with Egypt.

July: in Lebanon, where following the Suez Crisis there had been a polarization between Lebanese and Arab nationalists, President Camille Chamoun invites in United States troops to maintain order. Eisenhower, in an attempt to support the pro-Western element in the Middle East, sends in 10,000 Marines who land near Beirut. Britain, with American assistance, flies troops into Jordan at the request of King Hussein, in what is in effect a joint Anglo–American invasion of the Middle East. Washington allows Lebanon to settle its own crisis and General Fuad Chehab is elected President. Lebanon pursues a more neutral policy. British troops are withdrawn from Jordan in October.

1961 Syria dissolves constitutional links with Egypt.

Kuwait terminates special relationship with Britain and joins Arab League. Kassem of Iraq threatens Kuwait's independence, but this countered initially by British military assistance, and then by an Arab League force from Jordan, Saudi Arabia, Sudan and the United Arab Republic.

1962 28 September: in Yemen, pro-Egyptian army officers stage a revolt against Muhammad al-Badr who had just succeeded his father, Imam Ahmad. Rebels capture the main towns and declare a republic. Badr and royalist supporters escape to Saudi Arabia and with help of Badr's uncle, Emir Hassan, secure support of tribesmen in Yemen. Egypt, in what becomes a lengthy commitment, intervenes in the civil war in Yemen on behalf of the republicans, and Saudi Arabia supports the loyalist tribesmen.

1963 Shah of Iran in 'White Revolution' extends vote to women, and institutes limited land reform which inspires opposition from religious officials, notably Ayatollah Rouhollah Khomeini.

Kassem overthrown in Iraq by armed forces, and socialist government formed consisting of an alliance of nationalist army officers and members of the Baath party.

Kuwait becomes a member of the United Nations.

1964 King Saud of Saudi Arabia hands throne over to his brother Feisal, who leads Saudi Arabia on a course of moderation in foreign affairs.

Rebellion in Oman by the Jibalis, the hill tribes of Dhofar, against Sultan's refusal to liberalize, inspired by Marxist regime of People's Democratic Republic of Yemen.

1967 June: Six-Day War in which Israel fights Syria, Jordan and Egypt. Israel occupies East Jerusalem which had been incorporated into Jordan (East Jerusalem annexed by Israel in 1967), the Jordanian West Bank, the Egyptian territory of Sinai and Egyptian-controlled Gaza, and the Syrian Golan Heights (annexed by Israel in 1982).

Jordan signs defence pact with Egypt; in Six-Day War loses West Bank; accepts 200,000 new Palestinian refugees.

22 November: Resolution 242, passed by the Security Council of the United Nations, provides for a 'just and lasting peace' within 'secure and recognized boundaries'; Israel is to withdraw 'from territories occupied in the recent conflict' and there is to be an acknowledgement of all states' 'sovereignty, territorial integrity and political independence' in the area.

November: in South Arabia, in the former British protected territory and colony of Aden, the National Liberation Front, a group of left-wing nationalists, proclaims the independent People's Republic of Southern Yemen (People's Democratic Republic of Yemen), after the British evacuation of Aden on 29 November.

1968 July: a *coup d'état* in Iraq enables Baathists to strengthen control of the state.

October: Kurds who had staged inconclusive rebellions in northern Iraq since 1961, are confronted by Iraqi military forces. Fighting continues throughout 1969, with the Kurds demanding autonomy and mediation by the United Nations.

1969 31 August/1 September: army officers, inspired by Nasser and led by Muammar al-Gaddafi, depose King Idris in Libya.

Libya signs friendship treaties with Egypt and Sudan.

1970 Yemen Arab Republic (North Yemen) established after Egyptian withdrawal of forces and end of Saudi support to dissident tribes and royalist forces who had been loyal to Imam al-Badr.

23 July: Qabus ibn Said deposes his father, the Sultan of Oman, and institutes programme of reform.

August: fighting breaks out in Jordan between Jordanian government forces and guerrilla organizations including al-Fatah. From 1967 these guerrilla organizations had increasingly controlled the Palestinian refugee camps and were widely supported by the Palestinians living in Jordan, who made up around two-thirds of its total population. Despite the threat of intervention of Iraq and Syria, by the middle of September Jordan was in a state of civil war. The guerrillas, assisted by Syria and three battalions of the Palestine Liberation army sent by Nasser, claim control of the North. King Hussein's confrontation with the Palestinians is settled after talks with the United States about direct military assistance, and diplomacy conducted by the Arab heads of state. On 27 September Hussein and Yasser Arafat (of the Palestine Liberation Organization) sign an agreement ending the civil war. Palestinian guerrillas expelled over the following few months by Jordanian army.

28 September: Nasser dies and is succeeded by Anwar el-Sadat, a fellow member of the Free Officers who had staged the revolution in Egypt in 1952, and Vice President at the time of Nasser's death. Sadat is appointed provisional President by the Cabinet and Party, and is later elected President in a national referendum.

November: General Hafiz al-Asad seizes full executive power in Syria.

1971 August: Bahrain becomes sovereign state. Special relationship with Britain which had had responsibility for defence and foreign affairs is ended.

Bahrain also becomes member of United Nations Organization and the Arab League.

September: referenda in Libya, Egypt and Syria approve the constitution of the Federation of Arab Republics. This followed initiatives in the late 1960s by Gaddafi for a federation of Egypt (then the United Arab Republic), Libya and Sudan, and later moves towards securing Syria's adherence. These federation proposals had helped to precipitate a crisis in Egypt in April 1971, after which Sadat had mounted a purge of his opponents, and held new elections in July. In September 1971 a new constitution approved in Egypt, replacing the name 'United Arab Republic' with the 'Arab

Republic of Egypt'. The Federation of Arab Republics is officially inaugurated on 1 January 1972 but has little practical significance.

Qatar and Britain end treaty relationship. Qatar does not join the envisaged Gulf Federation, a proposal to follow the withdrawal of British influence from the Gulf with a federation of the seven Trucial states, Bahrain and Qatar. Qatar becomes an independent state.

December: after termination of British treaties with the seven Trucial states in the Gulf, the United Arab Emirates is formed. Ras al-Khaimah does not join until February 1972.

1972 22 February: in Qatar Sheikh Khalifa ibn Hamad Al Thani deposes Sheikh Ahmad ibn Ali Al Thani who had taken little interest in government. The new Sheikh introduces some reforms but maintains the Islamic basis of the state.

1973 National Assembly elected in Bahrain.

Gaddafi announces cultural revolution in Libya, the 'Third Universal Theory', aimed at purging both capitalism and communism from Libyan society.

6 October: Syria and Egypt, having co-ordinated their plans, attack Israel during the Islamic fast of Ramadan and the Jewish fast of Yom Kippur. In subsequent October War Arabs achieve stunning initial victories, but Israel stages a rapid recovery and is assisted by a huge airlift of weapons from the United States. By 15 October Israeli forces are within fifty miles of Cairo and have surrounded and cut off Egypt's Third Army in Sinai. United States and Soviet Union sponsor a Security Council resolution calling for a cease-fire and negotiations for a peace settlement.

During final days of October War the Arab oil producers ban the supply of oil to the United States and the Netherlands, and though Britain and France are exempt, supplies to Western Europe generally are reduced. The Arabs, using the 'oil weapon', raise the oil price and create balance of payments problems for many Western countries.

22 October: United Nations Security Council passes Resolution 338 which calls for the implementation, after the cease-fire, of Resolution 242 of 1967 'in all of its parts', and decides on 'negotiations between the parties concerned under appropriate auspices, aimed at establishing a just and durable peace in the Middle East'.

1974 20 July: Turkey invades Cyprus to forestall the threatened imposition of *Enosis*, or union with Greece, by Greece and supported by Greek Cypriots. On 14 August Turkey establishes the boundaries of an autonomous Turkish Cypriot administration.

September: General Assembly of the United Nations agrees to include 'the Palestine question' on its agenda and invites the Palestine Liberation Organization to take part in the debate.

October: Arab summit at Rabat recognizes the Palestine Liberation Organization under Yasser Arafat as the only legitimate representative of the Palestinians. King Hussein of Jordan accedes to this consensus and abrogates a Jordanian parliament that had included representatives from the West Bank.

13 November: Yasser Arafat addresses the General Assembly of the United Nations. The Palestine Liberation Organization achieves semi-official status in various international bodies.

1975 March: Shah of Iran announces the formation of a single party system, the Iran National Resurgence Party, with the Prime Minister as Secretary-General. This is an effort to solve the problems of internal opposition in Iran, which had become particularly evident in 1971 with the preparations for the lavish celebrations of the 2,500th anniversary of the Persian monarchy held in October 1971. The unequal distribution of the oil profits and the Shah's suppression of opposition by the SAVAK, the government security agency, had exacerbated this dissent at a time when the Shah was turning Iran into a modern Western state.

April: in Lebanon, where the Palestinian refugee problem has undermined the confessional system, Palestinian gunmen shoot the bodyguard of the (Christian) Phalangist leader, Pierre Gemayel. Phalangist gunmen retaliate by killing a bus full of Palestinians. Inter-communal fighting between Christians and Muslims quickly spreads in Lebanon. Syria, worried about the possibility of Israeli military intervention in southern Lebanon, sends troops into Lebanon in May 1976. The civil war in Lebanon continues until October 1976 when leaders of Egypt, Syria, Lebanon and the Palestine Liberation Organization agree to a cease-fire and the formation of an Arab peacekeeping force.

August: in Bahrain the National Assembly is dissolved by decree of the Emir and constitution is suspended. This follows industrial unrest that had surfaced in June 1974 over delays in the establishment of trade unions and a considerable rise in the cost of living. Unrest continues and there are arrests of agitators.

September: Israel withdraws in Sinai to behind Mitla and Gidi passes in terms of disengagement agreement negotiated by Henry Kissinger, the American Secretary of State.

Shah of Iran renounces Iranian claims to islands of Bahrain; this renunciation is not recognized by Islamic Republic of Iran when it replaces the Shah's administration.

December: defeat of rebels in Oman by Omani troops partly led by British officers.

1976 August: Emir of Kuwait suspends the National Assembly for four years. This follows criticisms of the administration, particularly on the slow pace of nationalization of the oil industry.

1977 9 November: Sadat tells the Egyptian parliament that he is prepared to go to the Knesset (the Israeli parliament) itself to negotiate a peace treaty with Israel. Through American intermediaries the Israeli Prime Minister, Menachem Begin, pursues this idea. Sadat faces the disapproval of his own ministers. Despite increasing Arab hostility, Sadat flies to Jerusalem on 19 November and offers Israel recognition and permanent peace based on agreements that would lead to the return of occupied Arab territories, including Arab Jerusalem, recognition of Palestinian statehood, and secure boundaries subject to international guarantees. Libya severs relations with Egypt after Sadat's visit to Jerusalem.

1978 4–17 September: President Jimmy Carter of the United States acts as an intermediary between Begin and Sadat at a meeting at Camp David, the presidential lodge in Maryland. On 17 September Carter announces that he has witnessed the signing of two basic documents by Sadat and Begin in which the two Middle Eastern leaders agree, among other things, to conclude a peace treaty within three months which would provide for an Israeli withdrawal from Sinai and the normalization of relations between Egypt and Israel.

1979 15 January: Shah leaves Iran after failing to counter political unrest by promising that his government would observe Islamic tenets, dissolve the SAVAK (the security police), support Palestinians, and stop the export of oil to South Africa and Israel.

February: Ayatollah Khomeini arrives in Iran from Paris; foments Islamic revolution. Shapour Bakhtiar's 'last chance' government resigns. By May, constitution of Islamic Republic of Iran is approved by referendum. (See chronology 9: The rise of revolutionary Islam and the Khomeini revolution in Iran.)

16 July: Saddam Hussein replaces General Bakr as President of Iraq.

1979–80 Saudi Arabia experiences disturbances fomented by

Sunni extremists, possibly incited by Iranian Islamic revolutionaries. King Khalid promises to operate government on Islamic principles.

1980 September: President Saddam Hussein of Iraq invades Iran. Subsequent war lasts until July 1988 when Iran announces unconditional acceptance of United Nations Security Council resolution of July 1987 for a cease-fire. (See chronology 12: The Iran–Iraq War.)

1981 May: against the threat of an Iranian victory in the Iran–Iraq War and the Russian invasion of Afghanistan, in a defensive measure, Kuwait, Bahrain, Oman, Qatar, Saudi Arabia and the United Arab Emirates form the Gulf Co-operation Council. The ultimate objective of the Council is to achieve some sort of political and economic fusion of the member states.

6 October: in Egypt Sadat is assassinated by a group of Islamic extremists. Group had hoped to stage a *coup d'état* and declare Egypt an Islamic republic. The Egyptian government imposes martial law and tries to purge armed forces of fundamentalists. Vice President Muhammad Hosni Mubarak succeeds to the presidency. Mubarak, through talking to the opposition in Egypt over a number of years, manages to quieten the domestic front and to rehabilitate Egypt's reputation in the Arab world, while still maintaining the peace treaty with Israel and a good relationship with the United States.

1982 March: rest of Sinai returned by Israel to Egypt by terms of the Treaty of Washington (29 March 1979) which had followed the Camp David accords and ended the state of war between Israel and Egypt that had lasted for thirty-one years.

6 June: Israel launches 'Operation Peace for Galilee' and invades the Lebanon. The objective is to destroy units of the Palestine Liberation Organization in Lebanon, and so protect Israel's sixty-three Galilee settlements and towns from raids across the northern border. A partnership with the Maronite Christians could assist this objective. There are also hopes that this could lead to the Palestinians overthrowing Hussein in Jordan and so give weight to the policy proclaimed by Yitzhak Shamir, the Israeli Foreign Minister, in Cairo, on 23 February 1982, that Jordan was the Palestinian state. Israelis besiege Beirut for two months. (See chronology 11: War in Lebanon.)

1985 By June Israel has withdrawn from most of Lebanon but maintains its influence in a buffer zone in the south.

1986 March: after claiming that Libya was sponsoring international terrorism, United States sinks Libyan naval vessels in Gulf of Sirte. Gaddafi claims Gulf as Libyan territorial waters; the United States maintains that it is international waters.

14 April: United States bombs Tripoli and Benghazi, following explosion, attributed to Libyan terrorists, in West Berlin discothèque that is frequented by American servicemen.

July: Emir of Kuwait suspends the National Assembly for the second time. Suspension follows discontent over the Kuwait stock market crash and domestic unrest.

1987 8–20 December: first wave of riots in popular uprising of Palestinians settled on the West Bank and Gaza. Known as the 'intifada'. (See chronology 10: The Palestinian refugee issue and the uprising in the occupied territories.)

1988 31 July: King Hussein of Jordan announces that the Jordanian government is giving up its administration of the West Bank. Hussein dissolves the Jordanian parliament which had had West Bank representation, and cancels Jordan's West Bank development scheme. The Palestine National Council (the parliament of the Palestine Liberation Organization) announces that it will take over the responsibilities and Jordan stops paying the salaries of 21,000 Arab school teachers and civil servants on the West Bank.

1989 15 November: the Palestine National Council, after a three-day meeting in Algiers, proclaims the establishment of the state of Palestine with Jerusalem as its capital, in terms of the United Nations resolution of November 1947 which had partitioned Palestine. Members of the council are divided on whether to accept United Nations Resolution 242 of 1967, which would have meant recognition of the state of Israel, but Arafat says that he wants this as a mandate with which to pursue peace. In the interim period the occupied territories should be administered by the United Nations. The Palestine National Council rejects terrorism, and confines the use of violence to Israel and the occupied territories.

14 November: Arafat, addressing a plenary session of the General Assembly held in Geneva, explicitly states that the Palestine Liberation Organization accepts United Nations Resolutions 242 and 338, recognizes Israel's right to exist, and renounces resort to terrorism. The United States starts a dialogue with the Palestine Liberation Organization in Tunis.

1990 May: Yemen Arab Republic and the People's Democratic

Republic of Yemen are unified after a century of separate development.

11 June: elections take place in Kuwait for a new National Assembly.

2 August: Saddam Hussein invades Kuwait and later annexes the Emirate as the nineteenth province of Iraq. (See chronology 13: The Gulf War.)

1991 17 January: after the expiry of a United Nations deadline for the withdrawal of Iraqi forces from Kuwait, the coalition headed by the United States and including Britain, France and other European nations, as well as Saudi Arabia, Egypt, Syria, the United Arab Emirates, Bahrain and Turkey, launches Operation Desert Storm and bombs Iraq and Kuwait. As Iraqi Scud missiles land in Tel Aviv and Haifa, the United States mounts the largest airlift of military equipment for Israel since the October War. The Israeli government follows 'a policy of remarkable restraint' which wins it widespread international sympathy and financial rewards. Palestinians see Saddam Hussein as the first Arab leader to pay more than lip-service to the Palestinian cause and to attack the heart of the Zionist state. Gulf War polarizes divisions in the Arab world: whereas Jordan and the Palestine Liberation Organization support Saddam Hussein, Saudi Arabia, its allies in the Gulf Co-operation Council, Egypt, and Syria oppose the Iraqi leader.

26–7 February: after launching of allied ground offensive on 24 February, Kuwait City is liberated and Iraqi forces are defeated. Iraqi government announces that it accepts unconditionally the United Nations resolutions on Kuwait.

6 March: President George Bush in his victory speech to the United States Congress insists that: 'A comprehensive peace must be grounded in the United Nations Security Council Resolutions 242 and 338 and the principle of territory for peace. This principle must be elaborated to provide for Israel's security and recognition, and at the same time for legitimate Palestinian political rights.'

April–June: Saddam Hussein, after crushing Kurdish rebellion in Iraq, precipitates Kurdish flight to Turkey and Iran. The British Prime Minister, John Major, suggests a policy of 'safe havens' in Iraq to which the Kurdish refugees could return. British and American troops go back to Iraq to set up these refuges, and Saddam Hussein in talks with Kurdish leaders agrees to the principle of Kurdish 'autonomy'.

June–August: James Baker, United States Secretary of State, in a series of diplomatic shuttles around the Middle East, secures Arab support, including that of President Asad of Syria, for regional peace conference to discuss the Palestinian question and the Arab–Israeli dispute. Israeli Prime Minister, Yitzhak Shamir, agrees to attend the conference, scheduled for October, provided a solution to the problem of Palestinian representation to the talks is achieved.

20 October: publication of book by Seymour Hersh, *The Samson Option* claiming that: Israel had over 100 nuclear bombs and had contemplated using one against Egypt during the October War of 1973; that successive American presidents had turned a blind eye to their manufacture; that the bombs were targeted against Arab oil installations and cities and the southwest cities of the former Soviet Union; that Israel's bombing of Iraq's nuclear reactor had been made possible through American intelligence information; and that British newspaper proprietor, Robert Maxwell (who died in mysterious circumstances shortly afterwards and was interred with full Israeli state honours on the Mount of Olives), had close links with the Mossad and had assisted in the tracking of Vanunu who had earlier leaked details of Israel's nuclear programme.

30 October–1 November: under the sponsorship of the United States and the Soviet Union delegations from Israel, Syria and Lebanon, and a joint Jordanian–Palestinian delegation attend the opening session of a Middle East peace conference in Madrid.

3–4 November: bilateral talks result in statement that further negotiations would be 'two track': discussing Israeli–Palestinian and Israeli–Jordanian issues.

10–18 December: scheduled bilateral talks in Washington founder on Israeli insistence that it would only deal with a separate Palestinian 'track' if it were under Jordanian auspices.

1992 13–16 January: bilateral talks in Washington achieve agreement on separate Palestinian representation within the joint Jordanian–Palestinian delegation.

end January: against background of multilateral Middle East peace talks in Moscow at which Palestinians boycott session and insist on inclusion of Palestinians from the diaspora in their delegation, the withdrawal of minority parties from the Israeli government means that an Israeli election is scheduled for 23 June.

October: Oman signs an agreement with Yemen on the demarcation of their border, and this is ratified in December.

1993 13 September: Israel and the Palestine Liberation Organization sign an accord, known as the Declaration of Principles, in Washington, DC. This follows secret talks between the two parties in Oslo, Norway, and Israel's recognition of the Palestine Liberation Organization, and Arafat's acknowledgement of Israel's right to exist in peace and security. The Declaration of Principles provides or Palestinian self-rule for the Gaza Strip and the West Bank town of Jericho, and Israeli sovereignty over the Jewish settlements in the occupied territories as an interim stage, with talks on permanent settlement to follow within two years.

1994 April–7 July: following legislative elections in Yemen on 27 April 1993, divisions emerge as the southern areas feel that they have lost influence. After an attempt with the 'Document of Pledge and Agreement' of 18 January 1994 to evolve a system of devolved government, clashes occur between rival military units from the north and the south, followed by the bombing by the south of targets in the north, including airports and power stations, with northern aircraft bombing the airport at Aden on 5 May 1994. The civil war wages against the background of United Nations' attempts to get the belligerents to talk, but through the action of the Saudi Arabian ambassador at Washington drafted resolutions make no reference to Yemeni unity. The north accuses Saudi Arabia of encouraging the southern secessionists with the aim of creating a new petroleum emirate in the Wadi Hadrumat under Saudi influence with an outlet to the Indian Ocean. Washington warns Saudi Arabia against interfering in Yemeni affairs, and supports a united Yemen. Northern forces advance and Aden surrenders on 7 July.

26 October: Israel and Jordan sign a peace treaty under which Jordan agrees that the Palestinian refugees in Jordan would stay there and forfeit their right to return to their homes in return for United States aid, and the Jordanian custodianship of the holy places in East Jerusalem is acknowledged. The Israeli–Jordanian border is similar to that demarcated at the time of the British mandate in 1922.

1995 September: Israel and the Palestine Liberation Organization sign an agreement in Washington for interim Palestinian self-rule in the West Bank under the Palestinian Authority together with the withdrawal of Israeli troops from seven West Bank towns by December, joint control by Israel and the Palestinian Authority of 450 Palestinian villages, and continued Israeli control of 128 Jewish settlements.

2. The birth of the State of Israel

1781 After Declaration of Independence, a certain degree of emancipation for Jews in the United States.

1790 After French Revolution, a certain emancipation of Jews in France. Napoleonic armies liberate Jews in many European countries.

1819 Following Napoleon's defeat, there is some reaction to Jewish liberation: the Hep Hep riots start in Wurzburg and spread throughout the German states and into Austria, Hungary, Poland and Denmark, reflecting a suspicion of Jewish financiers and bankers, and suggesting that the Jews were responsible for economic difficulties.

1830 Further riots. Some Central European Jews emigrate to the United States.

1858 Baron Lionel de Rothschild, a professing Jew, is elected to the British House of Commons.

*c.*1860 Word 'anti-Semitism' appears and with it a new challenge to the position of Jews, based not on grounds of creed but of race.

1881 March: assassination of Tsar Alexander II. After this Russia's difficulties are attributed to Jewish corruption and Jews are massacred in a series of attacks in which the government either acquiesced or connived. These became known as pogroms. By 1914 over 2 million Jews have fled from Russia and most have settled in the United States.

1882 Leo Pinsker in his pamphlet *Auto-emancipation* argues that anti-Semitism would persist wherever the Jews were a minority: they needed a homeland of their own.

Jewish immigration to Palestine starts in significant numbers following the Russian pogroms.

1886–91 Word 'Zionism' probably first used by Nathan Birnbaum in a series of articles.

1896 February: Theodor Herzl, who as a reporter had been shaken by the apparent hostility to the Jews that the trial of a Jewish officer of the French general staff, Alfred Dreyfus, unleashed in France in 1894, publishes *Der Judenstaat* in Vienna. Argues that anti-Semitic fervour made the establishment of a state for the Jews an urgent necessity.

1897 First Zionist Congress meets in Basle. Idea of a Jewish 'home' adopted instead of state. Out of the Basle programme emerged the World Zionist Organization, a national flag, a national anthem and the Jewish National Fund.

1897 Number of Jews in Palestine, an area of the crumbling Ottoman Empire subject to the Turkish Sultan, has probably reached around 50,000 with the creation of eighteen settlements or 'agricultural colonies'. Colonization organized partly by Baron Edmond de Rothschild, partly by the Lovers of Zion societies founded mainly in Russia, later by the Jewish Colonization Association under the Baron de Hirsch. As early as 1891 there had been evidence that some Arabs in Palestine, struggling against Ottoman domination and misrule, regarded the increasing flow of Jewish settlers as a threat to their own nationalist aspirations. In the late 1890s, Arabs warn the Zionist movement that its programme is not feasible. Because of the administrative structure of the Ottoman Empire, knowledge of the Zionist programme spreads to the Arabs outside Palestine. It is evident that the Arabs distinguish between the 'Ottoman' Jew and the 'foreign' Jew, and see only the former as deserving equal rights in a decentralized administration. The Arabs also know the difference between Jew and Zionist.

1903 Joseph Chamberlain suggests to Herzl part of East Africa as an area for Jewish colonization.

1904 Chaim Weizmann, a Jew born in Russia who had attended university in Berlin, chooses to settle in Britain. Considers it the one country likely to sympathize with the Zionist movement. Later, while researching chemistry at Manchester University, founds what becomes known as the Manchester School of Zionism. Its followers include Simon Marks, Harry Sacher and Israel Sieff.

1905 Zionist Congress rejects East Africa scheme, and those in favour of it, under Israel Zangwill, break away.

1907 Weizmann visits Palestine. Argues that diplomatic pressure alone is not going to convince governments of Europe; practical work necessary, particularly in the field of colonization in Palestine.

1914 Around 85,000 Jews settled in Palestine. They own about 2 per cent of the land. Some estimates based on 1922 census figures argue that the number was considerably lower.

Weizmann forges contacts with C.P. Scott, the editor of the *Manchester Guardian*, David Lloyd George, and Herbert Samuel, a Cabinet minister who prepared a memorandum about a Jewish state in Palestine.

1915 March: Samuel's revised memorandum suggests that it would be too costly and dangerous for the Zionist movement to est-ablish an autonomous Jewish state in Palestine immediately; rather, there should be a British protectorate that could be a safeguard to Egypt.

1916 April: British Palestine Committee formed by journalist Herbert Sidebotham, Harry Sacher, Israel M. Sieff and Simon Marks. Under guidance of Weizmann, committee relates Zionist aspirations to the British war effort.

December: Lloyd George becomes Prime Minister and Leopold Amery Secretary to the Committee on Territorial Change. Amery convinced by Mark Sykes of the importance of Zionism for Britain's strategic requirements.

1917 April: Zionism has achieved a new status in British political thinking. Not only is Palestine necessary for the security of empire, but it is thought that Zionist sympathies for the allied cause could help the war effort. Zionists in Russia could stop that country's drift out of the war; in the United States Zionists could speed up the American contribution following the United States declaration of war on 3 April.

19 June: meeting between Lord Rothschild, Arthur James Balfour, the Secretary of State for Foreign Affairs, and Weizmann. Balfour asks for a draft of Zionist aspirations.

31 October: Balfour tells War Cabinet that a declaration in favour of Zionism would help propaganda in Russia and the United States. By 'national home', Balfour understands some form of British, American and other protectorate enabling Jews to build up 'a real centre of national culture and focus of national life'.

2 November: letter from Balfour to Lord Rothschild saying that Britain viewed with favour the establishment in Palestine of a national home for the Jewish people, it being understood that nothing would be done to prejudice the civil and religious rights of existing non-Jewish communities in Palestine, nor the rights and political status enjoyed by Jews in any other country. The letter is published and is known as the Balfour Declaration.

35

1918 Weizmann heads Zionist Commission to Palestine to put Balfour Declaration into practice. Emir Feisal, the third son of the Sherif of Mecca and leader of Arab revolt, tells Weizmann in June that he refuses to consider Palestine as a British protectorate, or an area for Jewish colonization.

1919 Weizmann as principal Zionist speaker at Paris peace conference explains that the Zionists want to send 70,000 to 80,000 Jews annually to Palestine. The hope is that a nationality would gradually be built up to 'make Palestine as Jewish as America is American or England English'.

1920 Draft of British mandate for Palestine prepared by Zionists in Paris and accepted by British officials, Forbes Adams and Robert Vansittart. Curzon objects to the phrase 'recognizing the historic connection of the Jewish People with Palestine', and writes a minute dated 6 August: 'I do not myself recognize that the connection of the Jews with Palestine, which terminated 1,200 years ago, gives them any claim whatsoever.'

After Arab riots in Jerusalem, Herbert Samuel appointed to head a new civilian administration in Palestine.

1921 Amin al-Husseini becomes Mufti of Jerusalem and leads Arab opposition to creation of Jewish national home in Palestine.

1922 Churchill's White Paper allows further development of Jewish community in Palestine, but states that immigration should not exceed the economic capacity of the country.

22 July: League of Nations approves the Palestine mandate.

1924 United States imposes a quota system for immigrants. Jewish immigration into Palestine continues. After reaching a peak of 34,386 in 1924 it drops to 3,034 in 1927. Between 1919 and 1931 Jewish population of Palestine grows from around 60,000 to 175,000, an increase from 8 to 17.7 per cent of the total population.

1929 August: Jewish and Arab riots in Palestine following disagreements over the removal by the police of a screen placed near the 'Wailing Wall' (Western Wall) to separate Jewish men and women at prayer.

1930 March: a commission of enquiry under Sir Walter Shaw reports that Zionist immigration demands had aroused Arab apprehension about Jewish political domination.

Sir John Hope Simpson reports that the land in Palestine is not even sufficient to provide the Arab population with a decent livelihood. Pending development, there is no more room for Jewish settlers. This report forms the basis of the 1930 Passfield White Paper, which intimates immigration restrictions.

1930–1 Zionist lobby in Britain, including Weizmann, Baffy Dugdale (Balfour's niece), and Lewis Namier (at that time in the pay of the Jewish Agency, later Professor of Modern History at Manchester University), mount orchestrated campaign that shakes consensus in parliament on Palestine and strains Anglo–American relations.

1931 13 February: Ramsay MacDonald sends a letter to Weizmann, based on a memorandum provided by Leonard Stein, in which he reaffirms Britain's intention to stand by the mandate – viewed as an obligation to world Jewry – to uphold the policy of the Jewish national home by further land settlement and immigration, and to condone the Zionist insistence on Jewish labour for work on Jewish enterprises. Dubbed the 'Black Letter' by the Arabs.

1933 Hitler becomes Chancellor of Germany. Persecution of Jews increases, particularly with the Nuremberg laws of 15 September 1935 which effectively bar Jews from German society. Zionists in their publicity link the need for Jewish immigration to Palestine with the Nazi persecution. Jewish immigration to Palestine, most of it originating in Germany, reaches a peak of 61,844 in 1935.

1936 Arab rebellion in Palestine put down with 20,000 troops.

1937 June: Peel Commission recommends that Palestine be divided into three parts: an Arab state; a Jewish state; and also certain areas of strategic or religious importance that would remain under a British mandate.

8 December: Neville Chamberlain appoints a technical commission under Sir John Woodhead. Commission not bound by Peel Report and which can make representations that partition would be unworkable.

19 September: Weizmann, David Ben-Gurion, a leader of the Jewish community in Palestine, and Baffy Dugdale learn from Malcolm MacDonald that, fearing Germany, Italy and the Arabs, Britain intends to abandon partition. With the Munich crisis Britain wants to restore friendly relations with the Arabs: Iraq with its oil and communications would be important in war, and Egypt would be an area of battle. The High Commissioner in Palestine, Harold MacMichael, and Lieutenant-General Robert Haining, the General

Officer Commanding Palestine, insist that only postponement of partition and the complete cessation of immigration would bring peace to Palestine.

9 November: Woodhead commissioners' report published, ruling out partition as the two states envisaged would not be economically viable and would entail large-scale movements of population.

1939 February–March: London Round Table Conference at which the Arabs refuse to speak to the Zionists. MacDonald reports that to win Arab friendship Britain needs to decide the final number of Jewish immigrants.

17 May: British White Paper published, in which it is stated that it is not British policy that Palestine should become a Jewish state. Britain wanted an independent Palestine with Arabs and Jews sharing authority in government in a way that secured their essential interests. Over the following five years, 75,000 Jewish immigrants would be allowed into Palestine and after that immigration would be subject to Arab consent.

1942 May: at the American Zionist Conference at the Biltmore Hotel in New York, Weizmann's programme of demanding a 'Jewish Commonwealth' in the whole of western Palestine is adopted. Afterwards Weizmann's 'gradualist' tactics are replaced by Ben-Gurion's 'activist' programme. Ben-Gurion advocates that the United States should be stimulated into supporting a revolutionary change of Palestine policy to which Britain would have to acquiesce.

1943–4 Zionist Emergency Council lobbies systematically in Washington and throughout the United States. This takes place against the background of the publication in the *New York Times* of an 'extermination' list of the 1,700,000 people who had died in Nazi concentration camps. Five hundred rabbis petition President Roosevelt to open up Palestine and the countries of the United Nations to Jews.

1944 27 June: Republican Party in the United States adopts an electoral platform calling for the opening of Palestine to unrestricted immigration for the victims of Nazism, unrestricted Jewish land ownership, and Palestine as a free and democratic commonwealth.

15 October: Roosevelt promises in letter to Robert Wagner of the American Palestine Committee that if re-elected president he would help to bring about 'the establishment of Palestine as a free and democratic Jewish Commonwealth'.

15 November: American economic mission to the Middle East under William S. Culbertson advises: 'Perhaps the price the United States pays for the privilege to hold its widely publicized views on the Jewish state is worth all it costs. The mission wishes only to emphasize that the price is considerable and that apparently the American people do not realize how considerable it is.'

British Foreign Office argues that Britain should retain its pre-eminence in the Middle East: if it embarked on partition in Palestine on its own, it would cede that position to the United States.

17 November: following the assassination of Lord Moyne, the Minister Resident in the Middle East, by Zionist terrorists, Churchill tells House of Commons that he will have to reconsider his position and that plans for Palestine cannot be considered in such a climate.

1945 5 April: Roosevelt assures Ibn Saud that he will make no move against the Arabs.

United States administration has details of the plans of Haganah (the Zionist army and underground organization): any solution condemning Jews to a permanent minority status in Palestine would be countered by military activity, and resistance from the civilian population including a general strike. The Yishuv (the Jewish community in Palestine) was 'a bridgehead in the conquest of the empty sixty per cent of Palestinian land, where homes can be made for millions of distressed Jews in Europe'. Haganah would carry on illegal immigration.

31 August: bearing in mind the significance of the Jewish vote in a forthcoming election in New York, Truman writes to Attlee suggesting that the main solution lies in the quick evacuation of Jews to Palestine. Earl G. Harrison's committee, sent by Truman to investigate displaced persons in Europe, had recommended that 100,000 be admitted.

8 September: British Palestine Committee decides Arab attitude of first importance as the Middle East is a region of 'vital consequence' for Britain and the Empire. A policy unfavourable to the Arabs in Palestine could lead to widespread disturbances in Arab countries and endanger Britain's imperial interests.

9 November: Ernest Bevin announces the appointment of an Anglo–American commission of enquiry, and suggests that it should prepare a trusteeship agreement for Palestine as well as a permanent solution for submission to the United Nations.

November–December: leaders of the American Palestine Committee, aghast at the enormity of the Jewish tragedy – 5,700,000 had died at the hands of the Nazis – argue that Palestine is the only safe haven for the remainder. They do not regard the United States as a

39

suitable haven. Truman drafts a letter he does not send: 'I don't think that you or any of the other Senators, would be inclined to send half a dozen Divisions to Palestine to maintain a Jewish state'. Despite Truman's requests for delay, in the middle of December the Senate and the House of Representatives endorse a resolution mentioning Truman's request for the immediate entry of 100,000 refugees, and referring to a 'democratic commonwealth' in Palestine.

1946 30 April: Truman endorses recommendation of Anglo–American commission of enquiry that 100,000 certificates for Jewish immigration to Palestine be issued and two other aspects favourable to Zionism. The clauses conciliatory to the Arabs dismissed as long-range considerations. British public outraged: British soldiers had just been murdered by Zionist terrorists.

July: Anglo–American Cabinet Committee meeting in London recommends scheme of provincial autonomy. Becomes known as Morrison–Grady plan. Truman initially endorses three recommendations, but after representations from members of the American Christian Palestine Committee, who insist on the need for a Jewish state, and warnings from Zionists that 90 per cent of the 4 million American Jews were pro-Zionist and were influential in elections in large urban centres, Truman informs Attlee on 31 July that he can no longer agree to the plan as a joint Anglo–American venture.

1 October: Bevin sees Weizmann and other Zionist delegates. Weizmann prepared for a transitional period of several years before partition. Hopes are that the Jewish delegates could be brought into conference even before the return of the Arab delegates to the consultations in London.

4 October: Truman, going against the advice of the State Department and the Chiefs of Staff, but following that of Robert E. Hannegan, the Chairman of the Democratic National Committee, says in his Day of Atonement speech that a solution along the lines of partition originally proposed by the Jewish Agency on 5 August would 'command the support of public opinion in the United States'. Truman felt threatened by a speech by his likely opponent in the presidential election of 1948, Thomas E. Dewey, envisaged for 6 October, and designed to catch the Jewish vote in five major eastern states that tended to dominate the presidential elections.

December: against background of impasse in attempts to re-negotiate the Anglo–Egyptian treaty, the British Cabinet decides to move a further division of troops from Egypt to Palestine. Britain's unsatisfactory relations with Egypt make the Palestine base more essential for the maintenance of British strategic interests.

1947 15 January: influenced by the military arguments that the retention of Britain's position in the Middle East was cardinal for the future defence of the Commonwealth, Bevin suggests to Cabinet that the Morrison–Grady proposals could be amended to point towards a unitary state.

7 February: after meeting both Zionist and Arab delegates in London, Bevin warns Cabinet that if the parties do not acquiesce to a plan envisaging self-government in Palestine, leading to independence after a transitional period of five years under trusteeship, Britain would have to submit the Palestine problem to the United Nations without making any recommendations.

May: United Nations Special Committee on Palestine (UNSCOP) set up, with broad powers of investigation.

13 May: Truman writes to David Niles, a presidential adviser and the Zionist contact in the White House, that the Palestine problem could have been settled but for American politics: 'terror and Silver are the contributing cause of *some*, if not all of our troubles'. Truman is referring here to the Zionist terrorist outrages in Palestine, such as the blowing up of the King David Hotel, and to Rabbi Abba Hillel Silver of the Zionist Emergency Council, who annoyed Truman with his frequent lobbying.

31 August: UNSCOP'S majority plan suggests partition into an Arab state, a Jewish state and the city of Jerusalem under international trusteeship. Britain would administer the mandate during the interim period and admit 150,000 refugees into the Jewish state. The minority plan proposed an independent federal state.

20 September: British morale low in Palestine after terrorist hanging of two sergeants and the booby-trapping of their bodies, as well as the *Exodus* incident, in which Britain had suffered international vilification for returning an illegal immigrant ship from Palestine to Marseilles (because of French co-operation with the Zionists, the refugees ended up back in Hamburg). Bevin tells the British Cabinet that, failing a satisfactory settlement, Britain should announce its intention to surrender the mandate of Palestine, and plan for an early withdrawal of British forces and administration.

29 November: General Assembly of United Nations votes for partition. Prior to vote, American Zionists had exerted unprecedented pressure on the United States administration, on delegations to the United Nations and on their governments, to secure the necessary majority.

December: fighting breaks out between Arabs and Jews throughout Palestine. British forces try not to get involved.

1948 10 January: when an irregular Arab force from Syria attacks a Jewish village, British forces assist settlers to repel the invasion.

16 January: Secretary of Defense, James V. Forrestal, tells American Cabinet that without access to Middle Eastern oil the Marshall Plan could not succeed, the United States could not fight a war or even maintain the peace-time tempo of its economy. It would be stupid to endanger permanently relations with the Muslim world, or stumble into war over Palestine.

19 February: Truman tells George Marshall to pursue a course over Palestine in the light of the United States's interests and to 'disregard all political factors'.

February: Republicans running campaign on a militantly pro-Zionist platform win an election victory in New York.

March: Arab terrorists, assisted by British deserters, and other Europeans, some of whom were on the run, seriously hamper communications throughout Palestine.

18 March: at Zionist instigation and through the intervention of the President's old business associate, Edward Jacobson, Truman finally sees Weizmann who impresses on the President the need to include the Negev area in the future Jewish state.

19 March: Warren Austin, the American representative at the United Nations, urges the Security Council to suspend its efforts to implement partition, and to establish instead a United Nations temporary trusteeship without prejudice as to the character of the eventual settlement.

25 March: Truman tells press conference that he remains in favour of partition at some future date.

April: Zionists in Palestine have around 30,000 men under arms, 10,000 others for local defence, with another 25,000 in a home guard. Short of heavy weapons, armour and aircraft.

April: British forces in Palestine at times help Arab populations to leave some cities, at times arrange cease-fires to allow Zionist settlers to evacuate their children and wounded. Haganah uses information of one withdrawal to take control of Haifa, and under a British-arranged truce most of the Arab population of 100,000 leave their homes. At end of April, Irgun, the Zionist terrorist organization led by Menachem Begin, under Haganah command attacks the Arab city of Jaffa.

20 April: Warren Austin, the United States representative at the United Nations, speaking at the United Nations, calls for a truce in Palestine and the establishment of a trusteeship.

21 April: British military authorities in Haifa area start withdrawing their forces. Zionists and Arabs clash. Arabs start fleeing.

7 May: Max Lowenthal, a White House consultant with Jewish Agency connections, sends Clark Clifford, Truman's electoral adviser, a memorandum calling for the recognition of the Jewish state before 15 May. Such a move would 'free the Administration of a serious and unfair disadvantage' in the forthcoming November elections.

9 May: contingents of the Irgun and Stern gang, under Haganah command, encounter strong Arab resistance in the village of Deir Yassin, and slaughter 245 men, women and children. Massacre thought by the Arabs to have been perpetrated with the approval of Ben-Gurion and the Haganah leadership to terrorize the Arab population into fleeing from their land.

12 May: Clifford urges Truman to give prompt recognition to the Zionist state. Marshall objects that this is just 'straight politics'.

13 May: Jaffa officially surrenders to Zionist forces. Only about 3,000 of the Arab population of 70,000 remain. Arabs besiege convoy of Jewish doctors and nurses on the road to Mount Scopus and kill 77.

14 May: as the British troops evacuate Jerusalem, the Israelis and Arabs seize appropriate positions in the city and prepare for battle. The Israelis have already secured a major strategic advantage: the face of the Samarian and Judean mountains facing west.

14 May: in a museum in Tel Aviv, David Ben-Gurion, under a portrait of Theodor Herzl, proclaims the establishment of a Jewish state in Palestine to be called Israel. Immediately recognized by the United States, followed by the Soviet Union. Israel is later admitted to the United Nations, but on conditions concerning Jerusalem and the Arab refugees that have not been fulfilled. The Arab states refuse to recognize Israel and insist that Israel is usurped Arab territory.

3. The significance of oil

1901 The Shah of Iran grants William Knox D'Arcy, an English prospector who had made money in gold mining in Australia, the first oil concession, to last for sixty years. D'Arcy gives him £20,000 and promises £20,000 in shares.

1908 First important well discovered east of Abadan.

1909 Anglo–Persian Oil Company founded.

1912 Turkish Petroleum Company formed against background of interest in Mosul fields. Company in German, Dutch and British ownership.

1914 British government acquires largest share of company operating the Persian concession so that the Royal Navy could be independent of Dutch and American firms who had control over the production and marketing of oil.

1916 In Britain, on the recommendations of Admiral Slade, a start made to form a British National Oil Company to check the dominance of Royal Dutch Shell and the American Standard Oil.

1918 July: at instigation of Sir Reginald Hall, the Admiralty Director of Naval Intelligence, Slade circulates a memorandum on the significance of oil fields in the Middle East.

   1 August: Colonel Sir Maurice Hankey urges Balfour to read this vitally important paper: oil could take the place of coal in the next war, or would be at least of equal importance. The only potential supply under British control is in Persia and Mesopotamia. Balfour argues that the securing of these oil wells would be imperialistic, but Hankey overcomes his resistance.

   13 August: British Foreign Secretary tells a conference of Dominion Prime Ministers that it would be unthinkable to allow Iraq to revert to Turkish or Arab rule, and that Mesopotamia would have to be the exception to the policy of no expansion of the British Empire as a result of the war.

1919 21 December: France and Britain sign an agreement on oil rights. France will get a 25 per cent share of the Turkish Petroleum

Company, placed under British control. France agrees to Britain's building two pipelines, and also a railway to transport oil from Mesopotamia and Persia through the French area in the Middle East to the Mediterranean.

1920 April: at San Remo conference France and Britain reach an agreement on oil similar to the one of December 1919.

1927 Major discoveries of oil in Iraq, particularly at the Kirkuk oilfield.

1928 Red Line agreement between partners in the Turkish Petroleum Company not to secure separate concessions in the Asian lands of the Ottoman Empire, apart from Kuwait and the Khanaqin district in Iraq.

1929 Private agreement, following negotiations started in 1925, between the British owners of the Turkish Petroleum Company, the French Compagnie des Petroles, and two American companies, Standard Oil of New Jersey and Socony–Vacuum, to form the Iraq Petroleum Company. This followed objections from the American oil companies, supported by the State Department, to the arrangements between Britain and France which excluded American interests from oil developments in Iraq. The Anglo–Persian Oil Company gave the American group half its holdings, the Americans thus gaining an overall share of 23.75 per cent. In return the Americans agreed to hold to the Red Line agreement.

1930 In Bahrain Standard Oil of California and the Texas Company form the Bahrain Petroleum Company (BAPCO), registered in Canada and secure the concession.

1931 Concession given to Iraq Petroleum Company to lands in the Baghdad and Mosul provinces east of the Tigris, except for those areas where the Anglo–Persian Oil Company had rights. Iraq Petroleum Company agrees to build a pipeline system to Haifa and the Syrian coast, and to make annual payments against future royalties. Royalties fixed at four shillings a ton for twenty years. Pipeline built from Kirkuk with one branch going to Haifa and the other to Tripoli. Both branches start delivering oil in 1934.

1932 Oil in commercial quantities discovered in Bahrain.

1933 April: new concession signed by Iranian government and the Anglo–Persian Oil Company. This followed wide variations in the amount Iran received under the 16 per cent profits agreement, for example: £1,400,000 in 1926; £307,000 in 1931. Iran's sterling balances also depreciated when Britain went off the gold standard. Britain tried to take the case to the League of Nations and the International Court of Justice when, in 1932, the Shah cancelled the concession to the Anglo–Persian Oil Company, but they ruled that they did not have jurisdiction. Under the 1933 agreement the company relinquished its exclusive rights to build and operate pipelines in Iran, and agreed to pay four shillings per ton (22 cents per barrel) on all oil sold in Iran or exported.

In Saudi Arabia, Ibn Saud gives a concession to the Standard Oil Company of California and receives an advance of 30,000 gold sovereigns. The concession is to run for sixty years, and four gold shillings per ton to be paid to Saudi Arabia.

1934 Bahrain first Arab-ruled country to export oil.

In Kuwait, following disagreements between an American and a British company over concession applications in 1932 and 1933, the two companies apply jointly for a concession which is granted for seventy-four years to the Kuwait Oil Company.

1936 First oil refinery in Gulf region built at Sitra in Bahrain.

1938 Burgan field, south of Kuwait city, shown to have oil. Thought to be the largest known reserve of oil in the world.

Considerable oil finds at Dhahran in Saudi Arabia. Saudi Arabia starts exporting oil with first shipment to Bahrain in November.

Fifty-seven per cent of Britain's oil comes from United States and Western hemisphere. Only 22 per cent comes from Middle East, and of that, 18 per cent supplied by Iran. Middle East provides around 6 per cent of the total output of world oil: Middle East producing 16 million tons per annum; 320,000 barrels per day.

1939 May: Ibn Saud opens Ras Tanura terminal. Saudi Arabia starts direct export of oil. Further oil wells located and Saudi Arabia considered a future oil-producing state.

1939–45 Little development of oil production in Middle East, as safer to transport oil to Europe from American continent.

1943 March: United States presidential committee under Senator Harry S. Truman reports that future American demand for oil likely to be in excess of domestic production. The committee expresses the view that possibly the United States is providing a disproportionate share of the Allies' oil and speculates that Britain had managed to bring about this state of affairs to further its own imperial interests.

1944 Texas Oil Company, Standard Oil of New Jersey and Socony–Vacuum join Standard Oil of California to form the Arabian–American Oil Company (ARAMCO). United States army requests building of refinery at Ras Tanura.

February: Secretary of State, Cordell Hull, commenting on a congressional resolution advocating the establishment of an independent Jewish state in Palestine, warns that the Arabs could 'play hell' with American oil interests.

1945 September: British Palestine Committee concludes that Middle East is the Empire's main reserve of oil.

1946 Oil production starts in Kuwait.

Following oil companies' protests over suggestion that United States government buy shares in ARAMCO and finance a pipeline from Dhahran to the Levant coast to cope with the demand for petroleum products in the Mediterranean, ARAMCO secures capital for the construction of the pipeline. Standard Oil of New Jersey and Socony–Vacuum acquire 30 and 10 per cent respectively of ARAMCO stock.

1948 16 January: Secretary of Defense, James S. Forrestal, tells American Cabinet that without access to Middle Eastern oil the Marshall Plan could not succeed, the United States could not fight a war or even maintain the peace-time tempo of its economy.

Earlier feelings in Middle East that Western oil concessions had been too generous are accentuated. Increasing complaints that concessions too large in area, for too long a period, offered poor financial terms to host countries, that oil companies had too much authority and that host countries could not control drilling or exports.

Income tax law passed by newly elected democratic government in Venezuela, giving the government 50 per cent of the oil companies' profits. In 1949 delegation goes from Venezuela to Gulf to explain system. Oil companies offer same deal to Middle Eastern governments. New system introduced in Saudi Arabia in 1950, and in Iraq and Kuwait in 1951. Profits divided equally between companies and governments. Increased producing countries' revenue per barrel from 22 cents to about 80 cents.

1948–9 Kuwait and Saudi Arabia grant concessions in their halves of the Neutral Zone to independent American companies, Aminoil and Getty.

1948 Construction of Saudi Arabian pipeline to Mediterranean halted with First Arab–Israeli War. Jordan, Lebanon and Syria insist that as long as the United States supports the partition of Palestine and the creation of the State of Israel there will be no line. Oil companies organize Trans-Arabian Pipe Line Company. Line completed by this company to run between Dhahran and Sidon, 1,068 miles (1,719 kilometres) in 1950. Initially line carries between 300,000 and 500,000 barrels of oil a day. In 1952 Saudi Arabia's oil production reaches 40 million tons.

1949 In Qatar, start of commercial exploitation of oil which had been discovered in the late 1930s.

Arab states use economic tactics against Israel. Their boycott consolidated by the closing of both the Suez Canal and the oil pipe-lines to Israel. Iraq Petroleum Company transfers its headquarters from Haifa to Tripoli. Israel has to rely on oil imported by tankers, and starts to explore for this commodity in the occupied territories. Israel tries using the port of Eilat on the Gulf of Aqaba, but Saudi Arabia leases islands at the mouth of the gulf to Egypt, who then establishes shore batteries, in December 1950, at Sharm el-Sheikh and Ras Nasrani on the southern tip of Sinai to close the gulf to Israeli shipping.

1951 The Iranian parliament under Prime Minister Mossadeq nationalizes the oil industry. Abadan refinery closed in April. British experts leave and production stops.

1952–5 A Saudi expedition seizes Buraimi oasis, the possession of which was disputed between Oman, Abu Dhabi and Saudi Arabia, in August 1952. Saudis tempt the Americans with offers of oil concessions. British-led Omani scouts drive the Saudis out. Kermit Roosevelt of the Central Intelligence Agency tries to bribe people in Abu Dhabi to cede Buraimi oasis to King Saud in order to open the way to the American firm ARAMCO, and to close it to the British-controlled Iraq Petroleum Company. But Britain is informed and takes the dispute to an international court where the Central Intelligence Agency tries to bribe the arbitrators.

1953 July: Mossadeq overthrown in Iran and the Shah returns. Subsequent negotiations with oil companies recognize principle of nationalization. (See chronology 5: The Mossadeq crisis in Iran, 1950–4.)

1954 August: a consortium of oil companies reaches an agreement with Iran. National Iranian Oil Company formed. The former Anglo–Iranian Oil Company, now known as British Petroleum, sells 60 per cent of its holdings and keeps only 40 per cent in the new consortium. Five American companies hold 40 per cent. In 1955 these companies each give up a 1 per cent share and nine other American companies join. Royal Dutch Shell holds 14 per cent. The French petroleum company, Compagnie Française des Pétroles, holds 6 per cent. This means that the share of British capital invested in the oil industry of the Middle East drops from 49 to 14 per cent, and the British share of oil production from 53 to 24 per cent. The American share increases from 44 to 58 per cent, and the American companies control 42 per cent of the capital.

1955 Middle East's share of the world's oil production increases from 16.7 per cent in 1950 to 21.2 per cent. Middle East's estimated share of the world's reserves increases from 45 per cent in 1950 to 75 per cent in 1956. In 1955, the Middle East supplies 79 per cent of Europe's oil; 45 per cent of this goes through the Suez Canal; 33 per cent is carried by the Syrian pipelines; and 4 per cent around South Africa.

1957 National Oil Company of Italy, ENI, leads change in profit-sharing agreements. Offers Iran 75 per cent of profits. Later enters into a similar partnership with Egypt and the Sinai oilfields.

1959 Oil discovered at Zeltan in Cyrenaica, Libya. Oil production in Libya largely managed by American companies, rises from 5 million metric tons in 1960 to 70 million tons in 1966.

1960 Director of petroleum affairs for Saudi Arabia in Baghdad establishes the Organization of Petroleum Exporting Countries (OPEC). Founder members are Iran, Iraq, Kuwait, Saudi Arabia and Venezuela. Qatar joins in 1961, Libya and Indonesia in 1962, Abu Dhabi in 1967, Algeria in 1969, Nigeria in 1971, Ecuador in 1973, and Gabon in 1975. Membership of Abu Dhabi transferred to United Arab Emirates in 1974. OPEC aims to stabilize world oil prices, ensure fair profits for oil companies, ensure oil supplies to consumers, and arrange boycotts of companies that do not co-operate.

1961 In Iraq, Kassem (head of government since 1958 revolution) expropriates over 99.5 per cent of the concession held by the Iraq Petroleum Company group. Claims companies not exploiting area.

1962 Production of crude oil starts in Abu Dhabi.

1967 Libya joins three-month Arab boycott of oil supplies to Britain, United States and West Germany following Six-Day War. Closure of Suez Canal makes Libyan crude oil more attractive to Western European markets.

1968 Kuwait, Libya and Saudi Arabia form the Organization of Arab Petroleum Exporting Countries (OAPEC). Membership confined to Arab states in which oil production a major part of the economy. Sheikh Yamani, Saudi Arabian oil minister, demands ARAMCO accept Saudi Arabian participation in producing, refining, transporting and marketing of oil, starting with a 20 per cent share.

1969 Production of crude oil starts in Dubai.

1971 At meeting of OPEC in Tehran, twenty-two oil companies agree that 55 per cent of profits should go to the producing countries. Companies also agree to a considerable increase in the 'posted price', the base from which profits are calculated, of crude oil. Also agree on a formula to change posted price in line with fluctuations in value of dollar. This gives OPEC considerable control over petroleum markets. Between 1970 and the end of 1972 the price of crude oil doubles to $3 a barrel.

December: assets of British Petroleum Company nationalized in Libya.

1972 Iraq nationalizes Iraq Petroleum Company.

1973 World consumption of oil jumps more than 4 million barrels a day. The Gulf area provides most of the increase in production.

May: in preparation for the October War against Israel, King Feisal of Saudi Arabia and President Boumedienne of Algeria make arrangements to control the radical oil producers. On 25th anniversary of creation of State of Israel Arab oil producers stop production for one hour to mark the anniversary of 'the usurpation of Palestine'.

17 October: OAPEC decides to reduce oil production.

OPEC twice raises price of oil. By end of year posted price set at $11.65 a barrel. Gulf oil $18 a barrel at auction.

1974 Oil prices quadrupled in roughly two years. By end of year, average posted price of Saudi Arabian crude oil stood at between $11 and $12 a barrel. World economy seriously disturbed. Recession starts.

Production of crude oil starts in Sharjah.

Qatar agrees to divide revenues from Bunduq oilfield with Abu Dhabi. Qatar agrees to buy 60 per cent of Qatar Petroleum Company and Shell Qatar.

1975 Assembly in Kuwait votes for full nationalization of oil. Kuwait agrees to sell oil to companies for five years. Kuwait starts to limit oil production and embarks on policy of leaving oil in the ground. Production reduced to 2 million barrels a day.

1976 Oil revenues in Kuwait worth nearly $8 billion. Kuwait's per capita income reaches $11,500, the highest in the world.

1976–7 Budget of Saudi Arabia jumps to $32.5 billion. Investment abroad $12 billion or more a year. Saudi Arabia at Doha in December, supported by the United Arab Emirates, refuses to agree to increase in oil prices demanded by other OPEC members.

1977–8 Iran's budget, 90 per cent of which consists of oil income, estimated at $49 billion. Revenues for 1973-4 had been $11.7 billion. Iran did not reduce oil production during the October War.

1977 December: at OPEC meeting oil prices remain frozen. Saudi Arabia supported by Iran, Kuwait, the United Arab Emirates and Qatar.

1979 Strikes in Iran against the Shah's regime which affected oilfields from October 1978 lead to crisis over oil prices. Saudi Arabia tries to hold down prices by increasing production, but when peace treaty signed between Egypt and Israel, shows displeasure to United States by stopping increased production in April. In September Nigeria breaks the $23.50 a barrel 'ceiling' by imposing a further premium on the price of its crude oil, and so starts off another round of price increases.

1981 Saudi Arabia responsible for 43 per cent of OPEC output. Has power to dictate oil prices. In May, Yamani, Saudi Arabia's Minister of Petroleum and Mineral Resources, asks for a freeze on oil prices to give Western economies time to breathe and recover. Saudis want a unified price structure which is achieved at meeting at Abu Dhabi in December.

1982 Oil refining starts at Mina al-Fahal in Oman.

1983 OPEC cuts official oil prices, assigns production quotas, and allows Saudis to vary production in relation to world demand.

1984 Production of crude oil starts in Ras al-Khaimah, a member of the United Arab Emirates, situated on the Gulf.
  New oil reserves discovered in Kuwait. Estimated to be 200 years of petroleum in reserve at prevailing rates of extraction.

1984–5 Despite creation of Ministerial Executive Council under Sheikh Yamani to allow checks on member countries' petroleum sales, pricing and production, the official price structure is eroded by abuse. Saudi Arabia's oil production at a twenty-year low in 1985 at 2.2 million barrels a day. Saudis unilaterally cut oil prices and increase output.

1986 By middle of year Saudi Arabia producing 5.5 million barrels of oil a day. Oil prices fall to the lowest level for six years. OPEC agrees to Saudi strategy for restrictions on output and pricing.

31 October: King Fahd of Saudi Arabia dismisses Sheikh Yamani, Minister of Oil since March 1962. Reason given for Yamani's dismissal is his opposition to Faud's demand for the restoration of a fixed price of at least $18 per barrel for oil.

1988 28 November: all OPEC countries agree on a quota system. Production limited to 18.5 million barrels of oil a day. Iraq and Iran have limits of around 2.6 million barrels each.

1989 27 January: representatives from 13 non-OPEC oil-exporting nations met with OPEC counterparts and agreed to support efforts to stabilize oil prices.

June: Kuwait demands exemption from agreed production quotas.

Oil producers in Middle East and North Africa control around 70 per cent of the world's known oil reserves, are responsible for 30 per cent of world production, and provide more than half the crude oil in the international trade.

(See chronology 13: The Gulf War, for an account of developments in 1990 and 1991.)

1992 22 May: at OPEC meeting agreement reached to maintain production ceiling at 22,982 million barrels per day, but Kuwait is allowed to produce more than its previous quota to compensate for production lost during the Iraqi occupation.

1993 June: oil prices below the targeted level of $21 per barrel that OPEC had hoped to sustain by re-introducing what in effect was the quota system that had been abandoned during the Gulf War.

1994 July: oil prices strengthen in response to the decision taken in June by OPEC to freeze production at 24.52 million barrels per day for the rest of 1994.

1995 July: petroleum prices weak, and increased demand for crude petroleum has been met by non-OPEC suppliers.

1996 20 May: Iraq and United Nations agree to the sale of Iraqi petroleum up to $4,000 million of oil a year to purchase food and medicines, and to pay for United Nations' operation in Iraq. Falls in petroleum prices following the announcement are not sustained.

4. Terrorism

1919 February: Arab terrorist group known as Black Hand formed in Palestine and attacks Jews. Changes name in May to the Self-Sacrificers.

1921–9 Palestinian terrorist activities, directed by the Mufti of Jerusalem, attempt to stop Jewish land settlements by raids. Arabs who oppose Mufti's leadership assassinated.

1929 Jewish communities in Jerusalem, Hebron and Safed attacked after 'Wailing Wall' incident. Police in Jerusalem had forcibly removed a screen illegally placed near the 'Wailing Wall' to separate Jewish men and women at prayer. To the Jews the Western Wall, the lower courses of the outer wall of Herod's temple, is a sacred sanctuary and a reminder of past glory. To the Arabs it is part of Haram al-Sherif, where Muhammad had tethered his horse after his journey from Mecca to Jerusalem, while he ascended to the seventh heaven.

1931 Terrorist group led by Izz al-Din al-Qassam established in Palestine. Inspired by the duty of jihad (holy war), Qassam advocates a strict adherence to Islam. Qassam and followers attack Jewish settlements from hills on West Bank.

1936 Followers of Qassam spearhead Arab rebellion in April by murdering two Jews. Mandatory police try to stop cycle of retaliatory killings on both sides.

1937 Irgun Zvai Leumi (National Military Organization), an underground body, founded by militant Zionist, David Raziel. Leads terrorist campaign against Arab population.

Arabs subsidize a group of volunteers led by Fawzi al-Qawuqji, born in Lebanon and an officer in the Iraqi army. These volunteers operate mainly in countryside, mine roads and interfere with the transportation network. Mufti directs operations of Arab terrorists from Baghdad.

1939 February: against background of London Round Table Conference, and Arab elation over rumours of an agreement along the lines of the Anglo–Iraqi Treaty, Zionists start new tactics: on 27 February thirty-eight Arabs die in a series of bomb explosions throughout Palestine.

1940 Abraham Stern, after refusing to observe the truce between the Irgun and the British on the outbreak of war with Germany, breaks with the Irgun and forms the Lohame Herut Israel (Fighters for the Freedom of Israel) which becomes widely known as the Stern Gang. Attacks British in Palestine and moderate Jews who oppose use of terrorism.

After a pro-Axis coup in Iraq, British negotiate with the Arab Higher Committee, but the Mufti orders continuation of the Arab rebellion. Later the Mufti goes to Italy and Germany where he works as a propagandist. After 1945 he directs activities from Cairo.

1942 Menachem Begin arrives from Poland and becomes leader of Irgun. Blames Britain for not saving the Jews of Central Europe.

1944 February: Begin changes tactics. Instead of attacking Arabs he concentrates on the edifices of British rule. Irgun bombs immigration offices, police stations and government buildings.

23 March: Stern Gang kills seven British policemen in Tel Aviv.

April: Foreign Office and State Department officials discuss Palestine. Britain feels that it can control the situation provided that the American Zionists can be kept quiet, but wants firm action against Zionist terrorism in Palestine lest there be attempts to assassinate prominent British officials. The Americans warn that in election year there will be support for Jewish agitation.

6 November: Lord Moyne, the British Minister Resident in the Middle East, murdered in Cairo by the Stern Gang.

17 November: Churchill tells House of Commons that 'if our dreams for Zionism are to end in the smoke of assassins' pistols and our labours for its future to produce only a new set of gangsters worthy of Nazi Germany, many like myself will have to reconsider the position we have maintained so consistently in the past'. Plans for the future of Palestine could not be considered in such a climate.

November: the Jewish Agency (widely regarded as the unofficial Zionist government in Palestine) and Haganah, the defence force of the Jewish colonists in Palestine, launch the 'Hunting Season', hounding members both of the Irgun and the Stern Gang, and hand many of them over to the British.

1945 April: United States administration has details of Haganah's new plans. Any solution condemning Jews to a permanent minority status in Palestine to be countered by military activity, resistance from the civilian population, including a general strike and the proclamation of death sentences against any Jews collaborating with the British. In the sections of Palestine it held, Haganah would establish a Jewish government. The Yishuv, the Jewish community in Palestine, was 'a bridgehead in the conquest of the empty sixty per cent of Palestine land, where homes can be made for millions of distressed Jews in Europe'. Haganah would carry on illegal immigration, even if this led to clashes with Britain or any outside authority. If Britain attempted to stop or drastically curtail immigration, Irgun and the Stern Gang would submit themselves to Haganah to form a united opposition.

October: alliance between Haganah, Irgun and Stern Gang operating effectively. British security force reaches 100,000. Zionist terrorists blow up bridges, railways, raid military camps and kill British conscript troops.

2 November: Bevin tells Weizmann that Jewish Agency can no longer be regarded as an innocent party in relation to terrorist outrages.

1946 25 April: Stern Gang kills seven British soldiers in arms raid in Tel Aviv.

1 May: in reply to Truman's endorsement of those aspects of the Anglo–American commission of enquiry's report favourable to Zionism, and the British public's outrage at the murder of British soldiers by Zionist terrorists, Attlee tells the House of Commons that a large number of Jewish immigrants could not be absorbed into Palestine in a short time unless the illegal organizations were disbanded and disarmed.

June: Zionist terrorists kidnap five British officers in a series of attacks. The British Cabinet decides to suppress illegal organizations; this necessitates raiding the offices of the Jewish Agency as there is evidence of its connections with Haganah. On 29 June military and police forces occupy buildings in Jerusalem and Tel Aviv, including the Jewish Agency, arrest about 2,000 people, and seize large quantities of documents which reveal the close connection between the agency and Haganah.

22 July: Jerusalem's King David Hotel, one wing of which is used as British army headquarters, blown up. Ninety-one people killed. Begin later claims that warning given, but nature of warning disputed. After explosion the British army commander, Lieutenant-

General Sir Evelyn Barker, speaks of 'punishing the Jews in a way the race dislikes by striking at their pockets'.

1 October: Bevin warns Weizmann that the British government had not 'taken the initiative in blowing people up'. 'The destruction of the King David Hotel had burned deeply into the hearts of the British people.' Britain could not allow its young soldiers in Palestine to be slaughtered.

December: internal situation in Palestine deteriorates with increase in terrorist activities. On 27 December a sixteen-year-old Zionist, convicted of terrorism and too young to hang, sentenced to eighteen years' imprisonment and eighteen cuts with a cane, is duly beaten. On 29 December Irgun, under Begin's leadership, kidnap and flog four British officers administering each eighteen strokes with rawhide whips or a rope end. Terrorist implicated in floggings is one of the few later hanged by the administration. Palestine administration stops using judicial corporal punishment and the incident wears down British morale at a time when moves for withdrawal from Palestine being aired in official circles.

1947 January: Britain evacuates 2,000 non-essential staff from Palestine. Main post office, police headquarters and other government buildings enclosed in a wire security compound which becomes known as Bevingrad.

March: sensational kidnappings of British personnel by Zionist terrorists in retaliation for death sentences passed by mandatory authorities on Zionist murderers inflame people in Britain. Plans laid for the imposition of martial law in Tel Aviv; imposed briefly after twenty British soldiers killed in attack on the Jerusalem officers' club.

April: Attlee complains to Americans about report that the mayor of New York has initiated a Zionist drive to raise nearly £2 million for the purchase of 'men, ships, guns and money': £250,000 of this would be taken to Palestine to aid underground resistance before 4 July; £750,000 would be used for running illegal immigrant ships to Palestine; and the residue for the establishment of a provisional government for Palestine. Attlee complains: 'the guns which are being subscribed for in America can only be required to shoot at British soldiers in Palestine, and it is a matter for the greatest regret that they should be supplied from the United States'.

29 May: Foreign Office protests to Lewis Douglas, the American ambassador in London, about the probability of funds openly collected in the United States being passed on to Irgun. In particular it objects to Ben Hecht's encouragement of the terrorists by advertisements. The profits from Hecht's Zionist musical *A Flag is Born* go to Irgun, tax free, as contributions to charity. Eleanor Roosevelt active in fund-raising campaign.

31 July: bodies of two British sergeants, one of whom has a Jewish mother, found hanged and booby-trapped. Perpetrated by Irgun in retaliation for execution of Zionist terrorists. This act determines the fate of the illegal immigrants on board *Exodus*, as with widespread outbreaks of anti-Semitism in Britain Bevin left with no alternative but to send them back to Germany.

August: British public blames the Americans for giving the terrorists money; the *Daily Mail* on 1 August appeals to the feelings of 'American women whose dollars helped to buy the rope'. Press and some Members of Parliament demand an early evacuation of British troops from Palestine: Britain could no longer support the moral and financial drain.

24 November: Bevin tells Marshall that anti-Semitism is growing in Britain. The callous murder of the two sergeants is responsible. Before that act Bevin felt that the situation in Palestine could be held.

1948 March: Arab terrorists, assisted by some British deserters, Yugoslavs, Germans and Poles, seriously hamper communications throughout Palestine.

13 April: Arabs besiege a convoy of mainly Jewish doctors and nurses on the road to Mount Scopus: seventy-seven killed. Convoy expects to be relieved by British troops but these do not appear.

9 May: contingents of the Irgun and the Stern Gang, under Haganah command, encounter strong Arab resistance in the village of Deir Yassin, and slaughter 245 men, women and children. The massacre of Deir Yassin thought by the Arabs to have been perpetrated with the approval of Ben-Gurion and the Haganah leadership to terrorize the Arab population into fleeing from their land. Begin later speaks of the 'heroic' acts of his men at Deir Yassin, and attributes the Arab flight from the new state of Israel to this incident.

June: during first cease-fire of the First Arab–Israeli War, Irgun apparently defies authority of Israeli government and tries to bring in arms openly from the ship, *Altalena*. Official forces, initially led by Moshe Dayan, take action. After a short engagement Irgun withdraws. On 28 June the entire Israeli army take oath of allegiance.

17 September: United Nations mediator Count Bernadotte murdered on decision of Stern Gang Centre of which Yitzhak Shamir is a member. After this Ben-Gurion orders the dissolution of Irgun and the Stern Gang. Over 200 arrested, but eventually they are released without trial.

1953 14–15 October: Qibya raid in which Israeli soldiers kill sixty-six men, women and children of the village. Even sympathetic American newspapers compare the incident to the Nazi massacre of 185 men of the village of Lidice in Czechoslovakia in 1942 in reprisal for the assassination of an SS chief.

1954 17 March: Arabs ambush an Israeli bus on Scorpions' Pass, in eastern Negev: eleven Israelis killed. In retaliation Israeli raiders later hit the village of Nahhaleen, and kill nine inhabitants.

July: possibly at the instigation of Ben-Gurion, a group of rather amateur Israeli agents try to sabotage British and American property in Egypt in the hope of giving the impression that violent elements in Egypt oppose the *rapprochement* with Britain and the United States, and that the Egyptians could not control these dissident elements. The operation fails, and the Egyptians later release details of the ring and hang two members on 31 January 1955. The Israeli Defence Minister, Pinchas Lavon, is seen by some as being responsible, but he tries to blame the affair on Shimon Peres, the Director-General of the Ministry of Defence, Moshe Dayan, and General Benjamin Givly, the chief of intelligence.

1955–6 Fedayeen raids mounted from Egyptian-controlled Gaza Strip.

1956–7 Yasser Arafat, born in Jerusalem and educated in Cairo where he had been connected with the Muslim Brotherhood, founds al-Fatah, the Palestine National Liberation Movement, in Cairo. Initially sponsored by Nasser, but after cease-fire agreement Arafat moves to Kuwait in 1957.

1957 Following Sinai campaign, fedayeen operate under Egyptian direction in Iraq, Jordan, Syria and Lebanon.

1962 Fatah's 'Palestine Office' opened in Algiers. Believes in the armed struggle to liberate Palestine.

1964 May: Ahmad Shukairy calls a Palestine conference in Jerusalem, attended by all the Arab foreign ministers, and forms the Palestine Liberation Organization, the PLO. Its aim is to unite all expatriate Palestinians, including those on the West Bank. There will be a government in exile with headquarters in Gaza; an army to be recruited from the Palestinian refugees. Nasser offers the PLO Egyptian instructors and equipment.

1965 1 January: military wing of Fatah, al-Asifah (the Storm) mounts first commando action. Operates from West Bank and Gaza. Claims responsibility for thirty-nine commando actions in 1965.

1968 21 March: Israeli retaliatory raid on a Fatah base in the Karameh refugee camp in Jordan. Israelis suffer casualties and incident hailed as PLO victory.

1969 Fatah moves to Jordan where other Palestinian terrorist groups are operating, including the Marxist-Leninist Popular Front for the Liberation of Palestine (PFLP), the Popular Democratic Front for the Liberation of Palestine (PDFLP); the Syrian-sponsored al-Saiqa and the pro-Iraqi Arab Liberation Front. All agree on necessity of confrontation with King Hussein of Jordan, regarded as a Western Zionist puppet.

18 February: Palestinian terrorism spreads to international level with attack by PFLP on El Al Boeing 720 at Zurich. Three terrorists killed.

1970 6 September: PFLP start hijacking aircraft to Dawson Field, a strip about 30 miles (50 km) from Amman. They demand the release of fedayeen in British, German and Swiss gaols, and say that they will keep Israeli and American-Israeli passengers until guerrillas released from Israeli gaols. Until this episode Arab terrorism has followed the sort of tactics used by Begin and Irgun, with the connivance of Haganah, against the British in the Palestine mandate; on the whole, terrorism directed against Israeli citizens and sympathizers. This new departure, involving Western nationals, is probably based on their feeling that the West is responsibile for the plight of Palestinian refugees. On 9 September a BOAC jet hijacked from Bahrain and flown to Dawson Field. PFLP demand release of Leila Khaled from a British gaol. On 12 September three planes blown up. Apart from fifty-four passengers kept as hostages, others allowed to leave. Arab League secures their release as part of deal entailing release of terrorists held in European gaols.

Dr George Habash, leader of the PFLP, founds the Free Jordan Movement with the aim of overthrowing Hussein. Arafat denounces Habash, but Hussein decides that no agreement is possible with the Palestinian guerrillas. In July Hussein attacks their camps, but full battle is not joined until 17 September – 'Black September' – when the Jordanian army is sent into action against the PLO militia. By July 1971 the PLO guerrillas have moved to Lebanon.

1972 May: Black September group, formed to avenge the defeat in Jordan in 1970, attempts unsuccessfully to hijack a Belgian Sabena aircraft at Israel's Ben-Gurion airport. On 30 May three members of Japanese Red Army, acting for PFLP, fire machine-guns and throw grenades in arrivals lounge at Ben-Gurion airport, killing twenty-four people.

September: Black September murders eleven Israeli athletes at the Munich Olympics. Black September later secures release of three of the terrorists captured at Munich by hijacking a Lufthansa aircraft flying between Beirut and Ankara. Israelis respond by air raids on Palestinian terrorist bases in refugee camps in Lebanon.

1974 April: attack on the Military Technical Academy at Heliopolis, outside Cairo, by radical Islamic group led by Salih Siriyya.

April: Popular Front for the Liberation of Palestine–General Command attacks an apartment block in the town of Qiryat Shmona in the north of Israel, in which the three terrorists and eighteen Israelis, eight of whom are children, die. According to the Israelis, the terrorists went in and killed. The Popular Front version is that their members seized hostages, demanded the release of Palestinian prisoners, and when the Israelis stormed the building, the terrorists blew it up.

May: at the village of Ma'alot, ninety Israeli school cadets are taken hostage by the Popular Democratic Front for the Liberation of Palestine in an attempt to secure the release of twenty-six prisoners, one for each year of Israel's existence. When the school is stormed, twenty children and three terrorists die, and seventy people are wounded. Together with the outrage at Qiryat Shmona, the massacre at Ma'alot provides a context for the increase in American arms supplies to Israel.

1975 April: in Lebanon, Palestinian gunmen shoot the bodyguard of the Maronite Christian Phalangist leader, Pierre Gemayel. Phalangist gunmen retaliate by killing a bus-load of Palestinians. Precipitates factional fighting in Lebanon between Christians and Muslims, and Lebanese civil war.

November: General Assembly invites the PLO to take part in United Nations debates on the Middle East.

1976 PLO, assisted by Syrian artillery, attack Christian town of Damour just outside Beirut. Cut off food and water supplies and refuse to allow Red Cross to take out wounded. Infants and children die of dehydration. Town transformed into a PFLP stronghold.

June: PFLP hijack an Air France plane to Entebbe, Uganda and demand release of imprisoned Palestinians. Foiled by raid on Entebbe airport by Israeli paratroopers.

1977 July: kidnapping and murder of former Minister of Religious Endowment in Egypt by radical Islamic group, Society of Muslims (Jamaat al-Muslimin), popularly known as Jamaat al-Takfir wa'l-Hijra (Society of Emancipation and Flight).

9 November: in response to rocket attack by Palestinian terrorists on a settlement in the north of Israel, the Israeli air force bombs refugee camps in the south of Lebanon.

1978 11 March: PLO launches a series of raids from south of Lebanon by land and sea to attack near Tel Aviv, leaving thirty-seven dead and seventy-six wounded Israeli civilians. The Israeli Defence Forces retaliate on 14 March by mounting a massive operation across the northern frontier and establish themselves six miles into Lebanese territory.

1979 4 November: Iranian militants take sixty-six hostages in the American embassy in Tehran. Only released on 20 January 1981 when Reagan becomes President.

20 November: Grand Mosque in Mecca is attacked by group of Islamic zealots led by Juhayman al-Utaybi.

1980 February: after the killing of an Israeli settler on the West Bank, the Israeli Cabinet allows, in principle, Jewish settlement in Hebron, the site of the Cave of Patriarchs and a site holy to both Jews and Muslims. Arabs on West Bank riot.

May: the PLO kills six Jewish settlers following the shooting of a Palestinian youth by an Israeli officer. The Israeli authorities react by blowing up houses near the scene of the terrorist ambush, and deport the mayors of Hebron and Halhul. United Nations Security Council condemns Israeli action.

Settlers sponsored by Gush Emunim (an organization of young Israeli activists that pioneered Israeli settlement in historical Judea, which was populated by Arabs), and two Israeli army officers are charged with attempted assassinations of three West Bank Palestinian mayors.

1981 Begin responds to PLO retaliatory attacks on settlements in Galilee with raids on Beirut itself.

6 October: President Sadat is assassinated in Cairo by a group of Islamic extremists. Group had hoped to stage a *coup d'état* and declare Egypt an Islamic republic.

1982 3 June: Palestine National Liberation Movement led by 'Abu Nidal' (Sabri Khalil al-Banna, the dissident Fatah leader) attempts to assassinate Israeli ambassador in London. Israeli intelligence tells Begin that Abu Nidal's objective is to provoke an Israeli attack on

PLO strongholds in Lebanon. Begin refuses to pass this information on to the Cabinet. The Israeli airforce bomb PLO targets in Lebanon, penetrating as far as West Beirut. PLO respond by shelling Israeli settlements in Galilee. This provides the Israeli justification for the invasion of Lebanon.

21 August: start of evacuation of PLO fighters from Lebanon.

September: Lebanese Maronite Christian Phalangist militia with survivors from Damour allowed by Israeli commander, Sharon, and Bashir Gemayel, the Maronite President-elect of Lebanon, to clear remaining 2,000 PLO fighters out of refugee camps of West Beirut. Israeli troops surround the camps at Sabra and Shatila and open a way through for the Phalangists. Estimates of dead range from 1,000 to 2,000.

1983 18 April: American embassy in Beirut blown up; forty-six dead. Islamic Jihad (Holy War), inspired by the Ayatollah Khomeini of Iran, says that it is responsible.

23 October: suicide bomb attacks wipe out the headquarters of both the American and French contingents of the Multi-national Force in Beirut: 265 marines and fifty-eight French soldiers killed. A Shiite group with Iranian connections says that it is responsible.

12 December: series of bombings in Kuwait City kills seven and injures sixty. Iraqi and Lebanese Shiites, thought to be members of Islamic Jihad, arrested. Become known as 'Kuwait 17'.

1984 18 January: murder of Malcolm Kerr, President of the American University of Beirut. Claimed by Islamic Jihad.

March, May, December: kidnapping of several Americans in Beirut claimed by Islamic Jihad.

1985 January: explosions in sea-front cafés in Kuwait City kill eleven and injure ninety. Arab Revolutionary Brigade claims responsibility. Intention apparently to exacerbate relations between Sunni and minority Shiite populations.

14 June: two Lebanese Shiites, possibly members of Hezbollah, a Lebanese Shiite fundamentalist group, hijack a TWA aircraft with 153 people on board. One hundred hostages released in Beirut and Algiers, then plane returns to Beirut on 16 June. On 17 June Nabih Berri, leader of the Shiite militia, Amal, announces that forty-two hostages, mainly American, taken to secret hideouts in Beirut and demands release of 766 Lebanese prisoners held in Israeli goals. Israel refuses unless asked to do so by United States government. Release of hostages secured by Asad of Syria and his contacts with Berri and Amal.

25 May: attempted assassination of Emir of Kuwait, Jabir al-Ahmad Al Sabah, by suicide car-bombing probably carried out by militant Shiite group, Hizb al-Dawa al-Islamiyya (The Islamic Call Party).

25 September: three Israelis murdered on a yacht in a marina at Larnaca, Cyprus. Israelis claim that this was the work of an élite commando from Fatah's Force 17. PLO denies this and says that the three Israelis were Mossad (secret service) agents reporting arms shipments to Lebanon.

1 October: using satellite intelligence information provided by Jonathan Jay Pollard, the Israeli spy at the United States Naval Security and Investigative Command, eight Israeli F–16 aircraft bomb the headquarters of the PLO outside Tunis: fifty-six Palestinians and fifteen Tunisians killed. Arafat escapes. Although condemned by the United Nations and European leaders, Israel supported in this action by US President Reagan, who describes the raid as a legitimate response to terrorism.

7 October: Muhammad Abu Abbas, leader of a minor Palestinian faction, the Popular Liberation Front, instigates the hijacking of an Italian liner, the *Achille Lauro*, with 400 passengers and crew. PLO condemn action and persuade hijackers to surrender to Egyptian authorities. Hijackers murder a crippled American Jew. While being flown to Tunis, hijackers diverted by American fighters to a NATO base in Sicily. Italians stop Americans from taking hijackers into custody.

1986 15 April: explosion in nightclub in West Berlin used by American servicemen, killing two and injuring more than 200. American bombers from bases in Britain then raid Tripoli and Benghazi, killing many civilians. Libya considered by United States as sponsor of international terrorism.

17 April: Israeli guard discovers Semtex in bag of Ann Murphy about to board an El Al flight to Tel Aviv. Placed there by Jordanian boyfriend, Nizar Hindawi. Syrian airforce intelligence possibly involved; but Asad and government probably did not know of operation. Leads to Britain breaking diplomatic relations with Syria in October 1986.

November: revelations of secret arms deal between Iran and the United States, initiated by Israel on the pretext that it could lead to the release of American hostages.

1987 January: following bomb attacks on oil installations, eleven Shiites arrested in Kuwait.

18 May: six members of a terrorist organization recently formed in the occupied territories, Islamic Jihad (separate from the Lebanese Islamic Jihad), escape from security wing of Gaza Central Prison. Strike Israeli targets and assassinate two Arabs suspected of collaborating with Israel. Some killed in gun battle with Israeli forces on 6 October. Help to spark off the Palestinian uprising which becomes known as the intifada.

25 November: hang-glider flown by a member of the Popular Front for the Liberation of Palestine–General Command (PFLP–GC) across Lebanese border results in death of six soldiers in an Israeli army camp. Palestinian morale boosted.

1988 April: Lebanese Shiites led by a member of Hezbollah hijack a Kuwaiti Airlines plane flying between Bombay and Kuwait. Release of 'Kuwait 17' demanded. Following two weeks of bargaining at Larnaca airport in Cyprus and in Algiers, all hostages released except for two Kuwaiti Sunnis who are murdered on board. 'Kuwait 17' not released.

November: Palestinian National Council, the parliament in exile of the PLO, rejects terrorism and confines the use of violence to Israel and the occupied territories.

1989 13 January: first official British contact with PLO: William Waldegrave, Minister of State at the Foreign Office, after meeting with Arafat, compares terrorism of the PLO with that of Shamir's Stern Gang and its assassination of Lord Moyne in Cairo in November 1944.

1990 Release of some Western hostages who had been held captive in Lebanon.

5 November: Meir Kahane, leader of the banned Kach Party in Israel which stood for the expulsion of Palestinians from Eretz Israel (the land of Israel) and a state based on the Torah, assassinated in New York.

1991 August: British hostage, John McCarthy, is released by Islamic Jihad (Lebanon). American hostage Edward Tracey who had been kidnapped by members of the Revolutionary Justice Organization is also freed. Islamic Jihad sends a letter to the Secretary-General of the United Nations, Pérez de Cuéllar, indicating that they might free other hostages if 'detainees around the world' are released. This gives rise to hopes that ten other Western hostages held in the Middle East, including Terry Waite, the Archbishop of Canterbury's emissary, might be freed. The key to the situation is seen to be the over 300 Shiite detainees held by Israel in its security zone in Southern Lebanon, and the fate of Sheikh Abdul Karim Obeid, the Hezbollah leader kidnapped by Israeli commandos in Southern Lebanon in 1989 and imprisoned in Israel. Israel insists that the fate of seven Israeli servicemen, captured during the Israeli invasion of Lebanon in 1982 and afterwards, and either dead or held by various groups presumably in Lebanon, is central to any potential deal.

8 August: Shapour Bakhtiar, the last Prime Minister of Iran under the Shah, assassinated in Paris. Thought to be an attempt to embarrass the Iranian government for assisting with the release of John McCarthy.

22 October: Islamic Jihad (Lebanon) release American hostage Jesse Turner who had been held since 1987.

1 November: at Madrid conference Syrian Foreign Minister, Faruq al-Shara, replies to Shamir's attacks on his country as a harbourer of terrorist organizations by brandishing a wanted poster of Shamir and saying: 'he himself recognizes that he was a terrorist and that he participated in the assassination of Count Bernadotte (the United Nations mediator) in 1948'.

6 November: Georges Habash announces that the PFLP is suspending its membership of the PLO Executive Committee following the Madrid agreements.

9 November: announcement made in Damascus that agreement had been reached in principle between Syria and the PLO for the opening, after eight years' closure, of the offices of al-Fatah the largest constituent group within the PLO.

13 November: following a joint British–American investigation into the explosion of Pan American 747 over the Scottish village of Lockerbie on 21 December 1988 which killed all 259 people on board and eleven villagers, London and Washington file charges against two alleged Libyan government intelligence officials. Previously it had been suggested that Syrian, Iranian or Palestinian groups might have been involved. Now Lockerbie bombing thought to be an act of revenge for American bombing of Tripoli in April 1986.

18 November: following further United Nations mediation over a three-way exchange covering Western hostages, Arabs held by Israel, and Israelis held in Lebanon, Terry Waite, who is suspected of being involved with Oliver North and the American exchange of arms for hostages in Iran (the Iran–Contragate affair), is released by Hezbollah, and the American citizen Thomas Sutherland, kidnapped on 9 June 1985, is released by Islamic Jihad (Lebanon).

December: apart from two German aid workers abducted in 1989 and held by the Hamadi clan affiliated to Hezbollah as a ransom for the release of two of its sons held in German jails on murder, hijack and kidnap charges, remaining Western hostages, including Joseph Cicippio and Terry Anderson, are freed.

1992 16 February: in retaliation for the killing of three Israeli soldiers in northern Israel, Israeli helicopter gunships kill Sheikh Abbas Mousawi, the most senior Hezbollah leader, in an attack southeast of Beirut.

May: in Egypt fighting between militant Islamists and Coptic Christians leads to fourteen deaths, mainly Coptic Christians in Asyut governorate in Egypt. There follows an intensification of campaign by Islamists to overthrow Egyptian government and to establish an Islamic state.

9 June: Farag Fouda, a writer and critic of militant Islam, murdered by Islamic Jihad. At the trial of those accused, a year later, Sheikh Muhammad al-Ghazali, a leading Islamist scholar, claims that it is legitimate to kill any Muslim opposed to the application of Islamic law.

July: People's Assembly in Egypt enacts a new law to fight terrorism, including the death sentence.

December: in Egypt eight Islamists sentenced to death for conspiring to overthrow the government. It is reported that Islamist violence has led to seventy deaths, including foreign tourists who have become targets for the first time. The leader of one of the extremist Islamist groups, Jamaah al-Islamiyah, had attacked the idea of foreign tourism in Egypt and had threatened to destroy the Pharonic tourist sites. In 1992 the number of tourists fell by 40 per cent, and there was a loss of foreign earnings of $1,500 million as a result.

1993 January–December: in Egypt more than 250 terrorist outrages result in 274 deaths. Those attacked include the Prime Minister, Atif Sidqi, the Minister of Information, Muhammad el-Sharif, and the Minister of the Interior, Muhammad Hussein el-Alfi. Some of these attacks are attributed to the Vanguards of Conquest, a faction of Islamic Jihad. Tourists are also killed, and many international tour operators leave Egypt: revenue from tourism falls by around $800 million to $1,300 million.

April: in Egypt Mubarak dismisses the Minister of the Interior, Muhammed Abd el-Halim Moussa, as he has been willing to talk to imprisoned leaders of Islamic Jihad and Jamaah al-Islamiyah. General Hussein Muhammad el-Alfi, the new Minister of the Interior, stops indiscriminate mass arrests, and in August there are criticisms by courts of previous police practice and allegations of torture of suspects.

July: following bomb attacks against Jewish property resulting in considerable deaths in London and Buenos Aires, Washington accuses Iran of being behind the outrages. But Argentinian authorities are unable to find sufficient evidence to press charges against four Iranians.

October: in Egypt, after being reappointed Minister of the Interior, Hussein Muhammad el-Alfi states that new government will face terrorism with 'extreme force, resolution and firmness'. Military courts continue to be used for the trial of militant Islamists.

1994 January: bomb attacks on cinemas in Amman and Zarqa, Jordan, attributed to Islamist extremists.

February–March: in Egypt Jamaah al-Islamiyah sends faxes to international news agencies warning that foreign investors and tourists should leave Egypt. This policy is condemned by Vanguard of the Conquest on the grounds that it would increase the hardships of Muslim peoples. There are attacks on tourist trains in Upper Egypt and on Nile cruise ships. Jamaah al-Islamiyah warns Egyptians to close their accounts at banks practising riba (usury). Egyptian security forces jail around 29,000 Islamist militants.

25 February: Baruch Goldstein, an American-born member of Kach, resident of Kiryat Arba, the Jewish settlement in Hebron, massacres twenty-nine worshippers in the Ibrahim Mosque in Hebron with automatic gunfire. Alleged that Israeli soldiers did not stop Goldstein from entering mosque, and closed the doors preventing those inside from fleeing. Massive Palestinian protests follow, and a further thirty-three Palestinians are killed over the following eight days.

October: following stabbing in Cairo of Naguib Mahfouz, the Egyptian novelist who had been awarded the Nobel Prize and denounced as an 'infidel' by Muslim extremists, the Ministry of the Interior announces that the attack has been ordered by Jamaah al-Islamiyah.

Hamas kidnaps an Israeli soldier, Nachshon Waxman, and demands the release of 500 Hamas followers from jails. Israeli Defence Force mounts unsuccessful rescue operation. Then Hamas, in a suicide bombing attack, kills twenty-two Israelis in a bus in Tel Aviv.

2 November: Hani Abed, a leader of Islamic Jihad in Gaza, is blown up in booby-trapped car. Thought to be an Israeli undercover operation.

12 November: Islamic Jihad mounts a suicide attack at an Israeli Defence Force checkpoint in Gaza, killing three Israeli soldiers.

1995 22 January: against the background of new settlement programmes and confiscation of Palestinian land, two Islamic Jihad suicide bombers kill twenty-two Israelis, most of whom are soldiers, in a planned attack at Beit Lid. Arafat condemns the bombing and detains Islamic Jihad cadres. Israel closes Gaza Strip and West Bank.

31 March: Israeli helicopter gunships attack car carrying Hezbollah official, Rida Yasin, killing him and his companion. Hezbollah retaliates with rocket attacks on northern Israel.

2 April: an explosion in an apartment block in Gaza City kills four Palestinians, including important members of Izz al-Din al-Qassam, the military wing of Hamas, and injures thirty others. Hamas accuses the Palestinian Authority of collaborating with Israel in bombing the building. Palestinian Authority representatives assert explosion is a result of bomb manufacturing.

9 April: Hamas and Islamic Jihad retaliate for Gaza apartment-block explosion with two suicide attacks on soldiers and settlers in Gaza that leave eight dead and fifty wounded. Israel closes West Bank and Gaza Strip.

26 June: an unsuccessful attempt to assassinate President Mubarak of Egypt in Addis Ababa in Ethiopia. Mubarak accuses Sudan. Jamaah al-Islamiyah claims responsibility.

25 July: Hamas, against the background of talks between the Palestinian Authority and Israeli authorities about a phased Israeli withdrawal from Hebron and the position of the 300 Israeli settlers there, mounts a suicide bombing on a bus travelling through a Tel Aviv suburb, killing six Israelis.

21 August: Hamas female suicide bomber kills five Israelis on a Jerusalem bus, followed by another closure of the Gaza Strip and the West Bank.

September: Kusrat Rasoul Ali, the Kurdish Prime Minister, survives a bomb attack in Arbil.

26 October: Fathi Shaqaqi, the leader of Islamic Jihad, assassinated in Valeta, Malta. Thought to be a Mossad operation, something the Israeli government refused to confirm or deny.

4 November: Yitzhak Rabin, the Israeli Prime Minister, shot by Yigal Amir, a religious Jewish nationalist, while leaving a peace rally in Tel Aviv.

November: in Egypt Jamaah al-Islamiyah advises foreign tourists to leave and resumes attacks on tourist trains.

13 November: in Riyadh in Saudi Arabia offices of the United States training mission to the Saudi Arabian national guard are bombed, and five Americans and two other foreign nationals are killed, and around sixty wounded. Several organizations claim responsibility, including the Islamic Movement for Change, which had warned of such attacks if foreign troops did not withdraw from the Gulf, and the Tigers of the Gulf. In April 1996 four Saudi nationals are accused and claim to have been influenced by Islamist elements from outside. They are executed.

1996 January: Abdul al-Karim al-Karabiti, the Prime Minister of Jordan, admits that there have been thirty-six attacks by terrorists aimed at destabilizing Jordan.

January–February: in Bahrain there are several bomb attacks in the Manama business district. Islamic Front for the Liberation of Bahrain claim responsibility for an explosion in the Diplomat Hotel in February which wounds several people. The subsequent closure of mosques provokes renewed violence, and eight opposition leaders are arrested.

4 January: Yahya Ayyash, known as the 'Engineer', thought to have been the organizer of the Hamas bus bombings in Israel, killed in Gaza by a booby-trapped mobile telephone. 100,000 Palestinians attend his funeral, and his death ends a *de facto* cease-fire that has been observed by Hamas.

25 February: on the second anniversary of the Hebron mosque massacre, Palestinian suicide bombings in Jerusalem and Ashkelon kill twenty-five Israelis and wound fifty-five more.

March: in Bahrain seven Bangladeshi workers are killed in a fire-bomb attack on a restaurant in Sitra.

3–4 March: further waves of bombings in Tel Aviv and Jerusalem leave thirty-two Israelis dead. Izz al-Din al-Qassam claims responsibility but contradictory statements suggest a rift within the Hamas leadership. Palestinian Authority outlaws five Palestinian militias including Izz al-Din al-Qassam. Israel closes West Bank and Gaza Strip for an indefinite period.

April: in Cairo seventeen Greek tourists outside the Europa hotel are killed by four gunmen shouting 'God is great'. Jamaah al-Islamiyah claims that it had intended to shoot a group of Israeli tourists in revenge for Israeli strikes against Hezbollah in Lebanon.

18 April: during 'Operation Grapes of Wrath' mounted by Israel against Lebanon in retaliation for Hezbollah's action in the self-declared Israeli security zone in south Lebanon, Israeli shells land on a United Nations base at the village of Qana, killing 105 civilian refugees and wounding many others, including United Nations soldiers. Israel claims shelling is a result of technical and procedural errors, but this is rejected by the Secretary-General of the United Nations, Boutros-Boutros Ghali.

early June: in Bahrain government organizes a press conference to reveal that ten prisoners had confessed to being members of Hezbollah Bahrain, a terrorist group created on the instruction of

Iran's Revolutionary Guards. Claims are made that Shiites from Bahrain had been trained in Qom and in the Bekaa valley, and that the previous eighteen months of violence had been a result of a 'terrorist campaign of sabotage' perpetrated by Hezbollah Bahrain with the object of replacing the government with a pro-Iranian regime. Subsequently doubts cast on these claims.

4 June: in Al-Khobar, near Dhahran, Saudi Arabia, an explosive device attached to a petroleum tanker detonates outside United States military housing and kills nineteen United States personnel, and wounds 400 others. Two unknown groups, the Legions of the Martyr Abdullah Huzaifi and Hezbollah-Gulf, claim responsibility.

mid-July: following re-introduction of Israel Defence Force undercover units to West Bank, including into areas under Palestinian Authority control, one unit is thought to be responsible for the killing of an Islamic Jihad activist in Ramallah in an area under Palestinian security control.

1997 17 November: fifty-eight tourists and four Egyptians are killed at the temple of Hapshetsut near the Valley of the Kings outside Luxor, the site of the staging in October of the opera Aida, which had been intended to show that the Egyptian security forces had managed to pacify the south. The killers shoot the victims and then attack them with knives, singing and dancing. A pamphlet at the site of the massacre claims responsibility in the name of Jamaah al-Islamiyah's 'battalions of havoc and destruction'. Most international tourist operators halt tourism to Egypt, though some parties, including those of Thomas Cook, opt to continue their planned itineraries in Egypt. On 23 November the Egyptian President, Hosni Mubarak, says that Britain and other states have brought terrorism to their own people by sheltering Islamic militants whom he says are behind such attacks. Iran condemns the slaughter at Luxor as 'vile and inhuman'. President Omar Sashir of Sudan asks God 'to preserve Egypt from these demons'. The Palestinian organization, Hamas, 'utterly condemned this attack on civilians'. From Lebanon, Hezbollah damns the killings as 'bloody aggression' that only serves the purposes of the 'Zionist enemy'.

5. The Mossadeq crisis in Iran, 1950–4

1948 Against background of financial crisis, British government requires all British companies to limit dividend payments. This affects Iran's income as dividends paid to Iranian government by the Anglo–Iranian Oil Company (AIOC) are reduced. Iranian nationalists angered.

1949 New agreement negotiated between AIOC and Iranian government, doubling payments stipulated in 1933 schedule. But at same time AIOC's report for 1948 published, showing that Britain received $79 million in taxes from AIOC while the Iranian government received only $37.8 million in royalties.

1950 June: Shah appoints General Razmara as Prime Minister in an attempt to secure ratification by Majlis (Iranian parliament) of oil agreement.

1951 March: after attempts by Razmara to secure concessions from AIOC, oil agreement submitted to Majlis without amendments; Dr Muhammad Mossadeq, a veteran politician of aristocratic background, demands that Iran recover assets that should never have been granted to a foreign company and that the oil industry be nationalized. Razmara assassinated by a Muslim fanatic.

29 April: Senate and Majlis name Mossadeq, leader of the National Front, a loose grouping of parties that had come into existence in 1944, as Prime Minister.

c. **May**: C.M. Woodhouse, a senior officer in British external intelligence, MI6, arrives in Tehran together with Robin Zaehner, who has extensive Iranian contacts from Second World War. They form a team in British embassy under instructions from Foreign Secretary, Morrison, later confirmed by Eden, to arrange downfall of Mossadeq.

2 May: decree nationalizing Iranian oil industry; retroactive to 20 March. Britain contests this unilateral abrogation of 1933 treaty.

26 May: Britain pleads case for arbitration to International Court of Justice.

28 May: Iran refuses to recognize International Court of Justice's jurisdiction.

3 July: AIOC decides to transfer field operations to Iranians and to send British personnel from fields to Abadan for possible evacuation. In effect this means that AIOC on strike; all oil exports from Iran stop by end of month.

5 July: International Court of Justice issues an interim injunction that the AIOC and the Iranian government should not aggravate the dispute. Accepted by Britain on 7 July, but rejected by Iran on 9 July.

9 July: President Truman urges compromise.

15 July: Truman sends Averell Harriman to attempt to implement his compromise policy.

30 July: Britain sends note to Tehran recognizing nationalization of AIOC, provided Iranian authorities agree to negotiations suggested by Harriman to ensure availability of oil from fields in large quantities.

3 August: Richard Stokes, the Lord Privy Seal, leaves for Iran with an eight-point scheme which Iranians refuse to discuss. Returns on 23 August.

12 September: Iranian government sends Britain an ultimatum.

27 September: Iranian authorities occupy Abadan. British Cabinet discusses possibility of seizing Abadan island by force, but Law Officers advise that such action illegal unless authorized by United Nations Security Council.

4 October: Britain completes evacuation of Abadan.

10 December: Iran agrees to go to International Court of Justice over oil nationalization.

1952 Iran orders closure of British consulates. Britain refuses to comply.

25 April: United States agrees to resume military aid to Iran, having suspended it for four months.

Shah refuses Mossadeq right to appoint War Minister. Mossadeq resigns. Shah appoints Ahmad Qavam in place, a man approved of by British officials. Qavam overthrown in riots, and Mossadeq reinstated.

July: Woodhouse flies arms from British airforce base in Iraq to Iran. Hopes to use them to strengthen local tribesmen sympathetic to Britain.

22 July: International Court of Justice rules that it has no jurisdiction in oil dispute.

11 August: Iranian parliament confirms dictatorial powers for Mossadeq for six months.

22 October: Iran breaks off diplomatic relations with Britain, following Britain's rejection of Mossadeq's terms for settlement of nationalization dispute.

c. **October:** Eden (Foreign Secretary) authorizes Woodhouse to set up a joint operation with American Central Intelligence Agency (CIA) to overthrow Mossadeq.

November–December: MI6 makes proposals to CIA. Kermit Roosevelt, head of CIA operations in Middle East, takes charge of envisaged coup.

1953 19 January: Majlis agrees to extend Mossadeq's dictatorial powers for one year. Senate objects. Mossadeq later wins referendum on issue. Now supported by Tudeh Party and Soviet Union sponsors. Former allies begin to desert Mossadeq. Islamic leaders alienated by his schemes to nationalize businesses and enfranchise women.

29 July: Eisenhower tells Mossadeq there will no further American aid until he settles nationalization dispute with Britain.

July: Kermit Roosevelt takes charge of coup operation. Shah hesitates to sign decrees dismissing Mossadeq and appointing General Zahedi as Prime Minister. But convinced finally that British and American governments support plan by codes inserted in a speech by Eisenhower and a Persian-language broadcast by the BBC.

August: Mossadeq warned. Tudeh Party supporters demonstrate with anti-royalist slogans. Provocateurs used by Western intelligence to frighten Iranians into believing that a victory for Mossadeq would be against Islam and mean Soviet influence. Zahedi takes refuge in American embassy compound and Shah flies to Rome. Roosevelt helps to organize allies of Shah. On 19 August Mossadeq deposed by troops. Shah returns on 22 August. Zahedi becomes Prime Minister.

5 September: United States announces aid to Iran of $45 million.

1954 5 August: Iran reaches agreement with Western oil companies. Under new terms AIOC (now British Petroleum) owns only 40 per cent of the assets of the new company. Initially the other 40 per cent is held by five American companies, 14 per cent by Royal Dutch Shell, and 6 per cent by the French Petroleum Company.

6. The rise of Nasser and the attempts to export his philosophy of the revolution

1918 Gamal Abdul Nasser is born in Assyut district; later educated in Cairo, reads law, and graduates from military academy in 1938.

1941 Nasser is instructor at military academy in Sudan.

1948–9 Nasser commands Egyptian battalion during First Arab–Israeli War.

1950 Nasser elected president of the Free Officers' Executive Committee. The 'Free Officers' are a group of young army officers who are planning a *coup d'état* against King Farouk.

1952 January: Nasser in unit that helps to restore order to Cairo mob after Black Saturday riots, the anti-British demonstrations on 26 January in which the symbols of the British in Egypt, Shepheard's Hotel, Thomas Cook's and BOAC (British Overseas Airways Corporation) offices were ravaged and seventeen British subjects killed. Encouraged by demonstration of militant action.

23 July: coup against King Farouk, originally scheduled for August, brought forward. Almost bloodless. Anwar el-Sadat tells Egyptian people in name of General Muhammed Neguib that army has seized power to purge the country of traitors and weaklings who had dishonoured Egypt. Farouk goes into exile. Revolution starts social and land reforms that later become known as Arab socialism.

1953 18 June: Egypt proclaimed a republic with Neguib as President and Prime Minister, and Nasser as his deputy.

1954 July: Nasser instigates wireless broadcasts in Swahili supporting Mau Mau terrorism in Kenya against the British, and inciting Black British subjects in East Africa to rebellion.

October: a member of the Muslim Brotherhood, a fundamentalist religious body, attempts to assassinate Nasser. Several thousand, thought to be supporters of the Muslim Brotherhood, are arrested and tried, and some are sentenced to death.

19 October: Anglo–Egyptian agreement signed. The terms of the agreement included the maintenance of the Suez base in peace-time by British and Egyptian civilian technicians; provision for placing the base on a war footing if certain Arab states or Turkey attacked; the withdrawal of British armed forces from Egypt within twenty months of signature; confirmation of the 1888 convention of freedom of navigation in the Suez Canal.

14 November: Neguib, accused of being involved in a Muslim Brotherhood conspiracy against the state, is arrested and deprived of the office of President. Nasser becomes acting Head of State.

Nasser publishes *The Philosophy of the Revolution*, authorship of which has been disputed, in which he outlines his plans. *The Philosophy of the Revolution* states that Egypt is located at the coincidence of three circles: the Arab circle, the African circle and the Islamic circle. Egypt's wealth, size, population and religious and intellectual qualities make it the obvious leader of the Arab world. The emerging Black African nations would also look to Egypt, as link between Africa and the outside world. Cairo, with its ancient university, is also seen as the major focal point in the Muslim world.

1955 February: Eden meets Nasser in Cairo. Nasser hostile to envisaged alliance of Northern Tier states (later emerges as Baghdad Pact), as increasingly attracted to philosophies of neutralism and does not want Arab world dragged into conflict between East and West.

28 February: after Israel attacks Egypt with raid on Gaza, Nasser decides that it is necessary to increase Egypt's armaments.

Nasser unsuccessfully solicits arms and money from West to build his new Egypt.

April: *en route* to conference of non-aligned nations at Bandung, Nasser meets Chou En-lai in Rangoon. Chinese delegate agrees to present Nasser's difficulties over arms supplies to Russians.

20 July: Soviet Union tells Nasser that as talks with Americans progressing well at Geneva, arms will have to come through Czechoslovakia.

September: Washington learns of Nasser's need for money to build Aswan dam which he hopes will move Egypt into modern age.

21 November–16 December: discussions in Washington on Aswan dam loan. Contingent on Anglo–American grants, the World Bank would lend $200 million.

1956 January–February: Nasser's suspicions of Anthony Eden confirmed by British efforts to secure Jordanian accession to Baghdad Pact.

April: alarmed by Khrushchev's statement about arms embargo in Middle East, Nasser worried that arms supply from Soviet Union threatened and so hastily recognizes Communist China.

26 July: following cancellation of Aswan dam loan, Nasser, speaking at Alexandria, refers to his revolution's restoring Egypt's sense of dignity and describes the West's terms for the Aswan dam loan as 'imperialism without soldiers'. Gives signal for seizure of Suez Canal Company's premises. (See chronology 7: The Suez Crisis of 1956.)

October: Khrushchev warns Nasser, before the Anglo–French invasion, that the Soviet Union will not get involved in a Third World War for the Suez Canal. Nasser decides that world opinion will evict the 'aggressors'.

1957 April: Nasser tries to implement Arab circle of his *Philosophy of the Revolution* by attempting to secure Egyptian influence in Jordan through the Prime Minister, Suleiman Nabulsi. Thwarted by Hussein, with American help.

1958 1 February: union with Syria, largely on Egypt's terms, called United Arab Republic. Baath in Syria hesitant about union but pushed by a group of young officers. Nasser becoming the Arab 'hero'. Hussein of Jordan and Feisal of Iraq respond by joining together their countries, both of whose ruling houses belonged to the Hashemite dynasty.

June–July: in Lebanon, Chamoun becomes convinced that Nasser wants to destroy the Christian ascendancy in that country. As Cairo and Damascus radios incite the Muslim community to revolt, Chamoun invites in the American marines.

14 July: King Feisal and Nuri al-Said murdered in Iraq. King Hussein of Jordan asks for British assistance which is despatched immediately. Nasser sees his Arab revolution threatened and goes in secret to Moscow.

1959 With the arrival in Syria of officials of Egyptian origin who hold influential positions, Nasser alienates the Baath in Syria, and plots an abortive coup in Mosul (Iraq) against Kassem.

1961 28 September: army units march into Damascus and proclaim Syrian independence.

1961 Worried that increasing Soviet influence in Arab states will undermine his own revolution, Nasser tries to improve relations with West. Kennedy sends an Arabist ambassador and Britain re-establishes full diplomatic relations. Nasser arrests Egyptian

Communists but manages to secure Russian finance for Aswan dam and Egypt's arsenal is filled with Russian weapons.

1960–2 Nasser tries to further African circle of his *Philosophy of the Revolution*. In July 1960 supports Patrice Lumumba in the Congo. Cairo radio broadcasts propaganda to Black Africa. Nasser tries to win sympathy of Black Africa by breaking off relations with Pretoria on the apartheid issue. Courts leaders of the former French colonies of Guinea and Mali. Nasser wants a united African state of Egypt, the Sudan and the Congo, with Cairo as capital.

1962 March: Nasser initiates a coup in Syria, and during succeeding months an unsuccessful reunion with Egypt attempted.

September: Nasser involves Egypt in Yemen and tries to stop spread of Saudi hegemony over the Arabian peninsula. By 1970 70,000 troops, or nearly half the Egyptian army, tied down in Yemen.

1964 13 January: heads of thirteen Arab states meet in Cairo. Nasser proposes that ways of stopping Israel's diversion of the Jordan River be studied, and that a unified Arab command be set up under General Ali Ali Amer of Egypt to protect Arab frontiers from Israeli attacks.

September: at summit in Alexandria, Nasser secures endorsement of PLO as the first step towards the liberation of Arab Palestine.

1965 September: Nasser warns third Arab summit in Casablanca that war against Israel is not possible; Arab countries lack the necessary weapons and training.

1966 4 November: Damascus and Cairo sign a defence agreement. Aggression against either state to be regarded as an attack on the other.

1967 26 May: in a speech to the Arab Trades Union Congress, Nasser says that the Arab states are determined to destroy Israel.

5 June: Israeli planes destroy Egyptian air force. In subsequent Six-Day War, Israeli 'pre-emptive counter-attack' becomes spectacular military victory.

1967–8 Egyptian people refuse to accept Nasser's resignation following Six-Day War. Nasser virtually abandons his *Philosophy of the Revolution* and tries to promote Egyptian neutralism. Seeks *rapprochement* with Britain and resists a Soviet attempt to obtain a warmwater port and naval base in Egypt. Tries to heal breaches in Arab world and acknowledges that a failure in the Arab struggle had been the absence of a Palestinian element.

1968–70 Nasser leads War of Attrition against Israel.

1970 January: Nasser secures promise of latest Russian missiles, SAM–3s, technicians to man them, MiG–25 reconnaissance aircraft and eighty other Russian planes.

28 September: Nasser dies. National mourning in Egypt. Nasser is succeeded by Anwar el-Sadat, a close associate and Vice President at the time of Nasser's death. Initially thought of as a caretaker, Sadat is later elected President in a national referendum and by the middle of 1971 exercises a firm personal control of the government of Egypt. Sadat stages new elections for trade unions and professional bodies, as well as for his political party, and institutes a new Egyptian constitution which makes provision for personal freedoms as well as changing the name of the country from the United Arab Republic to the Arab Republic of Egypt.

7. The Suez Crisis of 1956

1955 November–December: Nasser, following Czechoslovak arms deal, lets Washington know that he would prefer to finance Aswan dam, his scheme to move Egypt into the modern age, with American money and so maintain his neutral posture. American response slow, as President Eisenhower's advisers – George Humphrey, United States Secretary of the Treasury, and Herbert Hoover Jr, Assistant Secretary of State – regard the scheme as a greedy ploy mounted by British manufacturers and construction companies. At discussions in Washington (21 November–16 December) it is agreed that the United States would provide $56 million and Britain $14 million for the first stage of the construction, and consider later grants up to $200 million. Contingent on the Anglo–American grants, the World Bank would lend $200 million.

1956 1 March: King Hussein of Jordan dismisses Sir John Glubb (Glubb Pasha), the British-born Commander-in-Chief of the Jordanian armed forces. Nasser congratulates Selwyn Lloyd, the British Foreign Secretary, on Britain's removing Glubb to improve relations with Egypt. Anthony Eden, the British Prime Minister, initially thinks that Nasser is behind Glubb's dismissal, but the former head of the Arab Legion probably persuades the Prime Minister otherwise. The young King Hussein dismisses Glubb as he fears that many see Glubb as the ruler of Jordan, at a time when there is internal resistance to moves in the direction of Jordan's joining the Western-orientated Baghdad Pact.

12 March: Eden speaks to Guy Mollet, the French Premier, about the possibility of an Anglo–French alignment against Nasser.

21 March: British Cabinet meeting suggests that Nasser could be isolated by Anglo–American action. Britain could use Iraq to overthrow a regime sympathetic to Nasser in Syria, while the United States could use Saudi Arabia. Action to be taken against Nasser could include cancelling Aswan dam loan.

27 April: Khrushchev makes a speech about Russia preferring an arms embargo in the Middle East. Nasser thinks this threatens his arms supply from the Soviet Union, and hastily recognizes Communist China. John Foster Dulles, the United States Secretary of

State, furious. British MI6 and CIA investigate possibility of a coup against Nasser, but Dulles prevaricates. From this point Dulles and Eden in overall agreement about objective of Anglo–American policy: the removal of Nasser.

13 June: last British troops withdraw from Canal Zone.

17 June: Moshe Dayan, Israeli Chief of General Staff, and Shimon Peres, Director General of Israeli Defence Ministry, meet members of the French secret service and learn that Paris prepared to provide Israel with the arms it wants. Earlier Eisenhower had agreed to the sale of twelve French Mystère aircraft to Israel; later commented that these multiplied like rabbits. Israel had also negotiated the purchase of aircraft and Centurion tanks from Britain, who had agreed to sell six Meteor night-fighters.

13 July: Dulles informs Eisenhower, recovering from ileitis, about difficulties in Congress over Aswan dam loan. Having decided to run again as President, Eisenhower resents having to take any political risks domestically for Nasser.

19 July: Dulles sees Egyptian ambassador, Ahmad Hussein, and tells him that anyone who built the Aswan dam would earn the hatred of the Egyptian people because the financial burden would be crushing: the United States was leaving that pleasure to USSR.

20 July: Cabinet decides that Britain also has to withdraw from dam project, but Egyptian ambassador told that decision an economic one and that Britain still wanted good relations with Egypt.

26 July: Nasser nationalizes the Suez Canal Company. British chiefs of staff instructed to produce a study of the forces needed to seize the Canal, and how they would be disposed if military action were necessary.

29 July: French defence officials start to draw up contingency plans for a possible operation with Israel, independent of any military moves with Britain.

30 July: Harold Macmillan, Chancellor of the Exchequer, with Eden's acquiescence, impresses on Robert Murphy, US Deputy Under-Secretary, that Britain and France prepared to participate in a military operation. Murphy advises that American public opinion not prepared for use of force.

31 July: Paris accepts British command of forces that might be used. Dulles meets Eisenhower to discuss a report that Britain had decided to 'break Nasser': it would take six weeks to mount a military operation. Eisenhower despatches Dulles with a message for Eden asking for a conference of maritime nations before corrective measures taken. If American forces were to be used, it would be necessary to show that every way of resolving the matter peacefully had been tried.

1 August: Dulles sees Selwyn Lloyd, Foreign Secretary, and Christian Pineau, the French Foreign Minister, in London. Washington did not exclude the use of force but it would have to be backed by world opinion. Dulles concedes that Nasser would have to be made to 'disgorge'.

5 August: Eden writes to Eisenhower that he does not think Nasser a Hitler, but that the parallel with Mussolini is close.

16–23 August: meeting of maritime nations in London. Dulles, in line with Eisenhower's thinking, suggests an international Suez Canal Board, and it is agreed that Sir Robert Menzies, the Australian Prime Minister, will take the suggestion to Nasser.

17 August: Dulles assures Eden that Britain can always count on the moral support and sympathy of the United States. Eden offers details of the Anglo–French military preparations, but Dulles says that it would probably be better if Washington did not know.

24 August: Macmillan tells Dulles that Britain and France determined that if diplomatic pressure does not work, they will have to use force.

1 September: Dayan told of Anglo–French military plans and that Admiral Pierre Barjot thought that Israel should be invited to take part.

2 September: Eisenhower writes to Eden that American public opinion flatly rejects the use of force: the President doubts whether he could get congressional support for the lesser support measures Britain might want. Peaceful means must be exhausted first.

7 September: Barjot meets an Israeli emissary in Paris and soundings taken as to Israel's likely attitude.

8 September: Eisenhower in letter to Eden, while stressing that American public opinion not yet ready for use of force, implies that it might be necessary if Nasser resorts to violence.

12/13 September: Britain and France agree to Dulles's scheme for a Suez Canal Users' Association. But British government's precarious position in House of Commons undermined when Dulles says that United States does not intend to shoot its way through the canal.

20 September–1 October: Macmillan in United States. Sees Eisenhower and Dulles. On return assures Eden that Eisenhower determined to stand up to Nasser, and that Dulles had given no indication that he did not recognize Britain's right to use force. Macmillan later acknowledges that he should have given greater weight in his advice to the date of the presidential election.

25 September: Peres reports to Israeli Cabinet that Paris has invited discussions on joint military action against Egypt. Ben-Gurion determined that this should be a co-operation of equals, and that Britain should ensure Jordan's neutrality. Hopes to gain control of the Straits of Tiran so that Eilat could become a large port and the Negev flourish.

28 September: Ben-Gurion sends Golda Meir, Peres, Dayan and Moshe Carmel to France. Pineau tells Israelis that he wants action before the American presidential election: Eisenhower would not want to appear to the electorate as one prepared to accommodate the Russians and sacrifice Britain and France. Discussions reveal that France does not have the bombers to take out the Egyptian aircraft which could bomb Israeli cities. British participation would be decisive.

1 October: joint Franco–Israeli talks start in Jerusalem. Ben-Gurion emphasizes need for British participation – otherwise Israeli cities could be bombed.

5 October: London warns Ben-Gurion that an Iraqi division going to enter Jordan: Britain would go to Jordan's aid if that country were attacked. Eden, whose health has been weakened by a faulty gall-bladder operation, collapses, and has to resort to benzedrine.

12 October: conferences start in Paris between French and Israelis to discuss Barjot and General Paul Ely's plans for Franco–Israeli action, based on the assumption of British and American neutrality. Israel would only attack if guaranteed Britain's neutrality. Israel's action near the canal would be token: its operation would concentrate on securing the Straits of Tiran. Lloyd warns Security Council against exaggerated optimism following Egypt's agreeing to principles governing the operation of the Suez Canal. Eisenhower undermines Britain's position with a statement about these developments: 'it looks like here is a very great crisis that is behind us'. Dulles tells Lloyd not to pay too much attention to what people say in the middle of an election campaign.

13 October: Lloyd warns Eden that Egypt might feel that the critical phase is over.

14 October: Albert Gazier and General Maurice Challe meet Eden and Anthony Nutting, Minister of State for Foreign Affairs, at Chequers. Challe outlines a plan for Britain and France to gain physical control of the Suez Canal. Israel should be invited to attack Egypt across Sinai. Once Israel had seized all or most of the area, Britain and France would then order Egypt and Israel to withdraw from the canal and allow an Anglo–French force to occupy it to safeguard it from damage. Eden gives non-committal response.

16 October: Eden and Lloyd see Mollet and Pineau in Paris. Mollet and Pineau give no indication of the state of their planning with Israel. Eden agrees that, subject to the approval of their Cabinets, Britain and France should implement the Anglo–French military plan, Musketeer Revise, to safeguard the canal and stop the spread of hostilities.

18 October: British Cabinet agrees that Britain and France should intervene to protect the canal if Israel should attack Egypt.

19 October: Paris transmits a document to Israel, probably without Eden's authorization, signed by Eden, stating that Britain would not aid Egypt if there were war with Israel; Britain would, however, defend Jordan if it were attacked; Britain and France would intervene to ensure the operation of the canal if either Egypt or Israel did not withdraw.

21 October: French emissaries arrive in Israel and try to negotiate on proposal in document of 19 October, described as a British proposal, but in reality a French proposal. In evening an Israeli delegation including Ben-Gurion, Dayan and Peres flies to Paris. A government opposed to the West is elected in Jordan.

22–4 October: at Sèvres, outside Paris, Britain, France and Israel discuss operational plans. Dayan refuses to give details of Israel's plan to the French and British. On 24 October a document is typed outlining a 'large-scale' Israeli attack on Egyptian forces on 29 October with the aim of reaching the Canal Zone the following day; an Anglo–French ultimatum followed by an attack on Egypt early on 31 October; Israeli occupation of the west shore of the Gulf of Aqaba and the islands in the Straits of Tiran. Provided Israel did not attack Jordan, Britain would not go to its ally's aid; all parties were enjoined to strictest secrecy. British delegates do not expect anything to go on paper and sign document merely as a record of discussions.

Revolt breaks out in Hungary, in which Hungarians rise against the occupying Soviet forces.

23 October: British Cabinet told by Eden that from secret conversations which had been held in Paris with representatives of the Israeli government it now appeared that the Israelis would not launch a full-scale attack against Egypt by itself. The British and French governments were confronted with a choice between an early military operation or a relatively prolonged negotiation.

25 October: Eden tells Cabinet that Israel likely to attack Egypt on 29 October. There should be an Anglo–French ultimatum so that the two countries would seem to hold the balance. Disapproving noises are anticipated from the United States, but it is thought that in view of its behaviour Washington would have no reason to complain.

28 October: Dulles knows of impending Israeli attack.

29 October: Israel mounts an attack 30 miles (50 km) from the Suez Canal. By 3 November Israel occupies nearly all of Sinai. Israel virtually ignores Anglo–French operation because of British delay in bombing Egyptian airfields owing to American evacuation in progress, and so makes nonsense of Anglo–French ultimatum to withdraw 10 miles (16 km) from the canal when it is still 30 miles (50 km) away.

31 October: Britain and France attack Egyptian airfields.

2 November: at a time when Soviet Union taking repressive action against Hungary, Dulles denounces Britain and France in the United Nations. After this, the Uniting for Peace Resolution is used to overcome veto. Dulles enters hospital for cancer operation.

4 November: Egyptians block Suez Canal by sinking ships.

5 November: British and French paratroopers dropped at Port Said and Port Faud. Soviet Union threatens military action against Britain, France and Israel.

6 November: Americans re-elect Eisenhower as President, but Eisenhower is furious as news of unsatisfactory Republican returns in Congress announced.

November: Eisenhower and George Humphrey, Secretary of the Treasury, co-ordinate economic sanctions against Britain: the American Federal Reserve sells quantities of sterling; holds up emergency supplies to Europe; block Britain's drawing rights on International Monetary Fund. In effect, forces Britain to stop a successful military operation before it has secured both ends of the canal, as the parity of sterling is considered important.

7 November: Anglo–French cease-fire.

mid-November: Dulles protests from sickbed to Eisenhower and Lloyd about Britain not going through with the venture and dispensing with Nasser.

15 November: United Nations forces arrive in Egypt.

November: Winston Churchill, former British Prime Minister, writes to Eisenhower about Soviet Union attempting to move into dangerous vacuum in Middle East. Suggests that the theme of the Anglo–American alliance is more important than at any time since 1945.

27 November: Eisenhower replies to Churchill that nothing would please the United States more, nor help it more, than to see 'British prestige and strength renewed and rejuvenated in the Mid-East'.

3 December: British and French withdrawal from Egypt announced.

4 December: United Nations Emergency Force moves into Sinai.

10 December: Britain secures $561.47 million from International Monetary Fund.

21 December: United States Export-Import Bank announces authorization of $500 million line of credit for Britain.

22 December: Britain and France complete withdrawal from Egypt.

1957 5 January: Eisenhower Doctrine for Middle East announced in Congress: economic strength for nations of Middle East; flexibility of President to use funds; provision to use armed forces of United States.

9 January: Eden resigns as Prime Minister and is succeeded by Harold Macmillan.

18 January: British Cabinet Committee on Middle East hopes that the Americans might take over Britain's long-term commitments in Jordan and Libya, but feels that Britain has a special position in Iraq which it might not want to abandon in favour of the Americans. The best hope of securing British aims, however, 'lay in co-operation with the US which was now taking an increased interest in the Middle East'.

March: at Bermuda conference, Macmillan concludes that Eisenhower 'appeared to be genuinely anxious fully to restore the traditional relationship between the two countries'. Eisenhower had devalued Britain to the status of merely being one among a number of allies when he became President, and there had been no 'special relationship' between Britain and the United States during the Suez Crisis.

7–8 March: Israeli troops withdraw from Gaza Strip and Straits of Tiran.

March: Eisenhower proposes a joint planning operation be undertaken to work out a common Middle Eastern policy between Britain and the United States.

24 April: American ship, the *Kernhills*, docks in Eilat after United States has helped Israel to secure freedom of passage through the Straits of Tiran.

April: United States operates Eisenhower Doctrine in Jordan to ensure position of Hussein.

August: during Syrian crisis Macmillan comments that it is good to be working so closely with the Americans again.

October: following the Russian launch of sputnik, the first satellite sent into orbit (this has immediate implications for Western defence and also indicates a possible Soviet lead in arms technology). Macmillan, during his visit to Washington, finally succeeds in 'regaining the special relationship with the US which we had previously enjoyed'.

1958 March: British and American working group prepare a paper on 'Measures to forestall or counter an anti-Western *coup d'état* in Jordan or the Lebanon'.

July: Anglo–American invasion of Jordan and Lebanon: the United States goes into Lebanon to support President Camille Chamoun in terms of the Eisenhower Doctrine; Britain into Jordan in response to a request from King Hussein. On 17 July Macmillan writes to Eisenhower of his great consolation that 'we are together in these two operations in Lebanon and Jordan'.

December: British Joint Planning Committee of Chiefs of Staff recommends that London should be prepared to consider with Washington the conditions under which force could be used in the Middle East to prevent a country from coming under complete Russian domination.

1982 May: Henry Kissinger, American Secretary of State 1973–7, publicly regrets United States action over Suez, in which Eisenhower had been seen as humiliating Britain and France, and argues that it forced the United States to take over Britain and France's burdens in the Middle East.

8. The Arab–Israeli wars and the peace process

1947 28 November: David Ben-Gurion, a Zionist leader, sends Ehud Avriel to Europe to establish the organization for the secret purchase and shipping of arms. Many of these come through Communist sources in Czechoslovakia, and are paid for by tax-free contributions from American citizens at the height of the Cold War.

29 November: General Assembly of United Nations votes for partition of Palestine. Jihad (holy war) proclaimed by the Mufti of Jerusalem. Arabs refuse to accept partition of Palestine, feeling that such a move goes against 1,800 years of Palestine's history. In 1947 Jews own less than 10 per cent of land and are less than one-third of the population. Partition awards the Jews 55 per cent of the land area of Palestine. Zionists regret that the partition plan does not give them control of Jerusalem.

December: fighting breaks out between Arabs and Jews throughout Palestine. British forces try not to get involved.

1948 22 March: British Cabinet rejects American suggestions that order should be maintained in Palestine by joint forces from Britain, France and the United States. Instead it instructs the chiefs of staff to investigate accelerating the British withdrawal. Office of Near Eastern and African Affairs tells George Marshall, the United States Secretary of State, that support for temporary trusteeship could lead to American troops in Palestine and the shedding of American blood. Without full Anglo–American co-operation, no Palestine policy could be successful; difficult unless Britain were assured that US administration refused to be influenced by Zionist pressure.

24 March: London informs Marshall that there is overwhelming popular demand in Britain to get the boys back home from Palestine: the long experience of being shot at by both sides and being vilified by Zionists and by some countries has 'so calloused that British conscience that it is insensate on this particular subject'.

25 March: President Truman of the United States tells a press conference that he remains in favour of partition at some future date. In the Foreign Office, Harold Beeley minutes that the President has 'destroyed the possibility of Arab co-operation in discussions on the basis of trusteeship'.

15 April: Ernest Bevin, British Foreign Secretary, tells Lewis Douglas, the American ambassador, that any British statesman suggesting further British responsibility for Palestine would not survive a moment. Bevin wonders, as the Jews would be reluctant to fight Americans, whether the United States could not send troops into Palestine.

20 April: Warren Austin, the American representative, speaking in the United Nations, calls for a truce in Palestine and the establishment of a trusteeship.

21 April: British military authorities in Haifa area start withdrawing their forces. Zionists and Arabs clash. Zionists win and the Arabs start fleeing. Arab states complain that this British withdrawal contrary to the understanding under which they agreed to refrain from intervention in Palestine until 15 May. They accuse Britain of giving the Zionists an advantage.

28 April: Bevin and Clement Attlee, British Prime Minister, meet American ambassador. Bevin says he has the impression that American policy is to allow no Arab country to help their fellow Arabs anywhere, while the United States assisted the Zionists to crush the Arabs within Palestine and then allow the slaughter to continue, and then ask the British government to restrain Abdullah, the King of Transjordan. The Jews appeared to be aggressive and arrogant, and to disregard United Nations' appeals. Bevin and Attlee insist that any 'little acts' the Arabs had committed had been exaggerated: 'After all, Palestine was an Arab country.' Attlee asks whether it is aggression for the Arabs to come into Palestine from their own countries, and non-aggression for Jews to come in by sea to the tune of thousands?

4 May: Washington proposes a ten-day cease-fire and the extension of the mandate for ten days. Bevin refuses: only a deadline would force the Zionists and the Arabs to negotiate.

13 May: London authorizes a plan for a truce in Palestine drawn up by members of the British, American and Canadian delegations to the United Nations. American delegation recommends plan to Washington. Chaim Weizmann, the Zionist leader and future President of Israel, writes to Truman hoping that the United States 'which under your leadership has done so much to find a just solution, will promptly recognize the Provisional Government of the new Jewish State'.

14 May: first committee adjourns to allow the United Nations General Assembly to meet at Flushing Meadows. Marshall prepares a statement on Palestine: the American representatives were using all their influence to secure a truce; a catastrophe could be avoided and there might be time to develop an acceptable solution. As British troops evacuate Jerusalem, Israelis and Arabs seize appropriate positions in the city and prepare for battle. At General Assembly, effort to push through final truce and mediation proposal, assumption being that United States had no intention of recognizing one party. When state of Israel declared, Truman recognizes it immediately.

15 May: various Arab armies enter Palestine: the Arab Legion goes into the area allocated to the Arabs in Judea and Samaria; the Egyptian army moves through Gaza and Beersheba; the Lebanese go into Arab Galilee; the Iraqis eventually go alongside the Arab Legion; Syrians are held near the border.

1949 24 February: armistice signed at Rhodes between the Egyptians and the Israelis. Further agreements soon signed with the Lebanon and Jordan, and finally with Syria. By these Israel gains 21 per cent more land than it had under the 1947 partition plan; indeed it covers almost 80 per cent of the area of the Palestine mandate. But Israel also acquires insecure frontiers.

1950 25 May: Tripartite Declaration made by Britain, the United States and France. Acknowledges that the Arab states and Israel need to maintain a certain level of armed forces for the purposes of legitimate self-defence of the area as a whole. Three powers agree to consider all applications for arms or war materials by the countries of the Middle East in the light of these principles.

1955 January: France overrides British objections and agrees to sell Mystère aircraft to Israel. France replaces United States as Israel's sponsor.

17 February: David Ben-Gurion becomes Minister of Defence. Brings with him philosophy that only way to secure Israel is to force the Arabs, probably by military measures, to accept peace with Israel. Great Power and United Nations intervention are to be avoided, and the Arabs are to be made to sue on Israel's terms. In doing this, Israel could also add to its territory.

28 February: two Israeli platoons of paratroopers storm an Egyptian encampment at Gaza and kill thirty-eight. United Nations Mixed Armistice Commission and Security Council condemn Israel for 'a prearranged and planned attack ordered by Israeli authorities'. Ben-Gurion's policy of direct confrontation is under way.

April: Egyptian general headquarters establish fedayeen, special units of 'self-sacrificers' who raid Israel from surrounding countries.

September: Egypt blockades the Straits of Tiran, effectively stopping the movement of ships from the Red Sea to Eilat, and flights of El Al (the Israeli airline) to South Africa.

29 September: Cairo radio threatens that Israel's defeat is at hand. Moshe Dayan, Israeli Chief of General Staff, holidaying in France, summoned home by Ben-Gurion and told to make preparations for the capture of the Straits of Tiran to ensure the passage of shipping through the Gulf of Aqaba.

2 November: general elections in Israel had meant that Ben-Gurion had become Prime Minister as well as retaining portfolio as Minister of Defence. But new Cabinet opposes scheme to take Straits by force.

1956 2 January: Ben-Gurion warns Knesset (Israeli parliament) that Nasser's Czechoslovak arms deal has changed the balance between Egypt and Israel in a most serious and dangerous manner.

11 April: first eight Mystères arrive in Israel. Follows accession of Mollet ministry to power in France and consent of President Eisenhower to Israel acquiring twelve Mystères. Israel also negotiating purchase of aircraft and Centurion tanks from Britain, which agrees to sell six Meteor night-fighters. United States maintains its arms embargo.

17 June: Dayan and Shimon Peres, Director General of the Israeli Defence Ministry, meet members of French secret service and learn that France is prepared to supply Israel with weapons in quality and quantity to balance Nasser's supply from Czechoslovakia.

18 June: gradualist Moshe Sharett resigns as Foreign Minister and is replaced by the activist Golda Meir.

20 June: two destroyers bought in Britain, with crews trained by the Royal Navy, sail into an Israeli port. Large quantities of arms arriving in secret from France.

1 September: Dayan told by French of Anglo–French plans for invasion of Suez Canal. Admiral Pierre Barjot thinks that Israel should be invited to take part.

7 September: Barjot takes soundings as to Israel's likely attitude from an Israeli emissary in Paris.

25 September: Peres reports to Israeli cabinet that Paris has invited discussions on joint military action against Egypt. Ben-Gurion is determined that this should be a co-operation of equals, and that Britain should ensure Jordan's neutrality. Ben-Gurion hopes to gain control of Straits of Tiran so that Eilat can become a large port and the Negev flourish.

28 September: at discussions between Israelis and French it is decided that, as France does not have the bombers to take out Egyptian aircraft which could bomb Israeli cities, British participation would be decisive.

12 October: conversations start in Paris between Israelis and French under General Gazin. Israel will only attack if guaranteed British neutrality. Israel's action near the canal would be token: its operation would concentrate on securing the Straits of Tiran.

22–4 October: in conversations at Sèvres between British, French and Israelis it is agreed that Israel will act on its own and not in partnership with Britain and France. Dayan refuses to give details of Israel's operational plans to French and British.

24 October: Dayan orders his chief of operations to mobilize Israeli units in secrecy, and to give the impression that this is aimed against Jordan.

29 October: Dayan's forces mount an attack 30 miles (50 km) from the Suez Canal. Israel maintains its independent action. It merely uses the dispute over the Suez Canal to secure the Straits of Tiran.

1957 24 April: freedom of passage through the Straits of Tiran secured when an American ship, the *Kernhills*, docks in Eilat carrying a cargo of crude oil. Outcome of Suez–Sinai War means that it is an Egyptian administration but not the Egyptian army that returns to the Gaza Strip.

1956–66 Israel increases its military strength substantially and develops a sophisticated military doctrine and organization.

1960 Yigal Allon, an Israeli strategist, argues in *Curtain of Sand* that the closing of the Straits of Tiran would be regarded by Israel as an 'act of open warfare'.

1963 August: Israel starts to divert 75 per cent of the waters of the Jordan for its own industrial and agricultural development. Syria sends in troops. Israel threatens retaliation. United Nations achieves a cease-fire.

1964 13 January: heads of thirteen Arab states meet in Cairo. Nasser proposes that ways of stopping Israel's diversion of the Jordan River be studied, and that a unified Arab command be set up under General Ali Ali Amer of Egypt to protect Arab frontiers from Israeli attacks.

1965 September: Nasser warns third Arab summit in Casablanca that war against Israel is possible: Arab countries lack necessary weapons and training.

1966 4 November: Damascus and Cairo sign a defence agreement: aggression against either state to be regarded as an attack on the other.

13 November: in retaliation for an incident in which an exploding mine killed three Israeli soldiers near the Jordanian frontier, an Israeli armed force attacks the village of Samu, just inside Jordan, destroying 125 houses and killing eighteen Jordanian troops. Palestinians in Jordan riot against King Hussein. Amman criticized for not sending assistance to repel the Israeli assault.

1967 January–March: clashes along border between Israel and Syria.

7 April: an exchange escalates into a tank battle and clashes between the Israeli and Syrian air forces.

15 May: absence of armoured formations from Independence Day parade in Jerusalem gives Nasser impression that an Israeli attack on Syria is imminent. Declares state of alert in Egypt and sends Egyptian troops into Sinai.

16 May: Nasser requests United Nations Emergency Force (UNEF) commander to withdraw a limited number of forces so that Egypt could occupy certain positions on the border between Sinai and Israel. Nasser told that partial withdrawal not possible.

18 May: taunted by fellow Arabs, Nasser asks for total withdrawal of UNEF forces.

21 May: Nasser gives in to scorn from Amman radio and some Egyptian officers and allows Egyptian troops to occupy Sharm el-Sheikh.

22 May: Cairo closes the Gulf of Aqaba to Israeli ships and others sailing to Eilat with strategic cargoes.

23 May: Levi Eshkol, the Prime Minister of Israel, tells Knesset that interference with shipping in the Gulf of Aqaba and the Straits of Tiran constitutes a violation of international law, and an act of aggression against Israel.

24 May: Abba Eban, the Foreign Minister of Israel, tells meeting at Israeli Ministry of Defence that Israel must think like a nation whose soil has already been invaded. But Israel's predicament is international not regional, and it has to look to the United States to neutralize the Soviet menace. Dayan favours military action against Egypt after forty-eight hours on a battleground close to the Israeli border. Agreed that reservists should be mobilized.

25 May: French President Charles de Gaulle warns Eban that Israel should not fire the first shot; in London, Prime Minister Harold Wilson shows 'unembarrassed sympathy'.

26 May: US President Lyndon Johnson of the United States tells Eban that he wants a little time and that Israel should not initiate hostilities. In speech to Arab Trades Union Congress, Nasser says that Arab states are determined to destroy Israel.

30 May: Jordan initiates a mutual defence pact with Egypt.

31 May: pressure to include Dayan in Israeli ministry considerable. Offered deputy-premiership but will only accept Ministry of Defence. Menachem Begin, former leader of Irgun and a bitter opponent of Ben-Gurion, also invited to join.

2 June: Dean Rusk, the American Secretary of State, informs Israelis of American negotiations in Cairo for modifications in the Egyptian blockade, and that the Vice President of Egypt is to go to Washington to make the arrangements. Dayan argues for an Israeli attack without delay.

3 June: Meir Amit, the Israeli emissary, reports after seeing Robert McNamara, Secretary of State for Defense, and others that the United States will not take the necessary action to open the Straits. If Israel went to war, the United States would not act adversely and might even help in the United Nations.

4 June: Dayan advocates a pre-emptive strike to ministerial defence committee. While Eshkol speaking, message arrives from Johnson that action to ensure the freedom of shipping through the Straits of Tiran could not be taken by the United States alone. Eshkol thinks this disappointing and in effect gives the army latitude to launch an attack when it considers the moment right. Dayan formally proposes this. Cabinet agrees.

5 June: Israeli planes destroy the Egyptian air force.

7 June: Jordan cedes Arab Jerusalem, Nablus, Jericho and the rest of the West Bank.

8 June: Israel controls area from Gaza to the Suez Canal and down to Sharm el-Sheikh.

10 June: Israel presses into Syria and secures the Golan Heights. Israel's 'pre-emptive counter-attack' becomes a spectacular military victory in the Six-Day War.

1972 12 April: President Anwar el-Sadat of Egypt tells Leonid Brezhnev, Head of State of the Soviet Union, that the Russians had not supported their friends as actively as the United States had Israel. Objects to flow of Russian Jews to Israel, many of whom were intellectuals and scientists helping to build up the Zionist state. Informs Brezhnev that Egypt could not become a trusteeship territory of Russia.

18 July: Sadat announces that 15,000 Russian military advisers and experts to leave Egypt within a week; equipment and installations established in Egypt after 1967 to become Egyptian property.

30 November: Sadat decides to go to war against Israel. The emerging *détente* between Russia and the United States could mean that Egypt would not have another chance, as the superpowers could accept the *status quo* in the Middle East or impose a humiliating settlement in their own interests. A war, even if only partly successful, could lead to the opening of the Suez Canal and a source of revenue for Egypt. It could also restore Egypt's flagging position in the Arab world. New Commander-in-Chief of the Egyptian armed forces, General Ahmad Ismail Ali, develops a strategy based on principle that superpowers would prevent a complete military victory by either side. Superior Israeli equipment had to be matched by exploiting the weakness in Israeli manpower and fighting a two-front war with Syrian assistance.

1973 31 January: armed forces of Syria and Egypt put under a unified command.

Dayan publicizes schemes for a new port of Yamit at Rafah which will isolate Egypt from the Gaza Strip.

April: Dayan refers to his vision of a new state of Israel stretching from the Jordan River to the Suez Canal.

May: Sadat tells King Feisal of Saudi Arabia that he is confident that the Egyptian army could cross the Suez Canal and advance into Sinai; at the same time Syria could cope with the Israeli forces on the Golan Heights. Feisal agrees to provide money and restrict oil production and to see that the Gulf states co-operate.

14 May: on BBC television Dayan speaks of Israel remaining till the end of time on the West Bank: if the Palestinian Arabs did not like that, they could go to another Arab country.

15 May: Arab oil producers stop production for one hour to mark the anniversary of the 'usurpation of Palestine'.

30 July: Dayan tells *Time* magazine that Palestine is finished.

10 August: Israeli jets force a Lebanese airliner back to Beirut on pretext that a Palestinian terrorist leader could be on board. Projects image of Israeli power.

22–8 August: eight Egyptian and six Syrian officers meet in Alexandria and finalize plan for simultaneous attack on Israeli forces in Sinai and the Golan Heights. Day and hour of attack still to be decided.

3 September: Syria sacrifices several aircraft to prevent Israeli reconnaissance planes from discovering the new SAM batteries around the port of Tartous. Syrian military intelligence also responsible for raid by Palestinian commandos leading to closure of transit camp at Schoenau Castle (Austria), diverting attention from Arab military preparations.

mid-September: Hafiz al-Asad, President of Syria, consents to 2 p.m. on 6 October attack: weather conditions, moonrise and tides would be favourable then for the crossing of the canal.

1 October: Sadat warns Russian ambassador that breach of cease-fire likely.

3 October: Dayan advises Golda Meir, Prime Minister of Israel, just back from Vienna, of Syrian and possibly Egyptian weapon reinforcements. Intelligence thought Egyptians just on annual manoeuvres.

5 October: Israeli general staff order 'C' alert, the highest alert for the army, and also a full alert for the airforce.

6 October: Dayan told at 4 a.m. that Syria and Egypt going to attack later that day. Reserves mobilized immediately and a pre-emptive strike by the airforce considered. Egyptians launch attack, on the Jewish holy day of Yom Kippur and during the Muslim religious fast of Ramadan, breaking down the sandbags of the defensive Israeli Bar-Lev line with water jets, cross the Suez Canal on pontoon bridges, and enter Sinai. The Syrians break through Israeli lines on the Golan Heights. By third day of war Egypt has occupied the East Bank of the Suez Canal and is advancing to the strategic Mitla pass in Sinai. The Syrian forces are within five miles of the Israeli frontier in the Golan. Israel then drives Syrian forces back, and Syrian forces are joined by an Iraqi armoured division and aircraft, as well as a Jordanian armoured brigade. Israel is assisted by a massive American airlift ordered by President Richard Nixon.

18 October: with Israeli forces driving back the Arab armies, Moscow proposes a joint Soviet–American cease-fire resolution in the United Nations. Nixon does not like the terms as it implies pre-1967 boundaries.

20 October: Henry Kissinger, United States Secretary of State, flies to Moscow and together with the Soviet leader, Brezhnev, drafts a cease-fire agreement: a cease-fire in place; a general call for the implementation of United Nations Resolution 242 of 1967 after the cease-fire; negotiations to establish a just and durable peace in the Middle East. This is accepted by both sides with 22 October as the day for implementation. But there are violations and the Egyptian Third Army of 20,000 men is encircled by Israelis on the East Bank of the Suez Canal.

24 October: second cease-fire effected. American intelligence receives information on Soviet military alerts; Brezhnev insists that Israel is fighting, and that the United States and Russia should immediately send military forces to the Middle East. Washington, regarding this as a threat of unilateral Soviet intervention, uses shock tactics and American bases throughout the world are put on nuclear alert. Brezhnev gives way.

5 November: Kissinger starts shuttle diplomacy between Arab countries and Israel following conclusion of October War.

1974 18 January: first disengagement agreement signed; while separating Egyptian and Israeli forces, it allows limited Egyptian troops on the East Bank of the Suez Canal, a disengagement or no-man's-land supervised by the United Nations in the western parts of Sinai, and limited Israeli forces west of the strategic Giddi and Mitla passes.

31 May: after Kissinger manages to convince the Israelis that the Syrian leader, Asad, is genuine in his assurances that the Golan would not become guerrilla country, Israeli and Syrian military representatives at Geneva sign an agreement providing for a separation of forces in the Golan and supervision and inspection by a third party, the United Nations Disengagement and Observer Force.

21 September: General Assembly of United Nations votes to include the Palestinian question on agenda.

November: Yasser Arafat, the Chairman of the Palestine Liberation Organization (PLO), outlines a plan for a democratic secular state in Palestine, in which Jews and Arabs could co-exist in terms of equality.

1975 August: against background of Gerald Ford's administration's new Middle East policy of considering a comprehensive peace settlement including Palestine, Kissinger bargains a second disengagement agreement between Israel and Egypt: the Israeli army to withdraw just east of the Gidi and Mitla passes while the passes themselves to constitute a buffer zone as Sadat had initially proposed; Egypt to regain control of the Sinai next to the Gulf of Suez, in which the Abu Rudeis and Ras al-Sudr oilfields are located. But there is also a confidential American–Israeli 'memorandum of understanding' providing for increased American aid, including the delivery of vast quantities of new sophisticated weapons, compensation for Israel's oil losses, and a pledge not to initiate moves in the Middle East without prior consultation with Israel. Washington also agrees to insist that negotiations between Israel and the Arab countries should be bilateral and not multilateral, and undertakes not to recognize the PLO or to negotiate with it without Israeli consent, until the PLO has formally recognized Israel's right to exist.

November: General Assembly of United Nations establishes a committee to see how the Palestinian right to self-determination and national independence could be implemented. It also invites the PLO to take part in United Nations' debates on the Middle East and describes Zionism as 'a form of racism and racial discrimination'.

Gush Emunim (Community of Believers or Bloc of the Faithful), a party of young Israeli activists, decides on the policy of settlements on all of the West Bank leading to the annexation of the area by Israel. Gush Emunim's tactic is to establish the settlements, and then to use divisions among the Labour Party leaders to secure concessions.

1976 April: municipal elections organized by the Israelis on the West Bank show widespread support for the PLO.

1977 May: in general elections in Israel, Likud and the National Religious Party increase their number of seats, and Menachem Begin leads a right-wing administration committed to maintaining control of the West Bank. Impressed by Revisionist Zionism and the concept of a Jewish state in the whole of the historic land of Israel, Begin seems to challenge President Jimmy Carter's schemes for a settlement of the Arab–Israeli conflict.

1 October: Washington and Moscow, in a joint statement, call for a Middle East settlement ensuring the legitimate rights of the Palestinians.

9 November: Sadat tells Egyptian parliament that he is prepared to go to the Knesset (the Israeli parliament) itself to negotiate a peace treaty with Israel. Begin pursues this idea through American intermediaries.

19 November: Sadat flies to Jerusalem and offers Israel recognition and permanent peace based on agreements that would lead to the return of occupied Arab territories, including Arab Jerusalem, recognition of Palestinian statehood, and secure boundaries subject to international guarantees.

1978 11 March: PLO launches a series of raids from the south of Lebanon by land and sea to attack near Tel Aviv, leaving thirty-seven dead and seventy-six wounded Israeli civilians.

14 March: Israeli Defence Forces mount a massive operation across the northern frontier and establish themselves six miles into Lebanese territory.

20 March: at time of cease-fire in Lebanon, Israelis occupy area as far as the Litani river apart from Tyre.

13 June: on withdrawing from Lebanon, Israelis hand over their positions to Maronite Christian Lebanese militia with whom they have collaborated, and not to United Nations Interim Force in Lebanon (UNIFIL), creating problems for the Syrian-dominated Arab peacekeeping force.

4–17 September: following invitation from Carter, Sadat and Begin meet at the US presidential lodge at Camp David in Maryland.

17 September: Carter announces on American television that he has witnessed the signing of two basic documents by Sadat and Begin. In one, the two leaders undertake to conclude a peace treaty within three months to provide for an Israeli withdrawal from Sinai and the normalization of relations between Egypt and Israel. The other, 'The Framework for Peace in the Middle East', designates Resolution 242 as the basis and states that Egypt, Israel, Jordan and the representatives of the Palestinian people should participate in the resolution of the Palestinian problem.

1979 26 March: Sadat and Begin sign, in Washington, a peace treaty between Egypt and Israel which generally follows the provisions of the Camp David framework.

31 March: in response to Egypt's signing of the peace treaty, the Arab League imposes a political and economic boycott on Egypt and announces that its headquarters would be moved from Cairo to Tunis.

October: Tehiya, a party dedicated to establishing Jewish settlements on the whole of the West Bank, founded.

1980 May: following the shooting of a Palestinian youth by an Israeli officer, the PLO kills six Jewish settlers on the West Bank. The Israeli authorities react by blowing up houses near the scene of the terrorist ambush, and deport the West Bank mayors of Hebron and Hallul. The United Nations Security Council immediately condemns the Israeli action.

May: in reaction to new Israeli settlement, plans which include the Gaza Strip as well as the West Bank and a bill in the Knesset which describes Jerusalem as Israel's indivisible capital, Egypt postpones negotiations with Israel indefinitely.

July: Sadat resumes talks with Israel to help Carter with his election. By this time Egypt and Israel have exchanged ambassadors and there are regular flights between Ben-Gurion airport and Cairo.

1981 7 June: Israel bombs Iraqi nuclear plant outside Baghdad, claiming that Iraq would shortly be able to make nuclear bombs. Begin knows that this is not so, and that the raid is unnecessary. His opponent, Shimon Peres, accuses him of electioneering.

June: election in Israel marked by social divisions between the European (Ashkenazi) and Oriental (Sephardi) Jews; Begin's invective and hardline foreign policy result in his retaining power in a coalition with the religious parties. Ariel Sharon becomes Minister of Defence.

24 July: cease-fire achieved in Lebanon to halt conflict in which Israel had intervened on 28 April. Cease-fire achieved by American negotiator, Philip Habib, who with the assistance of the Saudis manages to achieve an understanding between Begin, Asad of Syria, and Arafat of the PLO.

6 October: Sadat assassinated.

1982 23 February: Yitzhak Shamir, the Israeli Foreign Minister, publicly proclaims in Cairo the policy increasingly associated with Begin and the Likud: Jordan is the Palestinian state.

25 April: Hosni Mubarak, Sadat's successor, takes back the key strategic positions of Rafah and Sharm el-Sheikh in terms of the peace agreement between Egypt and Israel.

June–August: Israel invades Lebanon, besieges Beirut, and in the cease-fire arranged through American mediation, the PLO fighters are evacuated from Lebanon. (See chronology 11: War in Lebanon.)

24 September: after revelations about Israeli complicity in massacres in Palestinian refugee camps in Lebanon at Sabra and Shatila, 400,000 attend a demonstration in Tel Aviv organized by Peace Now and the Labour Alignment.

1983 15 September: after resignation following the death of his wife, Begin is succeeded by Yitzhak Shamir of the Likud alignment. Shamir is associated with the terrorist organization, the Stern Gang and the assassinations of Lord Moyne (British Resident in the Middle East) in 1944, and UN mediator, Count Bernadotte, in 1948; known for his opposition to Camp David accords.

1984 23 July: general election in Israel against background of Israeli invasion of Lebanon which resulted in higher Israeli casualties than Six-Day War and cost about $1 million a day, at a time when domestic inflation was around 15 per cent a month and the country was virtually bankrupt. Election inconclusive, enabling ultra orthodox religious factions to dictate a government of national unity, with Peres (Labour) as Prime Minister and Shamir (Likud) as Foreign Minister, the two men to exchange posts after eighteen months.

25 September: Hussein makes Jordan the first Arab country to re-establish diplomatic links with Cairo, broken after the peace treaty with Israel, and is followed by sixteen other Arab countries.

9 October: Mubarak stresses that Egypt's commitments to the Arab world have precedence over the treaty with Israel.

1985 January: Israel announces a unilateral withdrawal from Lebanon to be completed by July, but retains the commitment to intervene if threatened.

11 February: Hussein and Arafat sign the Amman agreement, which allows for Palestinian self-determination within the framework of a Jordanian–Palestinian confederation.

1986 19 February: Hussein formally announces the end of his collaboration with the leadership of the PLO, giving as his reason the organization's refusal to accept Resolution 242.

1987 December: beginning of the intifada, the Palestinian uprising in the occupied territories. (See chronology 10: The Palestinian refugee issue and the uprising in the occupied territories.)

1988 January: at meeting of Arab foreign ministers in Tunis, Palestine is restored to top of Arab agenda and members of the Arab League are obliged to contribute to a fund for the sustaining of the intifada.

5–11 February: the Assistant Under-Secretary, Richard Murphy, outlines an American plan on a shuttle tour of the Middle East: Israel and a joint Jordanian/Palestinian delegation to decide on a form of interim autonomy for the occupied territories; the Israeli military to withdraw from the West Bank, with municipal elections for Palestinian officials in 1989; an international conference to be held, though it would have no power to impose a solution; a settlement envisaged within three years.

June: the Arab League, meeting in Algiers, rejects the American plan. The Arab League communiqué insists on an independent Palestinian state and the participation of the PLO in an international conference.

31 July: the option of a Palestinian confederation with Jordan, often favoured by the Labour Party in Israel and the Americans, ceases when on 31 July Hussein announces that Jordanian government to give up its administration of the West Bank. The Palestine National Council, the Palestinian parliament in exile, says that it will take over Jordan's responsibilities.

1989 Early that year Shamir, the Israeli Prime Minister, proposes a peace plan which had been discussed through an intermediary with the leadership of the PLO: if the intifada stopped, there could be elections in the occupied territories.

May: Shamir rejects the idea of exchanging land for peace and the American Secretary of State, James Baker, warns against the vision of the 'Greater Israel'.

September: Memorandum of Understanding signed by Israel and the United States, by which the United States is to lend Israel war materials for research and development; this is followed by an agreement under which the United States is to stockpile $100 million of military supplies in Israel which Israel could use in a crisis.

October: Washington stops the flow of Russian Jews into the United States, which in effect means that many more go to Israel to be settled in the occupied territories.

10 October: following peace initiatives by Mubarak, James Baker releases a five-point framework which is an unofficial proposal to help Israel and the Palestinians to talk. But the planned meeting in Cairo does not materialize, and the overtures come to little.

1990 30 May: a seaborne terrorist attack against Israel by the Palestinian Liberation Front. Dialogue between the United States and the Palestinians break down after Arafat's hesitations in denouncing the attack.

June: formation of a new right-wing Israeli Cabinet which promises to retain the occupied territories and crush the intifada.

8 October: twenty-one Palestinians killed and 150 wounded on Temple Mount in Jerusalem by Israeli forces in a stoning incident involving Jewish worshippers. United States votes to condemn Israeli action in Security Council.

1991 January: with the Western and Arab state coalition attacks on Iraq and Kuwait launched on 17 January, Israeli army places some districts of East Jerusalem under curfew, and then the rest of the occupied territories. As Iraqi Scud missiles land in Tel Aviv and Haifa, the United States mounts the largest airlift of military equipment for Israel since the October War, with thirty Galaxy transport planes flying in American Patriot surface-to-air missiles to counter the Scuds. Despite pressure from its generals the Israeli government follows what Marlin Fitzwater, the American spokesman, describes as 'a policy of remarkable restraint', which wins widespread international sympathy as well as financial support.

Palestinian support for Saddam Hussein (see chronology 13: The Gulf War) increases with the Scud attacks: Saddam Hussein is seen as the first Arab leader to pay more than lip-service to the Palestinian cause and to attack the heart of the Zionist state.

The Gulf War polarizes divisions in the Arab world: whereas Jordan and the PLO support Saddam Hussein, Saudi Arabia, its allies in the Gulf Co-operation Council, Egypt and Syria, oppose the Iraqi leader.

6 March: President Bush, in Gulf War victory speech to Congress, insists that: 'A comprehensive peace must be grounded in United Nations Security Council Resolutions 242 and 338 and the principle of territory for peace. This principle must be elaborated to provide for Israel's security and recognition, and at the same time for legitimate Palestinian political rights.'

April: after efforts by American Secretary of State, James Baker, to secure concessions from Israel, David Levy, the Israeli Foreign Minister, promises on 26 April that Israel would agree to attend 'open-ended regional peace talks'. Levy is supported in this by only one member of the Israeli Cabinet, and on 28 April Shamir announces that Israel opposes such meetings. The Prime Minister says that if decisions are made in an international forum, unacceptable conditions could be imposed on Israel by the other parties, and Israel could be forced to trade captured Arab lands for peace. Shamir prefers separate negotiations with Arab states and individual peace agreements.

17 June: Eran Hayet, a spokesman for the left-wing Peace Now movement, reveals plans by Israeli officials to colonize large areas of the occupied territories. The documents show that 16,100 new houses are to be built around the Palestinian city of Hebron. This would increase the Jewish settler population from 8,000 to 80,000. 13,500 new houses are planned for the Gaza Strip, increasing the number of Jews there from 4,000 to 50,000. An Israeli ministry spokesman, while not denying the authenticity of the documents, says that the 'figures were exaggerated out of proportion'. Ariel Sharon, the housing minister, had said that reports of large-scale building projects for Israeli settlers in the occupied territories were untrue.

18 July: after a meeting with James Baker, Assad, the Syrian President, agrees to direct negotiations with Israel on the grounds of a comprehensive peace settlement based on Resolution 242.

31 July: Washington and Moscow announce that they will act as joint chairmen of a Middle East peace conference scheduled for October 1991 at which United Nations and European Community representatives would attend as observers.

4 August: Israeli Cabinet agrees to attend the peace conference on condition that Israel has a veto over the composition of any Palestinian negotiating team. At a time when Jordan, Egypt and Lebanon are accepting the American proposals for a peace conference Israel inaugurates a new West Bank settlement.

August–October: disputes among Palestinians over Israeli threat to veto a Palestinian delegation that included residents of East Jerusalem. Resolved that Palestinian delegation should include an advisory body made up largely of East Jerusalem residents.

30 October–1 November: peace conference meets in Madrid. Little achieved as Israel offers no prospect of withdrawal from the occupied territories and the Arabs insist that there could be no peace without territorial compromise. The Palestinians have the same time as the other Arab delegations to make representations and so achieve a procedural victory. Palestinians also accept that a period of autonomy could precede self-determination in the occupied territories.

4 December: further negotiations start in Washington at American initiative. The Israeli delegation arrives late and then refuses to negotiate on Palestinian issues other than with a team under Jordanian auspices. At the conference it is leaked that the Israeli government had approved a programme of Jewish settlement in Arab areas of East Jerusalem, continuing the 1991 programme of building Jewish settlements in the occupied territories, the largest for twenty-five years.

1992 16 January: at renewed talks Israel drops its objections to separate Palestinian representation, and insists that Jewish settlements in the occupied territories did not affect the autonomy talks and could only be negotiated when the final status of the territories was decided.

end January: multilateral regional talks held in Moscow with eleven states attending. The Palestinian delegation refuses to attend as Americans issue invitations to plenary sessions only to Palestinians from Gaza and the West Bank and exclude those from Jerusalem and the diaspora.

February: Baker makes a complete halt to Israeli settlement in the occupied territories a condition for an American guaranteed load of $10,000 million for the settlement of immigrants from the former Soviet Union.

end April: fifth round of bilateral talks held in Washington in shadow of Israeli election campaign initiated by the resignation of far-right Moledat and Tehiya parties from the Israeli government over the discussion of Palestinian autonomy in the occupied territories. Israelis propose phased municipal elections in the West Bank and Gaza, later described by Palestinian delegate, Hanan Ashrawi, as 'a dead-end'.

23 June: in Israeli elections the Likud defeated by unexpectedly large Labour gains, and Yitzhak Rabin becomes Prime Minister with Shimon Peres as Minister of Foreign Affairs. Labour victory welcomed in West as thought that it would accelerate the peace process, and with some optimism in Arab capitals. Islamic and left-wing Palestinian factions fear success of autonomy proposals and divisions between al-Fatah and Hamas leads to internecine fighting.

October: Washington, in a sign of support for Rabin, grants the $10,000 million to house the immigrants from the former Soviet Union.

December: eighth round of bilateral Israeli negotiations in Washington interrupted on 16 December by the deportation by Israel of more than 400 alleged Hamas members to Lebanon in response to the deaths in the occupied territories of five members of the Israeli security forces, and the murder by Hamas of an Israeli border policeman.

18 December: United Nations Security Council unanimously approves Resolution 799 demanding the return of those deported. Palestinians during the next few months insist on the full implementation of this resolution as a condition of resuming negotiations.

1993 12 February: President of Security Council, following Israel's concessions made under pressure from the new Democratic administration of President Bill Clinton, with Warren Christopher as Secretary of State, announces that the deported Palestinians could return by the end of 1993. Madeleine Albright, the new United States ambassador at the United Nations, warns that Washington will veto any move to impose sanctions on Israel.

March: Israel seals off the West Bank and the Gaza Strip after outbursts of violence between Palestinians and Israeli security forces in the occupied territories.

27 April: ninth round of bilateral Middle East negotiations resumes in Washington. Palestinians agree to attend under pressure from other Arab governments, and after Israel allows Feisal Husseini from East Jerusalem to take part. But in a testimony to the Congressional foreign affairs subcommittee on the Middle East, Edward Djerejian, the Assistant Secretary of State, did not object to Israel using the American loan guarantees to finance 'natural growth' of existing Jewish settlements in the occupied territories. Husseini, disillusioned, resigns.

30 August: Israeli Cabinet unanimously approves the Oslo Accords, but Likud warns that they constitute the foundation of a Palestinian state, and that when in power it would not honour the agreement.

31 August: eleventh round of bilateral negotiations starts in Washington. This follows secret negotiations between Israel and the PLO in Oslo, Norway, where agreement was reached on a plan for staged Palestinian autonomy in the West Bank and Gaza Strip, and mutual recognition. The Fatah Central Committee supported the Oslo Accords, but it was rejected by Hamas and by many Palestinians in the diaspora. Edward Said, the Palestinian-American academic responsible for the concept of 'Orientalism', condemns this transformation of the PLO from a national liberation movement to a municipal council.

early September: Arafat secures support of Mubarak and King Hussein for the Oslo Accords, which also have a qualified endorsement from the Gulf Co-operation Council. Assad objects that the Accords will make an Israeli withdrawal from the Golan Heights and southern Lebanon less likely, and from Lebanon President Hariri warns that Palestinian refugees would not be allowed to settle permanently in Lebanon.

13 September: Declaration of Principles signed by Peres, the Israeli Minister of Foreign Affairs, and Mahmud Abbas, the PLO spokesman on foreign policy. Arafat and Rabin shake hands. Declaration of Principles lays out a timetable for Israel's disengagement from the occupied territories, and envisages a transition period of Palestinian self-rule from 13 December 1993, leading to a permanent settlement of the Palestinian question to be achieved by December 1998. Hamas agreed to accept the new reality, and there are celebrations in the occupied territories.

15 September: Israeli and Jordanian representatives in Washington sign an agreement on an agenda for negotiations.

13 October: PLO–Israeli joint liaison committee meets for the first time. Agreement reached to meet frequently to monitor implementation of the Declaration of Principles.

13 December: failure to negotiate details of Israel's military withdrawal from the Gaza Strip and Jericho. Israel would not give in to PLO insistence that Palestinians control border crossings as that could imply recognition of Palestinian sovereignty.

1994 24 January: bilateral negotiations resume in Washington between Syria and Israel.

9 February: Israel and PLO agree to share control of two future international border crossings, but Israel to control access routes to Jewish settlements in Gaza Strip.

25 February: Baruch Goldstein, a member of Kach, massacres twenty-nine worshippers in the Ibrahim Mosque in Hebron. This is followed by widespread unrest in the occupied territories and among Israeli Arabs: a further thirty-three Palestinians are killed. Jordan, Lebanon and Syria suspend participation in the peace process. Palestinians demand the disarming of Jewish settlers and the dismantling of settlements.

10 March: United Nations Security Council adopts Resolution 904 condemning the Hebron massacre and urging protection for the Palestinians in the occupied territories. Washington abstains on two paragraphs referring to Jerusalem and the territories seized in 1967 as 'occupied Palestinian territory': Madeleine Albright justifies this on grounds that Washington does not want to prejudice the course of final status negotiations. Viewed by the Palestinians as a departure by the Clinton administration from previous American assurances that it regarded all of the 1967 territories as occupied.

April: on 6 April seven Israelis killed by a car bomb in Afula, and a week later five killed in Hadera: Hamas claims this as a retaliation for the Hebron massacre. Al-Fatah and Hamas agree to stop clashes between their factions for a month in Gaza.

4 May: confusion at signing in Cairo by Israeli and Palestinian officials of autonomy agreement for Gaza and Jericho over size of Jericho enclave, and leads to renewed criticism of Arafat's autocratic leadership.

10–17 May: Israeli Defence Force hands over to Palestinian forces in Jericho and Gaza.

25 May: Israelis kidnap Mustafa al-Dirani, a leader of a resistance organization in Lebanon supported by Iran, and later attack a Hezbollah camp in the Bekaa Valley, suggesting a move to the right by the Israeli government.

June: countries which, at the international donor's conference held in Washington in October 1993 that had pledged $2,300 million to the Palestinians, agreed to release $42 million to help establish a Palestinian administration. This move came against the background of financial chaos in the autonomous territories and difficulties experienced by Arafat in making appointments to the Palestinian Authority, at a time when Israel was limiting the admission of workers from Gaza.

1 July: Arafat arrives in Gaza and speaks of the Gaza and Jericho enclaves being a move towards an independent Palestinian state with Jerusalem as its capital. Followed by attacks in East Jerusalem by Israeli settlers on Palestinian settlers and property, as well as on Israeli security forces trying to keep the peace.

17 July: at the Eretz checkpoint Palestinian labourers riot and clash with units of the Israeli Defence Force over documentation checks.

25 July: in Washington King Hussein and Rabin end the state of belligerency between their two nations. This follows promises by Clinton to move to waive Jordan's $900 million debt to the United States, to offer military assistance, and to urge Saudi Arabia and the Gulf states to end their boycott of Jordan. A paragraph referring to Jordan's role as guardian of the Muslim holy sites in Jerusalem arouses Palestinian fears over Palestinian political sovereignty.

26 September: Rabin approves the construction of 1,000 new housing units at a Jewish settlement inside the West Bank, apparently defying the freeze on new construction in return for the American loan guarantees. At the end of 1994 it is reported that the number of Jewish settlers in the occupied West Bank had increased by 10 per cent during the year.

26 October: King Hussein signs peace treaty with Rabin in presence of Clinton, following settlement of outstanding disputes over territory and water.

October–November: a series of terrorist incidents mounted by Hamas and Islamic Jihad against Israelis in Israel leads to Arafat detaining Hamas activists, Israeli reprisals and counter-reprisals by the Islamic organizations.

mid-December: Rabin states that Palestinian elections would have to take place with Israeli armed forces present, or be postponed for a year.

1995 22 January: a suicide bomb attack at Beit Lid in Israel for which Islamic Jihad claims responsibility kills twenty-one Jews, mostly soldiers. After this the Israeli Cabinet closes the borders with

Gaza and the West Bank, and postpones the release of 5,500 Palestinian prisoners. Support for Likud increases.

early March: Arafat and Peres meeting in Gaza agree that 1 July 1995 be the date by which an agreement on the expansion of Palestinian self-rule in the West Bank should be concluded. Target was not met as there was no agreement as to where the Israeli troops on the West Bank would be deployed, nor over the security arrangements for the remaining 130,000 settlers on the West Bank.

18 April: following suicide bomb attacks in the Gaza Strip which killed seven Israeli soldiers, the responsibility for which was claimed by Hamas and Islamic Jihad, Palestinian Authority officials attempt to negotiate a limited cease-fire with the Islamic organizations.

late April: Israeli government approves plans to seize fifty-four hectares of mainly Arab-owned land in two areas of East Jerusalem to construct Jewish neighbourhoods and facilities.

early May: Israeli expropriation of Arab land condemned by Arab League, and in the Security Council the United States vetoes a resolution demanding that Israel rescind its decision. Madeleine Albright states that the Security Council was an inappropriate forum. This is the thirtieth time since 1972 that Washington has exercised its veto to protect the Zionist state. Israel suspends its plan after a threatened no confidence motion drafted by Hadash and the Democratic Arab Party which Likud was likely to support.

28 September: following talks at Taba on the Red Sea to implement the envisaged second stage of the Oslo Accords, Israel and the PLO sign Israeli–Palestinian Interim Agreement on the West Bank and the Gaza Strip. This provides for the withdrawal of Israeli forces from Nablus, Ramallah, Jenin, Tulkaram, Kakilya and Bethelem, and a partial redeployment away from Hebron; national Palestinian legislative elections to an eighty-two-member Palestinian Council, and for a Palestinian Executive President; and the release in phases of Palestinian prisoners held in Israel.

mid-October: Israel Defence Force begins its phased redeployment on the West Bank, Jenin being relinquished on 25 October.

4 November: Rabin murdered by Yigal Amir, a Jewish nationalist opposed to the peace process, as he was leaving a peace rally in Tel Aviv. Rabin's widow accuses Benjamin Netanyahu, the Likud leader who had not opposed verbal attacks by Jewish settlers on the Prime Minister, as being morally responsible for his death.

December: Peres as acting Prime Minister oversees Israeli withdrawal from Tulkaram, Nablus, Kakilya, Bethlehem and Ramallah.

1996 10 January: King Hussein starts visit to Tel Aviv during which Israel and Jordan sign agreements on normalization of economic and cultural relations.

late January: Palestinian presidential and legislative elections held. 676 candidates contest eighty-eight seats. Arafat has 88 per cent of the vote for his position as President of the Palestinian Authority. Al-Fatah wins fifty seats in the Legislative Council, with some others going to independent activists like Hanan Ashrawi.

25 February: on second anniversary of Hebron massacre Palestinian suicide bombings in Jerusalem and Ashelon kill twenty-five Israelis. Followed on 3 and 4 March by bombings in Tel Aviv and Jerusalem, killing thirty-two Israelis. Military wing of Hamas, the Izz al-Din al-Qassam brigades, claims responsibility and there is speculation that there is a split in the organization between the Gaza leadership and political radicals abroad.

3 March: Palestinian Authority outlaws the Izz al-Din al-Qassam brigades and arrest many Islamists, while Israel closes the West Bank and Gaza Strip indefinitely and restricts commerce and travel between autonomous areas on the West Bank. Palestinian security forces co-operate with the entry of Israeli Defence Forces into Palestinian villages with the aim of arresting suspects.

13 March: 'Summit of the Peacemakers', and anti-terrorism conference organized by the United States opens in Sharm el-Sheikh. Attended by twenty-seven countries, including twelve Arab states and the Palestinians. Syria and Lebanon do not attend. Conference pledges to support peace process and combat terrorism.

11 April: Peres announces the start of 'Operation Grapes of Wrath', an attempt to restrict Hezbollah's military capabilities. This is in response to Hezbollah's killing of six Israeli soldiers around the Israeli security zone in south Lebanon, followed by the Israeli killing of two Lebanese civilians in Yatar, and the firing by Hezbollah of Katyusha rockets into northern Israel. Israeli attack extends past Beirut, but evident that it is unsuccessful and that ground troops would be necessary to restrict Hezbollah.

18 April: Israeli shells hit a United Nations base at the village of Qana in Lebanon, killing 105 civilian refugees as well as wounding soldiers serving with the United Nations. United Nations report subsequently rejects Israeli claims that shelling was a technical and procedural error.

24 April: Palestine National Council revokes those articles of the Palestinian Charter denying Israel's right to exist.

27 April: cease-fire negotiated following attempt by Warren

Christopher, the United States Secretary of State, to implement a six-point plan which included the disarming of Hezbollah and a guarantee of Israel's northern border by Lebanon and Syria, but which was dismissed as being pro-Israeli. Instead Hervé de Charette, the French Minister of Foreign Affairs, achieves a return to the *status quo*.

end April: Peres visits Washington where Clinton endorses 'Operation Grapes of Wrath', provides technological and military aid, and hints at a formal defence treaty between Israel and the United States. Seen as an attempt to bolster Peres's election campaign.

5 May: Palestinian and Israeli negotiators start what are supposed to be final talks on issues such as settlements, Jerusalem, refugees and borders.

29 May: Likud's Benjamin Netanyahu wins election for Israeli premiership by a margin of one per cent. Despite repeatedly stated opposition to Palestinian self-determination and a commitment to treble the number of Israeli settlers in the West Bank, Netanyahu pledges to continue the peace process, but declines to meet Arafat.

21–3 June: Arab summit meeting held in Cairo and resolves that if Israel reneged on Oslo Accords Arab states would reconsider their support of the peace process. King Hussein agrees to support Syrian demands for an Israeli withdrawal from the Golan Heights.

July: Ariel Sharon appointed Minister of Infrastructure, responsible for infrastructural development on the West Bank, after threats of resignation that could have endangered the Likud alliance. Israel announces plans to establish eight new settlements on West Bank towards fulfilling election promises to increase Jewish population there to 500,000 by the year 2000. The Minister of Defence, Yitzhak Mordechai, re-introduces Israeli Defence Force undercover units to the West Bank and into areas under the control of the Palestine Authority.

mid-July: speaking to Congress in Washington Netanyahu dismisses the 'land for peace' formula and states that Middle East peace has to be based on security, reciprocity and democracy.

4 September: Netanyahu and Arafat meet at the Eretz crossing point between Israel and Gaza and confirm their commitment to the interim agreement.

25 September: following Israel's decision to open in the Arab quarter the north end of the Hasmonean tunnel which runs beneath the al-Aqsa Mosque in East Jerusalem from the Jewish quarter near the Western (Wailing) Wall, violence erupts between Palestinian security forces, Palestinian civilians and the Israeli forces in which at least fifty Palestinians and eighteen Israelis are killed, the worst fighting since the end of the intifada. Muslims regard the opening of the tunnel as a threat to their holy sites and implying an eventual 'Judaization' of Jerusalem.

1–2 October: Clinton hosts meeting of Netanyahu, Arafat and Hussein in Washington, and, after further United States mediation, it is announced that Israel is prepared to negotiate partial withdrawal of forces from Hebron.

13 December: Israeli Cabinet approves extra funds for the 150,000 settlers in the West Bank and the Gaza Strip. All settlers to have 'priority A' status, giving entitlement to tax concessions and government grants. Israeli government officials are reported as saying that the hope was that these incentives would raise the number of settlers to 500,000 by the year 2000.

1997 1 January: a nineteen-year-old off-duty Israeli soldier empties his automatic rifle into a market in central Hebron injuring seven Palestinians. Netanyahu telephones Arafat to condemn the attack, and so does Clinton.

15 January: Israel and Palestinians, following American mediation, sign an agreement to provide for an Israeli troop redeployment in Hebron.

17 January: Israel withdraws most of its troops from Hebron, though some 2,500 Israeli troops remain in Hebron to guard Jewish settlers.

2 February: meeting at Davos in Switzerland, Arafat and Netanyahu agree to resume negotiations on 6 February to speed up implementation of the thirty-four issues left over from the Oslo Accords, but the resumption is postponed after the death of seventy-three Israeli servicemen in a helicopter crash near the Lebanese border on 4 February.

16 February: first session of the new Israeli–Palestinian talks takes place between the chief Palestinian negotiator, Mahmoud Abbas, and the Israeli Foreign Minister, David Levy.

26 February: Israeli government approves the construction of a 6,500-unit Jewish settlement at Har Homa, known to the Palestinians as Jabal Abu Ghneim, in Arab East Jerusalem. Decision condemned by Palestinians, Arab states and most of the international community.

7 March: United States vetoes draft resolution on the Security Council calling for Israel to reconsider its plans to build at Har Homa.

18 March: Israeli government orders the start of construction work at Har Homa in East Jerusalem, and Israeli troops protect the site which is declared a closed military zone. Netanyahu states that: 'There is no good time to build in Jerusalem because there are always objections to such building. We intended to build. We promised to build. And we are building.'

21 March: Hamas claims responsibility for a suicide bomb attack in a Tel Aviv café killing three Israelis, the first such attack within Israel since Netanyahu assumed office in July 1996.

16 April: Israeli police recommend the indictment of Netanyahu for breach of trust over the so-called Bar-On affair, an alleged corruption scandal surrounding the appointment of Roni Bar-On as Attorney-General in January 1997. But it is announced on 20 April that no charges will be filed against Netanyahu.

5 May: the Minister of Justice of the Palestinian Authority announces that Palestinians who sell their land to Israelis will face the death penalty under a former Jordanian law.

6 May: the first high-level contact since the collapse of talks in March is made between Israeli and Palestinian negotiators when Arafat meets Ezer Weizmann, the Israeli President.

30 July: suicide bombing in Jerusalem kills sixteen people, including the two bombers, and results in Israel withholding £66 million tax revenues collected by Israel for the Palestinian Authority.

5 September: twelve Israeli soldiers killed in an ambush in southern Lebanon, Israel's greatest humiliation in Lebanon since 1985. Hezbollah success reportedly the result of a double-agent leading Israelis into a minefield.

11 September: Madeleine Albright asks Israel to take a 'time-out' from settlement activity: 'Israel should refrain from unilateral acts, including what Palestinians perceive as the provocative expansion of settlements, land confiscation, home demolitions, and confiscation of IDs.' In response to the priority given by Madeleine Albright to Israeli security and dealing with terrorism, Leah Rabin, the widow of Yitzhak Rabin, referring to the campaign of the Irgun against the British in the Mandate, observes: 'I have doubts about how much terrorism can be uprooted. We were also terrorists once and they didn't uproot us and we went on dealing in terrorist activities. Despite all the efforts of the British army in the land we went on with terrorism.'

19 September: Arafat calls the compromise, under which the eleven Jewish settlers sponsored by the American millionaire, Irving Moskowitz, in the previously Palestinian district of Ras al-Amoud in

East Jerusalem are to be replaced by ten seminary students who will guard and renovate the largest villa that the settlers have occupied, a 'trick'. Moskowitz observes: 'This is the first time in millennia that Jews come to the Mount of Olives not to be buried but to live there.' Netanyahu, in effect, has changed the *status quo* in East Jerusalem. The settlers say that by establishing the start of a new Jewish settlement at Ras al-Amoud they have ringed Jerusalem and broken up the continuity of Palestinian districts in the city, with the intention of making it impossible for the Palestinians to base their capital in East Jerusalem.

6 October: it is revealed that the Israeli release of Sheikh Ahmed Yassin, the founder and spiritual leader of Hamas, is part of a deal with Jordan to secure the release of two Mossad agents arrested for attempting to assassinate a senior Hamas official in Amman. Mossad agents carried Canadian passports, and Canada recalls ambassador from Tel Aviv to Ottawa. Observers comment that revelations of Israeli actions will make it difficult for Netanyahu to put pressure on Arafat on the subject of terrorism. Deal also includes the release of twenty-two Palestinian prisoners, and permission for Yassin to return to Gaza.

23 November: Netanyahu promises that Jewish settlements in Palestinian areas will continue to grow. This follows criticism from British and American Jews of the impasse he has helped to create in the peace process, and threats by Clinton and Albright of a possible rupture with Washington.

5 December: Ariel Sharon, one of the four members of the 'kitchen Cabinet' appointed by Netanyahu to determine Israel's position on troop withdrawals from the occupied territories, outlines for the first time Israel's blueprint for any final settlement with the Palestinians. Speaking in the Jewish settlement of Paduel on the West Bank, Sharon insists that Israel would annex two proposed security zones, one 4 miles (10 km) wide, running east of the Green Line which divides Israel from the West Bank, and the other 8 miles (20 km) wide along the Jordan Valley, if Arafat, as threatened, declares a Palestinian state. Sharon announces that the newly designated security zones, 19 miles (30 km) wide on either side of the West Bank 'were red lines, not pink', which Israel would never cross in the final negotiations due to be completed by May 1999. Sharon is demanding 'adjustments and corrections' to the 1993 Oslo peace accord.

9. The rise of revolutionary Islam and the Khomeini Revolution in Iran

1928 Hasan al-Banna, a secondary-school teacher born in Ismailiyya in 1906, founds Society of Muslim Brothers (Muslim Brotherhood) in Egypt. Insists on strict adherence to shariah (Islamic law): members pledged to observe religious obligations; avoid usury, fornication, gambling, and alcohol. But adapts to modern interpretations of law: only with the advent of ideal Islamic society, free from poverty, would penalties such as amputation for theft apply.

1942 Muslim Brotherhood establishes a clandestine group, the 'secret apparatus' for the 'defence of Islam and society', which is given military training.

1948 December: Prime Minister of Egypt, Mahmoud Fahmi Nuqrashi, assassinated by member of Muslim Brotherhood.

1949 Egyptian government arranges Banna's assassination. Although he considered his own times similar to the era of ignorance before the coming of Islam, Banna never argued that the ideal Islamic order would be brought about by political control and the establishment of an Islamic state.

1952 Muslim Brotherhood, under the leadership of Hasan al-Hudabi, abolishes the 'secret apparatus'.

1954 After attempt on Nasser's life, six leaders of Brotherhood executed, many imprisoned, and others flee to Saudi Arabia, Jordan, Syria and Pakistan.

1964–70 Feisal, first as Prime Minister and then as King of Saudi Arabia, against the background of the civil war in the Yemen, asserts Saudi Arabia's leadership of the Islamic world as guardian of the holy cities in the Hejaz, thus countering Nasser's claims for Egyptian leadership.

1966 After plot against Nasser, Sayed Qutb, theorist of Muslim Brotherhood, is executed. In his book, *Signposts along the Road*, Qutb argued that the world was in a state of *jahiliyya*, the state of ignorance without Islam, and that the sufferings and injustices suffered by peoples under capitalism and colonialism were a result of

opposition to the rule of God as shown in observance of the shariah. Qutb wanted a new élite of Muslim youth to fight the state of
ignorance.

1967 Arab defeat in Six-Day War undermines Arab nationalist
leadership. With al-Haram al-Sherif (the Temple Mount in Jerusalem, on which the Muslims had built the al-Aqsa Mosque and the
Dome of the Rock), the third holiest shrine in Sunni Islam, now
under Israeli control, Islamic hatred of Israel and its Western back-
ers intensifies. Islam increasingly seen as a means of legitimating
political protest.

1970 Party for National Order founded in Turkey, aimed at align-
ing Turkish state with precepts of shariah.

1974 Members of radical Islamic Liberation Party, led by Salih
Siriyya, attempt an unsuccessful coup against President Sadat in
Egypt with the seizure of the Military Academy in Heliopolis.

Formation of Amal, Groups of the Lebanese Resistance, by Imam
Musa al-Sadr gives spurt to militant Shiite Islam in Lebanon.

1977 Sadat's peace overtures to Israel initially opposed by moderate wing of Muslim Brotherhood. Many Muslim radicals are annoyed by photographs of Sadat praying at the al-Aqsa Mosque, thus
seeming to recognize Israeli sovereignty over it. But Sadat's peace
policy is supported by the Ulema (the Muslim doctors of sacred
law) at the leading Sunni academy at al-Azhar. After this, the
moderate wing of the Muslim Brotherhood is persuaded to accept,
tacitly, the peace overtures.

1978 July: Gaddafi announces Islamic revolution in Libya. Government to be based on Koranic precepts. Gaddafi and his popular
committees have the right to interpret the law.

August: new Prime Minister of Iran announces that government
will follow Islamic tenets.

Amal leader, Musa al-Sadr, disappears in Libya, and Nabih Berri
becomes head of Amal.

1979 15 January: Shah leaves Iran.

January: Ayatollah Khomeini forms an Islamic Revolutionary
Council near Paris; increased pressure in Iran for his return.

1 February: Khomeini arrives in Tehran to overwhelming welcome.

6 February: Khomeini names Dr Mehdi Bazargan as 'Provisional
Prime Minister', but soon evident that real power lies in fifteen-man
Islamic Revolutionary Council, headed by Khomeini.

March: referendum in Iran votes almost unanimously in favour of an Islamic Republic.

1 April: Islamic Republic declared in Iran.

After opposition to Camp David peace treaty, Sadat attacks communists posing as Muslims; attempts to control students' unions.

August: Muslim Brotherhood massacre fifty Alawi cadets at Artillery School in Aleppo, Syria. The Alawis are a religious minority in Syria and members of the sect make up a disproportionately large part of the officer corps.

November: Grand Mosque in Mecca seized by an extremist group acting in the name of a Mahdi, a messiah who will restore justice and peace and who has received his authority directly from Muhammad in a vision, in this case a student at the Islamic University in Riyadh. At the same time, revolt by Shiites in Saudi Arabia's Eastern Province suppressed by police. Population appeased with removal of unpopular governor, building of new schools and roads.

1979–80 Following Islamic revolution in Iran, Shiite movement in Lebanon divides between those who identify with Khomeini's pan-Islamic ideas, and those who follow Berri and the concept of a community in a secular Lebanon.

1980 Gaddafi introduces new Islamic calendar dating from Prophet's death in 632.

March, May: elections in Iran return Islamic Republican Party which is identified with policies of Khomeini.

1981 Following elections to National Assembly in Kuwait, Islamic fundamentalists able to secure passing of laws on banning of mixed bathing, banning of mixing of sexes at universities, and television censorship.

September: Sadat tries to bring mosques under state control. Earlier Sadat had arrested Coptic Pope.

6 October: Sadat assassinated by Jihad group, inspired by Qutb's activist approach. Group had hoped to stage a *coup d'état* and declare Egypt an Islamic republic. Government imposes martial law and tries to purge armed forces of fundamentalists.

1982 February: Sunni militants, including members of the Muslim Brotherhood, take over Hama in northern Syria. President Asad quells rebellion at cost of 10,000 lives.

June: Syria allows 1,200 Iranian Revolutionary Guards to settle in Baalbek area in Bekaa valley. 'Islamic' faction of Amal propagate Khomeini's ideas. This develops into the Hezbollah, the party of

117

God. Shiite movement in Lebanon divides between Hezbollah supported by Iran and Amal supported by Syria.

After Israeli invasion of Lebanon Amal under pressure from Shiites in south of country who resent Palestinian presence.

1983 Islamic code enforced in Iran: amputation of hand for theft; flogging for use of alcohol, fornication, and many other offences; stoning to death for adultery.

Series of bombings in Kuwait City results in seven deaths and arrest of Iraqi and Lebanese Shiites presumed to be members of Islamic Jihad.

September: shariah imposed in Sudan by President Gaafar Nimeiri.

1984 Motherland Party government in Turkey encourages trade with other Muslim countries and allows growth of Islamic schools and colleges.

Muslim Brotherhood forms alliance with Wafd (revived nationalist party) in elections to People's Assembly in Egypt.

March: elections for reconvened National Assembly in Jordan; Islamic traditionalists make gains.

December: Egyptian government closes down University of al-Azhar, a leading Sunni theological college, after ten days of riots.

1985 April: demonstrations in Iran by young Muslim fundamentalists lead to stricter enforcement of Islamic law. Clashes between opponents of government and fanatics belonging to Hezbollah, who support continuation of Iran–Iraq War and rigid observance of Islamic code.

Egyptian government gives in to Islamic fundamentalism and stops serving alcohol on Egyptian airline flights and bans *Dallas*, the American television serial.

14 June: march on President of Egypt's palace to demand application of Koranic penalties postponed.

October: further fighting in Hama in Syria. Amnesty International reports that since start of Islamic revolution in Iran, 6,426 people executed.

Egyptian government places all mosques under official control.

1986 May: Islamic fundamentalism evident in disturbances at Yarmouk University in Jordan.

July: Islamic fundamentalist criticism of Kuwait government's education and finance policies a factor leading to Emir's decision to dissolve National Assembly.

1987 June: Khomeini approves proposal by Hashemi Rafsanjani (speaker of the Majlis) to disband the Islamic Republican Party in Iran.

August: massacre in Mecca of 275 Iranians during pilgrimage. The Islamic revolution in Iran led to unrest among the Shiites in Gulf area who were subject to Sunni rule, but the Saudis had thwarted attempts to make the annual pilgrimage to Mecca a demonstration against Saudi rule. In August Iranian pilgrims demonstrated around the Kaaba, the holiest shrine of Islam, showing placards denouncing Saudi Arabia, Britain, and the United States. Crowds then sacked the Saudi Arabian and Kuwaiti embassies in Tehran; Saudis responded by limiting the number of Iranian pilgrims. Shiites in Saudi Arabia did not react to the situation.

December: Islamic fundamentalism important factor in the Palestinian uprising (the intifada) in the Israeli occupied territories of Gaza and the West Bank. Islamic Jihad organization in Gaza particularly significant.

1988 April: Lebanese Shiites hijack a Kuwaiti Airlines plane. After two weeks of bargaining, Kuwaiti authorities refuse to release any of the 'Kuwait 17' imprisoned for 1983 bombings. Passengers released, apart from two Kuwaiti Sunnis who are shot. Sectarian feelings in Kuwait exacerbated.

May: Iran announces that it will not send pilgrims to Mecca following break in diplomatic relations with Saudi Arabia.

After prolonged fighting between Hezbollah and Amal militias, Syrians move into southern suburbs of Beirut. Hopes that Western hostages – including Terry Waite and John McCarthy – would be freed not realized. Hezbollah maintains control of side-streets.

1988–9 Islamic movement in Egypt suffers setbacks with scandals in Islamic Investment Houses.

1989 14 February: Khomeini issues a religious edict (*fatwa*) exhorting all Muslims to carry out a death sentence on British author Salman Rushdie and his publishers (Viking in New York and Allen Lane in Britain) for *The Satanic Verses* (1988), a work considered blasphemous by many Muslims.

March: local elections in Turkey show less than 10 per cent support for Islamic Party. Turkish state maintains secularist policy, prosecuting an official of the Islamic Welfare Party for statement that he was neither a lay person, nor an Atatürkist, but a Muslim.

3 June: Khomeini dies. Followed by hysterical mass mourning.

119

28 July: in presidential election in Iran Hashemi Rafsanjani returned by 95.9 per cent of votes.

8 November: in election for new parliament in Jordan, Islamic candidates score an unexpectedly large victory: the Muslim Brotherhood wins twenty-five out of eighty seats and at least eleven others elected are sympathetic to the Islamic cause.

1990 12 June: the Islamic Salvation Front, under guidance of Abbassi Madani, wins first multi-party elections in Algeria since independence. The Islamic Salvation Front, taking approximately 55 per cent of votes in local and provincial elections, deals stunning blow to the ruling – and secular – National Liberation Front (FLN).

1991 1 January: against background of wide Jordanian support for Saddam Hussein, King Hussein brings Islamic fundamentalist delegates into the Jordanian Cabinet: ministries controlled by fundamentalist Islamic delegates include Religious Affairs and Education.

May–June: Islamic Salvation Front (FIS) in Algeria precipitates public demonstrations against FLN-dominated government, mainly in response to electoral law promulgated earlier in the year. The new electoral law is widely seen as being biased in favour of the FLN and is resented by the FIS. Islamic opposition, principally the FIS, had been expected to win the majority of seats in the projected June election. In response to civil unrest, President Chadli Benjedid dismisses the FLN Prime Minister.

18 May: in Saudi Arabia, senior religious officials issue a statement urging on the King a system similar to that in Iran. They urge the creation of a Majlis al-Shura, or Consultative Assembly with the power to decide foreign and domestic affairs; the Islamization of all social, economic, administrative and educational systems of the nation; the creation of 'a modern, strong and independent Islamic army on the pattern of the Prophet's armies' together with a diversification of the sources of arms; the introduction of comprehensive social justice based on Islamic laws; punishment of corrupt elements; the equitable distribution of wealth among all members of the nation; the closure of corrupt media and the creation of strong Islamic media; the keeping of Saudi Arabia out of 'non-Islamic pacts' and the reform of its embassies abroad along Islamic lines; and the creation of a Supreme Judiciary Council to implement Islamic laws. The petition is followed by disturbances in Buraudah, *c*.350 km north-west of Riyadh and a centre of fundamentalist Islam. Petition is viewed as an attempt by the ulemas to balance the petition of the Western-educated élite, made at the end of the Gulf War, for a change to a constitutional monarchy, with respect for human rights, freedom of the press, votes for women, and the creation of political parties.

22 May: against the background of the signing of the Treaty of Brotherhood, Co-operation and Co-ordination by the Lebanese and Syrian presidents in Damascus, the pro-Iranian Lebanese Shiite Muslim group, Hezbollah, announces that it has elected a new Secretary-General, Sheikh Abbas al-Mousawi. Mousawi, who had led the political arm of Hezbollah, the Islamic Resistance Movement, is regarded as a hardliner. Another hardliner, Sheikh Ibrahim al-Amin is elected Deputy Secretary-General.

3 June: some senior religious officials in Saudi Arabia criticize the statement of 18 May urging the King to adopt a system similar to that in Iran, and take a pro-government stance.

9 June: King Hussein, in an attempt to quieten domestic unrest (particularly among middle classes) aroused by application of Islamic principles, proclaims a national charter calling for multi-party democracy, greater freedom for women, and greater press freedom. But also calls for legislation to conform with Islamic law. Hussein is admitted to hospital the following day with suspected heart trouble.

15 June: the leader of the Movement for Democracy in Algeria, Ben Bella, announces that he is to stand for President. He denies that he is in an alliance with the Islamic Salvation Front (FIS) to solve the crisis in Algeria.

15 June: the Foreign Minister of Iran, Ali Akbar Velayati, *en route* to the hajj, has discussions with officials from Saudi Arabia.

16 June: according to Islamic Republican News Agency, the Kurdish Islamic groups of Iraq plan to form a united front to carry on the struggle against the Baathist rulers. According to Badr Ismail (a member of the Kurdish Hezbollah of Iraq), founder members of the Kurdish Islamic Movement, the Kurdish Hezbollah, the Kurdish Mujahidin, the Kurdish Ansar al-Islam and others have been invited to join. The Kurdish Hezbollah, led by Adman Barzani, is opposed to compromise moves evidenced by some Kurdish factions.

16–17 June: hajj starts in Saudi Arabia. For the first time since 1987, when over 400 pilgrims were killed in clashes between Saudi Arabian security forces and Iranian pilgrims, Iranian pilgrims take part in the hajj; Iranian pilgrim quota raised to 110,000. The Saudi Arabians also agree to allow limited Iranian demonstrations against 'infidels' to take place during the period of the hajj.

17 June: the Jordanian Prime Minster, Mudar Badran, resigns. King Hussein asks the Foreign Minister, Tahir al-Masri, to form a new government. Masri is the first Prime Minister of Jordan of Palestinian origin in twenty years.

October: clashes reported in Tehran and elsewhere in Iran, including Qom, supposedly reflecting dissatisfaction with rising utility costs and fuel shortages, as well as a power struggle between the moderate supporters of President Rafsanjani (pragmatists) and those who want Iran's spiritual leader, Ayatollah Ali Khamenei, to be promoted to the rank of Grand Ayatollah.

16 November: al-Masri resigns as Prime Minister of Jordan. Resignation precipitated by a petition from an alliance of deputies from the Muslim Brotherhood, the Constitutional Bloc, the Democratic Alliance, and some independent Islamic deputies. Most of the petitioners object to peace negotiations with Israel, and others resent their exclusion from government.

21 November: following invitation from King Hussein to his cousin Field Marshal Zayd ibn Shakar to form a broader-based government, the Muslim Brotherhood, opposed to the peace talks, remains excluded.

10 December: in address to Islamic Conference Organization meeting in Dakar President Rafsanjani of Iran warns Islamic countries against negotiating with Israel: the continuation of the intifada was the only way to restore the rights of the Palestinian people.

25 December: in Egypt a novelist, Alaa Hamid is sentenced to eight years in prison on charges of blasphemy following publication of his novel, *The Void in a Man's Mind*. Seen as an alliance between religious authorities and conservative elements to suppress freedom of expression.

1992 29 January: amidst widespread repression of fundamentalist dissent in Saudi Arabia, Minister of Justice orders the deposition of Sheikh Abd al-Ubayan, the President of the main court in Riyadh, for criticizing the policies of the government in his Friday sermons as well as opposing the presence of United States forces in Saudi Arabia.

9 February: state of emergency declared in Algeria after clashes between Muslim fundamentalists and security forces.

11 February: President Chadli Benjedid resigns in Algeria following first-round victories for the Islamic Salvation Front (FIS) in the elections of 26 December 1991 and predictions for an outright majority in the National Assembly in the second round set for 16 January. The constitution is suspended. The military-backed authorities fill the vacuum with the High Security Council, supposedly a civilian body but three of its six members are army officers. The High Security Council cancels the elections and establishes a Council of State. The FIS describe the events following Chadli's resignation as a *coup d'état* against the Islamic state and the Algerian people.

May: confrontation between militant Islamists and Coptic Christians in the Asyut governorate in Upper Egypt, leaving fourteen dead, follows intensification of campaign by Islamist groups to overthrow the Egyptian government and establish an Islamic state.

November: King Fahd of Saudi Arabia denounces the spread of Islamic fundamentalism, speaks of 'foreign currents' destabilizing the kingdom, and warns the religious communities not to discuss secular matters on public platforms.

1993 January–December: more than 250 terrorist attacks by Islamists in Egypt on police, security forces, cinemas, video shops and Coptic churches, and also on foreign tourists.

1994 February: in Egypt Jamaah al-Islamiyah warns that tourists and foreign investors should leave Egypt.

Government of United Arab Emirates announces that murder, manslaughter, theft, adultery, and drug offences by foreigners will be tried by shariah courts.

June: in Oman members of the security forces clash with the members of the banned Muslim Brotherhood movement which has been trying to achieve greater political influence.

28 September: after the civil war in Yemen the House of Representatives in Sanaa adopts a series of constitutional reforms, including the recognition of the shariah as the only rather than the principal source of legislation, and specific mention of the rights of women are removed.

October: King Fahd of Saudi Arabia approves the establishment of a Higher Council for Islamic Affairs in what is interpreted as an attempt to limit the influence of militant clerics and to lessen the authority of the powerful Council of Ulema.

November–December: following civil war in Yemen, the Islamist Islah Party, mainly made up of the Hashed tribe from the north, with the support of the Muslim Brotherhood, strengthens its position.

1995 November: at the start of the winter tourist season in Egypt Jamaah al-Islamiyah advises foreign tourists to leave and resumes attacks on trains taking tourists south.

1996: in Kuwait Islamic politicians in the parliament elected in 1996 demand again, as they have from 1992, that the shariah be recognized as the only source of law.

January: the People's Assembly in Egypt passes a new *jesba* law to limit claims of un-Islamic conduct. This follows a series of cases instituted by Islamist lawyers against prominent Egyptians for contravening Islamic morality.

March–April: elections to the Majlis in Iran suggest power is shifting from the conservative to the more liberal element.

17 December: in Algeria the government-appointed legislature, the Transnational Council, passes legislation to enforce the use of Arabic in public life ('the process of generalizing the use of the Arabic language should be perfected') by 5 July 1998, and that Arabic should be the medium of instruction in all schools and universities by 5 July 2000.

1997 8 February: the end of Ramadan in Algeria marks the bloodiest fast since the height of resistance against the French in 1962. Around 1,200 are estimated to have been killed, and an upsurge in barbaric massacres in rural areas is noted.

23 May: in Iran, Seyyed Muhammad Khatami is elected President by a considerable margin. Khatami is regarded an open-minded politician and a tolerant religious leader.

10. The Palestinian refugee issue and the uprising in the occupied territories

1947 29 November: with announcement of United Nations partition plan, the Mufti of Jerusalem proclaims jihad and fighting breaks out in Palestine. United Nations partition resolution elaborates on Arab rights in projected Zionist state: in testimony before the United Nations Special Committee on Palestine in summer 1947, Zionists gave assurance that Arab minority in the envisaged Zionist state would enjoy full civil, national and cultural rights.

1948 9 April: contingents of the Irgun and the Stern Gang, under Haganah command, encounter strong Arab resistance in the village of Deir Yassin, and slaughter 245 men, women and children. Massacre of Deir Yassin thought by the Arabs to have been perpetrated with the approval of David Ben-Gurion and the Haganah leadership to terrorize the Arab population into fleeing from their land.

6 May: British Foreign Office has reports that an estimated 50,000 Arab refugees have fled from Palestine.

14 May: some estimates suggest that 400,000 Palestinian Arabs have left their homes and fled to neighbouring Arab territories.

June: Israeli Defence Force Intelligence Branch report states that, as of 1 June 1948, 240,000 Arabs had fled from the area designated by the United Nations partition vote for the Jewish state; 150,000 Arabs had fled from the area designated for a Palestinian state and from Jerusalem which was to have been internationalized. Seventy per cent of the Arab exodus is attributed to 'direct, hostile Jewish operations against Arab settlements' by the Haganah (later the Israeli Defence Force), Irgun and Stern Gang. Two per cent is attributed to Jewish psychological warfare, and a further 2 per cent to 'ultimative expulsion orders'. Evacuation orders by Arab leaders for local military reasons account for 5 per cent of the Arab exodus; general fear for 10 per cent; and local factors for between 8 and 9 per cent.

16 June: Ben-Gurion tells his Cabinet that the return of the Arabs should be prevented. They would have to bear the consequences of declaring war on Israel.

1 August: following requests by Count Folke Bernadotte, the United Nations mediator, to allow the Arabs to return, Ben-Gurion mentions conditions that make any such event unlikely in the foreseeable future.

1948–9 By end of First Arab–Israeli War it is estimated that from June 1948 a further 300,000 Arab refugees have fled, many as a deliberate policy of expulsion mounted by Israeli Defence Force commanders. Figures estimating the overall Arab flight range from between 600,000 and 760,000, and the legally certified number of Palestinian Arab refugees given in 1949 is almost 1 million.

1948–1952 At end of First Arab–Israeli War there are an estimated 156,000 Arabs remaining within Israel's borders; around 80 per cent of the population of Israel is Jewish. These Arabs continue to live in about 100 towns and villages inhabited almost exclusively by Arabs, as well as in Acre, Haifa, Jaffa, Ramle and Jerusalem alongside the Jewish occupants. Around 60 per cent of these Arabs live in Galilee, about 20 per cent in villages alongside the Jordanian frontier, and about 7 per cent live in the Haifa area and the Negev. The Arabs in the new state of Israel have the right to vote, to sit in the Israeli parliament (the Knesset – four are elected to the first parliament), to organize political parties, to have access to Arabic-speaking schools as well as to Israeli courts and public services. Arabs (apart from the Druze minority whose religion accepted state authority) exempt from military service in Israel. Until 1952 Israel does not have citizens, either native-born or naturalized. The Nationality Law is passed in 1952 by the Knesset. The provisions for proof of citizenship by residence were difficult for the Arabs in Israel to fulfil: many had no proof of Palestinian citizenship under the mandate; others had returned after the First Arab–Israeli War. But provisions of Nationality Law are not rigorously applied and many Arab residents acquire Israeli citizenship within the following five years. Under a conservative leadership most of the Arab citizens vote for Zionist parties and in particular the Mapai.

1948–57 567,000 Jews leave Muslim countries in North Africa and the Middle East and most settle in Israel. The population of Israel rises from 1,174,000 in 1949 to 1,873,000 in 1956.

1949–50 Around 300,000 Arabs leave the West Bank for Transjordan. In referendum, Arabs on West Bank agree to become part of Transjordan which becomes known as Jordan.

Arab refugees from Palestine go mainly to Gaza, Jordan, 100,000 to Lebanon, 70,000 to Syria and smaller numbers to Iraq and Egypt. They are looked after mainly by United Nations relief organizations in camps and are not absorbed by the host countries. By 1967 estimates of the numbers of Palestinian refugees range between 2 million and 2.5 million.

1961 Census gives Israel's population as 2,260,700, of whom 230,000 are Arabs.

1966 Arab community in Israel estimated to be 301,000.

1967 After Six-Day War, Arabs flee from West Bank to Jordan. Estimates of numbers are between 150,000 and 250,000, but some are as high as 380,000. These refugees create economic and social difficulties in Jordan. Almost 1 million Arabs remain under Israeli control in the newly occupied territories. Around 70,000 in annexed East Jerusalem are regarded as Israeli citizens. The rest live under military occupation.

September: Palestinian students protest against the establishment of Jewish settlements in the occupied territories after the Six-Day War.

1970 Palestinians in Lebanon increase to around 400,000 out of a population of 3 million. Palestinians initially arrived in 1948, more in 1967, then further influx with the Jordanian civil war.

1970–2 Conflict between Hussein's Jordanian authorities and Palestinian organizations results in civil war and expulsion of Palestinian Liberation Organization to Lebanon. Around 100,000 leave, but it is estimated that 800,000 Palestinians remain on East Bank.

1973 March: Gaza Strip to be incorporated into Israel. Jewish settlement in Strip will continue, and Arab inhabitants can circulate in Israel during daylight hours.

18 August: Israeli radio announces that another thirty-five settlements will be built in occupied territories, bringing total to seventy-seven.

1974 March: Israeli authorities hold elections for mayors and municipalities in leading Arab towns.

November: following Arafat's speech to United Nations demanding a democratic and secular state, Palestinian workers in towns and cities demonstrate.

1975–6 Divisions within the Arab world at the time of the Lebanese civil war, and American preoccupation with the presidential election campaign give the Israelis the opportunity to establish further settlements on the West Bank, in the Golan Heights and in Sinai.

1975 Arab population of Israel estimated at 411,000.

November: United Nations General Assembly establishes a committee to see how the Palestinian right to self-determination and national independence can be implemented. Invites the Palestine Liberation Organization (PLO) to take part in United Nations debates on the Middle East and describes Zionism as 'a form of racism and racial discrimination'.

1976 January: United States vetoes United Nations Security Council resolution affirming the right of the Palestinians to establish a state.

March: United States delegate to Security Council condemns the establishment by Israel of 'illegal' settlements in Arab Jerusalem and other occupied areas.

April: Rioting spreads from the West Bank and Gaza into Israel itself. In municipal elections organized by the Israelis on the West Bank, widespread support for PLO evident.

Unrest on West Bank continues with Palestinian school children taking part in demonstrations in Nablus, Ramallah and Arab Jerusalem. In October, Jews and Arabs riot in Hebron over prayer rights, and in December there is a hunger strike by Arabs detained in an Israeli prison at Ashkelon.

1977 15 February: after report by the United Nations Special Committee for the Investigation of Israeli Practices in the Occupied Territories, the United Nations Human Rights Commission asks Israel to adhere to the Geneva Convention in its treatment of civilians.

May: in Israeli general election Arab voters move from supporting the Labour Party (formerly the Mapai) to supporting the Communists.

29 June: leaders of the European Economic Community endorse the creation of a homeland for the Palestinians.

1 October: Washington and Moscow in a joint statement call for a Middle East settlement ensuring the legitimate rights of the Palestinians.

October: Israel states intention to establish six further Jewish settlements on the West Bank.

9 November: in response to rocket attack by Palestinian terrorists on a settlement in the north of Israel, Israeli airforce bombs refugee camps in south of Lebanon.

1979 September: after Camp David accords and Egyptian–Israeli peace treaty signed, Israel allows its citizens to purchase Arab land in the occupied territories.

October: Israeli nationalists found Tehiya, a party dedicated to establishing Jewish settlements on the whole of the West Bank, reacting against Israeli Supreme Court judgment that as a settlement near Nablus did not have a necessary military purpose, it should be taken down and the expropriated land returned to its original Arab owners.

1980 February: against background of talks between Egypt and Israel about Palestinian autonomy, unrest on West Bank. In reaction to the killing of an Israeli settler, the Israeli Cabinet allows, in principle, Jewish settlement in Hebron and riots break out.

May: PLO kills six Jewish settlers in retaliation for the shooting of a Palestinian youth by an Israeli officer. Israeli authorities react by blowing up houses near the scene of the terrorist ambush and deport the mayors of Hebron and Halhul. In reaction to new Israeli settlement plans, which include the Gaza Strip as well as the West Bank, and a bill in the Knesset which describes Jerusalem as Israel's indivisible capital, Egypt postpones negotiations with Israel indefinitely.

1981 14 December: Begin sees bill through Knesset formally annexing the Syrian Golan Heights.

1982 March: virtually a revolt on West Bank over Israeli policy of establishing 'village leagues' as an attempt to counter radical nationalism of the urban Palestinian leadership.

1984 July: general election in Israel held against background of trial of Gush Emunim settlers and two Israeli army officers for the attempted assassinations in 1980 of three West Bank Palestinian mayors, and other measures intended to drive the Palestinians from territories Israel had occupied in 1967. A majority of Arab voters in general election vote for non-Zionist parties: the six Arab seats go to the two anti-Zionist Rakach and Palestine Land parties.

1985 11 February: Hussein and Arafat sign Amman agreement, which allows for Palestinian self-determination within the framework of a Jordanian–Palestinian confederation.

Mrs Margaret Thatcher, the British Prime Minister, makes an abortive attempt to support Amman agreement, but undermined by threats from Abu Nidal and bombing of PLO headquarters outside Tunis by Israel following Larnaca incident (see p. 64). Jewish settlers on West Bank doubled in number to 42,500 over the previous two years. Riots in Palestinian refugee camps.

1986 Appointment of three Arab mayors by Israeli authorities in West Bank towns, the deportation of the editor of a Jerusalem newspaper hostile to Hussein's plans for the West Bank, and attacks on Palestinian communities by Israeli settlers lead to clashes between the Israeli army and Palestinian demonstrators, the deaths of two students at Bir Zeit University. Bir Zeit and al-Najah University in Nablus closed.

1987 18 May: six young members of Islamic Jihad escape from the security wing of the Gaza Central Prison. Escapade changes their image from fanatics to heroes in the eyes of many of the Palestinian youth.

10 October: Islamic Jihad calls for a general strike. Later almost entire population of Gaza clashes with Israeli occupiers. Religious brawls at al-Aqsa Mosque in Jerusalem and the Cave of the Patriarchs in Hebron. Bethlehem University closed after clashes.

10 November: seventeen-year-old girl shot in grounds of her school in Gaza by Jewish settler after his car stoned. Settler released on bail.

November: at Amman summit meeting of Arab League, concentration on uniting the Arab nations against Iran. For first time Palestinian issue does not have priority. Arab world no longer seems interested in plight of Palestinians.

25 November: Palestinian morale boosted when a hang-glider operation, mounted by the Popular Front for the Liberation of Palestine–General Command, crosses Lebanese border and kills six soldiers in an Israeli army camp.

8 December: Israeli vehicle kills four Arab labourers at a road block on the northern frontier of Gaza Strip. Rumour that this is a revenge killing widely believed in Gaza and West Bank.

8–20 December: first wave of riots of intifada spreads from funerals of victims of road-block crash to Jebalya, largest refugee camp in Gaza Strip, to Gaza City and Nablus. Demonstrations different from previous disturbances: Palestinians attack Israeli soldiers and even armed personnel carriers with a boldness not seen before. Israeli guns kill twenty-six Palestinians and injure 320; fifty-six Israeli soldiers and thirty civilians injured.

22 December: United States does not veto United Nations Security Council resolution denouncing Israeli violence in the occupied territories.

1988 January–February: intifada institutionalized, with formation of the Unified National Leadership of the Uprising (UNLU) which includes representatives from both the PLO and Islamic Jihad. Encourages around 120,000 Palestinians who work in Israel to stay away from jobs and organizes strikes.

January: Yitzhak Rabin stops use of live ammunition against demonstrators and substitutes tear-gas and beatings with batons as form of punishment. Meeting of Arab foreign ministers at Tunis restores Palestine to top of Arab agenda.

February–June: attack on Israeli administrative structure in occupied territories. Palestinians who work as police and tax collectors encouraged to resign; non-payment of taxes and a partial boycott of Israeli goods.

31 July: Hussein announces that the Jordanian government will give up its administration of the West Bank and puts an end to the 'Jordanian' option favoured by the Labour Party in Israel and the Americans.

July–November: PLO and local Palestinian leadership come together in the moves towards the declaration of Palestinian statehood.

12–15 November: Palestinian National Council meets in Algiers and at end of session proclaims the establishment of the state of Palestine with Jerusalem as its capital, in terms of the United Nations resolution of 1947. Also rejects terrorism, and confines use of vio-lence to Israel and the occupied territories.

November: in Israeli general election many Arabs vote for an Arab party. Shift in Arab voting behaviour away from Zionist parties attributed to both the rise of a new young radical leadership, and an increase in political consciousness of Israeli Arabs with the inti-fada.

14 December: following Arafat's explicit statement that the PLO accepted Resolutions 242 and 338, recognized Israel's right to exist, and renounced resort to terrorism, George Shultz, the Secretary of State, names the American ambassador to Tunisia, Robert Pelletreau, as Washington's contact with the PLO.

December: serious rioting in occupied territories after Israeli troops fire on funeral procession in Nablus. Plastic bullets replaced use of batons for crowd control.

1989 7 February: United States State Department statistics claim that 366 Palestinians have died and more than 20,000 have been wounded in the intifada. Also claims that the uprising has killed eleven Israelis and wounded 1,100. 10,000 Palestinians have been imprisoned, and some, it is alleged, have been tortured.

7 April: at Nahalin, outside Bethlehem, Israeli police attack people leaving the village mosque, and kill four.

1989 May: violence in Gaza such that Israelis seal off territory for month and introduce identity-card system. Palestinians in occupied territories form clandestine network.

5 July: Yitzhak Shamir, the Israeli Prime Minister, rejects forever the idea of a Palestinian state and excludes Palestinians in East Jerusalem from voting in the proposed elections.

October: Washington stops the flow of Russian Jews into the United States, which in effect means that many more go to Israel, possibly for settlement in the occupied territories.

1990 20 May: a lone and apparently unbalanced Israeli gunman kills seven Arab workers in a roadside field and sparks off serious riots in which seven more Arabs die. Israeli army loses control of parts of Gaza for a time.

August: after Iraq's occupation of Kuwait on 2 August, Arafat overrides Egyptian objections and issues a joint statement from Baghdad with Saddam Hussein, the Iraqi leader, that they were united in their struggle against the Israeli occupation and the American intervention in the Gulf. This results in the expulsion of Palestinians by Saudi Arabia and Gulf states, particularly Qatar. Palestinians are settled in fleeing Kuwaitis' homes. Saddam Hussein increasingly links any solution in the Gulf to the Palestinian question.

15 September: given number of Palestinians in Jordan and degree of enthusiasm for Saddam Hussein, King Hussein allows George Habash of the Popular Front for the Liberation of Palestine, and Nayef Hawatmeh of the Democratic Front for the Liberation of Palestine, banned for twenty years, back into Jordan to attend a conference of Arab Popular Forces.

8 October: twenty-one Palestinians killed on Temple Mount in Jerusalem by Israeli forces in stoning incident involving Jewish worshippers.

October: Israel refuses to receive or co-operate with any United Nations mission investigating the Temple Mount killings. Foreign Minister, David Levy, says that 'the United States is held captive by the coalition it has formed against Saddam Hussein': Israel could not receive a mission which failed to take account of the Arab stone-throwing at Jewish worshippers or which infringed Israeli sovereignty over Jerusalem. Shamir says that the United Nations mission's brief to find ways of 'protecting' the Palestinian population is an infringement of Israeli sovereignty. Israeli fears that the

United Nations will give in to Palestinian demands to replace the Israeli administration on the West Bank and in Gaza with United Nations troops, which will then allow a PLO state to develop *de facto* if not *de jure.*

20 December: United Nations Security Council, with American support, approves a resolution criticizing Israel for its deportation of four Palestinians from the Gaza Strip, and asks the Secretary General 'to monitor and observe' the conditions of Palestinians in the occupied territories. This takes place against the background of the deteriorating situation in the Gulf, and the insistence of the Iraqi Revolutionary Council on 1 December that any direct talks with the Americans should include the future of the Palestinians in the occupied territories.

1991 17 January: with the launch of Operation Desert Storm and the bombing of Kuwait and Iraq by the coalition, the Israeli army places some districts of East Jerusalem under curfew, and then the rest of the occupied territories. Palestinians in the Gaza Strip are already under a blanket curfew following the assassination in Tunis on 14 January of PLO leaders.

Palestinian support for Saddam Hussein increases with the Iraqi Scud missile attacks on Israel, which include hits on Tel Aviv and Haifa. Saddam Hussein is seen as the first Arab leader to pay more than lip-service to the Palestinian cause and to attack the heart of the Zionist state. The curfew in the occupied territories remains in force, and this hampers the distribution of gas masks to Palestinians – already a matter of some controversy when, on 1 October 1990, the Israeli military had announced that it would distribute gas masks to Israeli citizens, residents and visitors to Israel, and that Palestinians in the occupied territories could buy masks when further supplies arrived.

The underground leadership of the intifada cancels all strikes and for the first time since the start of the uprising does not urge attacks against Israeli soldiers and settlers.

5 February: curfew restrictions in the occupied territories are eased, but only a small number of Palestinians are allowed to enter Israel, and the economic difficulties in the occupied territories increase.

6 March: President Bush, in his speech celebrating victory in the Gulf War, refers to the principle of territory for peace, and legitimate Palestinian political rights.

12 March: first meeting between an American Secretary of State and a wide-ranging Palestinian delegation when James Baker talks to ten Palestinians in Jerusalem.

133

Within Israel itself, arbitrary knife attacks by Palestinians result in at least seven Israeli deaths, but interrogation of the captured killers fails to link them to any Palestinian organization. Motives range from revenge killings for relatives killed by Israeli security forces, to a statement from a medical orderly who had killed four unarmed women that 'it was a message to Baker'.

31 March: Israeli government votes for extraordinary measures against Palestinians, including deportation.

22 April: Gush Emunim, the group of radical Zionists committed to settling Jews in the occupied territories, confirms that it is preparing to open two more sites for settlement on the West Bank.

28 April–June: American efforts to set up an international peace conference are frustrated by Shamir, who dislikes the possibility that such a forum could force Israel to trade captured Arab lands for peace. The Israeli Prime Minister prefers separate negotiations with the Arab states.

4 June: Hamas (the Islamic resistance movement in the occupied territories), its guerrilla group Islamic Jihad, and the PLO attempt a truce to end rival faction-fighting that has broken out in Nablus and Gaza. It is estimated that support for the Islamic underground groups is around 10 per cent, whereas in Gaza it is put at 30 to 40 per cent of the 800,000 inhabitants. In Gaza fighting had broken out over the issue of *hijab*, the dress code of Islam which requires women to wear a veil or a headscarf. A group of schoolgirls had broken the custom observed by most women in Gaza. The incident is seen as symptomatic of a major divergence between the fundamentalists and the PLO under Arafat over the approach to the United States and the envisaged peace conference. The fundamentalists regard the United States as an enemy.

17 June: Peace Now, a left-wing Israeli movement which monitors the expansion of Jewish settlements in the occupied territories, reveals documents drawn up by Israeli officials for plans to build 16,100 new homes for Jewish settlers around the Palestinian city of Hebron. This would increase the settler population in that area from 8,000 to 80,000. Plans also revealed to build 13,550 new Jewish homes in the Gaza Strip, increasing the Jewish settler population there from 4,000 to 50,000. An Israeli housing spokesman claims that the figures are exaggerated, but does not deny the authenticity of the document.

20 June: curfew in Gaza Strip to start at 10 p.m. instead of 8 p.m. Also, 130,000 work permits for Israel are to be issued to Palestinians who live in the occupied territories, 20,000 more than in the previous year. Palestinians in the West Bank are to be allowed to take part in municipal elections for the first time since 1976. Hundreds of Palestinian detainees are expected to be released by the Israeli authorities. Ronnie Milo, the police minister, says that 'the majority of the Palestinians in the [occupied] territories are tired of [the intifada]'.

26 September: Israeli military authorities report widespread arrests of alleged Popular Front for the Liberation of Palestine (PFLP) activists in recent months.

23 October: general strike declared in occupied territories over Madrid conference.

end October: clashes reported in occupied territories between those opposed to Madrid conference and supporters of al-Fatah, the mainstream PLO organization. Hanan Ashrawi, the chief Palestinian spokesperson to the Middle East peace conference, tells a television team before she leaves for Madrid that the intifada will continue.

4 November: against background of rival demonstrations over the peace conference nationalists who had supported the meeting at Madrid won elections to thirteen of the sixteen seats to the Gaza Chamber of Commerce, the remaining three going to Islamic groups who had rejected the conference.

Israeli Minister for Housing opens new civilian settlement, Kela, on Golan Heights.

15 November: Israeli police recommend that Hanan Ashrawi be prosecuted for breaking Israeli laws forbidding contact with the PLO. President Bush expresses his concern.

21 November: Israel's opposition Labour Party recommends repeal of law forbidding contact with PLO, suggests a freeze for one year of new settlements in the West Bank and Gaza Strip and recognizes the 'national rights' of Palestinians while still rejecting the creation of a Palestinian state.

1992 January: an Israeli inter-ministerial committee approves a demand for the deportation of twelve leading Palestinians as a reprisal for the killing of a Jewish settler in the Gaza Strip.

January–February: increase in killings of alleged collaborators in occupied territories, and in attacks on Israeli settlers and soldiers. Israel increases use of undercover units to control the intifada and is accused by human rights organizations of summarily executing Palestinian activists.

October–November: despite hopes for peace that followed the election of the Labour government in Israel on 23 June, there are

violent clashes between Palestinians and the Israeli security forces
in the occupied territories, prompted by a hunger strike of Palestinian prisoners in Israeli jails. Since 1987, 959 Palestinians, 543 alleged Palestinian 'collaborators' and 103 Israelis have been killed in
the intifada.

December: with backing from Iran, Hamas kills four Israeli soldiers in Gaza and Hebron, and kidnaps and later murders another.
At the time of the fifth anniversary of the outbreak of the intifada,
the nature of the uprising has changed. The original popular committees have been weakened by Israeli action and infighting. The
United National Leadership of the Uprising (UNLU), and its bi-
weekly communiqués, no longer leads the resistance. The intifada
is sustained by activists in small groups.

1993 March: violent confrontations between Palestinians and Israeli security forces, particularly in the Gaza Strip, lead to the closure of the West Bank and the Gaza Strip. Situation as bloody as at
the beginning of the intifada, and exacerbated by Israeli Defence
Force tactics of firing rockets at houses it thinks harbours wanted
Palestinians.

1994 February: following talks between Arafat and Peres in Davos,
Switzerland, and Cairo, and agreement reached on the implementation of the Gaza–Jericho Declaration of Principles covering border crossings, and Israeli access to the settlements in Gaza, the ten
Palestinian rejectionist factions meeting in Damascus as the Alliance of Palestinian Forces (APF) announce their refusal to co-
operate with the PLO and to participate in the elections scheduled
for July 1994. APF form a new central council to rival that of the
PLO and state that the intifada will be escalated.

May: Palestinian autonomy achieved in Gaza and Jericho.

1995 9 February: the Israeli Information Centre for Human
Rights in the Occupied Territories announces that 1,396 Palestinians and 230 Israelis have died in the intifada.

1996 January: Palestine Legislative Council elected.

11. War in Lebanon

1932 French colonial administration census in Lebanon (the last conducted to date) shows a ratio of Christians to Muslims of six to five. Confessional system (one based on representation by religious affiliation) established later provides for a Maronite Christian President, a Sunni Muslim Prime Minister and a Shiite Speaker.

1967 Following Six-Day War, number of Palestinians – who originally arrived in Lebanon in 1948 at the time of the First Arab–Israeli War – increases. This exacerbates divisions between the Maronite Christian community in Lebanon, which has a disproportionately large share of the wealth, leading positions, and makes up the backbone of the armed forces, and the Arab Muslim majority. The Maronite Christians take a moderate stand on the existence of Israel, whereas the Arab majority maintains a militant position on this matter.

1969 October: unrest among Palestinian refugees. Syrian guerrillas in Lebanon attack the Lebanese army as well as Israel, and move their bases into more favourable positions from which to attack the latter; Israel retaliates. Consequently, Lebanese army attacks guerrilla camps.

Syria opposes Lebanese government's attempts to restore order in south border region; Nasser's intervention results in the Cairo accords. This settlement acknowledges that Beirut government has lost control in south border region to Palestinian fighters.

1970–1 Number of Palestinians increases in Lebanon with their expulsion from Jordan. Palestinians now number around 400,000 out of a population of 3 million. Many of Palestinians settle south of the Litani river, where most of the inhabitants are Shiites. Shiites have to accept Palestine Liberation Organization (PLO) fighters and Israeli reprisals.

1975 April: Palestinian gunmen shoot the bodyguard of the Phalangist leader, Pierre Gemayel. Palestinians resent demands of Phalangists that Lebanese government should control the Palestinian fighters. Phalangist gunmen retaliate by killing a bus full of Palestinians.

1976 May: worried that intercommunal fighting between Christians and Muslims in Lebanon could lead to Israeli military intervention in southern Lebanon, Syria sends troops into Lebanon and faces opposition from the PLO and virtual isolation in the Arab world.

October: leaders of Egypt, Syria, Lebanon and the PLO agree to a cease-fire and the formation of an Arab peacekeeping force.

1977 16 March: the chief of the Druze (the religious sect settled on Mount Lebanon) and leader of the Lebanese left, Kamal Jumblatt, assassinated by unknown gunmen. Revenge killings follow but no major factional fighting.

July: Shtaura Agreement tries to regulate Palestinian camps and introduces a reconstituted Lebanese army into the south border area. Syria, the PLO and the Lebanese government are all parties to the Shtaura Agreement.

1978 11 March: PLO launches series of raids from south Lebanon and attack near Tel Aviv, leaving thirty-seven dead and seventy-six wounded Israeli civilians.

14 March: Israeli Defence Forces mount massive operation across the northern frontier and establish themselves six miles into Lebanese territory.

20 March: cease-fire. Israelis occupy area as far as the Litani river apart from Tyre. 1,000 civilians killed and over 200,000 become refugees.

13 June: on withdrawing from Lebanon, Israelis hand over their positions to Maronite Christian Lebanese (with whom they have collaborated) and not to the interim United Nations peacekeeping force, UNIFIL, creating problems for the Syrian-dominated Arab peacekeeping force.

1981 March: Syria agrees that the Lebanese government can send troops to join UNIFIL in southern Lebanon. This leads to the Israeli-backed Phalangist militia under Saad Haddad fighting against Syrian troops as well as the Palestinians.

28 April: Israeli intervention in Lebanon leads to the Israeli air-force shooting down two Syrian helicopters. Syria later responds by placing SAM 6 anti-aircraft missiles inside Lebanon to protect its positions in the Bekaa valley.

May: President Reagan sends Philip Habib to negotiate with the warring factions, but Begin renews Israeli attacks on Lebanon and demands that Syria remove anti-aircraft missiles stationed within its own borders and threatens Israeli action to achieve this.

24 July: Habib, with assistance of Saudis, manages to achieve an understanding between Begin, President Hafiz al-Asad of Syria and Yasser Arafat, the leader of the Palestine Liberation Organization, and there is a cease-fire in Lebanon.

Threat of Syrian missiles convinces Israeli Chief of Staff, Rafael Eitan, that a large-scale military operation would be needed to protect Israel's sixty-three Galilee settlements and towns from raids across the northern border. Partnership with Maronite Christians could help. Ariel Sharon, Israeli Minister of Defence, concurs, as does Menachem Begin, the Prime Minister of Israel and the Likud alignment.

December: Israeli Cabinet has reservations about plan to install Maronite leader Bashir Gemayel as President of Lebanon; concern about the prospect of a major clash with the Syrians.

1982 3 June: attempted assassination of Israeli ambassador in London. Israeli intelligence informs Begin that this is the work of Abu Nidal, who hopes to provoke an Israeli attack on PLO strongholds in Lebanon. Begin refuses to pass on this information to Israeli Cabinet.

4–5 June: Israeli airforce bombs PLO targets in Lebanon, penetrating as far as West Beirut. PLO responds by shelling Israeli settlements in Galilee.

6 June: Sharon starts a massive military operation, in which the Israeli army quickly reaches the outskirts of Beirut. Disregarding Cabinet opinion, Sharon provokes Syria and destroys eighty of its aircraft and damages its SAM missile sites.

11 June: Israel agrees to cease-fire with Syria.

13 June–12 August: siege of Beirut, in which capital bombed almost continuously; 18,000 dead and 30,000 wounded, most of the casualties being civilians. Israel says it will only end siege if the forces of the PLO, totalling around 9,000 fighters, surrender or leave Lebanon together with Syrian troops still in Beirut.

August: through American mediation, the Lebanese government and the PLO agree to a cease-fire and the evacuation of PLO fighters from Lebanon. Evacuation starts on 21 August, the Palestinians going to different Arab countries. A multi-national force of American, French and Italian troops sees that the agreement is implemented.

23 August: Bashir Gemayel, Maronite military leader, is elected President of Lebanon. Afterwards has secret talks with Israel about an alliance that would eliminate the Palestinian and Syrian influence in Lebanon and establish a Maronite supremacy.

1 September: Bashir Gemayel meets Begin and Sharon in northern Israel. Israelis demand that their ally in south Lebanon, Haddad, be Minister of Defence.

12 September: Sharon and Bashir Gemayel agree on Phalangist militia's clearing out the remaining 2,000 PLO fighters concealed in refugee camps of West Beirut.

14 September: Bashir Gemayel killed by a bomb at Phalangist Party headquarters. Israeli army moves into West Beirut in violation of cease-fire agreement. Sharon tells Eitan (Israeli Chief of Staff) to allow Phalangists into the refugee camps. Begin not informed.

16 September: Sharon tells Phalangist commanders that they can destroy Palestinian terrorists, but there should not be uncontrolled attacks on civilians. Israeli troops surround the camps at Sabra and Shatila and open a way through for the Phalangists.

18 September: Sharon goes to Sabra and Shatila; despite his apparent orders, the Phalangists do not leave for four hours. As Israeli Cabinet attributes atrocity to a Lebanese unit, disinterred bodies are photographed by newsmen and estimates of dead range from 1,000 to 2,000.

21 September: Amin Gemayel, who wants an accommodation with Syria, takes over from his murdered brother.

24 September: demonstration against war in Lebanon, organized by Peace Now and the Labour Alignment in Tel Aviv, attended by 400,000.

1983 February: Israeli commission criticizes Begin, Yitzhak Shamir, the Foreign Minister, Sharon and Eitan. Sharon resigns as Minister of Defence but stays on in Cabinet.

18 April: after American marines go to Lebanon as part of multinational force, American embassy in Beirut is blown up: forty-six dead.

24 April: George Shultz, US Secretary of State, travels to Middle East and negotiates an agreement between Israeli and Lebanese governments.

17 May: agreement signed between Israel and Lebanon secures withdrawal of Israeli troops from Lebanon, but allows joint Israeli–Lebanese patrols to operate inside the Lebanese border. Israel makes its agreement contingent on a simultaneous Syrian withdrawal from the Bekaa Valley.

May–June: Syrian army helps Palestine National Liberation Movement under Abu Musa take over Palestinian positions in the Bekaa Valley. Asad forces Arafat to leave Syria.

20 July: against background of demonstrations and admissions that Lebanon operation had cost at least 500 Israeli lives, Israeli

Cabinet decides that Israeli troops should be withdrawn to the Awali river, a more easily defensible position.

23 July: Walid Jumblatt announces Shiite–Druze coalition, supported by Syria. Israeli retreat from Shouf mountains exposes American marines to cross-fire between the Lebanese army and this coalition.

28 August: Begin resigns and is later succeeded by Shamir.

23 October: suicide bomb attacks wipe out headquarters of both the American and French contingents of the multi-national force in Beirut: 265 marines and fifty-eight French soldiers killed. Reagan later says that if there were a collapse of order in Lebanon, the marines would leave.

1984 February: with the Lebanese army disintegrating along sectarian lines, and Druze militia linking up with their Shiite allies in the southern suburbs of Beirut, the Americans and the rest of the multinational force departs. Gemayel, sensitive to Muslim opinion, cancels the agreement of 17 May 1983 with Israel in return for guarantees about internal security from Asad.

1985 28 December: militia leaders, Walid Jumblatt of the Druze, Nabih Berri of Amal and Elie Hobeika of the Lebanese Forces (LF) sign an accord in Damascus providing for an immediate cease-fire and an end to the state of civil war within one year.

1986 22 January: clashes between rival factions start again in Beirut.

1987 21 May: Lebanese National Assembly votes to abrogate the agreement signed by Lebanon and Arafat in 1969 and so cancels any right of PLO to official Lebanese protection.

December: against background of intifada, Nabih Berri, leader of Amal, suspends campaign against PLO. Frees Amal forces to be used against Iranian-backed Hezbollah which aims at setting up an Islamic state in Lebanon.

1988 5 May: fighting breaks out between Amal and Hezbollah militias.

7 July: Arafat's last stronghold in Beirut captured by Abu Musa.

1989 April: General Aoun (Awn), a Maronite Christian, backed by mainly Christian forces, starts a campaign to expel Syrian forces from Lebanon.

August: France sends senior government envoys to Middle East in attempt to stop fighting in Lebanon. French diplomatic initiative condemned by Hezbollah as a 'military adventure' to assist Aoun.

7 September: United States closes embassy in Lebanon. Aoun's attempt to internationalize Lebanese conflict and to secure Western support for the expulsion of Syria fails.

October: Lebanese parliament, meeting in Taif, Saudi Arabia, agrees to plan whereby Syrian troops are to be withdrawn over a two-year period and a more even distribution of power among major sects is to be implemented.

24 November: pro-Syrian, Elias Hrawi, is elected President of the Lebanese Republic, but his power is curtailed by continuing revolt of General Aoun. Hrawi takes office after his predecessor, René Muawad, is assassinated only seventeen days after he took the oath of office.

1990 February–July: intense fighting takes place between forces of Aoun and rival Christian leader, Samir Geagea of the Lebanese Forces.

October: Aoun defeated by Syrian forces and takes refuge in French embassy after Syrian bombardment of predominantly Christian East Beirut.

21 October: Dany Chamoun, son of former president, Camille Chamoun, and leader of National Liberal Party, murdered. Had reluctantly supported Aoun against Phalangist rivals.

December: as a result of President Hrawi's partial implementation of the Taif plan, following the amendment of the constitution in September to allow for political reforms, the withdrawal of the various militias from greater Beirut is virtually complete. Lebanese army, with Syrian support, controls the capital. Before the militias' withdrawal from Beirut the leaders of the rival Shiite factions, Amal and Hezbollah, had signed a peace agreement, and on withdrawal the militiamen move south towards the Israeli border. Israel responds with military incursions into south Lebanon. Lebanese government starts rebuilding programme, and takes over the operation of Lebanon's principal ports. Hrawi follows Syria in opposing Saddam Hussein, and so ensures aid from Saudi Arabia.

1991 President Hrawi tries to establish broad-based government by bringing militia leaders into Cabinet. Samir Geagea, leader of the Christian Lebanese Forces, refuses to join and Walid Jumblatt, Druze leader, withdraws. The Cabinet of thirty members under Umar Karami is estimated to be around 90 per cent pro-Syrian.

22 May: Treaty of Brotherhood, Co-operation and Co-ordination signed by Lebanese and Syrian presidents in Damascus. Syria formally acknowledges Lebanon's independence. Under clause three,

Lebanon agrees that it will not be a source of threat to Syria's security, and will not be a corridor or springboard for any force, state or organization hostile to Syria. Israeli assessment is that Syria is taking over Lebanon. Syrian move probably assisted by an American indulgence following Syrian President Asad's support of the coalition during the Gulf War.

28 August: announced that following an amnesty law, Aoun is to be allowed to leave the French embassy and go into exile in France.

17 October: in terms of Treaty of Brotherhood, Co-operation and Co-ordination President Hrawi, Prime Minister Umar Karami, and the President of the National Assembly, Hussein al-Husseini, visit Damascus to attend the first session of the Lebanese–Syrian Supreme Council. Discussions cover co-operation between Syria and Lebanon at Middle East peace conference.

21–7 October: Hrawi visits France to discuss French military and financial aid for reconstruction of Lebanon.

2 November: Karami announces that Washington has asked Israel 'to cease all military activity in southern Lebanon at once because the Middle East peace process cannot afford such aggressive acts'. This follows clashes between the Lebanese army and the Israeli-backed South Lebanese Army which had erupted early in October and continued into the following year.

1992 10 January: Israel reasserts its presence in south Lebanon and attacks a Popular Front for the Liberation of Palestine–General Command base in the hills just south of Beirut.

January: Vice-President of Syria, Abd al-Halim Khaddam, visits Beirut to attempt a reconcilation between President Hrawi, Prime Minister Karami, and the President of the National Assembly Husseini, as well as the return to the Cabinet of the militia chiefs Walid Jumblatt and Nabih Berri.

22 October: following elections to the National Assembly under a new electoral law under which the number of seats in the Assembly was increased from 108 to 128, to be divided equally between Muslim and Christian deputies, Rafik Hariri, a Lebanese-born Saudi-Arabian entrepreneur, is invited to form a government.

31 October: Hariri appoints a new Cabinet, including technocrats, and with offices not, as previously, distributed on a confessional basis.

16 December: Israel deports to Lebanon more that 400 alleged Palestinian supporters of Hamas. Lebanon refuses to accept them and deportees are stranded between Israel's self-declared security zone and Lebanon.

1993 25 July: Israel attacks southern Lebanon with the intention of eradicating Hezbollah and Palestinian guerrillas: 300,000 civilians displaced and move to north.

1994 19 October: Israeli attack on village of Nabatiyeh in the south of Lebanon seen as retaliation for operations by Hamas inside Israel. Leads to Hezbollah rocket attacks into northern and western Israel, and an escalation of the conflict.

1995 March: conflict escalates further following assassination by Israel of a Hezbollah leader in southern Lebanon.

8 July: Israel responds to the killing of two Israeli soldiers by Hezbollah with an attack on Nabatiyeh with anti-personnel missiles, killing three children. Hezbollah retaliates with rocket attacks on northern Israel, and in August Israel attacks Hezbollah targets and inflicts heavy casualties.

19 October: National Assembly votes to amend constitution to extend the term of office of President Hrawi for a further three years.

1996 11 April: Israel launches 'Operation Grapes of Wrath', which includes attacks on the southern suburbs of Beirut. The stated intention is to end rocket attacks by Hezbollah on northern Israel.

18 April: an Israeli attack on the United Nations base at Qana kills more than 100 Lebanese refugees.

27 April: cease-fire agreement achieved between Hezbollah and Israel, following unsuccessful shuttle diplomacy by Warren Christopher, the United States Secretary of State, and successful negotiations by Hervé de Charette, the French Minister of Foreign Affairs.

August: elections take place under controversial new electoral law which divides Mount Lebanon, where the Maronite Christian community is concentrated, into five electoral constituencies.

12. The Iran–Iraq War

1930 30 June: Iraq formally achieves independence with signing of Anglo–Iraqi Treaty. Under mandate, British authorities had controlled Basra and the Shatt al-Arab waterway between Iraq and Iran.

1937 British support ensures that navigation rights on the Shatt al-Arab waterway go in Iraq's favour. This means that Iraq effectively controls shipping destined for Iranian ports.

1968 Baath Party firmly established in Iraq; regards itself as protector of Arab interests.

1971 When Britain withdraws from Gulf, Iran seizes islands of Abu Musa and the Tumbs, then under control of United Arab Emirates. Move regarded as statement of Iran's determination to control Gulf region and challenge Iraq and Saudi Arabia. Iraq reacts in the name of the Arab world by restricting access to Iran's port of Khorramshahr and the oil refinery at Abadan, both of which are on eastern shore of Shatt al-Arab.

1971–5 Iran retaliates by stirring up Kurdish question, supporting Kurdish *peshmerga* (lit: those who confront death) guerillas.

1975 Algiers Agreement signed between Iran and Iraq: in return for Iran ceasing to support Kurds, Iraq to accept a new frontier in the Shatt al-Arab, the Thalweg Line. The international frontier is now the line of maximum depth and not the eastern low-water mark.

1979 Rise of Ayatollah Khomeini in Iran disturbing to Iraq, as Khomeini had developed connections with Iraq's Shiites during his exile in southern Iraq. Fifty-five per cent of Iraq's population Shiite. Iraq's Baath policy of radical secularism was opposed to the fundamentalist Islam of Iran.

Saddam Hussein, who had joined the Baath Party in 1957 and had been exiled to Egypt 1959–64 after his involvement in the assassination of Kassem and had then risen through the hierarchy of the Baath Party to become Vice Chairman of the Revolutionary Command Council in November 1969, becomes President of Iraq and eliminates opposition.

December: Iraqi government arrests Shiite clerics in southern Iraq, including Muhammad Baqir al-Sadr, a close associate of Khomeini.

1980 January: President Jimmy Carter declares Gulf of 'vital interest' to the United States.

April: all Shiites of Iranian origin living in Iraq expelled to Iran. Iraqi Shiite organization, supported by Iran, attempts to assassinate Iraqi foreign minister. Iraqi secret services encourage rebellion in Khuzestan province of Iran.

4 September: Iranian artillery bombardments on Iraq border.

11 September: Iraqi border encroachments.

17 September: Iraq unilaterally abrogates the 1975 Algiers Agreement.

22 September: Iraq invades Iran at four border points along a 300-mile front including Khorramshahr and Abadan.

September: Iran and Iraq attack each other's oil facilities.

October: Iran's forces successfully resist Iraqi divisions in Gulf sector.

1981 Iran wins a number of victories in winter campaign.

1982 After being driven out of Khorramshahr, Iraq withdraws from Iran and asks for peace negotiations. Iran demands removal of Saddam Hussein and reparations.

July: Iran launches jihad against 'the satan' (Saddam Hussein) with new offensive into Iraq around Basra.

1982–5 As oil revenues fall, Iraq has difficulties in paying for war. Iraq's Gulf terminals destroyed at start of war. In April 1982 Syria closes the Kirkuk–Banias pipeline. Mitigated by oil revenues from Neutral Zone, assisted by arms and technical aid from Soviet Union and France, also supported financially by other Arab countries, especially Saudi Arabia and Kuwait, Iraq borrows $7 billion from Kuwait.

1983 October: Iranian troops occupy 270 square miles of Iraq. Iraq bombs Kharg Island oil terminal and Iranian towns. Iran threatens to block the Straits of Hormuz.

1984 February: Iran attacks near confluence of Tigris and Euphrates rivers and occupies sections of Majnoon oilfield in Hawizah swamps. 'Human wave' tactics often used in fighting, but begin to be complimented by more professional army techniques.

April: Iraqi airforce starts attacks on Iranian offshore oilfields and export terminals in Gulf.

November: United States re-establishes diplomatic relations with Iraq.

Iraq attacks Iranian ships, including tankers using Kharg Island terminal.

1985 March: Iran crosses Tigris with 50,000 troops and closes main road between Baghdad and Basra. Followed by Iraqi counter-offensive and heavy casualties on both sides. Iraq bombs Tehran, Isfahan, Shiraz and other Iranian towns. King Hussein of Jordan and President Mubarak of Egypt visit Baghdad to show support.

April: attempted intervention by Secretary General of United Nations. Iran does not respond to Iraqi cease-fires.

July: Iran refuses to negotiate and demands removal of Saddam Hussein. Iranian casualties estimated at over half a million.

Iran attacks in Kurdistan in north and near Hawizah marshes in south.

August: successful Iraqi air attacks on Kharg Island, the main Iranian oil export terminal. Later air attacks destroy the replacement floating terminals at Sirri and Lavan islands.

1986 January: Iraq claims to have retaken Majnoon Islands.

9 February: 85,000 Iranian troops cross Shatt al-Arab waterway and occupy Faw (Fao). Iraq's only access to Gulf threatened. Iran attacks Iraq's forces between Faw and Basra.

February: Iran opens second front in Kurdistan. United Nations Security Council calls for cease-fire.

May: Iraq invades Iran and occupies area around Mehran.

July: Iran recaptures Mehran.

December: Kuwait requests protection from Iranian attacks for its shipping. Soviet Union offers four tankers on charter.

1986–7 Following successful Iraqi air attacks, Iranian oil exports drop from 2.2 million barrels a day in mid-1986 to less than 1.5 million by 1988. Iraq aims to weaken Iranian economy.

1987 March: United States responds to Russian offer by deciding to reflag eleven Kuwaiti tankers under United States flag.

May: President Reagan describes accidental attack by Iraqi aircraft on USS *Stark* as being a result of Iranian aggression causing instability in the Gulf that had led to the Iraqi error.

July: United States ships escort Kuwaiti tankers in waters mined by Iran. Security Council resolution urging a cease-fire rejected by Iran. United States requests an arms embargo against Iran.

August: after attacks on ships in Gulf, Britain, France, and later other NATO nations support American naval effort in Gulf.

1988 February: Iraq resumes 'war of the cities'.

March: Iraq uses chemical weapons in an attack on Halabja, killing 4,000 Kurdish civilians. Kurdish guerrillas had supported Iranian forces, enabling them to establish bridgeheads, particularly in the Mawat region along the Iranian border.

April: United Nations report states that evidence of victims of chemical warfare on both sides of conflict. Mine attack on American naval vessel in Gulf followed by American attack on Iranian offshore oilfield installations and the sinking of six Iranian naval ships. Iraq reconquers Faw (Fao) peninsula.

June: Khomeini appoints Rafsanjani as acting Commander-in-Chief of Iranian armed forces following major defeats at Shalamcheh, near Basra, Majnoon Island in the Hawizah marshes, Mehran and in Kurdistan.

18 July: Iran announces unconditional acceptance of United Nations Security Council resolution of July 1987 for a cease-fire. Khomeini admits on Iranian television that he has done worse than drink poison in abandoning destruction of Saddam Hussein.

July: USS *Vincennes*, during a minor skirmish, mistakenly shoots down an Iranian passenger aircraft killing 290. Iraq admits use of chemical weapons during war.

August: United Nations experts report that Iraq has used mustard gas in attacks on Iranian civilians.

20 August: cease-fire in force under supervision of United Nations monitoring force.

25 August: peace negotiations start at Geneva.

1990 September: against background of Saddam Hussein's invasion of Kuwait, Iraq proposes a non-aggression pact to Iran. Plans are made to resume diplomatic relations. Iraq reiterates its resolve to stand by all previous treaties with Iran, including the 1975 Algiers Agreement on the Shatt al-Arab waterway. In essence Saddam Hussein yields to Iran the latter's objectives in the Iran–Iraq War. The estimated loss of life on both sides during the eight-year conflict exceeds one million; over fifty towns and cities ruined.

13. The Gulf War

1990 16 July: Tariq Aziz, Foreign Minister of Iraq, in letter to Arab League, accuses Kuwait of having stolen oil worth $2,400 million from the Rumayla fields in the early stages of Iran–Iraq War, of erecting military installations on Iraq's territory, and of reducing Iraq's oil income by keeping oil prices low through over-production. Aziz also complains that the United Arab Emirates (UAE) had exceeded its oil production quotas, and that both it and Kuwait refused to cancel Iraq's war debts.

17 July: Saddam Hussein, President of Iraq, blaming the production policies of Kuwait and UAE on American influence designed to undermine Arab interests, threatens force to make Arab oil exporters keep to production quotas.

18 July: Kuwait convenes emergency session of its National Council and sends emissaries to Arab states to discuss Iraqi accusations.

19 July: Kuwait informs Arab League that Iraq is drilling for oil in Kuwaiti territory, and sends message to Péres de Cuéllar, Secretary General of the United Nations, about relations with Iraq. Richard Cheney, United States Secretary of Defense, states that the United States is committed to defend Kuwait in case of attack.

21 July: 30,000 élite Iraqi troops mass on border with Kuwait; by end of July number grows to 100,000.

25 July: after meeting in Alexandria between President Hosni Mubarak of Egypt, King Hussein of Jordan and Aziz, statement is issued that Iraq has agreed to settle differences with Kuwait and the UAE, and that Kuwait has agreed to talks with Iraq to be held in Saudi Arabia to settle the border dispute.

31 July: representatives of Iraq and Kuwait hold talks in Jedda, which collapse on 1 August.

2 August: on pretext of supporting a group of Kuwaiti revolutionaries opposed to the ruling Sabah family, Iraq invades Kuwait and occupies oilfields. The United Nations Security Council passes Resolution 660, condemning Iraq's invasion and stating that unless Iraq withdrew immediately and unconditionally, sanctions and military force would be used.

3 August: fourteen out of twenty-one of the Arab League foreign ministers meeting in Cairo, while condemning the Iraqi invasion, caution against any foreign intervention in Arab affairs. Jordan, Mauritania, Sudan, Yemen and the Palestine Liberation Organization (PLO) abstain; Libya walks out of meeting. The Gulf Co-operation Council (GCC) insists that the Arab League's rejection of foreign intervention does not apply to Security Council measures as Arab League charter includes adherence to United Nations resolutions. In Moscow, James Baker, the United States Secretary of State, and Eduard Shevardnadze, the Soviet Foreign Minister, issue a joint statement condemning the Iraqi invasion and asking for a halt to arms deliveries to Iraq.

6 August: United Nations Resolution 661 imposes economic sanctions on Iraq.

7 August: accepting Saudi Arabia's invitation to allies to reinforce defences against Iraq, United States in 'Operation Desert Shield' sends paratroopers, an armoured brigade and jet fighters to protect Saudi Arabia from an Iraqi invasion.

8 August: Iraq proclaims union of Iraq and Kuwait and says that Iraq will not attack Saudi Arabia. On American television, President Bush says that the sovereign independence of Saudi Arabia is of vital interest to the United States. Britain announces the despatch of two fighter squadrons to the Middle East, and the strengthening of its naval patrol in the Gulf. France also announces strengthening of its naval presence in Gulf.

9 August: Resolution 662 is unanimously adopted by the Security Council: Iraq's annexation of Kuwait is declared to be null and void; a special committee is established to monitor compliance with trade sanctions.

10 August: twelve out of the twenty-one members of the Arab League, meeting in Cairo, vote to send troops to help defend Saudi Arabia and other Gulf states against Iraq. Libya and PLO support Iraq. Jordan, Mauritania and Sudan support the resolution but with reservations. Algeria and Yemen abstain. Tunisia is not present.

11 August: Syria announces that it will send troops to Saudi Arabia, while Egyptian and Moroccan troops land in Saudi Arabia.

12 August: Saddam Hussein links withdrawal of Iraqi forces from Kuwait with Syrian withdrawal from Lebanon, and Israeli withdrawal from Gaza, the West Bank, the Golan Heights and Lebanon. The 'linkage' is rejected by United States and Israeli governments. Hussein also demands that foreign troops in Saudi Arabia be replaced by Arab forces under United Nations auspices, that United

Nations resolutions regarding the Syrian and Israeli situations be implemented, and that those applied to Iraq after 2 August be discontinued. Bush orders United States forces to stop Iraq oil exports, and also all imports apart from food stuffs.

15 August: Iraq accepts Iran's peace terms for the ending of the Iran–Iraq War.

17 August: Speaker of Iraq's parliament, Saadi Mahdi Salih, announces that nationals of 'aggressive nations' will be held while there is a threat of war against Iraq.

18 August: Iraqi officials announce that foreigners held in Iran and Kuwait will be moved to military bases and other strategic areas to serve as 'human shields'. Resolution 664 is unanimously adopted by the United Nations Security Council: 'Iraq should permit and facilitate the immediate departure from Kuwait and Iraq' of foreign nationals.

19 August: United States rejects offer from Saddam Hussein to release Westerners if the United States withdraws its forces from Saudi Arabia, and the economic sanctions against Iraq are lifted.

23 August: televised meeting of Saddam Hussein with British hostages, including children; he tells them that their presence is to prevent scourge of war. Jordan, overwhelmed by refugees fleeing Iraq, temporarily closes its borders with Iraq.

28 August: Saddam Hussein, in a decree, declares Kuwait the nineteenth governate in Iraq's administrative structure. Also says that all foreign women and children detained in Iraq (presumably including Kuwait) will be able to leave.

1 September: 'inconclusive' ending to two days of talks between Pérez de Cuéllar and Aziz in Amman. Around 700 foreign women and children are allowed to leave Iraq.

2 September: Saudi Arabia announces that it is increasing its oil production by 2 million barrels per day.

7 September: in Saudi Arabia, deposed Emir of Kuwait promises $5 billion towards the costs of the American military operation. Saudi Arabia and the United Arab Emirates also offer to contribute to the costs.

9 September: at summit meeting in Helsinki, Presidents Bush and Gorbachev warn Saddam Hussein that the Soviet Union and the United States are prepared to take further action consistent with the United Nations charter and insist that nothing short of the implementation of all the United Nations Security Council resolutions concerning Iraq will be acceptable. Once Iraq withdrew from Kuwait and the government was restored, and hostages had been released, Bush and Gorbachev agreed that their countries' foreign ministers would be urged to 'develop regional security structures and measures to promote peace and stability' in the area.

14 September: Britain announces that it will send an armoured brigade and 6,000 combat troops to the Gulf.

15 September: France agrees to send a further 4,000 troops and three army air regiments; the French presence being 13,000 men, fourteen warships and nearly 100 anti-tank helicopters.

16 September: Egypt sends a further 15,000 troops, making 20,000 in all.

20 September: Britain and United States agree that British troops can be placed under American command in Saudi Arabia, but that military action will require consultation.

23 September: Saddam Hussein threatens to retaliate to the 'stifling of the Iraqi people' by destroying oilfields in the Middle East and by attacking Israel.

24 September: President Mitterrand of France proposes an international conference on the Middle East to discuss the settlement of all sources of conflict in the region, once Iraq had withdrawn from Kuwait and freed the hostages. The price of oil reaches $40 a barrel.

27 September: Britain and Iran agree to restore diplomatic links.

29 September: in his address to the General Assembly of the United Nations, the Emir of Kuwait, Sheikh Jabir al-Ahmad Al Sabah, compares the Iraqi invasion of Kuwait with the Israeli occupation of the West Bank and southern Lebanon.

23 October: in response to efforts made by Soviet Union and France, there is an Iraqi announcement that French citizens are free to leave Iraq. President Bush and British Prime Minister, Margaret Thatcher, reiterate that there can be no compromise on the Iraqi withdrawal from Kuwait.

25 October: President Ali Abdullah Saleh accuses Saudi Arabia of damaging Yemen's economy by expelling around 500,000 Yemenis from Saudi Arabia.

29 October: Resolution 674 adopted by Security Council holds Iraq liable for human rights abuses, economic losses since the occupation of Kuwait on 2 August, and war damages.

1 November: General H. Norman Schwarzkopf, the American commander of the multi-national forces in the Gulf, says that it may not be in the best interests of the United States and 'a long-term balance of power in this region' to destroy Iraq.

8 November: Bush orders a further 150,000 troops to the Gulf 'to provide an adequate offensive military option' to force Iraq from Kuwait; this will raise United States troop strength in Gulf to over 380,000 by early 1991. Saddam Hussein dismisses his Chief of Staff, Lieutenant-General Nazir al-Khazraji, who is thought to have opposed the invasion of Kuwait.

18 November: Saddam Hussein announces that all hostages will be released from Christmas Day onwards, 'unless something takes place that mars the atmosphere of peace'. Release of hostages starts before that.

19 November: Iraq's official news agency announces that Iraq is sending an additional 250,000 troops (including 150,000 reservists) to Kuwait to deter any attempt to retake Kuwait. Iraqi forces in southern Iraq and Kuwait estimated at 700,000.

23 November: Bush meets Syrian President Asad in Damascus and announces that Asad is lining up with coalition, with a commitment to use force in the Gulf.

26 November: while in Moscow, Aziz is told by Gorbachev that Iraq must leave Kuwait if it wants to avoid war.

28 November: Britain restores diplomatic relations with Syria after a four-year break.

29 November: Resolution 678 is passed by Security Council, authorizing all member states 'to use all necessary means' to implement Resolution 660 and subsequent resolutions on Kuwait if Iraq fails to withdraw from Kuwait by 15 January.

30 November: Bush announces that he has invited Aziz to Washington, and is prepared to send Baker to Baghdad for talks with Saddam Hussein between 15 December and 15 January 'to discuss all aspects of the Gulf crisis', to go 'the extra mile for peace'.

1 December: Iraqi Revolutionary Council accepts 'the idea of the invitation and the meeting' (Bush's offer of direct talks) and says that Iraq 'will call on representatives of countries and parties that are connected with unresolved disputes and issues to attend the meetings', also that the future of the Palestinians in the occupied territories will be high on the agenda.

2 December: Baker says that Iraq's reward for withdrawing from Kuwait would be that there would not be a military attack by the United States, and that there should be no 'linkage' between Kuwait and the Palestinian question.

3 December: Richard Cheney, United States Secretary of Defense, says that Iraq could withstand impact of sanctions for a year or more, and that United States cannot wait indefinitely for sanctions to take effect.

5 December: William Webster, Director of the Central Intelligence Agency, testifies to United States House Armed Services Committee that continued economic sanctions against Iraq would mean that the Iraqi airforce would lose its ability to fly regular missions within three months, and Iraq's ground forces would lose combat-readiness in nine months.

6 December: Saddam Hussein asks Iraqi National Assembly to allow all foreigners to leave. He indicates that this has been prompted by consultations with Jordan, Yemen, Palestine, Sudan and the Arab Maghreb, and also by positive signals from some sources in the United States and Europe.

11 December: President Chadli Benjedid of Algeria contacts Libya and begins tour of Arab capitals in an Arab peace initiative. Israeli Prime Minister, Yitzhak Shamir, after talks with Bush in the United States, says that he believes that the United States will not settle the Gulf crisis at Israel's expense.

16 December: the British embassy in Kuwait, the last to stay open, is closed.

18 December: majority of members of European Community (France, Italy, Spain and Greece dissenting) decide to cancel meeting between EEC Council President and Aziz, until the dispute over the timing of the United States–Iraq talks is settled.

27 December: 110 Democratic members of the House of Representatives urge Bush to allow more time for sanctions to work.

28 December: Cheney tells United States troops in Gulf that force will probably have to be used against Iraq, and that if there were war there had to be 'absolute total victory'.

1991 4 January: Aziz accepts invitation to meet Baker in Geneva on 9 January, and stresses the need to deal with the Palestinian question.

6 January: United States Department of Defense announces that journalists reporting on a Gulf war will have to operate in 'pools' under military supervision and submit all reports to a 'security review'.

7 January: both Baker and the new British Prime Minister, John Major, announce that there can be no extension of the United Nations deadline for Iraq to leave Kuwait.

9 January: in Geneva, Baker and Aziz fail to reach any agreement. In Egypt, John Major says that an international peace conference on the Palestinian issue should be held once the Gulf crisis is over.

12 January: United States Congress authorizes Bush to use force in Iraq.

13 January: Pérez de Cuéllar, after meeting Saddam Hussein, indicates that he has failed to achieve a resolution. Saddam Hussein invites Asad to Baghdad in response to an appeal from Syria.

14 January: Iraqi National Assembly unanimously votes to allow Saddam Hussein to use 'all jurisdiction and constitutional powers required in the showdown' against the multi-national force in the Gulf. Israel undertakes not to launch a pre-emptive strike against Iraq. Warnings of terrorist attacks lead to increased security precautions at world's airports.

15 January: Pérez de Cuéllar makes final appeal to stop a conflict that no one wants. The United Nations deadline for the Iraqi withdrawal from Kuwait expires at midnight New York time.

16 January: shortly before midnight Greenwich Mean Time, the multi-national air attack on Kuwait and Baghdad, code-named 'Operation Desert Storm' starts. In initial raids on Baghdad, the Defence Ministry, the airport, oil refineries, a chemical plant and the presidential palace are hit.

17 January: Iraqi Republican Guard units on border between Saudi Arabia and Kuwait are bombed. General Colin L. Powell, Chairman of the United States joint chiefs of staff, announces that the success rate of the bombing raids is 80 per cent.

17–18 January: seven Iraqi Scud missiles armed with conventional warheads land in Israel near Tel Aviv and Haifa. American Patriot missile destroys Iraqi missile aimed at American air base in Dhahran (Saudi Arabia). Oil price falls from $30 to $18 a barrel on evidence of overwhelming allied military strength. Oil price still below $20 at end of January, and around $18 at end of February.

19 January: Patriot missiles airlifted by United States to Israel.

20 January: General Schwarzkopf announces that Iraqi nuclear research reactors have been thoroughly damaged, and that Iraqi factories manufacturing chemical and biological weapons have suffered 'a considerable setback'.

24 January: American forces capture the island of Qura off Kuwait. Japan increases contribution pledged to the multi-national effort to $11 billion.

25 January: United States and Saudi Arabia accuse Iraq of creating an oil slick in the Gulf about 9 miles long from oil spills from tankers anchored off Kuwait and from the offshore Sea Island Terminal.

26 January: in the West, widespread peace demonstrations:

200,000 in Bonn; 50,000 in Paris; 100,000 in Washington and San Francisco. 'Smart bombs' from United States aircraft stem flow of oil from Sea Island Terminal.

26–8 January: about 80 Iraqi war planes are flown to Iran; this constitutes about 10 per cent of the Iraqi airforce. Iran says that it will impound the planes and intern the pilots for the duration of the war.

29 January: Iraqi troops capture Khafji, a small town in Saudi Arabia. German government increases earlier pledge for war effort of $2.2 billion by another $5.5 billion.

31 January: allies recapture Khafji.

3 February: United States announces that seven of the eleven marines who died in the battle for Khafji were killed by friendly fire.

4 February: President Hashemi Rafsanjani offers to meet personally with Saddam Hussein and to serve as a mediator with the United States.

12 February: Gorbachev's special envoy, Yevgeny Primakov, meets Saddam Hussein in Baghdad, and an announcement follows on Baghdad Radio that Iraq is prepared to negotiate a solution to the situation in the Gulf.

13 February: United States bombs destroy a structure in the Al Amiriya residential district of Baghdad, killing around 300 civilians. In response to Iraqi claim that building was a bomb shelter, United States Department of Defense insists that it was converted to a military command-and-control centre in 1985.

15 February: Iraq announces that it is prepared to withdraw from Kuwait, but makes withdrawal conditional on comprehensive cease-fire and the recission of the United Nations resolutions on Iraq passed during 1990. Bush states that conditions are unacceptable.

17 February: Bush informed of Soviet peace proposal, which Aziz is flying to Moscow to discuss.

19 February: Aziz meets Gorbachev, then carries peace plan, details of which are not released, to Rafsanjani.

22 February: back in Moscow, after second meeting with Gorbachev, Aziz accepts Moscow's peace plan which entails a cease-fire, withdrawal of Iraqi forces from Kuwait on the second day of the cease-fire with the withdrawal to be completed within twenty-one days, followed by the recission of the United Nations resolution on Iraq. Bush insists that Iraqi troops start leaving Kuwait on 23 February and that their withdrawal be completed within a week. Soviets then announce a revised peace proposal, shortening some of the times for the Iraqi withdrawal.

22–3 February: Iraq destroys Kuwaiti installations and sets fire to oil pumping stations.

23 February: the United States ambassador to the United Nations, Thomas Pickering, says that the Soviet peace plans 'fall short'.

24 February: ground offensive starts against Iraq: units of multinational force move towards Kuwait City and into southern Iraq.

25 February: according to Baghdad Radio, Iraqi forces have been given the order to withdraw from Kuwait to positions held before 1 August 1990, which is claimed to be in compliance with United Nations Resolution 660.

26 February: Bush says that as Iraq does not accept all the United Nations Security Council resolutions, the coalition forces will pursue the war. United States military announces that 517 of Kuwait's 950 oil wells have been set alight by Iraqi troops. Britain suffers its worst losses during the war, when nine British soldiers are killed in a mistaken attack on their Warrior armoured infantry vehicles by a United States A–10 'tankbuster' war plane.

27 February: Arab and United States troops take Kuwait City and airport. United States troops fight Iraq's Republican Guard 50 miles (80 km) west of Basra. Bush declares on American television that Iraq's army is defeated and Kuwait is liberated; that the coalition will cease hostilities at midnight Eastern standard time; and that Baker will undertake a tour of the Middle East. Schwarzkopf announces that the United States has lost seventy-nine troops killed, 213 wounded, and forty-four missing in action; Britain has lost thirteen; France, two; the Arab countries thirteen. There are no official figures given for the Iraqi losses, but later estimates range from 200,000 to 700,000.

28 February: Bush announces that Iraqi military leaders have agreed to work out terms of cease-fire with multi-national force commanders.

1 March: in a television address King Hussein of Jordan expresses sympathy for the Iraqi people, but stresses that the people of Jordan rejoiced with their 'Kuwaiti brothers'. King Hussein asks that the same criteria be applied to the Palestine question as had been applied to Kuwait.

1–5 March: on 1 March first signs of popular revolt against Saddam Hussein, when crowds demonstrate in Basra against ruling Baath party. Disturbances spread to other towns and cities in the

157

south, including Nasiriyah, and the Shiite holy cities of Karbala and Najaf. The Supreme Assembly of the Islamic Revolution in Iraq (SAIRI), led by Hojatolislam Muhammad Bakr al-Hakim, a Shiite group supported by Iran, is thought to have organized what is seen as a rebellion by Iraq's majority Shiite community.

2 March: United Nations Security Council passes Resolution 686, which demands Iraqi acceptance of the previous twelve relevant resolutions, release of civilian detainees, and acceptance under international law for the damage done to Kuwait. Iraq accepts resolution on 3 March.

4 March: Sheikh Saad al-Abdullah Al Sabah, the Crown Prince, returns to Kuwait as Prime Minster and administrator of martial law.

5 March: Saddam Hussein's élite Republican Guard, using tanks and heavy artillery, is managing to suppress rebels. Iraq announces that Revolutionary Command Council has 'annulled the annexation of Kuwait' and will comply with United Nations demands to return Kuwait's assets.

6 March: Saddam Hussein appoints his cousin, Ali Hassan al-Majid, as Minster of the Interior, with instructions to suppress the rebellion. Ali Hassan al-Majid was thought to have used chemical weapons against the Kurds in 1988, and also oversaw the occupation of Kuwait.

9 March: statement from the Supreme Assembly of the Islamic Revolution in Iraq, made in Beirut, claims that over 30,000 people have died during the uprising in the south.

13 March: meeting in Beirut, twenty-three Iraqi opposition groups agree to form a joint leadership to overthrow Saddam Hussein.

14 March: Kurdish rebels claim they control parts of northern Iraq.

16 March: at the same time as promising democratic reforms and a referendum on a new constitution when the rebellion is over, Saddam Hussein claims that his troops have suppressed the rebellion in the south, but admits that there is unrest in the Kurdish areas in the north.

18 March: an Amnesty International report claims that soldiers and civilians in Kuwait are arbitrarily arresting and torturing Palestinians.

22–3 March: United States airforce shoots down two Iraqi fighter-bombers flying in violation of the cease-fire agreement of 3 March. General Colin Powell says that United States forces will remain in Iraq until the arrival of an Arab regional security force.

23 March: Saddam Hussein appoints a Shiite Muslim, Saadun Hamadi, as Prime Minister, and Tariq Aziz moves from being Foreign Minister to one of two Deputy Prime Ministers.

26 March: United States State Department confirms that oil centre of Kirkuk under Kurdish control.

28 March: the Shiite leader, Hojatolislam Muhammad Bakr al-Hakim, concedes that Saddam Hussein's forces have retaken Karbala and other southern Iraqi towns.

31 March: Iraqi government announces that its forces have retaken Dohuk and two other towns in northern Iraq, Arbil and Zakho, from Kurdish rebels. As hundreds of thousands of Iraqi Kurdish refugees cross into Iran, relations between Iraq and Iran deteriorate. By this time it is reported that only seven of the 571 oil-well fires in Kuwait have been extinguished.

1 April: against the background of claims that Iraqi forces have retaken Kirkuk, Masud Barzani, the leader of the Democratic Party of Kurdistan, claims that around 3 million Kurds have fled into the mountains to escape the Iraqi government's programme of 'genocide and torture'. Barzani asks Britain, the United States, France and Saudi Arabia to request intervention by the United Nations.

3 April: Resolution 687 passed by United Nations Security Council, giving the terms for a cease-fire in the Gulf: Iraq is required to submit information concerning chemical and biological weapons stocks by 17 April; to accept on-site inspection of the destruction of weapons of mass destruction; to renounce international terrorism; to pay war reparations from a fund, administered by the United Nations, created from a levy on Iraq's oil export earnings. Resolution 687 is accepted on 5 April by Iraq's Revolutionary Command Council, and on 6 April by the National Assembly.

4 April: Iraqi Revolutionary Command Council chaired by Saddam Hussein, announces that Iraq has crushed sedition in the towns in Iraq, and offers an amnesty to all Kurds except those who had 'committed murder, rape and looting during acts of riots and treason', which is refused by the Democratic Party of Kurdistan on 5 April.

5 April: President Bush reiterates the United States government's policy of non-intervention in the internal affairs of Iraq, and says that it was not an objective of the coalition to overthrow Saddam Hussein. Security Council passes Resolution 688, which condemns the 'repression of the Iraqi civilian population in many parts of Iraq, including most recently in Kurdish populated areas, the consequences of which threaten international peace and security'.

Resolution makes no provision for stopping Iraq's repressive activities.

8 April: John Major, the British Prime Minister, outlines a plan to the European Community leaders attending a summit meeting in Luxembourg for the creation of a United Nations 'enclave' in northern Iraq to protect the Kurds. Major's plan is endorsed and the scheme becomes known as the 'safe havens' for the Kurds. Estimate by governor of south-eastern region of Turkey puts the number of Kurdish refugees in Turkey at 400,000.

9 April: United States spokesman says that United States has no position on 'safe havens' for the Kurds.

10 April: United States orders Iraq to stop all military activity north of the 36th parallel, an area passing just south of Mosul, but excluding Kirkuk, and extending to the Turkish border. United States also warns Iraq that any military interference in the international relief effort mounted for the Kurds will be met by force.

13 April: heavy fighting between Kurdish guerrillas (*peshmerga*) and Iraqi government troops is reported around the cities of Shaqlawa and Sulaimaniya, as well as the capture by Kurdish guerrillas of the northern Iraqi town of Dukan.

19 April: Amnesty International asks Emir of Kuwait to intervene on behalf of those detained on suspicion of collaborating with the Iraqis. It is alleged that the detainees are being held in deplorable conditions.

20 April: Emir of Kuwait, Sheikh Jabir al-Ahmad Al Sabah, names a new cabinet headed by the Crown Prince, Sheikh Saad al-Abdullah al-Salim Al Sabah. The new government includes technocrats but not members of the opposition or resistance movements. The Sabah family retains control of Defence, Foreign Affairs and the Interior ministries.

21 April: Iran asks United Nations to assume responsibility for the relief centres in the north of Iraq.

24 April: Jalal Talabani, the leader of the Patriotic Union of Kurdistan, announces that Saddam Hussein has agreed in principle to grant the Kurds a measure of autonomy, and appeals to Kurds to return to their homes.

26 April: number of Iraqi refugees in Iran estimated to be over 1 million, of which around 50,000 are Shiites from southern Iraq and the rest are Kurds.

28 April–June: American efforts to set up an international peace conference are frustrated by Shamir, who dislikes the possibility that such a forum could force Israel to trade captured Arab lands for peace. The Israeli Prime Minister prefers separate negotiations with the Arab states.

c. 1–7 May: according to the *Observer* (London) there are meetings between Richard Haass, United States Special Assistant for National Security Affairs in Near East and South-east Asia, and Majid, son of the Grand Ayatollah of the Shiites world-wide, Abul Qassem Khoei. Majid is told by National Security Council officials that the Shiites should avoid escalating their insurgency in the south of Iraq so as to avoid endangering a coup the United States was planning with Iraqi officials to overthrow Saddam Hussein. At this time Iran has indicated that it will support the Iraqi Shiites, and military camps have been set up on the Iran–Iraq border to house around 30,000 Iraqi volunteers who have been equipped with captured arms. But Iran insists that all fighting must be under the control of Bakr al-Hakim, who heads an émigré religious group under Iranian control. This disturbs the Shiites, who are apparently aiming for a democratic rather than a theocratic regime in Iraq. The Shiites see control by Bakr al-Hakim as a retrograde sectarian move.

8 May: Egypt announces that it is withdrawing all its forces (30–35,000 men) from Kuwait and Saudi Arabia. The forces had been supposed to stay on and be reinforced to provide, along with the Syrians, the military potential for the proposed Mutual Defence Organization (MDO) that the United States and its allies had been trying to establish. Egyptians are reported to be upset that the Kuwaitis and the Americans had agreed that the force to be established in Kuwait would be an American brigade, and that there had been no mention of Egyptian or Syrian troops playing a role in the Emirate. Furthermore, Egypt felt that it had not received sufficient economic benefits from its participation in the Gulf War: $14 billion of Egyptian debt had been cancelled but that had left $30 billion outstanding. Egypt also felt that it was not getting its fair share of Kuwaiti and Saudi Arabian reconstruction contracts, and resented that the 1 million Egyptian labourers who had fled were not being re-employed.

11 May: Saddam Hussein tells meeting of Iraqi journalists that they can write what they like.

13 May: United Nations sends eight food trucks through to Dahok in northern Iraq, under the aegis of the agreement secured by United Nations envoy Prince Sadruddin Aga Khan on 18 March to set up humanitarian, non-military centres to assist displaced Iraqis. This establishes a United Nations presence in Dahok. The United States military also hand over the administration of the

Zakho refugee camp to the United Nations. The Foreign Minister of Iraq rejects outright the suggestion that Security Council Resolution 688, which offered limited protection to the Kurds, could be used to establish a United Nations police force in northern Iraq.

19 May: trials start in Kuwait of 628 people, mainly Palestinian and Iraqi, who are accused of aiding the Iraqi forces during the invasion of Kuwait. The 'unceremonious' treatment by the martial law courts of the first twenty-two suspects leads to expressions of concern from the United States State Department and President Bush's request to show compassion.

20 May: Security Council adopts Resolution 678. This, alongside the Secretary General's report of 2 May, initiates the creation of a fund to come from Iraq's oil revenues to be used to meet the claims of foreign governments, nationals and corporations for loss and damage, including environmental damage, resulting from Iraq's occupation of Kuwait.

20–4 May: United States forces move into the provisional capital of north-west Iraq, Dahok; the Iraqi military leave. An American military spokesman insists that this is not an extension of the 75-by-30-mile (120-by-50 km) Security Zone, and is just a temporary measure agreed with the Iraqi command.

23 May: Brent Bernandet, the United Nations Secretary General's representative in Baghdad, signs an agreement with the Iraqis to allow between 100 and 500 United Nations security guards to move into northern Iraq to protect United Nations civilian workers and equipment. This is very different from the British proposal for a United Nations police force to protect the Kurds.

26 May: the Crown Prince of Kuwait, Sheikh Saad al-Abdullah al-Salim Al Sabah, tells a televised gathering of security chiefs that kidnapping of non-Kuwaitis by policemen and soldiers had to stop; Kuwait's international image was being damaged by the media coverage of its treatment of its expatriate population.

2 June: the Emir of Kuwait, Sheikh Jabir al-Ahmad Al Sabah, meets opposition demands and announces timetable for general elections to the National Assembly, which had been suspended in 1986. The election date is set for October 1992, and there are immediate protests that by that time the ruling Al Sabah family would have been able to take the key decisions about the future of Kuwait. The Emir gives the assurance that the Advisory National Council would be revived to operate for the intervening sixteen months. But this offer is thought to have little credibility with politically-concerned Kuwaitis.

6 June: Barzani, leader of the Kurdish Democratic Party, says that his delegation is nearing an agreement with the Iraqi government on Kurdish autonomy, based on the 1970 agreement which recognized the Kurds' cultural and national identity and gave them the right to run the three provinces of Iraq where they were in a clear majority. There appeared to be disagreement over the oil-rich Kirkuk province. The Iraqi government, however, had agreed to allow back the Kurds who had been displaced from villages on the Iranian border during the Iran–Iraq War, and the two sides had also agreed on 'a legal body' to arbitrate on disputes over the implementation of the future agreement.

7 June: Britain and the United States renew their commitment to withdraw their troops from Iraq and reject calls from the Kurdish leaders (who fear reprisals from Saddam Hussein) for the troops to stay. The United Nations operation for the protection of the Kurds (a scaled-down version of Prime Minister John Major's 'safe havens' policy) is facing a crisis: the United Nations Disaster Relief Co-ordinator's Office warns that lack of aid and an inability to recruit suitable guards could lead the returned refugees to flee from Iraq again. As the allied troops leave, all humanitarian functions in the 3,600 square mile (9,300 sq km) Security Zone are handed over to the United Nations High Commissioner for Refugees.

9 June: in the Security Zone in northern Iraq the number of allied troops declined from a peak of 21,700 on 21 May, to 17,400. It is understood that the rest of the troops will soon be gone.

c. 12 June: it appears that some of Egypt's troops, destined to be withdrawn after the announcement on 8 May, may stay in the Gulf area. This follows intense pressure from the West to make Egypt's Gulf allies more amenable to the idea of a permanent joint Arab defence force envisaged in the Damascus Declaration of March. Richard Cheney, the United States Secretary of Defense, had assured Cairo that Kuwait had requested the presence of Egyptian peacekeeping troops. Kuwait had also tried to reassure Egypt over complaints concerning the treatment of Egyptians in Kuwait, and had stated that Egyptians with savings in Kuwaiti banks would soon be able to draw on them.

13 June: reports from Iran, suspected to be exaggerated, state that the Iraqi army had started to dislodge the Shiite rebels from their strongholds in the southern marshes.

16 June: according to Islamic Republican News Agency, the Kurdish Islamic groups of Iraq plan to form a united front to carry on the struggle against the Baathist rulers.

17 June: after a meeting of European Community foreign ministers, Jacques Poos, the Foreign Minister of Luxembourg, announces that the negotiations between Saddam Hussein and the Kurds 'are at a dead end and the Kurdish people who decided to return to their homes in the protection zones in the north of Iraq feel terribly insecure'. Douglas Hurd, the British Foreign Secretary, says that the foreign ministers of Britain, France, the Netherlands and Italy have agreed not to end their operations in northern Iraq so long as the Kurds are threatened by the Iraqi regime.

20 June: the United States suspends its withdrawal of troops from northern Iraq pending discussions with its European allies on how to guarantee the security of the Kurdish safe havens in the future and pending the results of autonomy talks between the Kurds and Saddam's government.

30 June: a United Nations delegation arrives in Baghdad to investigate Iraq's nuclear facilities.

October: clashes between Kurdish guerrillas and Iraqi troops near Sulaimaniya result in around 400 dead, mainly civilians. After reports of disagreements among Kurdish leaders, Barzani on 29 October, challenges his rivals to an electoral test as to whether to accept Saddam's autonomy plan or resort to armed struggle.

11 October: Security Council unanimously adopts Resolution 715 aimed at eliminating Iraq's nuclear, chemical, and biological weapons arsenal.

12 November: Kurdish leaders announce withdrawal of guerrilla forces south of Arbil, in northern Iraq, in return for the end to an economic blockade that had lasted three weeks.

15 December: suggestion for Kurdish referendum replaced by a proposal for a parliamentary election in Kurdistan.

19 December: allies maintain commitment to maintain air cover for the Kurdish safe haven area: Ankara extends mandate of 'Provide Comfort II' force for six months.

1992 January: Iraqis tell Kurdish delegation that economic blockade will only be lifted if Iraqi army and security services were allowed to move north.

1993 September: Tariq Aziz, the Deputy Prime Minister of Iraq, discusses with the Secretary-General of the United Nations, the lifting of economic sanctions and the resumption of petroleum sales by Iraq. Reports that Iraq has used chemical weapons in the southern marshlands killing many hundreds.

1994 February: following mediation by Iraqi National Council, rival parties in the northern Kurdish-controlled enclave reported to have signed a peace agreement, but followed by repeated bouts of fighting.

6 October: the United Nations Special Commissioner on Iraq, responsible for monitoring the Iraqi defence industries, states that a system of monitoring is beginning to operate. Iraqi forces move towards the Kuwait border, presumably as a threat to achieve an easing of the sanctions against Iraq.

9 October: Kuwait sends forces to its side of the border with Iraq, and the United States despatches reinforcements to Kuwait and the Gulf.

10 October: Iraq anounces that it is withdrawing its troops towards the north.

10 November: National Assembly in Iraq votes to recognize Kuwait within the borders defined by the United Nations in April 1992 and May 1993.

1995 16 January: Saddam Hussein offers to mediate in Kurdish dispute, and Britain warns that conflict could provide Iraq with a pretext to reassert control in the north of the country.

March: Turkey moves 35,000 troops across its border in an attempt to destroy bases of the Kurdish Workers' Party (PKK) in the Kurdish enclave.

July: Turkey briefly moves 30,000 troops across border into Kurdish enclave.

November: United States State Department official attempts unsuccessfully to promote agreement between Kurdish factions, in an effort to counter Iranian efforts at mediation.

1996 January: it is reported that refugees are continuing to flee from southern marshlands of Iraq, and that 60,000 to 70,000 are living in camps, and that 200,000 people in southern Iraq have been displaced.

February: agreement between Turkey and NAO for the continuation of 'Operation Provide Comfort' under which British, American and French aircraft based in Turkey enforce the Iraqi exclusion zone north of latitude 36 degrees north to protect the Kurdish enclave. But attacks into Turkey from the Kurdish enclave mean that Turkish Prime Minister gives the Turkish National Assembly the assurance that arrangement will not continue beyond July 1996.

Two members of Saddam Hussein's clan, who had defected to Jordan, return to Baghdad, following a pardon, and are then assassinated.

20 May: Iraq accepts United Nations terms on the sale of its

165

petroleum, allowing the sale of up to $4,000 million of oil a year to purchase food and medicine, and to finance United Nations operations in Iraq.

31 October: following United States-sponsored peace talks a truce is signed between the Patriotic Union of Kurdistan and the Kurdish Democratic Party. There is a cease-fire to the fighting in Iraqi Kurdistan where it is feared that there would be renewed Iraqi intervention.

12 December: Saddam Hussein's eldest son, Udai Hussein, regarded as the chosen successor, is injured in an attack on his car in Baghdad.

1997 29 October: Saddam Hussein expels Americans from the United Nations weapons inspection team. The British and Americans take a firm stand and move troops to the Gulf.

20 November: Faced by a united front in the Security Council, Saddam Hussein agrees to allow all the United Nations weapons inspectors, including the Americans, to return to Iraq. President Clinton announces that Washington is resolute in its determination to prevent Iraq from threatening its neighbours with nuclear, chemical and biological weapons, and despatches a further expeditionary force to the Middle East. Robin Cook, the British Foreign Secretary, insists that no deal has been struck with Saddam. But observers note that Baghdad has gained two important concessions: a hint that the proportion of American weapons inspectors in the United Nations team will be reduced; and an expansion of the United Nations oil-for-food plan which will enable Iraq to buy a wider range of products.

1998 15–16 February: the United Nations Secretary-General, Kofi Annan, initiates a plan devised by France and Russia for a compromise with Iraq that would grant special arrangements for weapons inspections of eight presidential sites declared off-limits by Baghdad. This takes place against Anglo-American preparations for war against Iraq, with only Canada and Australia offering 'undefined' support. The Anglo-American alliance with which to confront Saddam Hussein was forged in Washington during the visit of Tony Blair, the British Prime Minister, early in February, against the background of revelations about Clinton's sex-life and Robin Cook's intention to appoint his mistress as his diary secretary in the Foreign Office. Some commentators observed that there was a danger that a war against Iraq would be launched to divert attention from domestic scandals.

SECTION II

Biographies

Abdullah (1882–1951): Emir of Transjordan 1921–46; King of Transjordan 1946–8; King of Jordan, 1948–51. Born in Mecca, second son of Sherif Hussein. Educated in Istanbul. Took part in Arab revolt of 1916. Winston Churchill while Colonial Secretary, with help of Lawrence of Arabia, established Abdullah as Emir of Transjordan in April 1921 on understanding that he would abandon plans to attack the French and restore Hashemite rule in Syria, and also claims to the crown of Iraq. Abdullah hoped for a union of Transjordan, Palestine, Syria and Lebanon under his crown in 'Greater Syria', and also a 'Fertile Crescent', made up of a federation of Greater Syria and Iraq. Loyal to Britain during the Second World War, his Arab Legion helped to put down Rashid Ali's rebellion in Iraq. When Britain granted Transjordan independence in May 1946, Abdullah became king. Negotiated with Zionist leaders before May 1948 but did not achieve an accommodation. The Arab Legion took over the West Bank and West Jerusalem during the First Arab–Israeli War and, after secret contacts with Israel and initial opposition from the Arab League, annexed them to Transjordan and formed the Kingdom of Jordan. This move introduced a dissident Palestinian element into Jordanian politics. On 20 July 1951 Abdullah was assassinated by a Palestinian when going into al-Aqsa Mosque in Jerusalem.

Abdul-Huda, Tawfig (1895–1956): Prime Minister of Jordan 1938–44, 1947–50, 1951–3, 1954–5. Born in Acre. Part of Feisal's administration in Damascus 1919–20. Joined Jordanian civil service in 1922. Director of Agricultural Bank, 1932–7. Foreign Minister, 1945, 1947. Resigned as Prime Minister in 1950 over Abdullah's attempts to make a peace agreement with Israel.

Aflaq, Michel (1910–89): founder of Syrian Baath Party. Born in Damascus of Greek Orthodox background. Educated in Paris where influenced by communism. Helped to found Arab Renaissance Party, which joined the Arab Socialist Party to form the Arab Socialist Renaissance Party in 1953. With split in Baath party in 1960s between civilian and military wings, ousted from Syria. Elected Secretary-General of the Baath National Command in 1970. It was announced when he died that shortly beforehand Aflaq had converted to Islam.

Ahad Ha'Am (1856–1927): Hebrew pseudonym, meaning one of the people, for Asher Ginsberg. Initially believed that Zionism should establish a cultural and spiritual centre in Palestine rather

169

than a political state, but after immigrating to Palestine in 1922 argued for a Jewish majority. A major influence on Chaim Weizmann.

Ala, Hussein (1883–1964): Prime Minister of Iran, 1951, 1955–7. Educated at University of London. Ambassador to London, 1934–6. Ambassador to Washington, 1946–50. During Mossadeq crisis attempted to achieve a compromise with British oil interests.

Albright, Madeleine (1937–): United States Secretary of State, 1997– . Of Czechoslovakian origin, she has explained that her 'mindset is Munich' and that the defining event of her political life was what she considers Neville Chamberlain's 'betrayal'. Originally a professor of political science at Georgetown University, she served as United States Ambassador at the United Nations from 1993–6, and distinguished herself for her strident anti-Iraq, anti-Cuba, and pro-Israeli stances. She repeatedly exercised the American veto to protect Israel. As Secretary of State she has urged Israel to restrain its settlement policies in occupied East Jerusalem.

Allenby, Edmund (Viscount) (1861–1936): leader of the British Expeditionary Force in Egypt, June 1917–18. Planned the attack on Turkish forces and entered Jerusalem on 9 December 1917. Took Damascus, Beirut and Aleppo in October 1918. Initially in charge of the provisional military administration of the occupied areas of the former Ottoman Empire, he served later as British High Commissioner in Egypt during the declaration of Egyptian independence in February 1922 and the assassination of Sir Lee Stack.

Allon, Yigal (1918–80): Israeli strategist, and Deputy Prime Minister 1966–77. Attended the Kadoorie Agricultural College and the Hebrew University of Jerusalem. Co-founder of the Ginnosar kibbutz in 1937. After serving with the British army he helped to found the Palmach and was its Commander-in-Chief, 1945–8. His strategy during the First Arab–Israeli War was partly responsible for the expulsion of the Egyptian army. Minister of Labour, 1961–8. He helped to form the Israel Labour Party in 1968. Minister of Immigrant Absorption, 1967–9. Foreign Minister, 1974–7.

Amery, Leopold (1873–1955): Assistant Secretary War Cabinet and Imperial War Cabinet, 1917. Involved in drafting of Balfour Declaration.

Antonius, George (1892–1942): historian of the Arab nationalist movement. Born in Egypt, he served in the Palestine administration 1921–30 and then joined the New York Institute of Current World

Affairs. He gave evidence to the Peel Commission in 1936–7, and took part in the London Round Table Conference of March 1939 as an adviser, as well as assisting with translations of the Hussein–McMahon correspondence for British government parliamentary papers in 1939. His book, *The Arab Awakening* (1938), is considered by some to have created a myth of a growing Arab movement and identity, but it has become a classic, and at the time of its publication it did much to further the Arab cause.

Arafat, Yasser (1929–): leader of the Palestine Liberation Organization (PLO). Born in Jerusalem. Educated in Egypt, he graduated from Cairo University in 1956 as an engineer. Connected with Muslim Brotherhood. Worked in Kuwait 1957–60. Became the spokesman of al-Fatah (Palestine National Liberation Movement) in 1968 after being a founder member of the organization in 1958. In February 1969 became chairman of the executive of the PLO. In October 1974 he outlined a plan for a democratic secular state in Palestine, in which Jews and Arabs could co-exist on terms of equality. Renounced terrorism in November 1988 and in his speech to the General Assembly in Geneva in December 1988 implied acceptance of the two-state solution to the Palestine question. In the early stages of the intifada no alternative leadership of the Palestinians emerged to challenge that of Arafat and the Palestine Liberation Organization. During the Gulf War, Arafat eroded a great deal of support and sympathy for the Palestinian cause in the West with his support of Saddam Hussein. Arafat became Chairman of the Palestinian Authority and Minister of the Interior in May 1994, and President of the Palestine Legislative Council in 1996. He shared the Nobel Peace Prize in 1994. Increasingly his efforts to achieve peace with Israel were opposed from within by the Islamists headed by Hamas and Islamic Jihad, and he was accused by Israel of harbouring terrorists.

Arens, Moshe (1925–): Israeli Ambassador to the United States 1982–3. Minister of Defence, 1983–4, 1990–2. Minister without Portfolio, 1987. Minister of Foreign Affairs, 1988–90. Educated in the United States, and a former Technicon professor of aeronautical engineering. A supporter of the Herut Party and regarded as a hardliner. Served in Likud alignments under both Begin and Shamir. After the Israeli invasion of Lebanon in 1982, advocated in 1983 a unilateral withdrawal of Israeli troops from the Shouf mountains to the Awali river line. As Minister of Defence opposed Jewish vigilante movements.

Asad, Hafiz al- (1930–): President of the Syrian Arab Republic 1971– . Born at Qardaha, a member of the minority Alawi sect (Shiite). Trained as a pilot in the Soviet Union. Appointed Commander of the Air Force in 1964 and Minister of Defence in 1966. Associated with faction in Baath party that promoted Arabism and supported the Palestine Liberation Organization. That faction seized power in November 1970 and opposed close ties with Moscow. Asad was re-elected President in 1978 and 1985. He is also Commander-in-Chief. Sided with Iran and the coalition against Saddam Hussein in the Gulf War and sent Syrian troops to the Gulf area. He thus managed to counter-balance the reputation Syria had achieved for master-minding international terrorism, and secured the reopening of diplomatic ties with Britain. Asad played an important role in the release of Western hostages held in Lebanon.

Ashrawi, Hanan (1946–): Palestinian academic and politician. A professor of English literature at Birzeit University on the West Bank who became the official spokeswoman for the Palestinian delegation to the peace conferences on the Middle East in 1991–3. She successfully presented a more acceptable image to the West of the Palestinian cause to those suspicious of Arafat's reputation, and was elected as an independent to the Palestinian Legislative Council in 1996.

Atatürk, Mustafa Kemal (1881–1938): first President of the Turkish Republic, 1923–38. Born in Salonika. Initially a supporter of the Young Turks but became disenchanted. Graduated from the Military Academy in Istanbul in 1905 and fought during the First World War in the Dardanelles and Arabia. From May 1919 he organized the Anatolian national resistance to the planned dismemberment of Turkey, and led the nationalists to victory in the War of Independence against both the Allies and the Ottoman Sultan's government. Elected first President of Turkey, which he changed into a modern, Westernized and secular state.

Austin, Warren (1877–1962): United States Representative to the United Nations, 1947–53. In 1948 initiated United States plan for the trusteeship of Palestine in the United Nations.

Aziz, Tariq (1936–): Iraqi Minister of Foreign Affairs 1983–91; Deputy Prime Minister of Iraq 23 March 1991– . Read English studies at the College of Arts, Baghdad. Started career as a journalist and was a member of the editorial staff of the *Al-Jumhuriya* newspaper (1958); chief editor of *Al-Jamaheer* (April 1963); worked for the

Baath press, Syria, in February 1963; was chief editor of *Al-Thawra* in 1969 and later became head of the Al-Thawra Publishing House. Member of the Revolutionary Command Council General Affairs Bureau, 1972; reserve member Arab Baath Socialist Party Leadership, January 1974; Minister of Information, 1974–7; Deputy Prime Minister, 1973. As Foreign Minister during the Gulf War went to Moscow in February 1991 to discuss Soviet peace plan, then carried the details of the plan to President Rafsanjani of Iran.

Badr, Muhammad al- (1927–): Imam of Northern Yemen 1962–70. Visited Russia in 1956 and the Peoples' Republic of China in 1958 as representative of his father the Imam Ahmad. Succeeded in September 1962 but overthrown by an officers' revolt and with Saudi Arabian assistance fought the republic proclaimed in Sanaa. With the reconciliation of the warring fractions, he was exiled in 1970.

Baker, James (1930–): United States Secretary of State, 1989–92; United Nations Special Envoy to solve Western Sahara Dispute, 1997– . Warned Yitzhak Shamir after the Israeli Prime Minister's rejection of the idea of exchanging land for peace in May 1989 against the vision of a 'Greater Israel'. On 9 January 1991 negotiated unsuccessfully with Tariq Aziz, Foreign Minister of Iraq, in an attempt to avert the Gulf War. Conducted first meeting between an American Secretary of State and a wide-ranging Palestinian delegation in Jerusalem in March 1991. Attempted to set up a general Middle East peace conference, but hindered by an Israeli insistence that it would only conduct bilateral talks with individual Arab states.

Bakhtiar, Shapour (1916–91): Prime Minister of Iran, January–February 1979. Deputy Minister in Mossadeq's National Front government. After Khomeini's return to Iran, Bakhtiar left for France, from where he led the National Movement of Iranian Resistance. His assassination on 8 August 1991 was thought to have been an attempt to embarrass the Rafsanjani government in Iran for assisting with the release of John McCarthy.

Balfour, Arthur James (1st Earl Balfour) (1848–1930): British Prime Minister, 1902–5. Attended meetings of War Cabinet, 1914–15. First Lord of Admiralty, 1915–16. Foreign Secretary, 1916–19. Balfour Declaration of 1917 bears his name. Some authorities have suggested that he did not really know of the existence of Arabs until he was stoned by them in Palestine in the 1920s. Some have also suggested that he was anti-Semitic.

Banna, Hasan al- (1906–49): born in Ismailiyya. Became a secondary school teacher. Founded Society of Muslim Brothers (Muslim Brotherhood) in Egypt in 1928. Though he considered that he lived in a period similar to the period of ignorance before the coming of Islam, he never argued that the ideal Islamic order would be brought about by political control and the establishment of an Islamic state. Egyptian government arranged his assassination after the murder of the Prime Minister of Egypt, Nuqrashi Pasha, by a member of the Muslim Brotherhood. The Muslim Brotherhood had acted after it had been dissolved by the Egyptian government. Banna did repudiate Nuqrashi's murder.

Bazargan, Mehdi (1905–95): named by Khomeini as 'Provisional Prime Minister' of Iran on 6 February 1979. In office until 5 November 1979. Bazargan resigned over the issue of the retention of the United States hostages. He was opposed to Khomeini's policy of keeping the hostages.

Beeley, Harold (Sir) (1909–): Secretary of Anglo–American Commission of Enquiry on Palestine, 1946. Between 1946 and 1948 involved in making of British policy towards Palestine in Foreign Office. Ambassador to the United Arab Republic, 1961–4.

Begin, Menachem Wolfovitch (1913–92): Prime Minister of Israel, 1977–82. Born in White Russia, he was influenced by Jabotinsky, the Zionist revisionist thinker, and led the Betar, the Polish youth movement, in 1919. Helped to organize the illegal immigration to Palestine and reached Palestine in 1942 with the Polish army. From 1943 to 1948 he led the Irgun, the Zionist organization which worked for the establishment of the State of Israel through terrorist tactics. He was involved in the blowing up of the King David Hotel in July 1946, the flogging of British army officers in retaliation for the judicial caning of an Irgun youth, December 1946–January 1947, and the hanging and booby-trapping of the bodies of two British sergeants in July 1947 which Ernest Bevin considered made a continued British presence in the mandate impossible. In 1948 Begin founded the right-wing Herut Party and represented it in the Knesset in 1949. He advocated a Zionist state on both sides of the Jordan and was opposed by Ben-Gurion. Begin was brought into the government on the eve of the Six-Day War as Minister without Portfolio. As Prime Minister of Israel and leader of the Likud bloc June 1977–82 he attracted the Sephardic vote, negotiated the Camp David accords and the peace treaty with Egypt, bombed Iraq's nuclear reactor, and invaded Lebanon.

Bell, Gertrude Margaret Lowthian (1868–1926): attached to military intelligence department, Cairo, 1915; liaison office of Arab Bureau in Iraq, 1916; Assistant Political Officer, Baghdad, 1917; Oriental Secretary to the High Commissioner of Iraq, Baghdad, 1920–5. Despatches influential in moderating draft of Balfour Declaration of 1917. Helped set Feisal on throne of Iraq in 1921.

Ben-Gurion, David (1886–1973): Prime Minister of Israel 1948–53, 1955–63. Born in Plonsk, Poland. Went to Palestine in 1906 and advocated a socialist Zionism. He leaned towards the Ottoman Empire, but was expelled from Turkey in 1914. Went to Palestine again in 1918 as a member of the Jewish Legion, and became Secretary-General of the Histradut, the General Federation of Labour in Palestine, and helped to found the Mapai in 1930. He was elected chairman of the Zionist Executive and the Jewish Agency in 1935. Pushed for the adoption of the Biltmore Programme in 1942. Helped to form a Jewish defence force in the lead up to the creation of the State of Israel. Became Prime Minister and Minister of Defence in 1948. During the First Arab–Israeli War he forced different factions into the Israeli Defence Force. As Prime Minister he oversaw the absorption of immigrants. In 1953 he handed over to Moshe Sharett, but following the Lavon affair returned as Minister of Defence, and became Prime Minister again in July 1955. He inspired the Franco–Israeli pact and was present at Sèvres in October 1956 which marked the 'collusion' of France, Britain and Israel. He resigned in June 1963 for personal reasons. When the Mapai split over the Lavon affair, Ben-Gurion established the Rafi. He retired from the Knesset in June 1970.

Ben-Yehuda, Eliezer (1858–1922): revived Hebrew as a spoken language. Emigrated from Lithuania to Palestine in 1881 and compiled a Hebrew dictionary. Advocated the use of Hebrew in daily life and saw it as a cornerstone of the Jewish rebirth.

Bernadotte, Folke (Count) (1895–1948): United Nations Mediator for Palestine, May–September 1948. Of Swedish origin. Supported the merger of the Arab part of Palestine and Jordan, as well as the annexation of the Negev and the repatriation of Arab refugees. He was assassinated in Jerusalem on 17 September 1948 by members of the Stern Gang.

Berri, Nabih (1939–): leader of Shiite Amal movement, 1978– . Member of National Salvation Front, 1984. Ally of the Syrians. Minister of Water and Electrical Resources and Justice, 1984– , Minister of State for the South and Reconstruction, 1984– . Led Liberation

Bloc in 1992 parliamentary elections. President of the National Assembly 1992– .

Bevin, Ernest (1881–1951): British Secretary of State for Foreign Affairs, 1945–51. Responsible for British policy towards Palestine. Believed that the Second World War had been fought so that the Jews could stay in Europe. Disillusioned with what he saw as Truman's irresponsible advocacy of the issuing of 100,000 certificates for immigration to Palestine to displaced persons in Europe, he tried to involve the United States in the problem with the Anglo–American Commission of Enquiry. After the United States's rejection of the Morrison–Grady Plan, worried about the possible rise of anti-Semitism in Britain as a consequence of Zionist terrorism. Furious over Truman's apparent endorsement of a Zionist state in his Day of Atonement speech on 4 October 1946. Having been branded as an anti-Semite in the United States, Bevin wanted to give up the British mandate. He was persuaded against this by military considerations at the time of the emergence of the Cold War, and instead handed the matter to the United Nations in February 1947. But the hanging of the two British sergeants by Irgun, and consequent outbreaks of anti-Semitism in Britain, convinced Bevin that Britain could not stay in the mandate. At the beginning of 1948 he resisted United States pressure on Britain to stay on. During the First Arab–Israeli War, Bevin was exercised by the Arab refugee question. He was widely regarded by Zionists as unsympathetic and even anti-Semitic. Bevin believed that the defence of the Middle East was one of the three pillars of British strategy, and as important as defence of the United Kingdom itself. He was not successful in renegotiating treaties with the Arab states, with the exception of Jordan. He believed that in the Middle East Britain should work with the peasants and not the pashas. In reality Britain found that it could best work with the pashas.

Bourges-Maunoury, Maurice (1914–): French Minister of National Defence, 1956–7. Prime Minister, 1957. Helped to consolidate the Franco–Israeli alliance in the run up to the Suez Crisis.

Bourguiba, Habib Ben Ali (1903–): President of Tunisia, 1957–87. Led Tunisia to independence (from France) in 1957. An opponent of Nasser, he suggested that the Arabs should negotiate with Israel, but after the Six-Day War resumed relations with Egypt. Initiated mediation in the civil war in Jordan in 1970.

Brezhnev, Leonid Il'ich (1906–82): Head of State of Soviet Union,

1960–82; Leader of Communist Party, 1964–82. His policy of *détente* led to Sadat's fearing that the superpowers would impose a solution on the Middle East and to the planning of the October War. During October War, suggested that as Israel was still fighting, the United States and the Soviet Union should immediately send military forces to the Middle East. Washington took this as a threat of unilateral Soviet intervention: shock tactics were decided on and American bases throughout the world were put on nuclear alert. Brezhnev gave way.

Brzezinski, Zbigniew K. (1928–): Assistant to the United States President for National Security Affairs, 1977–81. Influenced Carter with his view that it was futile for Israel to seek security through the acquisition of territory.

Bulganin, Nikolai Aleksandrovich (1895–1975): Prime Minister of the Soviet Union, 1953–7. Involved with Khrushchev's suggestion that the Soviet Union preferred an arms embargo in the Middle East which led to Nasser's thinking that his arms supply was threatened and his recognition of Communist China.

Bunche, Ralph (Dr) (1914–71): United Nations official. An American, he succeeded Bernadotte as United Nations mediator to Palestine in September 1948, and chaired the armistice discussions at Rhodes in 1949 that ended the First Arab–Israeli War. He supervised United Nations peacekeeping operations in 1956–7, keeping Egypt and Israel apart with the United Nations Emergency Force (UNEF), and later in Cyprus.

Bush, George Herbert Walker (1924–): Vice President of the United States, 1981–9. President of the United States, 1989–93 (Republican). In 1940 deeply affected by a lecture from former Secretary of State Henry Stimson on the moral case for intervention. Saddam Hussein's occupation of Kuwait offended Bush's simple code. In 1990 sent almost half a million American troops to Saudi Arabia as part of an international force to defend that country. Mrs Thatcher lent immediate British support to the venture and became one of his close confidantes. Organized a coalition of forces of Western and Arab countries to defeat Saddam Hussein in the Gulf War. Resolutely insisted that Saddam Hussein conform to United Nations resolutions on Kuwait. In his speech on 6 March celebrating victory in the Gulf War, he referred to the principle of territory for peace and legitimate Palestinian rights. Resisted moves by Congress to block aid to Jordan after King Hussein's support for

Saddam Hussein during Gulf War. With an eye to the forthcoming presidential election, and after Israel's policy of restraint during the Gulf War, tried to move Israel towards participation in a general Middle East peace conference while reaffirming the United States special relationship with the Zionist state. During and following the Gulf War pursued the policy of maintaining the integrity of Iraq, and refrained from overtly supporting the Shiite and Kurdish rebellions. Supported John Major's policy of 'safe havens' for the Kurdish refugees.

Carter, Jimmy (James Earl Jr) (1924–): President of the United States, 1977–81 (Democrat). In election campaign supported the United States's commitment to the security of Israel. As a Southern Baptist thought a homeland for the Jews ordained by God. Also saw Israel as a strategic asset that could thwart Soviet expansion in the area. Considered that depriving Palestinians of rights was contrary to moral and ethical principles. On 16 March 1977 Carter advocated a homeland for the Palestinians, and on 26 May 1977 he said that they should be compensated for the losses they had suffered. In July 1977 proposed to Begin the creation of a Palestinian entity as distinct from an independent nation. Gambled on inviting Sadat and Begin to the presidential lodge at Camp David for conference that lasted from 4–17 September 1978. Camp David meeting resulted in Egypt and Israel's agreeing to conclude a peace treaty within three months. Re-election as President damaged by the American Embassy hostage crisis in Tehran.

Catroux, Georges (1887–1969): de Gaulle's representative in the Middle East, 1941. Helped prepare for the conquest of Syria and Lebanon, which were held by the forces of Vichy France. On invading the countries on 8 June 1941 revoked the French mandate and declared their independence, though he and de Gaulle envisaged a privileged place for France. When he returned to Beirut in November 1943, his reinstatement of the National Government marked a French retreat from this position.

Ceausescu, Nicolae (1918–89): President of Romania, 1974–89. Used by Begin to sound out Sadat in preparation for Camp David meeting.

Chamoun, Camille (1900–87): President of Lebanon, 1952–8. Born a Maronite Christian. Elected member of parliament in 1929. Minister of the Interior, 1938, 1943–4. Minister in London, 1944. Leader of Lebanese delegation to United Nations, 1946. After forcing al-Khuri to resign, elected President in 1952 and pursued a policy of neutrality towards Arab countries while cultivating close relations with the West. In 1958, against the background of the formation of the United Arab Republic, he proposed a constitutional amendment to legalize his election for a second term which led in May 1958 to riots. He requested United States military help, under terms of the Eisenhower Doctrine for the Middle East. With the compromise settlement he withdrew his candidature, and in opposition formed a right-wing party, the National Liberal Party. He joined an alliance in the 1960s with the Phalangist leader, Pierre Gemayel, and the head of the Bloc National, Raymond Eddé. Appointed Minister of the Interior in 1975 during Lebanese civil war. Became leader of the right-wing Lebanese Front.

Chehab (Shihab), Fuad (General) (1903–73): President of Lebanon, 1958–64. Born into a leading Maronite Christian family, served with the special troops organized by the French during the mandate. Commander of the army in 1946. Refused to fire on crowds demonstrating against corruption in 1952, and during 1958 troubles insisted that army be a force for national unity. His election as President seen as a compromise. Moved Lebanon towards Egypt and strengthened the Muslim element.

Cheney, Richard B. (1941–): United States Secretary of Defense, 1989– . Signed a memorandum of understanding with Israel in September 1989, under which the United States would lend Israel war materials for research and development. On 19 July 1990 stated that the United States was committed to defend Kuwait in case of attack. Maintained on 3 December 1990 that the United States could not wait indefinitely for sanctions against Iraq to take effect. Insisted that 'absolute total victory' was necessary in the war against Iraq.

Christopher, Warren M. (1925–): United States Secretary of State, 1993–7. As Deputy Secretary of State in the Carter administration negotiated for the release of the American hostages in Iran in 1980. In Clinton's administration saw that Washington exercised the veto in the United Nations to avoid censure of Israel. Through shuttle diplomacy attempted to keep the peace process moving, but was widely viewed in the Arab world as pro-Israeli.

Churchill, Winston Leonard Spencer (Sir) (1874–1965): British Colonial Secretary, February 1921–October 1922; Prime Minister, 1940–5, 1951–5. Following a conference at Cairo in March 1921, and with the assistance of T.E. Lawrence, Churchill installed Feisal as King of Iraq and Abdullah as Emir of Transjordan. Issued the British White Paper of 1922, which limited Jewish immigration to the mandate to the economic absorptive capacity of the country, and in effect denied that the Balfour Declaration envisaged Palestine as a Jewish state. Often proclaiming himself a life-long Zionist, Churchill supported the report of the Peel Commission in 1937 and opposed MacDonald's White Paper of May 1939. During the Second World War he opposed the Foreign Office on Palestine and moved British policy towards supporting partition, but with the assassination of Lord Moyne in November 1944 was disillusioned by Zionist terrorism, and suspended British policy. While in opposition he supported the Zionist cause though thundered against Britain's giving in to terrorism in 1947 in stopping using corporal punishment in the mandate after terrorist atrocities following the judicial caning of an Irgun youth. Privately he scorned the Arabs and particularly the Egyptians, and as Prime Minister in the 1950s, fought Eden's attempts to reach a negotiated settlement with Nasser over a British withdrawal from the Suez Canal zone. He had a good personal relationship with Ben-Gurion and was anxious that Britain should not discriminate against Israel and favour the Arabs. After 'Black Saturday' in Cairo in 1952, in which British property was attacked by rioters, he suggested that the best way of dealing with the 'Gyppos' was to turn the Jews on them. He referred to the Egyptians as having crawled out of the gutter. The advent of the hydrogen bomb and the consequent change in strategic thinking led to Churchill's reluctantly agreeing to abandon the Suez base.

Clifford, Clark McAdams (1906–): Special Counsel to the President of the United States, 1946–50. Truman's election adviser for the 1948 presidential election. Advised initially that Palestine would not be an issue. Truman consequently allowed the State Department to pursue a Palestine policy in the interests of the United States without regard to domestic factors. American policy shifted from partition to trusteeship. Clifford changed his advice after the Republican victory in a February 1948 election in New York, and worked with the Zionists in the United States to override Marshall and the State Department and to secure Truman's recognition of the State of Israel.

Cox, Percy Zachariah (1864–1937): High Commissioner for Iraq, 1920–4. An imperial administrator, together with Gertrude Bell, he helped to create Iraq. Political Agent in Muscat, 1899–1904. Resident, Persian Gulf, 1904–13; Chief Political Officer to the British

Expeditionary Forces in Mesopotamia, 1914–18; Minister to Persia, 1918–20.

Curzon, George Nathaniel (Lord) (1st Marquess of Kedleston) (1859–1925): Lord President of the Council, 1916–19; Secretary of State for Foreign Affairs, 1919–24. Warned War Cabinet that Balfour Declaration would be open to manipulation. Objected to the terms of the mandate for Palestine: 'Here is a country with 580,000 Arabs and 30,000 or is it 60,000 Jews (by no means all Zionists). Acting upon the noble principles of self-determination and ending with a splendid appeal to the League of Nations, we then proceed to draw up a document which reeks of Judaism in every paragraph and is an avowed constitution for a Jewish State. Even the poor Arabs are only allowed to look through the keyhole as a non-Jewish community.'

Dayan, Moshe (1915–81): Israeli Minister of Defence, June 1967–74; Foreign Minister, 1977–9. As a member of the Haganah fought with Orde Wingate's special unit during the Arab rebellion, 1936–9. Sentenced to imprisonment by Britain for underground activity in 1940, he lost his left eye in Allied operations against Vichy France in Lebanon in 1941. A founder member of the Palmach, he was involved in the *Altelena* incident in 1948. He served as the commanding officer in Jerusalem during the First Arab–Israeli War and was the Israeli representative at the armistice talks in Rhodes. Chief of General Staff, 1953–8. Helped to forge the Franco–Israeli alliance; present at the 'collusion' meeting at Sèvres in October 1956. His tactics were successful in the Suez–Sinai War. Minister of Agriculture, 1959–66. Together with Ben-Gurion formed the Rafi party. In 1968 joined Rafi with Mapai to form the Israel Labour Party. Blamed for provoking the October War by pursuing expansionist policies, and for being unprepared when it came. Present at Camp David meeting.

de Bunsen, Maurice (Sir) (1st Baronet) (1852–1932): in 1915 chaired Committee on Asiatic Turkey to discuss British desiderata.

de Gaulle, Charles (General) (1890–1970): President of France, 1958–68. Defeated Vichy France in Lebanon and Syria in 1941. Led the move to grant independence to Algeria in 1962, as issue on which there had been bitter divisions within the French nation, and during this period sustained France's tacit alliance with Israel. Partly because disillusioned by Israel's attempts to diversify its arms supplies, but also to further his ambition to restore France's position as a great power, he moved France towards a pro-Arab stand. During the Six-Day War France was the only major Western country unsympathetic to Israel: he embargoed the supply of fifty Mirage jets to Israel just before the outbreak of the war. Afterwards he demanded Israel's withdrawal from the occupied territories. Some have accused him of anti-Semitic tendencies.

Dugdale, Baffy (Blanche Elizabeth Campbell) (died 1948): Head of Intelligence Department of League of Nations Union, 1920–8. Member of British Government's delegation to League of Nations Assembly, 1932. Niece of Arthur James Balfour. Lobbied for Zionist cause, especially 1929–31 and 1939. Wrote *Life of Arthur James Balfour. First Earl Balfour*, 2 vols, 1936.

Dulles, John Foster (1888–1959): United States Secretary of State, 1952–9. Visited Middle East in 1953 and, at a time when Eisenhower had devalued special relationship with Britain, tried to secure Nasser's agreement to British plans for withdrawal from the Suez Canal. Managed a United States Middle East policy at a time when the State Department had decided that Britain and France could no longer take the lead for the West in the Middle East. In 1956 agreed with Eden that Nasser had to go, but throughout the Suez Crisis followed the instructions of his president.

Eagleburger, Lawrence Sidney (1930–): United States Deputy Secretary of State 1989–92; Acting Secretary of State, August–December 1992; Secretary of State, December 1992–January 1993. Believed in close military relationship between Israel and the United States and served as Envoy to Israel during the Gulf War in 1991.

Eban, Abba (1915–): Israeli Foreign Minister, 1966–74. Born in South Africa. Educated at Cambridge. Ambassador to the United Nations, 1948–59, and to the United States, 1950–9. Minister of Education and Culture, 1960–3. Deputy Prime Minister, 1963–6. Sounded out Western politicians on attitude to Israel's position before outbreak of Six-Day War. Involved with Jarring mission. In run up to 1974 general election in Israel proposed as candidate for the premiership by Mapai wing of Labour Party. Regarded as a Labour centrist. In 1977 favoured a substantial withdrawal by Israel from the West Bank, but later rejected the idea of a Palestinian state.

Eden, Anthony (Sir) (Earl of Avon) (1897–1977): British Prime Minister, April 1955–January 1957. Studied Persian languages at Oxford. An Arabic speaker. As Foreign Secretary, 1940–5, helped to inspire the formation of the Arab League. Again as Foreign Secretary, 1951–5, favoured reaching an accommodation with Egypt over the evacuation of the Suez base but was opposed by Churchill. Having felt that he had held out the hand of friendship to Nasser, became disillusioned with the Egyptian leader's attempts to export his *Philosophy of the Revolution* and his challenge to the British position in the Middle East and Africa. Worked with the Americans on Operation Alpha in 1955, a plan to enforce a solution to the Arab–Israeli conflict. Instrumental in forming the Baghdad Pact in 1955. Viewed Middle East policies of the 1950s in the light of his experience of the 'appeasement of Europe' in the 1930s, as Neville Chamberlain's Foreign Secretary. By 1956 Eden considered Nasser another Mussolini and decided that it was necessary to thwart Egypt's apparent expansionism. Thought incorrectly that Nasser was behind the sacking of Glubb Pasha in Jordan in 1956, and subsequently agreed with the Americans that Nasser had to be removed. His attempt to do this with French and Israeli assistance in 1956 led to his resignation. Eden, misinformed by Harold Macmillan, miscalculated the significance of the American presidential election and Eisenhower's reaction.

Eisenhower, Dwight David (1890–1969): President of the United States, 1953–61 (Republican). On becoming President devalued special relationship with Britain and managed an American Middle East policy that moved away from an identity with Israel to a more even-handed approach. His policy during the Suez Crisis largely determined by domestic electoral considerations. Forced Britain out of the Suez Canal by arranging a run on sterling. Went out of his way to make amends at the Bermuda conference of March 1957, and restored special relationship. Eisenhower Doctrine for Middle East fitted in well with Britain's policy of reducing commitments in area as part of overall withdrawal, and getting the United States to take its place. Eisenhower agreed to joint Anglo–American planning and action in Lebanon and Jordan in 1958. Middle East policy then reflected the Anglo–American relationship based on 'mutual interdependence'.

Eitan (Eytan), Rafael (1929–): Israeli Chief of General Staff, 1978–83; member of Israeli Ministerial Defence Committee, 1990– ; Minister of Agriculture, 1990–1. In 1982 decided that threat of Syrian missiles necessitated a large-scale military operation into Lebanon to protect Israel's sixty-three Galilee settlements and towns from raids across the northern border.

Eshkol, Levi (1895–1969): Prime Minister of Israel, 1963–9. Born in the Ukraine. In 1913 emigrated to Palestine, where he served in the Jewish Legion, 1918–20, was active in the labour movement and a member of the Haganah High Command. As Director-General of Israel's Ministry of Defence he established Israel's arms industry. Minister of Agriculture, 1951–2. Minister of Finance, 1952–63. When Director of the Settlement Department of the Jewish Agency, 1949–63, he oversaw the absorption into Israel of immigrants. When Prime Minister, he split with Ben-Gurion over the Lavon affair. Resisted moves towards war against the Arabs but gave way to Cabinet pressure, and resigned as Minister of Defence, 1963–7, on eve of Six-Day War. Oversaw Israel's control of the occupied territories. After 1967 he headed the National Unity government.

Evans, Trefor Ellis (1913–74): Assistant Oriental Secretary and Private Secretary to the British Ambassador in Egypt, 1941–5; Head of the Middle East Secretariat, Foreign Office, 1949–52. Oriental Counsellor to His Majesty's Embassy in Cairo, 1952–6. Ambassador to Algeria, 1962–4, Syria, 1964–7, Iraq, 1968–9. Was the British contact with the Free Officers' movement, 1952–4. Reports helped to form British policy at the time of the Suez base negotiations.

Fahd (ibn Abdul al-Aziz Al Saud) (1923–): King of Saudi Arabia, 1982– . Minister of Education, 1953. Minister of the Interior, 1962. Tried to avoid Saudi Arabia's isolation and developed a closer relationship with the United States. Broadened base of government. In 1990 hosted international force from the United States, Britain, France and others, including Arab countries, in reaction to Saddam Hussein's invasion of Kuwait.

Fahmi, Ismail (1922–): Egyptian Foreign Minister, 1973–7. Resigned over Camp David accords.

Farouk (1920–65): King of Egypt, 1936–52. Educated in England and Egypt. Inherited Egyptian throne as a minor in May 1936; country ruled by regents until July 1937. Encouraged opposition to Wafd Party. Fearing his pro-Axis sentiments the British High Commissioner, Sir Miles Lampson, surrounded his palace with tanks in 1942 and forced him to appoint Mustafa al-Nahas, the Wafd leader, as Prime Minister. Farouk dismissed the Wafd in October 1944. Farouk's position undermined by Egyptian losses during First Arab–Israeli War. Deposed in July 1952 by the Free Officers' coup, he was exiled to Italy where he continued his sybaritic lifestyle.

Fawzi, Mahmud (1900–81): Prime Minister of Egypt, October 1970–January 1972. Born in Cairo. Educated at the universities of Cairo, Rome and Columbia. Served in New York, Japan, Jerusalem, Washington, and was Egypt's representative at the United Nations, 1945–7. Foreign Minister, 1952–64. Deputy Prime Minister for Foreign Affairs, 1964–7. Special Presidential Adviser on Foreign Affairs 1967–70. Considered to have pro-Western leanings and in domestic politics to be a liberal.

Feisal (ibn Abdul al-Aziz Al Saud) (1905–75): King of Saudi Arabia, 1964–75. Second son of Ibn Saud. Appointed Governor of the Hejaz in 1927. Often represented Saudi Arabia in negotiations abroad. After the accession of his brother, Saud, in 1953, Feisal was in effect though not in name, Prime Minister. The economic crisis of 1958 exacerbated divisions between the two brothers, and Feisal increased his powers. Through fiscal savings Feisal repaid Saudi Arabia's international debts by 1962. Saud was deposed, and on 2 November 1964 Feisal was proclaimed king. Feisal relied on Western countries, especially the United States, for arms. He challenged Nasser's claim to leadership of the Muslim world and collaborated with Iraqi and Jordanian forces in the Six-Day War. Played an important role in mediating between the Jordanian government and the Palestinians in July 1970. Used oil weapon at time of October War. Assassinated by a nephew on 25 March 1975.

Feisal I (ibn Hussein) (1885–1933): King of Iraq, 1921–33. Born in the Hejaz, the third son of the Sherif of Mecca. Childhood spent in Constantinople. Chosen by T.E. Lawrence as a leader of the Arab revolt. Entered Damascus in October 1918 as commander of an army and assumed control of Syria in the name of the Arabs. Represented the Arab cause at the peace conference in Paris. Terms of his agreements with Weizmann over Jewish settlement in Palestine are disputed. Crowned King of Syria by an Arab–Syrian national congress in March 1920, but driven out by French. Chosen by Lawrence and endorsed by Churchill as King of Iraq; installed following a plebiscite of August 1921. Maintained a close relationship with Britain, which oversaw Iraq's admission to the League of Nations as an independent state in October 1932, following the signing of the Anglo–Iraqi Treaty of 1930. Established the Iraqi constitution of 1925, which lasted until 1958.

Feisal II (ibn Ghazi) (1935–58): King of Iraq, 1939–58. Succeeded to the throne, aged three, on death of his father King Ghazi. Educated at Harrow. Assumed power in 1953. Seen as pro-British and an opponent of Nasser. Dined with Eden on the eve of the Suez Crisis in July 1956. Had little influence domestically. Murdered on 14 July 1958 in a coup.

Ford, Gerald Rudolph Jr (1913–): Vice President of the United States, 1973–4; President of the United States, 1974–7 (Republican). As President initially considered a comprehensive peace settlement in the Middle East including Palestine. Later agreed to let Israel know of any peace proposal before showing it to the Arabs.

Forrestal, James Vincent (1892–1949): United States Secretary of Navy, 1944–7; First Secretary of Defense, 1947–9. At beginning of 1948 emphasized the need for a Palestine policy which gave consideration to the United States future oil requirements.

Fuad (Ahmad Fuad) (1868–1936): King of Egypt, 1917–36. Fought to achieve greater Egyptian independence from Britain. Anglo–Egyptian Treaty of 1936 signed just after he died.

Gaddafi, Muammar al- (1942–): 'Guide of the Revolution'. Coming from a Bedouin family, he was born near Sirte. Expelled from high school for political activity, he studied history at the University of Benghazi; attended the Libyan Military Academy and the Royal Signals Corps School at Beaconsfield, England; commissioned in the Royal Libyan Army in 1965. Led the revolution in 1969 and served as Prime Minister, 1970–2. Elected General-Secretary of the General People's Congress secretariat in March 1977. In May 1973 proclaimed his answer to communism and capitalism, the Third Universal Theory, which advocated that committees should replace government administration. Led Libya into the Arab Maghreb Union consisting of Libya, Tunisia, Algeria, Morocco and Mauritania. At summit meeting of Arab Maghreb Union in Lanuf, Libya, on 10 March 1991, Gaddafi spoke of the role of the United Nations in defending 'international legality' but insisted that in its handling of the Gulf War 'the Security Council has plundered the sovereignty of the General Assembly'; he wondered whether the actions of coalition forces in the Gulf did not amount to a crusade or colonialism. In the aftermath of the Gulf War tried to re-establish Libya's international acceptability through offering to pay compensation for the death of a British policewoman in the Libyan embassy siege in London in 1984, but was told that Libya had to denounce international terrorism first. Libya had sponsored both Palestinian and Irish terrorist organizations and was accused of being responsible for a number of individual outrages including the explosions in a nightclub in West Berlin in April 1986 that led to the United States bombing raids on Libya.

Gemayel, Amin (1942–): President of Lebanon, 1982–8. Born in Bikfaya. Educated at St Joseph's University in Beirut. Practised as a lawyer. Member of the Lebanese parliament since 1971. Pro-United States policies antagonized some sects. Although a Phalangist deputy, not recognized as leader by some extremists.

Gemayel, Bashir (1947–82): elected President of Lebanon on 23 August 1982. Lebanese Maronite Leader. Met Begin and Sharon in northern Israel on 1 September 1982. Killed by a bomb at Phalangist Party headquarters on 14 September 1982.

Gemayel, Pierre (1905–84): founded the Phalangists in Lebanon in 1936. A pharmacist by profession, he was educated in Beirut and France. In 1958 his Christian faction led the resistance to the rebels, and he became one of the members of a caretaker government. In the 1960s he formed the 'Triple Alliance' with Chamoun's National Liberal Party and the Bloc National led by Raymond Eddé, pro-Western and Christian in orientation. Opposed the use of Lebanon as a base by Palestinian fighters. In 1975 he wanted to maintain contact with Syria, while his son, Bashir, hoped to counter Syrian influence by an alliance with Israel.

Ghazi (Feisal) (1912–39): King of Iraq, 1933–9. Born in the Hejaz. Educated in Baghdad, and, briefly, at Harrow. Disliked the British. Had little political influence. Was killed in a car crash.

Glubb (Pasha), John Bagot (Sir) (1897–1986): Commander-in-Chief of the Arab Legion, 1938–56. As a British army officer served during the First World War in France and Iraq. Served in the Iraqi civil service. Second-in-command of the Arab Legion, 1930–8. Led the Arab Legion during the First Arab–Israeli War. Although blamed by Arab nationalists for Jordan's losses during that war, his influence in the kingdom was such that the young Hussein felt threatened by him and dismissed him in 1956. Glubb then became an historian of the Arabs and a publicist of their cause.

Goldmann, Nahum (Dr) (1894–1982): President of the World Zionist Organization, 1956–69. Born in Poland. Helped organize the World Jewish Congress in 1936. Jewish Agency representative to the League of Nations, 1934–40. Member of the Executive of the World Zionist Organization and the Jewish Agency, and President of the World Jewish Congress, 1951–78. Played an important role in the restitution agreement with the Federal Republic of Germany. Advocated accommodating the Arabs.

Gorbachev, Mikhail Sergeyevitch (1931–): Executive President of the Soviet Union, March 1990–2. Chairman of the Praesidium 1988–90; Head of State, 1988–90. During Gulf War in February 1991 proposed a peace plan which Iraqi Foreign Minister Tariq Aziz took to President Rafsanjani of Iraq, but which the Americans felt did not go far enough.

Grey, Edward (Sir) (1st Viscount) (1862–1933): British Foreign Secretary, 1905–16. Approached by Arab National Congress in June 1913 about demand that Arabs should be able to exercise their political rights. Involved in Hussein–McMahon correspondence.

Habash, George (Dr) (1925–): leader of the Popular Front for the Liberation of Palestine (PFLP), December 1969– . A Greek Orthodox Christian born in Lydda, Palestine, he graduated in medicine from the American University of Beirut. A founder of the left-wing pan-Arab group, the Arab Nationalist Movement. Opposed Nasser and Baath in Syria. Established the Free Jordan Movement, aimed at overthrowing Hussein. Arafat (Leader of Palestine Liberation Organization) denounced Habash. Responsible for the hijacking of aircraft to Dawson Field, outside Amman, in September 1970. Accepted majority vote of Palestine National Council in November 1988 in Algeria, rejecting terrorism and confining the use of violence to Israel and the occupied territories.

Habib, Philip Charles (1920–92): Special United States Presidential Envoy to Middle East, 1981–3. Sent by Reagan in 1981 to negotiate with warring factions in Lebanon. Managed, with assistance of Saudis, to achieve an understanding between Begin, Asad and Arafat, and secured a cease-fire on 24 July 1981.

Haddad, Saad (1936–84): Phalangist military leader. Professional officer in Lebanese army. Trained in United States. Helped Israeli patrol that came into Lebanon in 1972. Officer with south battalion of Lebanese army, 1975–6. Broke with army and established private militia. In 1978 and 1982 showed himself to be a pro-Israeli commander in the south of Lebanon. In April 1979 proclaimed 'independent free Lebanon', an area of around 1,800 sq km adjoining the Israeli border. Supported by Israel, Haddad maintained his independence. Died of cancer on 15 January 1984.

Haig, Alexander Meigs Jr (General) (1924–): United States Secretary of State, 1981–2. In 1982 communicated with Begin about proposed Israeli invasion of Lebanon, and restrained Reagan from putting pressure on Begin over this issue.

Hammarskjöld, Dag (1905–61): Secretary-General of the United Nations, 1953–61. Swedish. In April 1956 compared Nasser to Hitler in 1935. Helped to establish the United Nations Emergency Force (UNEF) in November 1956, which took over from the British, French and Israeli forces in Egypt after the Suez invasion of 1956.

Heikal, Mohamed (Muhammad) Hassanein (1923–): Egyptian Minister of National Guidance, 1970. A journalist, became a friend and confidant of Nasser during the First Arab–Israeli War. Said to have written Nasser's *The Philosophy of the Revolution*. Became editor of the Cairo daily newspaper *Al-Ahram* in 1957. Frequently travelled with Nasser abroad. Also became a confidant of Sadat.

Herzl, Theodor (Binyamin Zeev) (Dr) (1860–1904): father of political Zionism. Born in Budapest. Studied law in Vienna. Became a journalist and was influenced by the French anti-Semitism evidenced at the Dreyfus trial, which he witnessed as a correspondent. Impressed by Cecil Rhodes's wresting of control of land from the Matabele and the Mashona in what became Rhodesia, as well as the way in which Rhodes secured financial backing and a sponsor. Herzl's book *Der Judenstaat* (*The State of the Jews*) was published in February 1896, and suggested that anti-Semitic fervour made the establishment of a state for the Jews an urgent necessity. He had two possible regions in mind: Palestine or Argentina. He organized the first Zionist Congress which met in Basle in August 1897. This adopted 'home' as a synonym for state, and out of the conference emerged the World Zionist Organization, a national flag, a national anthem, and the Jewish National Fund. Herzl tried to link Zionism to British imperial interests, and to play on the anti-Semitism of British statesmen concerned about the flood of Jewish refuges into England following the pogroms in Russia. Herzl initially rejected Joseph Chamberlain's proposal of 'Uganda' – in effect the Kenya highlands – as an area for Jewish colonization, but later warmed to the idea. He noted in his diary that at Basle he had founded the Jewish state: in fifty years everyone would know it.

Herzog, Chaim (1918–): President of Israel, 1983–93. Born in Belfast. Attended universities in Dublin, London and Cambridge. Also studied at Hebron's yeshiva. Went to Palestine in 1935. Served as a British major during the Second World War and on Allied General

Staff in Germany. In charge of security section of Jewish Agency between 1947 and 1948. Director of Israel's military intelligence, 1948–50, and 1959–62. First military governor of the West Bank from June 1967. Israeli ambassador to the United Nations from 1975 to 1978. Elected to Knesset as Labour Party candidate.

Hoover, Herbert William Jr (1918–). President of the Hoover Company, 1954–6. An American business executive who advised Eisenhower.

Humphrey, George Magoffin (1891–1970): United States Secretary of the Treasury, 1952–6. Helped Eisenhower to organize run on sterling during the Suez Crisis.

Hussein (ibn Ali) (*c.* 1852–1931): Sherif of Mecca, King of Hejaz, 1916–24. Exiled in Istanbul, he returned to the Hejaz after the Young Turks revolution and was appointed Emir of Mecca. His main rival was Ibn Saud. In 1914 he approached Lord Kitchener about British assistance should the Arabs rise against the Turks. Ten letters were exchanged between the British High Commissioner in Egypt, Sir Henry McMahon, and Hussein about recognition of Arab independence in return for a revolt against Turkish rule. Joined in starting the Arab revolt of 1916 and in October/November was recognized as King of Hejaz. Objected to the Sykes–Picot agreement and refused to endorse the peace treaties. Clashed with the Nejd tribes in 1919–20, and was saved by British intervention. In March 1924 proclaimed himself Caliph after the office abolished by the Turkish National Assembly in 1924, but was not recognized by Islamic leaders. Ibn Saud declared him a traitor and his Wahhabis attacked. Hussein forced to abdicate in favour of his son, Ali, but Mecca was captured by Ibn Saud in October 1924. Ali was overthrown in 1925, and Hussein went into exile.

Hussein (ibn Talal al-Hashemi) (1935–): King of Jordan, 1953– . Born in Amman. Educated at Victoria College, Alexandria, Harrow and Sandhurst. Policy to retain both friendship of Arab leaders and West. In 1956 expelled Glubb Pasha as this former British army officer was thought to have too great an influence in Jordan. After Suez Crisis resisted moves by his Prime Minister to move Jordan towards a Soviet orientation. Invited British troops into Jordan during the Lebanese crisis of 1958. Encouraged American influence in Jordan. During Jordanian civil war expelled the Palestine Liberation Organization (PLO). Survived because Bedouin remained loyal to him. Having lost the West Bank and East Jerusalem in the Six-Day

War, did not get involved in the October War. With Reagan plan of 1982 of self-government for the Palestinians in association with Jordan, Hussein requested mandate from the Palestinians. The Labour Party in Israel and the United States hoped that he might provide a 'Jordanian solution' for the Palestinian problem, but in early stages of intifada he cancelled Jordan's authority on the West Bank. In 1990, against background of strong domestic support for Iraq, tried to sustain a balancing act between Saddam Hussein and the countries sending troops against him. On 1 January 1991, King Hussein brought Islamic fundamentalist delegates into the Jordanian Cabinet. With coalition victory in Gulf War tried to ameliorate impression of Jordanian support for Saddam Hussein by saying that the people of Jordan rejoiced with their 'Kuwaiti brothers', and asked that the same criteria be applied to the Palestine question as had been applied to Kuwait. In June 1991, after proclaiming a national charter calling for multi-party democracy and greater freedom for women as well as legislation to conform with Islamic law, in an attempt to quieten domestic unrest, King Hussein was admitted to hospital with suspected heart trouble. On 17 June 1991 King Hussein appointed the first Prime Minister of Palestinian origin to serve in Jordan for twenty years. In the aftermath of the Gulf War managed to restore Jordan's relations with the West and the United States in particular.

Hussein, Saddam (1937–): President of Iraq, 1979– . Joined Baath Party in 1957. After involvement in attempted assassination of Kassem in November 1959, escaped to Egypt. Returned in 1964 and in 1966 became deputy Secretary General of the Baath Party and Vice Chairman of the Revolutionary Command Council in November 1969. Proclaimed President of Iraq and Chairman of the Revolutionary Command Council on 16 July 1979. Issued a plea for Arab solidarity in 1980. Wanted to overthrow the Islamic revolutionary regime in Iran (Shiite). Although a majority of the population of Iraq was Shiite, the leadership was dominated by Sunnis. Led his country in an eight-year war against Iran. In 1990 annexed Kuwait. Partly explained his action in terms of focusing attention on the Palestinian question. Tried to link his image to the historic leaders of Babylon. Was considered by many Palestinians and other Arabs as a great popular hero as he was seen to be the first Arab leader to strike the heart of the Zionist state with the Scud missile attacks on Tel Aviv and Haifa during the Gulf War. Western leaders appreciated that Saddam Hussein had managed to hold the very different elements of the Iraqi state together, and insisted that their policy was not to kill him. In the aftermath of the Gulf War, Western leaders refrained from supporting the Shiite and Kurdish uprisings against Saddam Hussein and so enabled the integrity of Iraq to continue. Saddam Hussein survived 'defeat' in the Gulf War and reasserted his authority over most of Iraq in the aftermath by force.

Husseini, Feisal al- (1940–): a chief spokesman of the Palestine Liberation Organization on the West Bank from the late 1980s.

Husseini, Hajj (Muhammad) Amin al- (*c.* 1897–1974): Palestinian politician. Educated in Jerusalem, Cairo and Istanbul. Sentenced for taking part in anti-Jewish demonstrations in Jerusalem in 1920, but pardoned, and appointed Mufti of Jerusalem by High Commissioner in 1921 on understanding that Husseini would use family influence to maintain peace. Elected President of the Supreme Muslim Council in January 1922. Encouraged Muslim character of Jerusalem and this formed background to disturbances of August 1929. President of the Arab Higher Committee, 1936, and helped to organize the Arab rebellion of 1936–7. Dismissed by mandatory authorities as President of the Supreme Muslim Council in October 1937 after banning of Arab Higher Committee. Went to Syria, Iraq, and later Italy and Germany where he supported Nazi war effort. In June 1946 elected President of Arab Higher Committee in absentia, and from Egypt opposed the partition of Palestine. In 1948 tried to form an 'All-Palestine Government' in Gaza.

Husseini, Jamal al- (*c.* 1892–presumed dead): Palestinian politician. Educated at Jerusalem and at the American University of Beirut. Secretary to the Arab Executive in Palestine, 1921–34. Secretary to the Supreme Muslim Council, 1928–30. Head of the Palestinian delegation to the Round Table Conference in London in March 1939. Established a new Arab Higher Committee in Palestine in 1946, but it was divided by factionalism, and after intervention of Arab League he was appointed Vice President of a new Committee. Presented Arab case before various committees of enquiry. Helped to persuade the Arab Higher Committee to reject the United Nations partition plan.

Husseini, Mussa Kazim al- (1850–1934): Mayor of Jerusalem, March 1918–20. Educated in Istanbul. Appointed mayor of Jerusalem, but as he did not stay out of politics was dismissed in 1920. Elected President of the Arab Executive, 1920–34, and led Palestinian delegations to London.

Ibn Saud (al-Aziz ibn Abd-Rahman Al Saud) (1880–1953): King of Saudi Arabia, 1932–53. Grew up in Kuwait. Captured Riyadh in 1901 and re-established the Saud dynasty in Nejd. Recognized by Britain in 1915 and paid a subsidy. Neutral during First World War. Defeated Hussein, Sherif of Mecca, 1918–19, but under British pressure did not pursue victory. Defeated Ibn Rashid, 1919–21, and took over his lands, calling himself the Sultan of Nejd and its dependencies. Conquered Mecca in 1924, and Jedda and the rest of the Hejaz in 1925. Proclaimed King of the Hejaz, Nejd and its dependencies in January 1926. Recognized by Britain in the Treaty of Jedda, 1927. In 1932 Ibn Saud took the title of King of Saudi Arabia. Fought the Yemen in 1934 and allowed the Imam of Yemen independence. American oil interests encouraged Roosevelt to give Saudi Arabia aid and Saudi Arabia supported the Allies in 1945. Opposed Zionism in his meeting with Roosevelt in February 1945, and in his correspondence with Truman. Ruled as a conservative monarch and promoted Wahhabi Islam, a form of the religion that is conservative and accepts only what is written in the Koran and early scriptures.

Idris, King **(Muhammad Idris al-Mahdi al-Sanussi)** (1890–1983): King of Libya, 1951–69. Grandson of the founder of the Sanussi Order, a Sunni religious order which had the stated intention of returning to the teaching of the Koran and was influential among the Bedouin in Cyrenaica. Born at Tughbub, Cyrenaica. Made contact with the British in Egypt in 1914 and assisted in the war against Turkey. Recognized by Italy in 1920 as Emir of Cyrenaica, but went into exile in Cairo in 1922. During Second World War helped to recruit a Sanussi force to fight the Italians in the North African campaign. With British assistance proclaimed Emir of Cyrenaica in 1949. Became king of a united Libya on 24 December 1951 and sustained a conservative personal rule until he was deposed in a military coup on 1 September 1969. Died in exile in Egypt.

Jabotinsky, Vladimir (Zeev) (1880–1940): Revisionist Zionist writer. Born and educated in Russia. Helped to form Jewish volunteer units during First World War. Organized defence of Jewish quarter in Jerusalem, 1920. Elected to Zionist Executive in 1921, but resigned in 1923 over British White Paper of 1922. In 1925 founded the World Union of Zionist Revisionists and the youth movement, Betar. In 1935 elected President of the New Zionist Organization, a Revisionist group dedicated to the immediate establishment of a Zionist state. Jabotinsky advocated a Zionist state in both Palestine and Transjordan, militant opposition to the British, and increased Jewish immigration into Palestine. He inspired Begin who, despite opposition from Ben-Gurion, oversaw his interment on Mount Herzl in Jerusalem in 1964.

Jadid, Salah (1929–): Deputy Secretary of the Syrian Baath Party, 1966–70. Born at Lataqia. Assisted the officers' coup of March 1963 and appointed army Chief of Staff. Led military wing of Baath Party. After being dismissed in September 1965, led a coup on 23 February 1966, establishing a regional and military leadership. Belonged to wing of Baath Party which felt that priority should be given to internal reform and the creation of a one-party state along neo-Marxist lines. Opposed by Hafiz al-Asad and the nationalist wing of the Baath Party which emphasized the need for a pragmatic attitude to the economy, improved relations with the Arab neighbours and a stand against Israel. By the end of 1968 Asad had won the power struggle, and after his seizure of power in November 1970 he imprisoned Jadid.

Jalloud, Abdul Salam Ahmad (Major) (1940–): Prime Minister of Libya, 1972– . Born in Tripolitania, he attended an Army Corps of Engineers school in the United States. Commissioned in the Royal Libyan Army in 1965. One of the officers who planned the revolution with Gaddafi. Led Libyan delegation to talks on evacuation of British and American bases in 1970. Influential in increase of oil prices in 1970, and nationalization of foreign oil companies in 1973. In 1986 took on greater responsibilities in security and foreign affairs.

Jarring, Gunnar (Dr) (1907–): United Nations Special Envoy to the Middle East, 1967–71. A Swedish diplomat, he attempted, through separate talks with the Arabs and Israelis, to achieve a settlement of the conflict. Talks suspended in 1969, but resumed in 1970 with little result.

Johnson, Eric (1896–1963): American businessman who drew up a plan for the distribution of the waters of the Jordan river, 1953–5. Arab leaders refused to agree to a scheme which could benefit Israel.

Johnson, Lyndon Baines (1908–73): President of the United States, 1963–9 (Democrat). Oversaw a swing in United States policy towards favouring Israel. Change marked by the visit to the United States of the Israeli premier, Eshkol, in 1964. Later a radical switch in the type of armaments supplied to Israel, from a moderate supply of defensive weapons to highly sophisticated offensive arms.

Jumblatt, Walid Kamal (1949–): hereditary leader of the Druzes. Born in Lebanon. Educated at American University of Beirut. One of the leaders of the revolt against Amin Gemayel in Lebanon in 1983. President of the Parti Socialiste Progressiste since 1977. Appointed Minister of Public Works and Transport in October 1990, but withdrew from the broad-based cabinet that President Hrawi had established in 1991.

Kahane, Meir (Rabbi) (1932–90): leader of the Kach Party in Israel, 1984–8. Born in the United States. During Bevin's visit to the United States at the end of 1946 pelted the Foreign Secretary with eggs and tomatoes as a gesture of protest over British policy towards Palestine. Moved to Israel in 1971 after being employed by Shamir when head of the Mossad. Tried to apply the ideas of Jewish self-defence he had developed in Brooklyn against the blacks to the Arabs. Elected to the Knesset in 1984, as head of the Kach Party, on the platform of expelling the 700,000 Palestinians who were Israeli citizens as well as the 1.3 million who lived in the occupied territories. Advocated that Israel became an all-Jewish theocracy where the Torah was the law. He proposed legislation to ban sexual relations between Jews and Arabs, and wanted non-Jews confined to ghettos in case they polluted the 'authentic Jewish spirit'. Prevented from standing for election again in 1988. Declared by the State Department in October 1985 to be no longer an American citizen. Assassinated in New York.

Kamel, Muhammad Ibrahim (1927–): Egyptian Foreign Minister, 1977–September 1978. Born in Cairo and educated in law at university there. Resigned over Camp David accords and peace treaty with Israel.

Karami, Rashid Abdul Hamid (1921–87): Prime Minister of Lebanon at various times between 1960 and 1987. Attempted to promote national reconciliation in Lebanon.

Kassem, Abd al-Karim (1914–63): 'Sole Leader' of Iraq, 1958–63. Born in Baghdad into a Sunni Muslim family. Was commissioned as an army officer in 1938 and served as a battalion commander during the First Arab–Israeli War. Chairman of the Committee of Free Officers which overthrew King Feisal II in July 1958. Nominated himself as Commander-in-Chief, Prime Minister, and acting Minister of Defence. Introduced agrarian reforms in 1958. Tried to keep Iraq outside Nasser's sphere of influence, and in alliance with Communists suppressed the pro-Nasser mutiny in Mosul led by Colonel

Shawwaf in March 1959. After this suppressed the Communists. Confronted by a Kurdish rebellion in 1961. On 25 June 1961 Kassem declared that since Kuwait had been part of the *vilayet* of Basra in Ottoman days, it was now part of Iraq. He considered Britain's treaty of 1899 with Kuwait a forgery. The arrival of British troops, later replaced by Arab forces, prevented Kassem from implementing this threat. Also had disagreements with Iraq Petroleum Company in December 1961. Overthrown by combination of Baath supporters and anti-Communist officers, captured and shot.

Khalid (ibn Abd al-Aziz Al Saud) (1913–82): King of Saudi Arabia, 1975–82. Oversaw the implementation of Saudi Arabia's second Five Year Plan (1975–80), and the preparations for the third. During his reign Crown Prince Fuad led the policy of industrialization and building up Saudi Arabia's infrastructure.

Khomeini, Ruhollah (Ayatollah) (1900–89): Leader of the Islamic revolution of 1979 and of the Islamic Republic of Iran. Educated at Khomein and at the theological school at Qom, where he later taught. Arrested in Qom after riots following Shah's land reforms of 1963. Exiled in Turkey, 1964–5, Najaf in Iraq, 1965–78, and in France October 1978–February 1979. Khomeini outlined his doctrine, that of *wilayat-e-faqih* (the trusteeship of the jurisconsult), in a series of lectures to his students in Najaf. He moved away from an acceptance of state authority and the implied acceptance of religion and politics, and argued that government should be entrusted directly to the ulema (Islamic scholars). Returned to Iraq in February 1979 and inspired the constitution of the Islamic Republic of Iran. Rallied Iranians behind the banner of the jihad after Saddam Hussein's invasion from Iraq. Considered to be an inspirational force behind the enforcement of the Islamic code in Iran in 1983: amputation of hand for theft; flogging for use of alcohol, fornication, and many other offences; and stoning to death for adultery. With the announcement of Iran's unconditional acceptance of the United Nations Security Council resolution for a cease-fire in the Iran–Iraq War, Khomeini admitted on Iranian television on 18 July that he had done worse than drink poison in abandoning the destruction of Saddam Hussein. In 1989 Khomeini issued a religious edict exhorting all Muslims to carry out a death sentence on British author Salman Rushdie and his publishers for *The Satanic Verses*, a work considered as blasphemous by many Muslims. Khomeini's death on 3 June 1989 was followed by hysterical mass mourning.

Khrushchev, Nikita Sergeevich (1894–1971): Head of the Soviet Communist Party and State, 1958–64. Tried to replace Western influence in Egypt with Soviet influence. Helped to finance Aswan dam and financed industrialization in Egypt.

Khuri, Faris al- (1877–1962): Prime Minister of Syria, 1944–5, 1954–5. A Protestant Christian, he was a member of Feisal's government in Damascus in 1920. After exile in Lebanon he became leader of the 'Bloc National' in Syria and was President of the parliament, 1936–9, 1943, 1945–9. From 1947 he was one of the leaders of the National Party.

Killearn, Lord (Sir Miles Lampson) (1880–1964): High Commissioner, 1934–6, then Ambassador in Egypt, 1936–46. Led British delegation to the talks on the Anglo–Egyptian Treaty of 1936. Surrounded Farouk's palace on 4 February 1942 with tanks and troops and forced the King to appoint a Wafd Prime Minister thought to be sympathetic to the British war effort. Opposed partition in Palestine, and in 1944–5 was influential in leading the British government away from that policy.

Kissinger, Henry Alfred (1923–): Special Assistant to United States President for National Security Affairs, 1969–75; Secretary of State, 1973–7. Prominent in negotiations for a Middle East cease-fire, 1973–4. Ensured an American dominance over the settlement that ended the October War with his shuttle diplomacy, and was awarded the Nobel Peace Prize in 1973 for his efforts.

Kitchener, Horatio Herbert (Lord/Earl) (1850–1916): British Agent and Consul General in Egypt, 1911–14; Secretary of State for War, 1914–16. Approached in February 1914 by Sherif of Mecca about possible British support for Arab independence.

Kollek, Teddy (1911–): Mayor of Jerusalem 1965–93. Born in Hungary, Kollek grew up in Vienna. He emigrated to Palestine in 1936. Became intelligence liaison officer for the Haganah, and was chief arms purchaser in the organization's New York office, 1947–8. Israeli Minister Plenipotentiary in Washington, 1951–2. Director-General of the Prime Minster's Office, 1952–4. As candidate of the Rafi Party elected Mayor of West Jerusalem in 1965. From 1967 also administered East Jerusalem. Had an ability to achieve compromises between Arabs and Jews in Jerusalem, and clashed with Orthodox Jews. Late in 1993 lost in the municipal elections in which he appealed unsuccessfully to the Arabs in East Jerusalem to vote for the Likud candidate, Ehud Olmert.

Lawrence, Thomas Edward (1888–1935): Lawrence of Arabia. Oxford educated. Acquired an attachment to Arabia through a personal relationship when working on archaeological expeditions. Attached to the Arab Bureau in Cairo in January 1916. Between October 1916 and September 1918 involved in the Arab revolt and the march on Damascus. The legend surrounding his activities at this time helped to make the world aware of the existence of Arabs: arguably, Lawrence helped to give the Arabs the concept of being Arab. Member of the British delegation to the Paris peace conference of 1919, where he acted as an adviser to Feisal. Appointed by Churchill as adviser on Middle East affairs to the Colonial Office, 1921–2, and helped to instal Feisal as King of Iraq, Abdullah as Emir in Transjordan, and attempted to settle with Hussein, the Sherif of Mecca. Lawrence probably felt in doing this he had repaid his debts to the Arabs for the march on Damascus and lost interest in their affairs.

Linowitz, Sol Myron (1913–): appointed by Carter in October 1979 as an American envoy with remit to get both Egypt and Israel to agree to a Palestinian homeland and safeguards for Israeli security. In post until 1981.

Lloyd, Selwyn (Baron Selwyn-Lloyd of Wirral) (1904–78): British Minister of State at the Foreign Office, October 1951–4; Minister of Supply, October 1954–April 1955; Minister of Defence, April–December 1955; Secretary of State for Foreign Affairs, 1955–60. Involved in 'collusion' negotiations during Suez Crisis of 1956. His version, *Suez 1956: A Personal Account,* was posthumously published. Largely instrumental in helping to restore the special relationship with the United States, 1957–8, and developed a good rapport with Dulles. Helped to oversee transfer of power in Middle East from Britain to the United States.

Lloyd George, David (1st Earl Lloyd George of Dwyfor) (1863–1948): British Prime Minister, 1916–22. Sympathy for Zionism a consequence of teaching of Old Testament religious history in school and church. A protagonist of Samuel's scheme in 1915 for a British protectorate over Palestine. Negotiated with the French to ensure that Palestine fell under British control.

MacDonald, Malcolm (1901–81): Secretary of State for Colonies and Dominions at various times between 1936 and 1939. Involved in Zionist lobby to secure change in British Palestine policy, 1930–1. In May 1939 issued White Paper limiting Jewish immigration into Palestine.

MacDonald, James Ramsay (1866–1937): British Prime Minister, 1929– 35. Name given to 'Black Letter' which revised British policy in Palestine and allowed further Jewish immigration and land purchases.

McMahon, (Arthur) Henry (Colonel Sir) (1862–1949): High Commissioner of Egypt, 1914–16; British Commissioner on Middle East International Commission at Peace Conference. Helped to shape Foreign Office response to approaches from Sherif of Mecca, 1915–16.

Major, John (1943–): Prime Minister of the United Kingdom, 1990–7. Son of an entertainer; after leaving grammar school early he trained as a banker but entered politics. Foreign Secretary, 1989; Chancellor of the Exchequer, 1989–90. Worked in close alliance with the United States during the Gulf War, and became a popular wartime Prime Minister. In January 1991, while in Egypt, said that an international conference on the Palestinian issue should be held once the Gulf crisis had passed. On 8 April 1991 outlined a plan to the European Community leaders for the creation of a United Nations 'enclave' in northern Iraq to protect the Kurds. The scheme became known as the 'safe havens' for the Kurds.

Mardam, Jamil (1888–1960): Prime Minister of Syria, 1936–9, 1946–8. Born in Damascus. Helped to found al-Fatat, the Arab nationalist association in Paris in 1911. Organized the first Arab congress in Paris in 1913. Member of Arab delegation at Paris Peace Conference in 1919. One of the founders of the 'Nationalist Bloc' in Syria.

Marks, Simon (Lord Marks of Broughton) (1888–1964): member of Manchester School of Zionism. Entered retail firm of Marks and Spencer in 1907 and later became chairman. Assisted Weizmann in lead-up to the Balfour Declaration. Honorary Secretary to Zionist Delegation at Paris Peace Conference.

Marshall, George Catlett (1880–1959): Chief of Staff of the United States Army, 1939–45; Secretary of State, 1947–8. Influential in securing State Department's policy of trusteeship as a solution to the Palestine problem. Oversaw aid to Greece and Turkey in 1947. Opposed Truman's recognition of the State of Israel in May 1948 as pure party politics. Refused to stay on as his Secretary of State in following administration.

Masri, Aziz Ali al- (1878–1965): Arab politician and Egyptian Ambassador to Moscow 1953–4. Born in Cairo. Educated at the military academy in Istanbul. A founder of the Young Turk movement. Anticipated Arab autonomy and a joint Arab–Turkish kingdom. In 1916 fought with Sherif Hussein's army as Chief of Staff in the Arab revolt. Pro-German, he was appointed Chief of Staff of the Egyptian army in 1939, but dismissed in 1940 as a result of British pressure. Helped to inspire the Free Officers movement in Egypt as a symbol of nationalist opposition to the British.

Meir (Myerson), Golda (1898–1978): Prime Minister of Israel, 1969–74. Born in Russia. Educated in the United States. Immigrated to Palestine in 1921. Member of the Executive Committee of the Histradut (General Federation of Labour in Israel), 1934. Head of the Political Department of the Histradut in 1936. Active in the struggle against the British, she was also involved with the Mapai, a Zionist-Socialist political party. In 1946 she became head of the political department of the Jewish Agency. In 1948 negotiated in secret with Abdullah of Transjordan. Appointed Minister to Moscow in May 1948. Minister of Labour, 1949–56. Foreign Minister, 1956–66. Initiated Israel's outward policy towards emerging African countries and established good relations with some. Appointed Secretary-General of the Mapai in 1965 she helped to form the Israel Labour Party in 1968. As Prime Minister succeeded in securing from Nixon an identification of the United States's interests with those of Israel. Reputation suffered from the Israeli lack of preparation for the October War. Resigned as Prime Minister in a demoralized state in April 1974, after an attempt to rebuild her coalition government.

Midfai, Jamil al- (1890–1958): Prime Minister of Iraq, 1933–4, 1935, 1937–8, 1941, 1953. Born in Mosul, educated in Istanbul, served in the Ottoman army but joined the Arab revolt in 1916. Military adviser to Feisal, 1918–19. Though took part in anti-British riots in 1920 was later a member of Nuri al-Said's pro-British faction.

Milner, Alfred (Viscount) (1854–1925): served in Egypt, 1889–92. As a member of the British War Cabinet was involved in the drafting of the Balfour Declaration. Initially Milner revised the Zionist draft to eliminate 'National' and made 'the' home merely 'an' home. Milner approved of an autonomous Jewish community in Palestine under a British protectorate, but not of an independent Jewish state. He later insisted on guarantees for the existing non-Jewish communities in Palestine, and with that inclusion allowed 'national' to creep back. In 1919 led a mission to Egypt, and his analysis formed the background of the treaty of alliance that maintained British strategic control of and influence in Egypt.

Mohieddin, Zakariya (1918–): Prime Minister of Egypt, 1965–6; Vice President 1961–5, 1966–7. Born in the Dakhaliyya region and graduated from the Officers' Academy with Nasser in 1938. Joined the Free Officers. Minister of the Interior, 1953–62, responsible for internal security. Head of government 1965–6, but disagreed with Nasser on economic policy. In 1967 on Nasser's resignation, appointed by Nasser as President, but withdrew after demonstrations in favour of Nasser. Considered a candidate for the Presidency in 1970.

Mollet, Guy (1905–75): Prime Minister of France, 1956–9. Nasser's apparent support of rebels in Algeria led Mollet to be persuaded by military advisers to embark on Suez adventure.

Mossadeq, Muhammad (Dr) (1882–1967): Prime Minister of Iran, 1951–3. Came from a wealthy Iranian landowning background. His father was a financial administrator and served in the Qajar court. Mossadeq took over one of his father's posts and became the financial administrator of Khurasan province. Educated abroad at universities in France and Switzerland; received a doctorate in law from the University of Neuchâtel in 1914. After First World War, campaigned against British political and economic influence in Iran. Elected to the Iranian parliament in 1924, where he advocated constitutional principles and campaigned against British influence in Iran. In 1925 he voted against the accession of Reza Khan as the first Pahlavi Shah. Advocating that Iranians should manage their own affairs, he complained of British attempts to manage the country through the Anglo–Iranian Oil Company and the British embassy in Tehran. He was exiled to the provinces in 1936 after protesting against the weakening of parliamentary government. He returned in 1941 after the abdication of Reza Shah and campaigned as a nationalist, being elected to the Iranian parliament in 1944. A considerable orator, he supported a law in December 1944 intended to prevent foreign exploitation of Iranian oil, and in 1946 denounced the Iranian–Soviet agreement on oil exploitation, which was declared void by the Iranian parliament in October 1947. In 1951, having been named Prime Minister by the Iranian parliament, Mossadeq nationalized the Anglo–Iranian Oil Company. Overthrown by a coup organized by British and American intelligence in 1953. Revered in pre-Khomeini Iran as a democratic and secular nationalist who stood for his country's national dignity.

Mubarak, Muhammad Hosni (1928–): President of the Arab Republic of Egypt, 1981– . Trained at the Cairo Military Academy and Air Academy, as well as in Soviet Union. After Six-Day War of 1967 appointed Director-General of the Air Academy, and in June 1969 Chief of Staff of the air forces. Appointed Commander-in-Chief of the Air Force in 1972. In 1975 appointed Vice President, and led Egyptian delegations to Organization of African Unity conferences. Elected Secretary-General of National Democratic Party in 1981. After assassination of Sadat, became President of Egypt in a national referendum in October 1981. Careful not to offend Israel. Oversaw handing back of last third of Sinai in April 1982. In 1980s handled domestic difficulties exacerbated by rise of fundamentalist Islam. Aligned Egypt with the coalition forces during the Gulf War and secured the cancellation of $14 billion of debts. His threat to withdraw Egyptian troops prematurely from the Gulf area, where it was hoped that they would form the basis for the envisaged Mutual Defence Organization (MDO), led to further concessions being made to Egypt.

Murphy, Richard William (1929–): United States Assistant Secretary of State for Near Eastern Affairs, 1983–9. In 1984 attempted to mediate with Syria to enable an Israeli withdrawal from Lebanon.

Nabulsi, Suleiman al- (1908–76): Prime Minister and Foreign Minister of Jordan, October 1956–April 1957. Born in Salt and educated at the American University of Beirut. Minister of Finance and Economy, 1946–7, 1950–1. Ambassador to London, 1953–4. Became leader of the Nationalist Socialist Party which had left-wing leanings and opposed the Hashemites. Precipitated a crisis in Jordan when established diplomatic relations with the Soviet Union in April 1957. Dismissed by Hussein, who was assisted by the Americans in terms of the Eisenhower Doctrine for the Middle East.

Nahas, Mustafa al- (Pasha) (1876–1965): Prime Minister of Egypt, 1928, 1930, 1936–7, 1942–4, 1950–2. Helped to found the Wafd Party and elected its head in 1927. As head of the Wafd government in 1936 negotiated the Anglo–Egyptian Treaty. Dismissed by King Farouk in 1937 but restored by Britain in 1942. Lead conference preparing for formation of Arab League in October 1944 in Alexandria, and dismissed by Farouk immediately afterwards. Returned to power in the 1950 elections, Nahas abrogated the Anglo–Egyptian Treaty in October 1951, announced the incorporation of the Sudan into Egypt, and refused to join a Middle East defence pact. Initiated demonstrations against the presence of British troops in the Suez

Canal base, and after the 'Black Saturday' riots early in 1952 his government fell in the Free Officers' *coup d'état.*

Nahayan, Zayid ibn Sultan Al (1916–): President of United Arab Emirates since 1971; ruler of Abu Dhabi since 1966. Helped to make Abu Dhabi a modern city. Played a leading role in the establishment of the Arab Gulf Co-operation Council.

Namier, Lewis (Sir) (1888–1960): member of Political Intelligence Department of the Foreign Office, 1918–20; Political Secretary of the Jewish Agency for Palestine, 1929–31. Influential in securing the reversal of British policy in Palestine, 1930–1, with the 'Black Letter', and in 1939 attempted unsuccessfully to lobby against the policy that was outlined in Malcolm MacDonald's White Paper of May 1939.

Nashashibi, Ragheb al- (*c.* 1875–1951): Mayor of Jerusalem, 1920-34. Educated in the Ottoman Empire, he served as a Turkish officer during the First World War. As Mayor of Jerusalem co-operated with the British and opposed the Supreme Muslim Council dominated by the Husseini family. Founded the National Defence Party in 1934 and became a member of the Arab Higher Committee in 1936, but resigned in 1937. First Governor of West Bank after its incorporation into Jordan, 1948. Minister of Agriculture and Transport in Jordan, 1950–1; also Guardian of the Holy Places.

Nasser, Gamal Abdul (1918–70): President of Egypt, 1956-70. Born in the Assyut district, he was educated in Cairo, read law, and graduated from the military academy in 1938. Instructor at military academy in Sudan, 1941. Commanded Egyptian battalion during the First Arab–Israeli War. A leader of the Free Officers' coup that overthrew Farouk on 22 July 1952. Replaced Neguib as Prime Minister in February 1954 after a power struggle. Published *The Philosophy of the Revolution* in 1954, describing Egypt as the centre of three circles: Arab, Islamic, and African. After Gaza raid of February 1955, opposed negotiations with Israel. Following conclusion of agreement on British withdrawal of troops from Egypt, moved towards neutralism, and in 1955 attended the Bandung conference. When refused arms from West he acquired them from Czechoslovakia in 1955. Hoped to bring Egypt into modern age with Aswan High Dam scheme, and after cancellation of loan, nationalized the Suez Canal. The Suez–Sinai War of 1956 left Nasser with enhanced prestige in the Arab world. Formed the United Arab Republic with Syria in 1958, but union dissolved in 1961. Nasser's attempts to export his philosophy of the revolution alienated his fellow Arabs. He was more successful in Africa, where he was sometimes seen as a rival to Kwame Nkrumah. Pushed into fighting the Six-Day War, he resigned after the resounding defeat, but was forced to withdraw his resignation by popular acclaim. After this he took an increasing interest in the Palestine question and in the late 1960s fought the 'War of Attrition' with Israel. Nasser's position was undermined by his involvement in the war in the Yemen from 1962.

Neguib, Muhammad (General) (1901–84): President of Egypt, 1953–4. Born in Khartoum, read law at Cairo University and graduated from the military academy in 1921. Fought in the First Arab–Israeli War, and was linked with the Free Officers group. Between 1952 and April 1954 was at various times Prime Minister, Minister of War and President. A follower of Islam Neguib, was conservative in outlook. Regarded by Nasser as a figurehead, he was forced out of presidential office in November 1954 after being accused of conspiring with the Muslim Brotherhood. Under house-arrest until freed by Sadat in 1971.

Netanyahu, Benjamin (Binyamin) (1950–): Prime Minister of Israel, 1995– . Israel's Ambassador to the United Nations, 1982–4; Deputy Foreign Minister, 1988–91. Became leader of the Likud in 1993. His book, *A Place among the Nations: Israel and the World* (1993), outlined his credo: Israel needs to retain the occupied territories, which he refers to as 'Judea' and 'Samaria', and to resist all calls for the establishment of a Palestinian state on the West Bank. Asserts that a Palestinian state already exists: 'The land of Palestine comprises the modern states of Jordan and Israel. It is large enough to accommodate both a small Jewish state, Israel, and a substantially larger state for the Arabs of Palestine which is today called Jordan.' Like his predecessors, Begin and Shamir, he attempts to equate 'anti-Semitism' and 'anti-Zionism'. Elected Prime Minister by a wafer-thin majority under a new direct electoral system in 1995, he has been accused by Arab critics of retarding the peace process by apparently giving in to pressure from his right-wing coalition members for continued Jewish settlement in the occupied territories and in particular in East Jerusalem.

Nixon, Richard Milhous (1913–94): Vice President of the United States, 1953–61; President of the United States, 1969–74 (Republican). Deepened and broadened the commitment made to Israel by President Johnson. In 1973 extended to Israel $2.2 billion in grants and loans. Israel became the single largest recipient of American aid. In early stages of Presidency, however, professed an even-handed approach in the Middle East. Against background of Water-gate, an internal scandal which ultimately led to his downfall, put American nuclear bases on nuclear alert during October War, and mounted an operation in support of Israel larger than the Berlin airlift of 1948–9.

Nuqrashi, Mahmud Fahmi (1888–1948): Prime Minister of Egypt, 1945–6, 1946–8. Trained as an engineer. Left the Wafd to form the Saadist Party in 1937. Minister of Transport, 1936–7. Minister of the Interior, 1940. Foreign Minister, 1944–5. As Prime Minister, raised the dispute with Britain over the Sudan in the Security Council, 1947. Banned the Muslim Brotherhood in 1948, and was assassinated by one of its members.

Nutting, Antony (1920–): British Under-Secretary of State for Foreign Affairs, 1951–4; Minister of State for Foreign Affairs, 1954–6. Involved in 'collusion' negotiations during Suez Crisis and resigned. His account recorded in *No End of a Lesson*. Also wrote an important biography of Nasser (1972).

Pachachi (Bajaji), Muzahim al- (n.d.): Prime Minister of Iraq, 1948–9. Educated in law in Istanbul and active in the Arab awakening, founding a newspaper and a National Scientific Club. In 1924 helped to draft the Iraqi constitution, though opposed the Anglo–Iraqi Treaty of 1930. Minister of Interior, 1931–3. Representative to the League of Nations, 1933–5. Minister to Italy, 1935–9, and to France, 1939–42. Appeared before Anglo–American commission of enquiry, 1946. In 1950 led the opposition to the law allowing Jews to leave Iraq.

Pahlavi, Muhammad Reza Shah (1919–80): Shah of Iran, 1941–79. Educated in Switzerland and at Tehran Military Academy. Acceded to throne on father's abdication. Allowed Allies to use Iran as a supply route to Soviet Union during the Second World War. In 1946 requested United Nations to help Iran resist Soviet occupation. Attempted agrarian reform, 1950–1. Left Iran briefly in August 1953 during Mossadeq crisis, but restored by combined American and British intelligence operation. Joined Baghdad Pact in 1955. Reinstituted land reforms in 1959, and in 1963 a plebiscite endorsed his social and economic reforms known as the 'White Revolution'. Attempted to secularize Iranian society, make it an ally of the West and particularly the United States, and to place women on an equal footing with men. Faced strong opposition which he attempted to suppress with the aid of the SAVAK, his secret police. Driven into exile on 16 January 1979 by an Islamic fundamentalist revolution.

Pahlavi, Reza Shah (Muhammad Reza Khan) (1878–1944): Shah of Iran, 1925–41. Born at Alasht. Served in Persian Cossack brigade and helped to engineer a coup in February 1921. Became Minister of War, then Prime Minister in 1923, and in 1925 had Shah Ahmad deposed by the Majlis. Chosen as Shah in December 1925, he founded the Pahlavi dynasty. His programme of Westernization was opposed by the mullahs. Suspicious of Britain and the Soviet Union, he refused to allow Allied supplies through Iran to the Soviet Union in 1941. He was considered a Nazi sympathizer, and after the Allied occupation he abdicated in September 1941 and was deported to South Africa.

Peres, Shimon (1923–): Prime Minister of Israel, 1984–6; Acting Prime Minister 1995–6. Born in Poland. Emigrated to Palestine in 1934. Attended Tel Aviv University. In charge of arms purchases during First Arab–Israeli War. Director-General of Israeli Defence Ministry, 1952–9. Deputy Minister of Defence, 1959–65. Joined Rafi Party in 1965, but rejoined Labour and was Minister of Communications and Transport, 1970–4, and Minister of Defence, 1974–7. In terms of rotation agreement, handed premiership to Shamir in 1986. Helped to strengthen Israel's aircraft industry and the nuclear reactor in Dimona. Maintained close contacts with France, particularly during build-up to Suez Crisis of 1956. In 1990, following the Temple Mount killings, he favoured Israel receiving a United Nations mission. Following Labour's victory in the 1992 election, was appointed Foreign Minister and was involved in talks with the Palestine Liberation Organization (PLO) in Norway in 1993. He was a prime mover behind the Israeli–PLO accord of September 1993 and the Jordanian–Israeli peace treaty of 1994. Shared the Nobel Peace Prize in 1994.

Philby, H. St John B. (1885–1960): British Resident in Transjordan, 1921–4. In 1917 Philby ensured Ibn Saud's neutrality in the Arab revolt. Between 1920 and 1921 he was adviser to the Iraqi Ministry of the Interior. Settled in Jedda in 1926 and became an oriental scholar and adviser to Ibn Saud. In 1939 elaborated a scheme whereby Ibn Saud would agree to a Jewish state in Western Palestine, provided Arabs in the rest of the Middle East secured independence, and in return for Jewish financial aid.

Pineau, Christian (1904–): French Minister of Foreign Affairs, 1956–8. Helped to cement the Franco–Israeli alliance. Involved with 'collusion' planning between Britain, France and Israel during Suez Crisis of 1956.

Qabus ibn Said Al Bu Said (1940–): Sultan of Oman, 1971–. Born in Dhofar. Privately tutored in England, then attended Sandhurst. Overthrew father on 23 July 1970 and liberalized Oman, defeated Dhofari rebels, and led country on to world stage.

Qavam al-Saltana, Ahmad (1874–1960): Prime Minister of Iran, 1922–3, 1923–4, 1942–3, 1946–7, July 1952. Negotiated with Soviet Union during Azerbaijan crisis of 1945–6. Appointed Prime Minister in July 1952 following resignation of Mossadeq, but resigned after pro-Mossadeq demonstrations.

Quandt, William B. (1942–): Served in Bureau of Near Eastern and South Asian Affairs, State Department, 1972–6; member of United States team at Camp David, 1978; member of National Security Council Staff, White House, responsible for Arab–Israeli affairs, 1977–9.

Qutb, Sayed (1906–66): theorist of Muslim Brotherhood. Influenced by conservative Sayyid Abul Ala Maududi of Pakistan who shared his fellow countryman, Muhammad Iqbal's idea of the shariah as a system of law suitable for the modern world. In his book, *Signposts along the Road*, argued that the world was in a state of *jahilyya*, the state of ignorance without Islam, and that the sufferings and injustices suffered by peoples under capitalism and colonization were a result of opposition to the rule of God as shown in observance of the shariah. Qutb wanted a new élite of Muslim youth to fight the state of ignorance. Imprisoned by Nasser.

Quwwatli, Shukri al- (1892–1967): President of Syria, 1943–9, 1955–8. Born in Damascus and was a leader of the al-Fatat society of 1911. Minister of Defence, 1936–9. Leader of the nationalist movement, the Nationalist Bloc, he was elected President in 1943, and deposed in a military coup in 1949. Re-elected in August 1955, he supported closer links with the Soviet Union and Egypt. After formation of United Arab Republic in 1958 proposed Nasser as President.

Rabin, Yitzhak (1922–95): Prime Minister of Israel, 1974–7; 1992–5. Born in Jerusalem and attended an agricultural college, 1936–40. Took part in Allied invasion of Syria in 1941. Member of the Haganah. A commander in the Israeli Defence Force during the First

Arab–Israeli War, and after holding various offices in the force became Chief of Staff, 1964–8. Ambassador to Washington, 1968–73. Leader of Labour Party, 1974–7. Resigned in run-up to election over breach of currency regulations. Became Minister of Defence in 1984 and oversaw Israeli withdrawal from Lebanon. Opposed Peres's support of autonomy for West Bank, bringing to a head long-standing rivalry. Oversaw the negotiations with the Palestine Liberation Organization in 1993, and marked the subsequent accord by shaking hands with Arafat on the White House lawn. Signed the peace treaty with Jordan in October 1994. After agreeing to self-rule for the Palestinians on the West Bank was assassinated by a right-wing Jewish extremist, Yigal Amir, in September 1995. Shared the Nobel Peace Prize in 1994.

Rafsanjani, Ali Akbar Hashemi (1934–): President of Iran, 1989–97. Studied in Qom under Khomeini. From 1977 helped to organize opposition movements in Iran. In July 1979 appointed Deputy Minister of the Interior. Elected Speaker of the Islamic Consultative Assembly, 1980–9. Acting Commander-in-Chief of the armed forces, 1988–9. Pursued a more conciliatory policy towards the West, but sensitive to power of Iranian conservatives who could command mass support. Condemned Saddam Hussein's invasion of Kuwait.

Razmara, Ali (1901–51): Prime Minister of Iran, 1950–1. Graduated from a military academy in France. Chief of the General Staff, 1946–50. Led the Iranian troops into Azerbaijan in December 1946. As Prime Minister attempted to initiate land reform, with Shah's support, but assassinated by a Muslim fanatic after statement that Iran was not ready for oil nationalization.

Reagan, Ronald Wilson (1911–): President of the United States, 1981–9 (Republican). Informed Begin in 1982 that United States would ensure Israeli military superiority. Alexander Haig recorded that 'Israel has never had a greater friend in the White House than Ronald Reagan'. Under his presidency the United States attempted various peace plans in the Middle East, including the Reagan Plan and the Shultz Plan. Involved in the Iran–Contragate affair over deals with Iran through the good offices of Israel to secure the release of American hostages. The most popular United States president of the century, Reagan's political reputation was not significantly harmed by this. Supplied Saudi Arabia with AWACS surveillance aircraft, overcoming congressional opposition.

Riad, Mahmud (1917–81): Egyptian Foreign Minister, 1964–72; Deputy Prime Minister, 1971–2. Graduated from the Egyptian military academy in 1939. Represented Egypt on the Egypt–Israel Mixed Armistice Commission, 1949–52. Director of the Department of Arab Affairs, 1954–5. Ambassador to Syria, 1955–8. Presidential Adviser on Foreign Affairs, 1958–61. Ambassador to the United Nations, 1962–4. Supported Egypt's connections with the Soviet Union. Opposed compromise on the Arab–Israeli conflict. Presidential adviser, January–June 1972. Secretary-General League of Arab States, 1972–9.

Roosevelt, Eleanor Ann (1884–1962): wife of President Franklin D. Roosevelt. A convinced Zionist. In March 1945 tried to balance Ibn Saud's influence over her husband and was prepared to risk a fight with the Arabs. But in 1946 suggested in her syndicated newspaper column that there was some truth in Bevin's statement that the Americans wanted the Jewish refugees to go to Palestine as they did not want them in New York. Active in fundraising campaigns for the Irgun in 1947. As a United States representative to the United Nations complained in May 1948 about Truman's recognition of the State of Israel as undermining the United States's credibility in that organization.

Roosevelt, Franklin Delano (1882–1945): President of the United States, 1933–45 (Democrat). In 1938 convened the Evian Conference on the refugee problem, which led to the establishment of the Inter-Governmental Committee for Refugees. In May 1943 promised Ibn Saud that 'no decisions altering the basic situation of Palestine should be reached without full consultation with both Arabs and Jews'. On 15 October 1944 promised, if re-elected, to help bring about 'the establishment of Palestine as a free and democratic Jewish Commonwealth'. Met Ibn Saud on the Great Bitter Lake on 14 February 1945, and was told that the Arabs would rather die than yield their land to Jews. Ibn Saud protested on 23 March 1945 about Zionist preparations 'to create a form of Nazi-Fascism' in the midst of Arab countries loyal to the Allied cause, and insisted that bringing Jewish immigrants into 'land already occupied and do away with the original inhabitants' was 'an act unparalleled in human history'. Thus on 5 April 1945 Roosevelt assured Ibn Saud that he would make no move against the Arabs. This correspondence later published by State Department.

Rothschild, Lionel Walter (2nd Baron) (1868–1937): a leading British Zionist Jew. Acted as intermediary with the British government over the Balfour Declaration.

Rushdie, Salman (1947–): British author, born in Bombay. Condemned to death by Khomeini on 14 February 1989 for his novel *The Satanic Verses* (1988), sections of which were considered as blasphemous by some Muslims. Episode soured relations between Britain and Iran.

Sabri, Ali (1920–91): Prime Minister of Egypt, 1962–5; Vice President of Egypt, 1965–7, 1970–1. Graduated from the Egyptian military academy in 1939. Liaised with the United States embassy during the Free Officers' coup. Appointed Minister for Presidential Affairs in 1960. Supported close relations with the Soviet Union. Chairman of the Arab Socialist Union, 1965–9. Considered responsible for street demonstrations of June 1967 which led to Nasser withdrawing his resignation. Dismissed as Vice President in 1971 and accused of treason. Released from prison May 1981.

Sacher, Harry (1881–1971): founder member of Manchester School of Zionism. Director of Marks and Spencer Ltd, 1932–62.

Sadat, (Muhammad) Anwar el- (1918–81): President of Egypt, 1970–81. A graduate from the Egyptian military academy in 1938, he was a Nazi sympathizer and between 1940–4 involved in pro-German underground activities. A member of the Free Officers involved in the coup of July 1952, he liaised with the Muslim Brotherhood and the Young Egypt Party. Chairman of the National Assembly, 1959–69. In 1960s managed relations with Yemen and acted as Nasser's emissary. Appointed Vice President of Egypt, 1969. As President consolidated his position within Egypt, planned the October War of 1973, and established relations between Washington and Cairo. After his visit to Jerusalem and the Camp David meeting, signed a peace treaty with Israel on 26 March 1979. Through his policy he isolated Egypt in the Arab world, though he was considered a great statesman internationally. Assassinated in 1981 by a group of Islamic extremists who had hoped to stage a *coup d'état* and declare Egypt an Islamic republic.

Said, Edward W. (1935–): American academic of Palestinian extraction who espoused the Palestinian cause. Serious illness prevented him from playing a leading role in the evolving Palestinian entity. Responsible for the intellectual concept of 'Orientalism': the assertion that the West has tended to judge the East and

Islam through the eyes and prejudices of the West rather than accepting it on its own terms.

Said, Nuri al- (1888–1958): Prime Minister of Iraq, 1930–2, 1938–40, 1941–4, 1946–7, 1949, 1950–2, 1954–7, 1958. Of mixed Arab–Kurdish descent, was born in Baghdad. Family of Sunni background. Graduated from Istanbul Military Academy and, though an officer in the Ottoman army, took part in the Arab revolt and became Feisal's Chief of Staff. Iraqi Chief of Staff, 1921. Minister of Defence, 1922–4, 1926–8. Negotiated Anglo–Iraqi Treaty. Dominated Iraqi politics for twenty years after 1938 and tried to secure British interests. Had ideas of a united Iraq, Syria, Lebanon and Jordan in a Fertile Crescent. Resented rejection of this scheme in the early 1940s in favour of the Arab League centred in Cairo. Hoped to counter Nasser's claims to lead the Arab world and accepted United States arms on American terms. Helped to lay foundation of Baghdad Pact in 1955. Dining with Eden at time of Nasser's nationalization of Suez Canal. Murdered on 14 July 1958 in the coup.

Sallal, Abdullah al- (1917–): President of the Yemen Arab Republic, 1962–7. Coming from a Zeidi family, graduated from Baghdad military academy in 1938. Appointed by Crown Prince al-Badr as commander of personal guard, mid-1950s, and Commander-in-Chief of the army during 1962. Collaborated with Egyptians in civil war and refused to compromise with royalists. After Egyptian defeat in Six-Day War, Sallal deposed while in Moscow. Initially exiled, he was allowed to return to a private life in Yemen.

Samuel, Herbert (Sir, later Viscount) (1870–1963): High Commissioner of Palestine, 1920–5. In a memorandum of March 1916 he suggested that rather than establishing an autonomous Jewish state in Palestine immediately, there should be a British protectorate which could be a safeguard to Egypt. Britain should assist the Jews through immigration and land purchases to become the majority, and achieve self-government. As High Commissioner, appointed known opponents of Zionism to senior positions. In May 1922 drew up a statement of policy on Palestine accepted by Churchill and published as a White Paper in June 1922: the development of the Jewish national home in Palestine did not mean the imposition of Jewish nationality upon the inhabitants of Palestine as a whole, but the further development of existing Jewish community, with the assistance of Jews in other parts of the world, so that it could become a centre in which Jewish people as a whole could take an interest.

Schwarzkopf, H. Norman (General) (1934–): Commander of allied coalition forces in Gulf War, 1990–1. Born into a military family, his father was a general. Educated at Bordentown Military Institute, near Trenton, New Jersey, at the age of twelve he went to Tehran with his father and then on to schools in Europe where he learnt German and French. Attended West Point Military Academy where he graduated in 1956. Served in Vietnam for two tours and was awarded the Silver Star three times. Became convinced that the failure in Vietnam was a consequence of the lack of public and political support for the military, and concluded that the United States should not again engage in a limited war with badly defined aims. 'Operation Desert Shield', the American plan to protect the Gulf area after the invasion of Kuwait, was Schwarzkopf's plan and had been rehearsed five days before Saddam Hussein's invasion. As the commander of allied forces Schwarzkopf showed considerable diplomatic skills, particularly in his handling of the Saudis. He also successfully orchestrated a war machine made up of forces from twenty-eight countries, including around 675,000 troops, hundreds of ships, and thousands of aircraft and tanks. His 'gung-ho' approach may have been the source of his nickname 'Stormin' Norman'.

Shaabi, Qahtan Muhammad al- (1920–81): President of South Yemen, 1967–9. Born in Lahej Sultanate. Became director of Lahej Land Department in 1955 but fled to Yemen in 1960, and in 1963 founded the National Liberation Front for Occupied South Yemen. His organization dominated the war in Yemen and power was transferred to it by the Geneva independence talks of November 1967. Resigned in June 1969 after a reported power struggle, and was succeeded by a more left-wing regime which moved towards the Soviet Union.

Shamir, Yitzhak (1915–): Prime Minister of Israel, 1983–4, 1986–92. Born in Poland. Emigrated to Palestine in 1935 where studied law. In 1937 joined the Irgun, but in 1940 left it and became part of the leadership of the Stern Gang, and is associated with the assassination of Lord Moyne in November 1944 in Cairo, and Count Bernadotte in 1948. Between 1948 and 1965 served abroad as an agent of the Mossad (Israeli intelligence) and later became its head. Joined the Herut Party in 1970. Elected to the Knesset in 1973. Speaker of the Knesset, 1977–80. Campaigned against the Camp David agreements. Foreign Minister, 1980–3, 1984–6. Supporter of the Greater Israel Movement. Acting Minister of the Interior, 1987–8. In 1990, following the Temple Mount killings, refused to receive a United Nations mission. During the Gulf War enhanced Israel's international reputation by following a policy of restraint in the face of Iraqi Scud missiles landing on Tel Aviv and Haifa. Assisted his housing minister, Ariel Sharon, to pursue the most rapid and extensive expansion of Jewish settlement in the occupied territories. In aftermath of Gulf War overrode his Foreign Minister, David Levy, and resisted American efforts to set up a general Middle East conference on the grounds that Israel would only conduct bilateral negotiations with Arab states; attended opening session at Madrid in October 1991. Resigned as leader of the Likud in 1993.

Sharett, Moshe (formerly Shertok) (1894–1965): Prime Minister of Israel, 1954–5. Born in Russia. Immigrated to Palestine in 1906 and served in the Ottoman army during the First World War. Active in the Labour movement and the Mapai. In 1933 appointed head of the Political Department of the Jewish Agency and became a leading Zionist spokesman. Fought the British and helped to form the Jewish Brigade Group in 1944 which oversaw Jewish immigration into the Palestine mandate. Arrested by the British in 1946. Foreign Minister, 1948–56. As Prime Minister, regarded as a gradualist in the tradition of Chaim Weizmann. Clashed with Ben-Gurion and his supporters. Chairman of the Zionist and Jewish Agency Executive, 1960–5.

Sharon, Ariel (1928–): Israeli Minister of Defence, 1981–3; Minister of Trade and Industry, 1984–90; Minister of Construction and Housing, 1990–2; Chairman of Cabinet Committee to oversee immigration from (former) Soviet Union, 1991–6; Minister of National Infrastructure, 1996–. Born in Palestine. Member of Haganah. Battallion commander in First Arab–Israeli War. In 1953 in charge of 'Unit 101' that killed sixty-six Jordanians in the retaliatory Qibya raid. His paratroopers failed to hold the Mitla pass in Suez–Sinai War of 1956. In 1962 appointed commander of the Israeli Defence Force's armoured brigade. Commanded a division in the Six-Day War and then handled resistance in the Gaza Strip. After differences with fellow officers in October War, became a Likud member of the Knesset, 1973–4. Adviser to Rabin, 1975–7. As Minister of Agriculture, 1977–81, encouraged Israeli settlement on occupied West Bank. Appointed Minister of Defence in 1982. Censored by Kahan Commission for Sabra and Shatila massacres. Retained by Begin as Minister without Portfolio, 1983–4. As housing minister initiated the most rapid and extensive expansion of Jewish settlements in the occupied territories, with the approval of Yitzhak Shamir, the Prime Minister. In the middle of 1991 Sharon predicted that suburban Jerusalem would one day cover the twenty miles to Jericho, the Palestinian town in the Jordan valley.

Shevardnaze, Eduard (1928–): Foreign Minister of the Soviet Union, 1985–91. Visited Middle East in February 1989 and suggested that Bush administration was prevaricating.

Shishakli, Adib (1909–64): President of Syria, 1953–4. Born in Hama and served with the special troops organized by the French during the mandate. Fought in the Arab volunteer force during the First Arab–Israeli War and then returned to Syrian army. Led military coups in December 1949 and November 1951. Though effectively ruling behind the scenes, he only assumed power officially in June 1953 when elected President in a referendum. Maintained stability in Syria through autocratic rule. Supported the West. Forced to resign after a coup on 25 February 1954.

Shukairy, Ahmad (1907–80): Chairman of the Palestine Liberation Organization, 1964–9. Born in Acre of a Muslim religious family. Trained as a lawyer. Member of the Arab Higher Committee, 1946. Member of the Syrian delegation to the United Nations, 1949–50. Under-Secretary for the political affairs of the Arab League, 1951–7. Saudi Arabian Ambassador to the United Nations, 1957–62. Nasser secured his appointment as Palestinian representative to the meeting of the heads of thirteen Arab states in Cairo on 13 January 1964, at which Shukairy proposed the establishment of a Palestinian national 'entity'. In May 1964 Shukairy called a Palestine conference in Jerusalem, attended by all the Arab foreign ministers, and formed the Palestine Liberation Organization.

Shultz, George Pratt (1920–): United States Secretary of State, 1982–9. Suggested an international conference on the Middle East, 1986–7. Banned Arafat's entry into the United States in 1988 on grounds that he was an accessory to terrorism.

Sidki, Ismail (1875–1950): Prime Minister of Egypt, 1930–3, 1946. A supporter of Saad Zaghlul but left the Wafd Party and founded the People's Party. As Prime Minister he tried to strengthen the monarchy. A member of the delegation that signed the Anglo–Egyptian Treaty of 1936. In 1946 achieved agreement with Britain on the evacuation of British forces from Egypt, but it was not ratified because of disagreements over the issue of Sudanese self-determination.

Sieff, Israel Moses (Baron) (1889–1972): founder member of Manchester School of Zionism, 1906. Joined Marks and Spencer Ltd (British and later international retail chain) in 1915. Secretary of Zionist Commission, 1918. President Anglo–Israel Chamber of Commerce, 1950–65. President of Marks and Spencer, 1967–72.

Stack, Lee (Sir) (1868–1924): Governor-General of Sudan and Commander-in-Chief of the Egyptian army, 1917–24. His assassination in Cairo led to a crisis in Anglo–Egyptian relations.

Stein, Leonard (1887–1973): Honorary Legal Adviser to the Jewish Agency for Palestine, 1929–39. Drafted what became known as Ramsay MacDonald's 'Black Letter', reversing the British policy in Palestine outlined in the Passfield White Paper. Wrote *The Balfour Declaration* (1961).

Stern, Abraham (1907–42): leader of the Stern Gang, 1940–2. Emigrated from Poland to Palestine in 1925 and later joined the Irgun. Broke with Irgun in 1940 over that organization's policy of co-operating with British in war effort, and formed the extremist Stern Gang, which attacked British army personnel and tried to reach an accommodation with the Axis powers. Killed by a British policeman in 1942.

Strauss, Robert Schwarz (1918–): Chairman of Democratic Party, 1972–7. Appointed by Carter as special negotiator to implement the Camp David accords in 1978.

Sulh, Riyad al- (1894–1951): Prime Minister of Lebanon, 1943–5, 1946–51. Born into a Sunni family. Studied law in Beirut and Istanbul. Part of Feisal's Arab administration in Damascus in 1918. In 1943 reached agreement with Maronite Christian leader al-Khuri on the National Pact which tried to establish an equilibrium between Christians and Muslims.

Tall, Wasif al- (1920–71): Prime Minister of Jordan, 1962–3, 1965–7, 1970–1. Educated at the American University of Beirut. Served in the British army during the Second World War. Fought in the Arab volunteer and the Syrian armies during the First Arab–Israeli War. Jordanian Ambassador to Iraq, 1961–2. Opposed Nasser and during his final premiership remained loyal to King Hussein and drove out the Palestinians after the civil war. Assassinated by Palestinian terrorists.

Thani, Khalifa ibn Hamad Al (1932–): Ruler of Qatar, 1972– . After serving as Director of Police and Internal Security, Director of

Education, Minister of Finance and Petroleum Affairs, Prime Minister and Deputy Ruler, overthrew his cousin Sheikh Ahmad ibn Ali Al Thani in February 1972. Established Advisory Council and instituted social and economic reforms. Supported Iraq in Iran–Iraq War. Condemned Saddam Hussein's invasion of Kuwait.

Thatcher, Margaret Hilda (Baroness) (1925–): Prime Minister of the United Kingdom, 1979–90. In September 1985, at a banquet in Amman, Mrs Thatcher spoke of a peace settlement taking into account the legitimate rights of the Palestinians. She later invited two members of the Executive Committee of the PLO to London to see the Foreign Secretary. After pressure from Washington, following the *Achille Lauro* incident, Britain asked the PLO members to sign a statement committing themselves to oppose all forms of terrorism, and the meeting was cancelled. In 1989, implied that Shamir's plan for elections in the occupied territories if the intifada stopped was not enough. In 1990 sent troops to Saudi Arabia as a reaction to Saddam Hussein's occupation of Kuwait.

Tlass, Mustafa al- (1932–): First Deputy Prime Minister of Syria (Defence), 1984– . Born near Homs, a Sunni Muslim, educated at Military Academy. Chief of Staff and Deputy Minister of Defence, 1968–72. Led Syrian forces in the October War.

Truman, Harry S. (1884–1972): President of the United States, 1945–53 (Democrat). In March 1943 in charge of a presidential committee that reported that future United States demand for oil was likely to be in excess of domestic production. In February 1944 recorded that he was willing to help fight for a Jewish homeland in Palestine. In June 1945 sent Earl G. Harrison to investigate the condition of displaced persons in Europe. Ignored Harrison's recommendation that reasonable numbers of Jewish refugees should be allowed into the United States, and instead wrote to Clement Attlee, the British Prime Minister, on 31 August recommending that Britain implement Harrison's recommendations and admit 100,000 Jewish refugees to Palestine. Truman's concern was the mayoral election in New York and the effect of the Zionist lobby. These concerns dominated his policy towards Palestine: his public endorsement on 30 April 1946 of only those sections of the Anglo–American commission of enquiry's recommendations favourable to Zionism; his rejection of the Morrison–Grady plan on 31 July 1946; his statement on 4 October 1946 that a solution along the lines of partition originally proposed by the Jewish Agency on 5 August would 'command the support of public opinion in the

United States'. Probably personally involved in securing success of partition vote in General Assembly in November 1947. When told Palestine not an electoral consideration, allowed State Department to take over policy January–February 1948, but after Democratic setback in New York election in February 1948 and change of advice on presidential election, took over Palestine policy again; on 14 May 1948 recognized the State of Israel. Truman resisted Soviet moves in the Middle East in March 1946 in Iran and Turkey, and again during the Dardanelles crisis in the middle of 1946, over which he was prepared to go to war. Moved towards taking over British responsibilities in Greece and Turkey with the Truman Doctrine of 1947.

Vance, Cyrus Robert (1917–): United States Secretary of State, 1977–80. Considered depriving the Palestinians of rights as contrary to moral and ethical principles.

Wagner, Robert (1910–91): Democratic Senator for New York and head of the American Palestine Committee (later the American Christian Palestine Committee), 1943–8. Influential in securing Roosevelt's support for a Jewish Commonwealth in 1944, and Truman's rejection of the Morrison–Grady plan in July 1946.

Waldegrave, William Arthur (1946–): British Minister of State at the Foreign Office, 1988–90. Made first British contact with PLO when he met Arafat in Tunisia on 13 January 1989. Compared terrorism of PLO with Shamir's Stern Gang and its assassination of Lord Moyne in Cairo in November 1944.

Weinberger, Caspar Willard (1917–): United States Secretary of Defense, 1981–7. In February 1982 visited Saudi Arabia, Oman and Jordan, and afterwards hinted that Washington might redirect its military support away from Israel and towards the Arabs. Drew analogies between Israel's action in the Lebanon in 1982 and the Argentinian invasion of the Falklands.

Weizmann, Chaim (1874–1952): President of Israel, 1948–52. Born in Russia. Attended university in Berlin. Influenced by Asher Ginsberg (Ahad Ha'Am) who saw Palestine as focus for the renaissance of Judaism, based on the positive love of Zion. Chose to settle in Britain as the country likely to sympathize with the Zionist movement. While researching in chemistry at Manchester University founded the Manchester School of Zionism. Visited Palestine in 1907 and decided that what was necessary was practical work, particularly in the field of colonization in Palestine. Guided the British Palestine Committee, formed in April 1916, to relate Zionist aspirations to the British war effort, and lobbied for Balfour Declaration. Led Zionist commission to Palestine in 1918, and met Feisal. Principal Zionist speaker at Paris peace conference, 1919. In 1930 helped to secure rejection of the Passfield White Paper and the change of British policy in Palestine reflected in Ramsay MacDonald's letter of 13 February 1931. In a speech at Tel Aviv on 23 April 1936 called the Arab–Zionist struggle one between the forces of the desert and destruction on the one side, and the forces of civilization and building on the other. In May 1942, at the American Zionist Conference in the Biltmore Hotel in New York, Weizmann's programme of demanding a 'Jewish commonwealth' in the whole of Western Palestine was adopted. After that, Weizmann's gradualist programme was replaced by the activist one of Ben-Gurion. On 19 November 1947 influential in securing Truman's support for inclusion of Negev in Zionist section under partition plan. On 18 March 1948 impressed on Truman the need for future Jewish state of the Negev area. No place reserved for Weizmann's signature on scroll proclaiming the State of Israel.

Weizmann, Ezer (1924–): President of Israel, 1993– ; Israeli Minister of Defence, 1977–80. Nephew of Chaim Weizmann. Attended Royal Air Force Staff College. Officer in Israeli airforce, 1948–66. Shot down five RAF planes during First Arab–Israeli War. Chief General Staff Branch, 1966–8. Minister of Transport, 1969–70. Influential in securing concessions from Begin at Camp David. Wanted moderate policy on West Bank and resigned from Begin's Cabinet on this issue. Minister of Communications, 1984–8. Minister of Science and Development, 1988–90. Head of Yahad party in National Unity Government, 1984–9. Resigned as minister after revalations by Shamir that he had broken the law by meeting a Palestine Liberation Official in Geneva.

Wilson, Arnold Talbot (Sir) (1884–1940): Acting Civil Commissioner for Mesopotamia, 1918–20. In charge of civil administration during the rebellion in Iraq when British authority broke down. The rebellion followed the destruction of the Arab dream of a free Arab confederacy under Feisal with the announcement of the mandate system. Quelling the revolt cost £40 million and 2,000 casualties. Wilson recommended that Feisal should head an Arab administration in Iraq.

Wilson, (James) Harold (Wilson of Rievaulx, Baron) (1916–95): British Prime Minister, 1964–70, 1974–6. Attributed his Zionism to upbringing based on Old Testament Christianity. During Six-Day War showed 'unembarrassed sympathy' with Israel. After resignation wrote *The Chariot of Israel, Britain, America, and the State of Israel* (1981).

Wilson, Woodrow (1856–1924): President of the United States, 1912–19 (Democrat). Shown the Milner–Amery draft of the Balfour Declaration and agreed to it, but insisted that his approval should not be mentioned. The twelfth of his Fourteen Points outlined to Congress on 8 January 1918 stated that the Turkish portions of the Ottoman Empire needed sovereignty, but the other nationalities 'should be assured an undoubted security of life and an unmolested opportunity of autonomous development'. Disregarded the report of the King–Crane Commission and in Palestine found an exception to his interest in self-determination.

Wingate, Orde Charles (1903–44): a British army captain and a proponent of Zionism. During the Arab rebellion of 1936–9 led 'special night squads' of mixed British and Zionist units against the rebels, and to protect the Iraq Petroleum Company's pipeline. His methods were ruthless and to the Arabs this appeared an alliance between Britain and the Zionists.

Woodhouse, Christopher Montague (1917–): Served in British Embassy in Tehran, 1951, and in the Foreign Office in 1952. Planned with American Central Intelligence Agency the coup that overthrew Mossadeq.

Yafi, Abdullah al- (1901–): Prime Minister of Lebanon, 1938–9, 1951–2, 1953–4, 1956, 1966, 1968–9. A Sunni, he studied law in Paris. Minister of Justice, 1946–7. An ally of Chamoun until the Suez Crisis of 1956, after which he urged that Lebanon become part of an Arab alignment under Egypt. Minister of Defence, February–October, 1968. Minister of Social Affairs, 1968–9. Minister of Education, 1968–9.

Yahya Hamid al-Din (1869–1948): Imam of Yemen, 1904–48. A younger son of a Zeidi family. Achieved autonomy for the sect under nominal Turkish sovereignty in 1911, and secured independence for Yemen in 1918. In a war with Saudi Arabia over the Asir region in 1934 he lost. An opponent of modernization he tried to keep Yemen free from outside influences.

Yahya (Al-Tikriti), Tahir (1915–): Prime Minister of Iraq, 1963–5, 1967–8. Born in Tikrit in northern Iraq, he served as an army officer. Helped to plan coup of 1958. Director-General of Police, 1958–9. Dismissed after taking part in pro-Nasser meeting. A leader of the coup of February 1963 which overthrew Kassem. Chief of Staff, Iraqi army, 1963–5. Vice President of Iraq, May 1967. Imprisoned for political reasons in April 1969.

Yamani, Ahmad Zaki (1930–): Minister of Petroleum and Mineral Resources in Saudi Arabia, 1962–86. Born in Mecca. Read law at Harvard. Legal adviser to the Council of Ministers, 1958–60. Secretary-General of the Organization of Arab Petroleum Exporting Countries (OAPEC), 1968–9. President of the Supreme Consultative Council for Petroleum and Mineral Affairs, 1975. The leading force behind the Organization of Petroleum Exporting Countries (OPEC), in 1973 used to pass messages to Americans that unless the United States took steps to secure justice for the Palestinian Arabs and the restoration to Muslims of Jerusalem's holy places, the increased Saudi oil production would stop. Regarded as a son by King Feisal, but sacked by King Fuad in 1986 when oil prices fell to lowest for six years. It has been claimed that Yamani was used as a scapegoat.

Young, Andrew (1932–): United States Permanent Representative at the United Nations, 1977–9. In September 1979 met the PLO observer to the United Nations. After Israeli protests, Young resigned, stating that the American refusal to talk to the PLO was ridiculous.

Zaghlul, Saad (1860–1927): Prime Minister of Egypt, 1924. Came from a fellahin family in the Delta region of Egypt. Trained as a lawyer. In 1906 appointed Minister of Education and then Justice. Led the delegation (*wafd*) demanding Egyptian independence in November 1918. The Wafd Party emerged from this. In August 1920 Zaghlul and the Milner mission agreed in London that although Egypt would become an independent constitutional monarchy, it would be bound by a treaty of alliance with Britain. Britain would be allowed to station troops in Egypt, and the British High Commissioner would remain pre-eminent in Cairo. Zaghlul organized a political crisis in Egypt, and on 8 January 1922 the Residency in Cairo accepted a deal whereby an Egyptian ministry would be formed, provided Britain recognized Egyptian independence. The murder of Sir Lee Stack by Egyptian nationalists effectively led to the fall of Zaghlul in Egypt.

Zahedi, Fazullah (Major General) (1890–1963): Prime Minister of Iran, 1953–5. Born in Hamadan and educated at the military academy in Tehran. Arrested by the British in 1942 as a Nazi sympathizer. Chief of Police, 1949. Minister of the Interior, 1950–1. Led the coup in 1953 which overthrew Mossadeq and restored the Shah. Permanent Representative to the Geneva Offices of the United Nations, 1960–3.

Zaim, Husni al- (*c.* 1896–1949): President of Syria, 1949. Born in Aleppo of a Kurdish family. Detained by British in Syria in 1941 as had remained loyal to Vichy. Commander-in-Chief of Syrian army, 1948. After organizing the military coup of 30 March 1949 he was elected President, but before he was able to carry through a programme of reform he was overthrown by Colonel Sami Hinnawi on 14 August 1949.

Pledges, treaties, alliances, settlements, reports, plans, and United Nations resolutions

Alexandria Protocol (1944) A document that emerged from a meeting of seven Arab states – Egypt, Transjordan, Iraq, Syria, Lebanon, Saudi Arabia and Yemen – and a representative of the Palestinian Arabs in Cairo late in 1944, envisaging a commonwealth of Arab states as a league of independent and sovereign states rather than as a federation.

Algiers Agreement (1975) Signed between Iran and Iraq: in return for Iran's stopping its support of the Kurds, Iraq would accept a new frontier in the Shatt al-Arab, the Thalweg Line, the international frontier being the line of maximum depth not the eastern low-water mark.

Anglo–American Commission of Enquiry (1946) Recommended in April 1946 that 100,000 immigration certificates should be issued immediately to Jewish war refugees from Europe wanting to go to Palestine. Referred to Palestine as continuing under the prevailing British mandate until a trusteeship agreement under the United Nations could be applied. Neither race to dominate the other in the envisaged state, and government to be based on equal rather than proportional representation. Palestine would become neither an Arab nor a Jewish state.

Anglo–American Convention of 1925 An agreement that United States consent was necessary for any modifications to the mandate for Palestine which affected American interests.

Anglo–Egyptian Treaty of 1936 In effect did not lessen Britain's power or prestige in Egypt. While British occupation formally came to an end, British troops remained in the country, though provision was made for their gradual withdrawal to the Suez Canal Zone and Sinai, and a limit of 10,000 land forces and 400 air personnel. In the event of war, Britain had the right of reoccupation and the unrestricted use of Egyptian roads, ports and airports. The Condominium Agreement of 1899 was reaffirmed, but Britain remained the predominant power, Egypt having only a share in the higher administration and judicial posts of the Sudan government.

Anglo–Egyptian Treaty of 1954 Signed on 19 October 1954. Britain agreed to give up its rights to the Suez base and to evacuate the Canal Zone within twenty months.

Anglo–Iraqi Treaty (30 June 1930) Under treaty Iraq formally achieved independence but was bound to have 'full and frank consultations with Great Britain in all matters of foreign policy'.

Anglo–Jordanian Treaty (22 May 1946) Britain recognized the independence of Transjordan and entered into an alliance with the new state.

Anglo–Jordanian Treaty (15 March 1948) Gave the appearance of an arrangement between equals and established a joint defence board responsible for external and strategic planning. Abrogated by Jordan in 1957.

Anglo–Soviet Treaty (29 January 1942) Guaranteed independence of Iran.

Baghdad Pact (1955) A defence treaty, the Pact of Mutual Co-operation, between Iraq and Turkey was signed on 24 February. Britain, Pakistan and Iran joined in 1955. Opposed by Nasser. The United States joined the military committee in March 1957. Iraq withdrew in March 1959 after the coup of July 1958. In 1959 what was left of the alliance was renamed the Central Treaty Organization (CENTO).

Balfour Declaration of 1917 On 31 October 1917 the British War Cabinet authorized the Foreign Secretary, James Arthur Balfour, to make a declaration of sympathy with Zionist aims: 'His Majesty's Government views with favour the establishment in Palestine of a national home for the Jewish people, and will use its best endeavours to facilitate the achievement of this object, it being clearly understood that nothing shall be done which may prejudice the civil and religious rights of existing non-Jewish communities in Palestine, or the rights and political status enjoyed by Jews in any other country.'

The letter was sent on 2 November from Balfour to Lord Rothschild. Care was taken to amend the original Zionist draft by Harry Sacher and Nahum Sokolow. Lord Milner, possibly influenced by warnings from Gertrude Bell (the Assistant Political Officer in Baghdad) that neither Arabs nor Muslims would accept Jewish authority, insisted on guarantees for existing non-Jewish communities in Palestine. Balfour told the War Cabinet on 31 October that a declaration in favour of Zionism would help propaganda in Russia and the United States for the war effort. Scientific development could enable Palestine to sustain a larger population. By 'National home' Balfour understood some form of British, American and other protectorate enabling Jews to build up 'a real centre of national culture and focus of national life'.

Biltmore Programme (May 1942) The endorsement by the Extraordinary Zionist Conference, meeting at the Biltmore Hotel in New York, of the declaration that Palestine should be established as a Jewish Commonwealth. Shortly after the conference, the Zionist movement furthered the programme by changing its tactics from working on the British government to using electoral 'blackmail' in the United States, and moving from 'gradualism' to 'activism'.

Cairo Agreement (November 1969) Signed between Lebanon and the Palestine Liberation Organization, outlining the principles of Palestinian residence in Lebanon.

Camp David accords (1978) On 17 September President Carter announced on American television that he had witnessed the sign-ing of two basic documents by Anwar el-Sadat of Egypt and Menachem Begin of Israel. In one, the two leaders undertook to conclude a peace treaty within three months which would provide for an Israeli withdrawal from Sinai and the normalization of relations between Egypt and Israel. The other, The Framework for Peace in the Middle East, designated United Nations Resolution 242 as its basis, and stated that Egypt, Israel, Jordan and the representatives of the Palestinian people should participate in the resolution of the Palestinian problem. A Palestinian self-governing authority, freely elected by the inhabitants of the West Bank, would exercise autonomy. As soon as possible, but not later than in the third year after the beginning of the transitional period, negotiations should start to determine the final status of the West Bank and Gaza and to conclude a peace treaty between Israel and Jordan. The security of Israel should be maintained during this time, and the refugee problem resolved. These 'framework' agreements were supplemented by letters exchanged by Carter, Sadat and Begin, mentioning the need for Knesset approval for the dismantling of Israeli settlements in the Sinai and covering the different treatment of Jerusalem by the three parties. In a separate letter from Harold Brown to Ezer Weizman, the United States undertook to help relocate Israeli air bases from the Sinai to Israeli territory.

Central Treaty Organization (CENTO) Name given to Baghdad Pact in August 1959 after Iraq's withdrawal in March 1959. As Pakistan moved towards the Soviet Union the original political intention receded, and CENTO concentrated more on economic planning and co-ordination.

Culbertson Mission Report (1944) William S. Culbertson led a special United States economic mission to the Middle East late in 1944.

In his report of 15 November he warned that, until it was settled, the Palestine question would remain a serious menace to the peace and security of the Middle East. The situation injured American prestige among the Arabs. 'Perhaps the price the United States pays for the privilege to hold its widely publicized views on the Jewish state is worth all it costs. The Mission wishes only to emphasize that the price is considerable and that apparently the American people do not realize how considerable it is.' The Culbertson report was highly influential in determining State Department policy towards the Middle East.

Egyptian–Israeli Peace Treaty of 1979 President Carter succeeded in getting Sadat and Begin to sign on 26 March 1979, in Washington, a peace treaty between Egypt and Israel which generally followed the provisions of the Camp David framework.

European Economic Community (EEC) On 29 June 1977 leaders of the EEC endorsed the creation of a homeland for the Palestinians. In 1979 the EEC formally criticized Israeli policy and mentioned, for the first time, the role of the Palestine Liberation Organization (PLO). At the Venice meeting on 13 June 1980, the EEC issued a statement that the Palestinian people had to be allowed to exercise fully its right to self-determination, and that the PLO should be associated with the negotiations.

Fahd Plan (August 1981) A Middle East peace plan suggested by Crown Prince Fahd of Saudi Arabia which indicated that Saudi Arabia might recognize Israel in return for withdrawal from the occupied territories and the setting up of an independent Palestinian state. Rejected by Menachem Begin as being intended to destroy Israel.

Feisal–Weizmann Agreement (1919) While visiting Palestine as head of the Zionist commission, Chaim Weizmann met Feisal, the future King of Iraq, near Aqaba on 4 June 1918. Feisal insisted that, as an Arab, he refused to consider Palestine as a British protectorate, or an area for Jewish colonization. While at the peace conference in Paris in January 1919, Feisal signed an agreement with Weizmann for Zionist money and financial advice in return for allowing the Zionists the right to enter Palestine and to settle even beyond its borders. But Feisal changed Weizmann's phrases 'Jewish state' and 'Jewish government' to 'Palestine' and 'Palestinian Government', and added a codicil to the document in effect making all this conditional on the Arabs attaining their independence. This codicil was abbreviated and misleadingly translated by T.E. Lawrence, who omitted 'independence'.

Fez Plan (9 September 1982) Emerged from an Arab summit meeting at Fez in Morocco. Almost identical to the Fahd Plan of 1981. Called for the creation of a Palestinian state in the occupied territories. Also implicitly recognized Israel's right to exist.

Franco–Lebanese Treaty (13 November 1936) Lebanon given considerable autonomy.

Franco–Syrian Treaty of Friendship and Alliance (1936) An agreement that the French mandate would end within three years. Syria to be admitted to the League of Nations. Alexandretta, the Druze and the Alawi territories were included in the state with special status (limited autonomy). Lebanon to maintain its individuality.

Hope Simpson Report (1930) Sir John Hope Simpson was sent to Palestine to investigate the land question. He reported that the amount of cultivated land in Palestine was considerably less than that estimated by the Zionists and the Commissioner of Lands. This land was not even sufficient to provide the Arab population with a decent livelihood. Pending development, there was no more room for Jewish settlers. This report formed the basis of the 1930 Passfield White Paper, which intimated immigration restrictions.

Hussein–McMahon Correspondence (1915–16) Ten letters exchanged between Hussein, the Sherif of Mecca, and Sir Henry McMahon, the British High Commissioner in Egypt, between 14 July 1915 and 30 March 1916. They negotiated the terms under which there might be a defensive and conditionally offensive alliance, under which Britain might undertake to assist the Arabs regain their freedom in return for the Arabs raising a revolt against Turkish rule. There was later debate as to whether Palestine had been excluded from the area designated for Arab independence, and in 1939 Britain published a parliamentary paper on the matter.

Israeli–Palestine Liberation Organization Accord (13 September 1993) (Oslo Accord) (Washington Accord) After secret talks in Norway between Israeli and Palestine Liberation Organization officials, a deal was initialled in Oslo in August 1993. Following Yasser Arafat's renunciation of violence and recognition of Israel's right to exist in peace and security, the accord, called the Declaration of Principles, was signed in Washington by Mahmud Abbas, the second-in-command of the Palestine Liberation Organization, and Shimon Peres, the Israeli Foreign Minister. The Declaration of Principles outlined the provisions for Palestinian self-rule for the Gaza Strip and Jericho on the West Bank, and for Israeli sovereignty over the Jewish settlements in the occupied territories, as an interim stage, with negotiations on permanent settlement to follow after two years. The talks on permanent settlement, including the status of East Jerusalem, were scheduled to start by 13 December 1995, and the permanent settlement was to take effect from 13 December 1999.

Jedda, Treaty of (1927) Britain acknowledged Ibn Saud as King of Hejaz and Nejd.

Jordanian–Israeli Peace Treaty (26 October 1994) Established the Jordanian–Israeli border along the lines demarcated at the time of the British mandate in 1922. In return for financial aid from the United States, Jordan conceded that the Palestinian refugees would be settled where they were in Jordan, in effect denying the right of the Palestinian refugees in Jordan to return home. Jordan's custodianship of the Muslim holy places in East Jerusalem was recognized.

King–Crane Commission (28 August 1919) A commission headed by two Americans, Charles R. Crane and Henry C. King, sent to Palestine to determine the wishes of the inhabitants as to a mandatory power. It reported Syrian opposition to a French mandate, and warned that the Zionist programme would have to be modified if the civil and religious rights of the non-Jewish inhabitants of Palestine were to be protected in terms of the Balfour Declaration.

Lausanne, Treaty of (24 July 1923) Followed negotiations between Turkey and Britain, France, Italy, Japan, Greece, Yugoslavia, and Romania. Turkey renounced its claims over the non-Turkish provinces of the former Ottoman Empire. Turkish sovereignty over Anatolia was reconfirmed, and in a separate agreement with Greece, an exchange of population between the two countries was arranged. A Convention of the Straits covering freedom of navigation for merchant vessels and warships under certain restrictions was also added to the treaty.

Lebanese–Syrian Treaty of Brotherhood, Co-operation and Co-ordination (May 1991) Outlined terms of co-operation between Lebanon and Syria, including the proviso that the two countries should not be a source of threat to one another's security. The treaty made provision for the formation of a Lebanese–Syrian military committee to decide on the number of Syrian troops in Lebanon and how long they would stay.

Lloyd George–Clemenceau Agreement (1 December 1918) Clemenceau apparently agreed to Britain's attaching Mosul to Iraq, and to Palestine being under British control. France would have a share in the oil resources from Mosul and have full control over areas of Syria.

Lowdermilk Plan (1944) A scheme, outlined in the book *Palestine – Land of Promise* by Dr Walter C. Lowdermilk of the United States Bureau of Agriculture, to use the waters of the Jordan river for irrigation and hydroelectric power. Favoured by Zionists at the beginning of 1945, it was later developed into the Johnson Plan.

Middle East Defence Organization (MEDO) An attempt, against the background of the joining of the Cold War, by the Western powers to align the Middle East countries against the Soviet Union in a multilateral defence pact. Arising out of the concept of a Middle East Defence Command, largely initiated by Britain, it foundered when Egypt refused to join at the end of 1951. It pointed to the formation of the Baghdad Pact in 1955.

Montreux Convention (20 July 1936) Replaced the agreement on the Dardanelles and the Straits of the Bosphorous, appended to the Treaty of Lausanne. The Montreux Convention was signed by Britain, France, the Soviet Union, Bulgaria, Greece, Romania, Yugoslavia, Australia, Japan and Turkey, and gave Turkey the right to remilitarize the Straits, and ban enemy ships when at war, or if it felt threatened, to allow the passage of foreign ships at its discretion.

Morrison–Grady Plan (July 1946) A scheme initially devised separately by Sir Douglas Harris of the Colonial Office and William Yale of the State Department for a trusteeship of Palestine. It envisaged provincial autonomy, with Palestine as neither an Arab nor a Jewish state. Accepted by the Anglo–American Cabinet Committee meeting in London in July 1946, and initially endorsed by Truman, it was later killed by the American President as a result of Zionist blackmail over the forthcoming American congressional elections (threats of using the Zionist vote). Britain tried to pursue the plan on its own, but Bevin's attempt to get the Arabs and Zionists to the talks was scotched by Truman's Day of Atonement speech of 4 October 1946, endorsing, in effect, the Zionist solution.

Mudros Armistice (1918) Marked capitulation of Turkey at the end of the First World War.

North Atlantic Treaty Organization (NATO) Established on 4 April 1949 it has one Middle Eastern member, Turkey.

Passfield White Paper (1930) A British parliamentary paper based on Sir John Hope Simpson's report on the land question in Palestine. It implied that the land was insufficient to provide the Arab population with a decent living, and that as there was a Jewish national home in Palestine Britain had fulfilled the Balfour Declaration. Further immigration into Palestine would affect the rights of the existing inhabitants.

Peel Commission Report (1936) Report of the Royal Commission that went to Palestine in 1936 to investigate the rebellion. It recommended that Palestine be divided into three parts: an Arab state; a Jewish state; and then certain areas of strategic or religious importance that would remain under a British mandate. As the Jewish state would include the best land, the report recommended that it should pay an annual subvention to the Arab state. A source of the idea of partition as a solution to the Palestine problem. Recommendations effectively rejected by Malcolm MacDonald's White Paper of 1939.

Portsmouth, Treaty of (15 January 1948) A draft treaty between Britain and Iraq to replace the Anglo–Iraqi Treaty of 1930 and to establish the relationship between the two countries on an equal footing. British air bases were to be handed to Iraq and strategic interests considered by a joint defence board. Demonstrations in Iraq led to the treaty's repudiation.

Reagan Plan (1 September 1982) Envisaged the restoration to the Arabs of the territories occupied by Israel in 1967. At the same time rejected a Palestinian state, and proposed instead self-government for the Palestinians in association with Jordan. Plan rejected by Israel, which then renewed its programme of settlements on the West Bank.

Red Line Agreement (1928) Partners in the Turkish Petroleum Company agreed not to secure separate concessions in the Asian lands of the Ottoman Empire, apart from Kuwait and the Khanaqin district in Iraq.

Resolution 242 (United Nations) (22 November 1967) At a time of waning enthusiasm for Israel's occupation of Arab lands, the

United Nations Security Council passed Resolution 242. This was a triumph for British diplomacy. The Americans told the British delegation that they could only accept a resolution that had Israeli endorsement. Under this pressure Lord Caradon, the British delegate, changed his draft to stipulate that the United Nations representative would merely have to 'promote agreement between the states of the region'. This gave Israel the necessary assurance, and the ambiguities of the wording provided the necessary loopholes for both sides. Resolution 242 provided for a 'just and lasting peace' within 'secure and recognized boundaries'; Israel was to withdraw 'from territories occupied in the recent conflict' and there was to be an acknowledgement of all states' 'sovereignty, territorial integrity and political independence'. The Arab states and the Soviet Union failed in an attempt to include withdrawal from 'all' the occupied territories. The Soviet Union and India supported the resolution on the understanding that the withdrawal envisaged was from all the territories. For many years the Palestinians rejected Resolution 242, as they argued that it implied a Palestinian recognition of Israel without reciprocal recognition. In November 1988, however, the Palestine National Council endorsed Resolution 242 at the same time as affirming Palestinian national rights.

Resolution 338 (United Nations) (22 October 1973) The October War secured serious Israeli security negotiations on the basis of Resolution 242. The Security Council Resolution 338 called for the implementation, after the cease-fire, of Resolution 242 'in all of its parts', and decided on 'negotiations between the parties concerned under appropriate auspices, aimed at establishing a just and durable peace in the Middle East'.

Resolution 598 (United Nations) (July 1987) Urged cease-fire between Iran and Iraq. Did not unambiguously condemn Iraq for the outbreak of war in 1980. Required protagonists to withdraw to national boundaries. Accepted by Iran on 18 July 1988. Cease-fire came into force on 20 August 1988.

Resolution 660 (United Nations) (2 August 1990) Security Council found that the invasion of Kuwait on 2 August 1990 constituted a breach of international peace. It condemned the invasion, demanded that Iraq withdraw immediately and unconditionally all its forces to the positions in which they were located on 1 August 1990, called upon Iraq and Kuwait immediately to begin intensive negotiations for the resolution of their differences. It supported all efforts in this regard, and especially those of the Arab League, and decided to meet again as necessary to consider further steps to ensure compliance with this resolution.

Resolution 678 (United Nations) (29 November 1990) Authorized all member states 'to use all necessary means' to implement Resolution 660 and subsequent resolutions on Kuwait if Iraq failed to withdraw from Kuwait by 15 January 1991.

Resolution 686 (United Nations) (2 March 1991) Security Council demanded that Iraq accept the previous twelve relevant resolutions referring to the Iraqi occupation of Kuwait, release all civilian detainees, and in terms of international law accept liability for the damage done to Kuwait.

Restitution Agreement (10 September 1952) Negotiations for an agreement between Israel and the Federal Republic of Germany initiated by Dr Nahum Goldmann and pursued by Moshe Sharett. The Federal Republic of Germany undertook to pay Israel to help resettle Jewish refugees from Germany in recognition for the 'unspeakable criminal acts' perpetrated against the Jewish people by the Nazis. Begin and the Herut party opposed the measure, as they believed that there should be no contact with the Germans.

Rhodes, Armistice of (24 February 1949) Signed between Egypt and Israel. Agreement to cease hostilities at the end of First Arab–Israeli War.

Rogers Plan (1969) Plan published on 9 December by William Rogers, the United States Secretary of State, as a solution to the Arab–Israeli conflict. Both sides had to make concessions: the United States did not support expansionism, and boundary modifications had to be confined to 'insubstantial alternatives required for mutual security'. Proposals rejected by Israeli Cabinet. On 23 July 1970 Nasser accepted Rogers's proposal for a cease-fire. After a Cabinet crisis Israel did the same, but reiterated its rejection of the Rogers Plan.

Saadabad Pact (8 July 1937) Treaty of non-aggression signed between Turkey, Iran, Iraq and Afghanistan. Against the background of increasing international tension, the four countries hoped to improve relations between themselves, encouraged by the West. The treaty, however, amounted to little and the council it established never met after the outbreak of the Second World War.

San Remo Conference (April 1920) The leading allied powers, – Britain, France, Italy, Japan, Greece and Belgium – decided the future of the Middle East. The form of the mandates was first to be decided by Britain and France, and then submitted to the League of Nations. The mandates for Syria and Lebanon were allotted to France, and those for Palestine and Mesopotamia to Britain. The mandatory power in Palestine was to implement the Balfour Declaration. At the same time, Britain and France agreed on French interests in oil rights in Iraq.

Seeb, Agreement of (1920) Made between Sultan Taimur and the people of Oman. Attempted to re-establish the Sultan's authority over government, trade, and movement between the tribal interior, and trading communities, Muscat and Sohar, on the coast.

Sèvres, Treaty of (10 August 1920) Signed between the Ottoman Empire and its opponents from the First World War. Dismembered the Ottoman Empire and Anatolia. The treaty was never ratified.

Shaw Commission Headed by Sir Walter Shaw, a British jurist and administrator. Went to Palestine to investigate the reasons for Arab unrest in 1929, and reported in March 1930 that Zionist demands on immigration had aroused Arab apprehension about Jewish political domination. Shaw thought the Zionist demands a breach of the principle, accepted by the Zionist Organization of 1922, that immigration should be regulated by the economic capacity of Palestine to absorb the new arrivals.

Shamir Plan (1989) In initial form originated by Yitzhak Rabin, and discussed through an intermediary with the leadership of the Palestine Liberation Organization: if the intifada stopped, there could be elections in the occupied territories. Similar to one developed by a presidential study group in Washington. In May, however, Yitzhak Shamir rejected the idea of exchanging land for peace.

Shtaura Agreement (July 1977) An attempt by the Syrian and Lebanese governments and the Palestine Liberation Organization to regulate Palestinian camps and to introduce a reconstituted Lebanese army into the south border area.

Shultz Plan (February 1988) Outlined by Richard Murphy, United States Assistant Under-Secretary of State, on a shuttle tour of the Middle East between 5 and 11 February 1988: Israel and a joint Jordanian/Palestinian delegation to decide on a form of interim autonomy for the occupied territories; the Israeli military to withdraw from the West Bank and municipal elections for Palestinian officials to be held in 1989; an interim conference to be held, though it would have no power to impose a solution; a settlement envisaged within three years. George Shultz saw leaders in the Middle East at the end of February. Shimon Peres had reservations but endorsed the plan. Yitzhak Shamir rejected it as impracticable, and warned that pressure to implement it could lead to a general election in Israel which the Likud might win outright. As there was no provision for a Palestinian state the plan was rejected by the Palestine Liberation Organization, and the leadership of the intifada dismissed it as a ruse to stem the growth of a world-wide sympathy for the rights of the Palestinians.

Sykes–Picot Agreement (May–October 1916) Initially a plan agreed by British and French officials, envisaging an Arab confederation in which France would have economic priority in the north and Britain in the south. In an area along the Syrian coast, France, and at the head of the Persian Gulf, Britain, could establish such direct and indirect administration as they desired. Britain took the ports of Haifa and Acre in Palestine, and Mosul fell within the French region of economic priority as did Homs, Hama, Aleppo and Damascus. Britain insisted on Russian consent. An exchange of letters between the three countries, May–October 1916, made the agreement official. British officials took care to ensure that there were no contradictions between the Hussein–McMahon correspondence and the Sykes–Picot Agreement.

Tripartite Declaration (25 May 1950) Made by Britain, the United States and France. Acknowledged that the Arab states and Israel needed to maintain a certain level of armed forces for the purposes of legitimate self-defence of the area as a whole. The three powers agreed to consider all applications for arms or war materials by the countries of the Middle East in the light of these principles.

United Nations Special Commission on Palestine (UNSCOP) (1947) A committee of enquiry on Palestine established by a special session of the United Nations on 15 May 1947, made up of representatives from eleven states: Australia, Canada, Czechoslovakia, Guatemala, India, Iran, Netherlands, Peru, Sweden, Uruguay and Yugoslavia. The Arabs refused to give evidence to the commission. The report was signed on 31 August 1947. The majority plan suggested partition into an Arab state, a Jewish state, and the city of Jerusalem under international trusteeship. Britain would administer the mandate during the interim period and admit 150,000 refugees into the Jewish state. The minority plan proposed an independent federal state.

White Paper of 1922 Drawn up by Herbert Samuel and accepted by Winston Churchill and the Cabinet. The document formed the basis of British policy in Palestine for almost a decade. On the one hand it attempted to reassure the Arabs: Britain had never contemplated the disappearance or the subordination of the Arab population, language or culture in Palestine. The Balfour Declaration did not envisage that Palestine as a whole would be converted into a Jewish national home. It said that such a home should be founded in Palestine. The development of the Jewish national home in Palestine did not mean the imposition of Jewish nationality upon the inhabitants of Palestine as a whole, but the further development of the existing Jewish community, with the assistance of Jews in other parts of the world, so that it could become a centre in which Jewish people as a whole could take an interest. To enable the Jewish community in Palestine to develop, it was essential that it should be known that it was in Palestine as of right and not on sufferance. The White Paper said that was the interpretation the British government placed on the Balfour Declaration. The Zionists formally accepted this document. An Arab delegation rejected it.

White Paper of 1939 British parliamentary paper published on 17 May 1939. Stated that it was not British policy that Palestine should become a Jewish state. Britain also could not accept that the Hussein–McMahon correspondence formed a just basis for the claim that Palestine should be converted into an Arab state. Britain wanted an independent Palestine, with Arabs and Jews sharing authority in government in a way that secured their essential interests. This was to be established within ten years. It would have treaty relations with Britain to meet the commercial and strategic interests of both countries. Over the following five years, 75,000 Jewish immigrants would be allowed into Palestine and after that immigration would be subject to Arab consent. In some areas no transfer of Arab land would be permitted; in others it would be restricted. There was no Jewish veto over the establishment of an independent state in Palestine. Became the basis of British Foreign Office policy for Palestine, 1943–5.

Woodhead Commission A 'technical' commission appointed by Neville Chamberlain on 8 December 1937 to investigate the practicability of the Peel Report. It was open to the commission, under Sir John Woodhead, to represent that partition would be unworkable. Its report was published on 9 November 1938 and ruled out partition, as the state envisaged would not be economically viable and would entail large-scale movements of population.

Religions and sects

Alawites (Alawis) (Nusseiris) Possibly the remnants of the Canaanite people from ancient times, they were little influenced by Christianity or Islam, but adhered to the Ismaili sect in the Middle Ages though broke away from it later. Only the initiated know the beliefs of the sect which hinge on a trinity of Ali, Muhammad, and one of the Prophet's companions. Small sections of the community live in Turkey and Lebanon but most are settled on the Syrian coast. The Alawite region was granted autonomy under the mandate for Syria, but this was ended when the French left at the end of the Second World War. The French policy of encouraging minorities to serve in the armed forces, in order to counter the nationalist tendencies of the Sunni majority, led the Alawites to form a disproportionately large part of the officer corps. President Asad is an Alawite.

Armenian Catholics Fled from Turkey during First World War and became refugees in Arab countries, especially Lebanon. Adopted Christianity before the meeting of the Council of Nicaea in the 4th century.

'Assassins' An Ismaili movement spread in the 11th century in the mountains of northern Iran around the fortress of Alamut by Husan-i Sabbah. He intimidated his enemies with political assassinations, often carried out by his followers acting under the influence of hashish. Addicts of hashish were known as *hashishiyyun*, which became 'assassins' in European languages. Disputed successions in the 12th century meant that the Assassins largely disappeared, but today there are still supporters of rival claimants: the Nizaris who support the claims of Nizar; and the Tayyibis who support Tayyib.

Bahais Deriving from Shiite Islam, the Bahai faith emphasizes the unity of all religions, world peace and universal education. It was started in Persia in 1862 by Mirza Hussein Ali Bahaullah. Few Bahais now live in the Middle East.

Chaldean Catholics Their origins lie in the early 19th century as a uniate offshoot of the Nestorians. They are found in Iraq, northwest Iran, south-west Turkey and Syria.

Christians Although a small minority in the Middle East, they are often from the best educated and cultured sections of the communities in which they reside. The basic tenets of the Christian faith – humility and forgiveness – contrast with many aspects of Islam. The most significant Christian creeds in the Middle East are: the Copts; the Coptic Catholics; the Nestorians; the Chaldean Catholics; the Armenians; the Western-influenced Latin and Protestant

Christians who follow the rites of the Roman Catholic Church or different Protestant creeds; the Maronites; the Syrian Catholics; the Syrian Orthodox (Jacobites); the Greek Catholics; and the Greek Orthodox. Christians are divided in their political attitudes: for instance, the Greek Catholics oppose the Palestine Liberation Organization while Greek Orthodox followers support it. Many Christians have left the Middle East in the last decade: it is estimated that around 50,000 Christians left Iraq, mainly for the United States in the aftermath of the Gulf War, and the exodus of Christian Palestinians from Jerusalem to the United States means that less than 2 per cent of that city is Christian. Christians, however, have stayed in secular Syria, particularly following President Asad's suppression of the Muslim rebellion in Hama in 1982.

Conservative Judaism Developed in the United States particularly in the 20th century. Allows modifications in rabbinical law to adjust to modern needs, but opposed to radical changes in the traditional observances.

Coptic Catholic Only existed officially since 1895. Most of the church's 100,000 members live in Cairo.

Copts Members of a Christian church based in Egypt, tracing its origin to St Mark's evangelism, which believes that the incarnate Christ has only one divine nature (monophysite). Many of its followers were converted to Islam with the Muslim conquest. In the 19th century the Copts developed a higher standard of living and education than most Egyptians and moved towards administering their own affairs. In the 20th century the Copts resented the increasing dominance of Islam in Egyptian life and claimed they were discriminated against.

Dervish Orders A form of Muslim mysticism, Sufism, the aim of which is to approach God through gnosticism (a mystic philosophy which sees the world as a hopeless mixture of the material and spiritual, and the chief purpose of people being to escape the material and find refuge in the spiritual being) and attain spiritual absorption in the divinity. The general practice is to reach ecstasy through the repetition of a religious formula or God's name. Some branches, like the Whirling Dervishes (Mevlevis) in Konya, Turkey, achieve this through dancing. At times influential in Egypt, Sudan and Turkey, the Dervish Orders have never enjoyed much influence in the Arab countries of the Fertile Crescent.

Druze An 11th-century offshoot from the Ismailis, the Druze sect settled on the slopes of Mount Hermon and later in the southern parts of Mount Lebanon. After clashes between the Christian Maronites, supported by the French, and the Druze, encouraged by the British, in 1860–1, a French expeditionary force established the semi-autonomous district of Mount Lebanon under a Christian governor and many Druze emigrated to the Houran mountains in southern Syria. In Lebanon, the Jumblatt and the Arslan clans fought for the leadership. The French had to put down a Druze revolt in Syria in 1927. In 1944 the Druze area in Syria lost its autonomy and Druze leaders have participated in various coups, including the one that overthrew Adib Shishakli in 1954. The Druze in Israel have fought alongside Jews against Arabs, and from 1957, at the community's request, Druze did compulsory military service. The Druze in Lebanon oppose Israel and its Christian allies. The tenets of the Druze religion are only known to the initiates, but the practice emphasizes moral and social principles and loyalty to the state ruling power. Around 200,000 Druze live in Lebanon, 100,000 in Syria, and 50,000 in Israel.

Greek Catholics Initially Christians in Syria who left the Greek Orthodox Church in the late 16th century. Their patriarchates of Antioch, Jerusalem and Alexandria united with the Roman Catholic Church, and recognized the supreme authority of the Pope, but they practice a Byzantine rite in Arabic. There is now only one patriarch who carries the names of Antioch, Alexandria and Jerusalem in his title. They are commonly known as Melchites/Melkites. They now live mainly in Lebanon, Syria, Egypt, Israel and Jordan.

Greek Orthodox The Greek Orthodox Church is now a universal communion whose patriarch is in Constantinople. Part of this wider communion is found in the Middle East, particularly the patriarchates of Constantinople, Alexandria, Antioch and Jerusalem. The origins of the Greek Orthodox Church lie in the churches which remained loyal to the Council of Chalcedon (451) when, first, the Nestorians were driven out of the empire into Persia in the late 5th century, and then the Monophysites formed their own church in the 6th century. In the Middle East, until the late 19th century, the priests were usually Greek, while the congregations wre Arab. Weakened by conversion to roman Catholicism, and by divisions following the conflict between Greece and Turkey (1920–3), the Greek character of the senior clergy was retained mainly in the Patriarchate of Jerusalem.

Ibadis Members of an Islamic sect which broke away early from mainstream Islam and who are often regarded as heretical. Thought to have had their origins in a group of Khawarijs (Kharijis) founded by Abd Allah ibn Ibad in Basra. In interpreting the law they allow for the Traditions, and if conditions are not suitable for rebellion they are prepared to live with other Muslims. They survive today mainly in Oman, where Ibadism is the state religion, and North Africa.

Islam Means submission to the will of God. A Muslim is one who does this. Muslims reject 'Muhammadan' as a term describing a practitioner of the faith of Islam: Muslims worship Allah and Muhammad is only the apostle of Allah. Muhammad is considered the final prophet in a line which includes Moses and Jesus. These prophets are revered but not worshipped. Muhammad, who around 610 started to announce a faith which he said had been revealed to him by the Archangel Gabriel, did little to change the ancient Arabian religion. The pilgrimage to the Kaaba in Mecca was retained. The revelations made to him were recorded in the sacred book, the Koran, in Arabic. Around 622 Muhammad, accompanied by a few faithful, left Mecca for Medina; this move has become known as the Hegira. Islam dates from this. The Tradition (Hadith) of Muhammad's practice (Sunna) at Medina until his death in 632 became part of the body of the law of Islam and supplemented many of the social principles laid down in the Koran. In the Islamic view the world has two parts: *Dar al-Islam*, the part under Islam; and *Dar al-Harb*, the area of war, or the part that has to be brought under Islam. Almost all Muslims accept the six articles of faith: belief in God; belief in God's angels; belief in the revealed books; belief in God's apostles; belief in the resurrection and the day of judgement; belief in God's predestination of good and evil. Five works are obligatory: *Shahada*, the recital of the belief; *Salat*, prayer at five appointed times during the day; *Zakat*, the payment of alms; fast during Ramadan (the ninth month of the lunar year); and the pilgrimage, hajj, to Mecca. Jihad, the concept of the holy war against the infidel, has never been accepted as an obligatory sixth practice.

An early schism in Islam lead to the growth of two dominant branches: Sunni and Shiite. Within these branches various sects emerged, including the Wahhabis, the Ismailis, the Alawis, the Druze, the Zeidis, the Ibadis and religious orders such as the Sanussi in Libya and the Muslim Brotherhood in Egypt. Around the 1970s a fundamentalist revival within Islam was evident. This took a practical form with the formation of an Islamic state in Iran under the Ayatollah Khomeini, and his stated intention to export the Iranian revolution. Many Westerners think of this sort of Islam as a return to violent Dark Ages. They see it as entailing the restoration of Turkey to the status of an Islamic state, the destruction of Israel or the 'Zionist entity', and the purging of Western influence from the Islamic world. Fundamentalist Islam has brought with it the return of women to a restricted position within Islamic society and a renewed emphasis on violence to secure its ends. Islam is the fastest-growing religion in the world: it has between 900 million and 1,000 million adherents and is the official religion in at least forty-four countries.

Ismailis (Fatimid Ismailis) A group of Shiites which does not recognize Musa al-Kazim (d. 799) as the seventh Imam, but consider Ismail, the other son of al-Kazim's father, Jafar al-Sadiq (d. 765) as the last Imam visible on earth. Fatimid Ismailis, for this reason, are sometimes also called the Seveners. Ismailis are divided as to whether they acknowledge Ismail as the seventh Imam, or one of his sons. When the Ismailis spread into North Africa in the 10th to 12th centuries the Fatimids of Egypt recognized a son of Ismail's son, Muhammad. The fourth Fatimid caliph founded Cairo in 969. See **Nizari Ismailis**.

Ithna'asharis (Twelvers) The largest Shiite school. It acknowledges a succession of twelve Imams. Ithna'asharis believe that Muhammad publicly designated Ali ibn Abi Talib, his cousin and the husband of his daughter, Fatima, to succeed him. Ithna'asharis believe that the community, in rejecting Ali, committed an act of infidelity. Ithna'asharis believe that each Imam designated his successor until the last known one, Muhammad al-Mahdi, the twelfth in line, who disappeared in 878. They believe that he is still alive and will reappear as the Mahdi, a messiah, before the Day of Judgement, and will rule personally by divine right. After the disappearance of the twelfth Imam, Shiites in Iraq were protected by the Buyids (932–1066) and a distinct system of law, jurisprudence and theology emerged. 'Twelver' Shiism is prominent today in Iran, southern Iraq, southern Lebanon, eastern Arabia, India and Pakistan.

Judaism The religion of the Jews. It is based on the belief in one God, all-powerful, with whom humans can have contact. The Torah, or the Pentateuch, the first five books of the Old Testament, are the written source. The Torah records God's revelations to Moses on Mount Sinai around 1,000 BC. The 613 commandments of the Torah form in effect what is a social as well as a religious creed: they cover matters of hygiene and food, as well as murder and sex. As it has developed, Judaism has refined the belief in the divine selection of the Jews to preach God's message. On the whole it is not a proselytizing religion. There are around 14 million Jews in the world, but increasingly many of these follow secular practices, even in Israel where it is estimated that around half the Jewish population has secular convictions. Around 6 million of the world's Jews live in the United States and over 3 million in Israel. The Nazi extermination of around 6 million Jews led to renewed emphasis on the part of Jewish leaders for the need for a separate Jewish state where Jews would not be a minority controlled by a majority. Israel is not a secular state, and considerable power rests in the rabbinical courts which handle interpretations of Jewish law. The rabbis, the religious leaders within the Jewish community, often play a significant social role, particularly in Israel on matters such as divorce. Fanatics in Judaism are usually called 'zealots'. Orthodox Jewish men often wear distinctive head-dress, beards and black clothes. Modern Judaism is practised in various forms: Orthodox, Conservative, and Reform or Liberal. Jews of German and East European descent are widely known as 'Ashkenazi' and the term 'Sephardi' is used to refer to Jews in Israel of North African and Middle Eastern backgrounds.

Khawarij (Kharijis) The dissenters. The oldest religious sect of Islam. Considered to be the antecedents of the Ibadis of Oman. Following the murder of the third Caliph, Uthman, in 656, his cousin, Muawiya ibn Abi Sufyan, rebelled against the fourth Caliph, Ali ibn Abi Talib, demanding revenge. Ali accepted arbitration, but some of his supporters, including those involved in Uthman's murder, insisted that judgement was God's prerogative. They insisted that only the Koran could lay down how a Muslim should believe and withdrew from the community. After about fifty years they were suppressed.

Maronites Originally members of a Christian Church which traced its foundation to the ascetic, Maro, who lived in northern Syria in the 5th century. In the 9th century the community was forced to migrate to the Lebanese mountains by the Arabs. The Maronite Church attempted links with Rome during the Crusades, and the authority of the patriarch was acknowledged in a 13th-century papal bull. Formal union with the Roman Catholic Church was established in the 18th century. Headed by a patriarch, the church practises its own liturgy. In the 19th century the Maronites moved southwards into a region of Lebanon where the Druzes lived. Through the intervention of the European powers, the autonomous district of Mount Lebanon was established in 1861 with a majority of Maronites. The Maronites, however, became a minority in Greater Lebanon (1920). From the 1930s until the political disruptions of the 1960s, the President of Lebanon was a Maronite. The Phalange, the paramilitary organization set up in the 1930s, was also dominated by the Maronites. Many fled from Lebanon during the civil war which started in 1975. It is estimated that between 1975 and 1997 around 500,000 of the more than 1 million Maronites left Lebanon.

Monophysites Followers of a Christian doctrine stemming from a schism at the Council of Chalcedon, 451, which holds that Christ has only one divine nature, as distinct from the usual Christian belief that Christ is both divine and human. Monophysite teaching was known before Chacedon, and the formal split came in the 6th century. The Monophysites doctrine is held by the Orthodox churches of the Copts, the Armenians, the Syrian Jacobites and the Ethiopians.

Muslim Brotherhood A fundamentalist Muslim religious and political association founded in Egypt in 1928 by Hassan al-Banna. A popular movement, it did not have parliamentary power and opposed political parties. Responsible for demonstrations and assassinations between 1945 and 1948, it forced Farouk to fight the First Arab–Israeli War. Banned, December 1948–51. Banned by the Free Officers in January 1954. Six leaders executed following an attempt on Nasser's life in October 1954. Student disturbances in the late 1960s were attributed to the Muslim Brotherhood. In theological terms the movement aims at a return to Islam and the shariah.

Nestorians Adhere to the teachings of Nestorius of Cilicia (d. 451) that Christ had distinct divine and human persons. Today they often refer to themselves as Assyrians, or members of the Assyrian Church of the East. The patriarch is resident in Tehran. In recent years there have been ecumenical discussions with the Roman Catholic Church and the Chaldeans with a view to unification between the Nestorians and the Chaldeans. Numbers are difficult to estimate, particularly as many left Iraq after the Gulf War, but around 35,000 probably live in Iraq and north-eastern Iran, and 15,000 in Syria and Lebanon.

Nizari Ismailis Following the destruction of the Assassin fortress at

247

Alamut in 1256 by Mongols it is claimed that the last Imam of Alamut sent his son for safety to Azerbaijan. In 1840 the Imam, Hasan
Ali Shah, who had taken the title Aga Khan, went to India, where
there were a number of his followers called Khojas. Today Khojas
live mainly in Gujarat, Bombay and East Africa. Nizari Ismailis who
also acknowledge the Aga Khan live in Salamiyya in Syria.

Orthodox Judaism Particularly practised in the Middle East, it insists that the practices outlined in the Torah and elaborated in the
Talmud, the main body of Jewish law, are sacrosanct.

Reform Judaism (Liberal Judaism) An increasingly popular form
of Judaism, particularly in Western countries, which is pragmatic.
Not especially rigorous in practices of ritual and dogma.

Samaritans A small sect who regard Mount Gerazim in Jordan as
sacred and who celebrate Passover there.

Sanussi Order (Sanussis) (Sanussiyya) A Sunni religious order
founded in Mecca in 1837. Stated intention to return to the teaching of the Koran. Influence considerable among the Bedouin in
Cyrenaica (Libya). Led by King Idris, tried to reach a compromise
with Italy, but failed in 1922 and the order was banned by the Italians in 1930. Helped Idris take over first Cyrenaica then the whole
of Libya in 1951. Influence declined after Gaddafi coup of 1969.

Shafeis A school of orthodox Sunni Islam, the adherents of which
live mainly in Yemen. Dominated from the 1960s onwards by the
Zeidi element.

Shiite (Shias) Shiite, meaning 'party', or the 'Party of Ali', are the
group who claim that the imamate belonged to Ali ibn Abi Talib,
Muhammad's cousin and husband of his daughter Fatima, and
father of the Prophet's only grandchild. Muslim leaders claiming
descent from Ali's son, al-Hasan, are called Sherifs (Sharifs), and
those tracing descent from Ali's second son, Al Hussein, are known
as *Sayyids*. They have certain privileges. Many of these leaders are
Sunnis. Shiite Islam is much the same in practice as Sunni orthodox Islam, as it is based on the same sources. But Shiite *mujtahids*
have greater power, at least in theory, as they can change the application of the law as spokesmen of the Hidden Imam. In Iran the
Khomeini regime emphasized the concept that the mullahs had the
trusteeship over the whole community delegated by the invisible
Imam, and aimed at a return to the ideal Islamic state. Shiites and
Sunnis differ mainly over the imamate. Shiites insist that the Imam

248

must be a descendant of Ali and Fatima, whereas Sunnis do not require an Imam to be a member of Muhammad's house. When the Safavids conquered Persia in the 16th century they took Shiite Islam there. Principal Shiite sects include the Ithna'asharis, the Ismailis, and the Zeidis in Yemen. Some Shiites, as they reject the Sunni belief that people under the authority of the divine law have the right to select the ruler of an Islamic society, try to overthrow Sunni regimes and set up clerics in their place. Around 15 per cent of Muslims are Shiites. Shiism is the official religion of Iran and most of that country's population is Shiite. Shiites are the largest group in Lebanon, make up a considerable proportion of Iraq's population, and around 20 per cent of the population of Pakistan. There are around quarter of a million Shiites in Saudi Arabia.

Sufis Islamic mystics, the name coming from a woollen garment they are supposed to have worn. Developed partly as an aesthetic reaction to the wealth acquired in Muslim conquests. Some practitioners borrowed ideas from neo-Platonism and gnosticism (see also p. 242). Sufic orders, brotherhoods, or *turuq* (singular, *tariqa*) as they developed emphasized an identification with the Supreme Being and an annihilation of self. This was sometimes achieved through hashish and opium. Sometimes exalted states came from repeating the name of Allah. Examples today are the Mawlawiyya, the 'Whirling Dervishes' in Konya, Turkey, and the Sanussi order in Libya.

Sunnis The mainstream of Islam, keeping to the Tradition in belief and accepting the orthodox successors or caliphs to Muhammad. The Sunni belief has spawned various mystic and fundamentalist sects. The Hashemite dynasty in Jordan and the Alawite dynasty in Morocco are Sunni, as were the rulers in Iraq and Libya. Orthodox Sunni Islam venerates the shariah (law). Four Sunni schools have emerged. The Hanafi, followers of Abu Hanifa (d. 767), emphasizes the use of reasoning. It was the official rite of the Ottoman Empire and is strong today in Turkey, Iraq, Syria, India and Central Asia. The Malikis school follows Malik ibn Anas (d. 795) who taught in Medina. Its emphasizes the Interpretation of Muhammad's practice at Medina and is predominant in the North African states, as well as being widespread in Sudan, Nigeria and Central and West Africa. The Shafeis follow Muhammad ibn Idris al-Shafi (d. 820) who helped to establish the authority of Tradition in Islamic law. Followers today live mainly in northern Egypt, South Arabia, the Hejaz, East Africa, and South-east Asia. The Hanbali school follows Ahmad ibn Hanbal (d. 855) who believed in a literal interpretation of the Koran and the practice laid down by Muhammad, established by the Tradition. It is the official legal school in Saudi Arabia. Under Islam all aspects of life are covered by the shariah. Generally Sunnis follow the Sunna, the way of Muhammad. Their Sunna is based on the Koran and the Six books of the Traditions (Hadith).

Syrian Catholics Live mainly in Lebanon, Egypt, Iraq and Syria. Have their own patriarch and are not subject to the authority of the Roman Catholic Church. Usually well-educated and influential.

Syrian Orthodox The Monophysite church of Syria. They are also known as Jacobites, after Jacob Baradaeus who led the split with Constantinople in the 6th century. Followers live in Lebanon, Syria, Iraq, and there are Syrian Orthodox communities in south-eastern Turkey around Mardin.

Tayyibi Ismailis (the Bohras) Arising out of the disputed Assassins succession in the 12th century, they believe in the concealment of the two-year-old al-Tayyib, and that there has been no revealed Imam since 1130. They give authority to the chief missionary, the Dai a-Dua. After persecution in Yemen his seat was moved to Bombay. Following a disputed succession, the group divided between the Daudi Bohras who live mainly in India, and the Sulaymani Bohras who live in Najran in Saudi Arabia.

Uniate The Uniate churches recognize the authority of the Pope and follow the dogmas of the Roman Catholic Church. They are headed by patriarchs and practise their own liturgical rites, some more Latin than others. In the Middle East they include the Greek Catholic, the Maronite, the Syrian Catholic, the Armenian Catholic, the Coptic Catholic and the Ethiopian Catholic Churches.

Wahhabis A conservative Sunni Muslim sect founded in the Arabian peninsula in the second half of the 18th century. It emphasizes the oneness of God, and accepts only what is written in the Koran and the early scriptures. Veneration of saints, luxuries, and decoration of mosques are banned. With Ibn Saud's conquest of the Nejd and the Arabian peninsula early in the 20th century, Wahhabism was formally established in the area, but in practice some of its edicts were modified.

Yazidis The Yazidi creed incorporates elements from Zoroastrism, Manicheism, Judaism, Christianity and Islam, and emphasizes transmigration of the soul as a means of expiation for the violation of divine law. One of their active forces is represented by Malak Taus, the peacock angel who ruled the universe after it had been created by God. The other name for Malak Taus is Shaytan, the same name as the Koran gives to Satan. This has led to the mistaken belief that the Yazidis worship the devil. Numbering around 100,000 they live in north-eastern Syria, northern Iraq and the trans-Caucasian republics. Although their scriptures are written in Arabic, they speak a Kurdish dialect.

Zeidis A Shiite sect recognizing a continuing line of Imams from Zeid who was killed around 740. Became an élite in Yemen. The imamate was abolished in 1962.

Zoroastrians Followers of a religion founded in Iran, in legend by Zoroaster (Zarathustra) around the 6th century BC. Views the cosmos in terms of a battle between good (*Ahura-Mazda*) and evil (*Ahriman*). Small number of followers in modern Iran, and also in India (Parsees).

Rulers, Prime Ministers, Foreign Ministers, political parties and movements

Bahrain

Heads of State
Under the British Protectorate 1880–1971
1869–1923	Isa (I) Al Khalifa
1923–1942	Hamad (regent 1923–33)
1942–1961	Salman (II) ibn Hamad Al Khalifa
1961–	Isa (II) ibn Salman Al Khalifa

Since independence in 1971
1971–	Isa ibn Salman Al Khalifa

Prime Minister
1973–	Khalifa ibn Salman Al Khalifa

Minister of Foreign Affairs
1971–	Muhammad ibn Mubarak ibn Hamad Al Khalifa

Egypt

British Protectorate 1914–36; monarchy until 1953

British High Commissioners
1914–1916	Sir Arthur Henry MacMahon
1916–1919	Sir Francis Reginald Wingate
1919–1925	Edmund Henry Hynman Allenby
1925–1929	George Ambrose Lloyd
1929–1933	Sir Percy Lyham Loraine
1934–1936	Sir Miles Wedderburn Lampson

Heads of State
1914–1917	Hussein Kamil (Sultan)
1917–1936	Ahmad Fuad I (King)
1936–1952	Farouk (King)
1952–1953	Ahmad Fuad II

Prime Ministers
1914–1919	Hussein Rushdi
1919	Muhammad Said
1919–1920	Yusuf Wahba

1920–1921	Muhammad Tawfiq Nasim
1921–1922	Adli Yegen
1922	Abd al-Khaliq Tarwat
1922–1923	Nasim
1923–1924	Abd al-Fattah Yahya Ibrahim
1924	Saad Zaghlul
1924–1926	Ahmad Ziwar
1926–1927	Yegen
1927–1928	Tarwat
1928	Mustafa al-Nahas
1928–1929	Muhammad Mahmud
1929	Yegen
1930	Nahas
1930–1933	Ismail Sidki
1933–1934	Ibrahim
1934–1936	Nasim
1936	Ali Maher
1936–1937	Nahas
1937–1939	Mahmoud
1939–1940	Maher
1940	Hasan Sabri
1940–1942	Hussein Sirri
1942–1944	Nahas
1944–1945	Ahmad Maher
1945–1946	Mahmud Fahmi al-Nuqrashi
1946	Sidki
1946–1948	Nuqrashi
1948–1949	Ibrahim Abd al-Hadi
1949–1950	Sirri
1950–1952	Nahas
1952	Maher
1952	Ahmad Neguib Hilali
1952	Sirri
1952	Hilali
1952	Maher
1952–1953	Muhammad Neguib

Foreign Ministers

1922	Tarwat
1922–1923	Mahmud Fakhri
1923	Ahmad Hismat
1923–1924	Tawfiq Rifaat

1924	Wasif Boutros Ghali
1924	Zaghlul
1924–1926	Ahmad Ziwar
1926–1927	Tarwat
1927–1928	Morqos Hanna
1928	Ghali
1928–1929	Hafiz al-Afifi
1929	Ahmad Midhat Yegen
1930	Ghali
1930	Afifi
1930–1933	Ibrahim
1933	Nahlal al-Muti
1933	Salib Sami
1933–1934	Ibrahim
1934–1935	Kamil B. Ibrahim
1935–1936	Abd al-Aziz Izzat
1936	Ali Maher
1936–1937	Ghali
1937–1939	Ibrahim
1939–1940	Maher
1940	Hasan Sabri
1940–1941	Hussein Sirri
1941–1942	Sami
1942–1944	Nahas
1944–1945	Mahmud al-Nuqrashi
1945–1946	Abd al-Hamid Badawi
1946	Ahmad Lutfi
1946	Ibrahim Adb al-Hadi
1946–1947	Nuqrashi
1947–1948	Ahmad Muhammad Hasaba
1948–1949	Ibrahim Dasqi Abaza
1949	Hasaba
1949–1950	Sirri
1950–1952	Muhammad Salah al-Din
1952	Maher
1952	Muhammad Abd al-Khaliq Hassuna
1952	Sirri
1952	Hassuna
1952	Maher
1952	Ahmad Muhammad Farraj Tayi
1952–1953	Mahmud Fawzi

Republic after 1953

Presidents

1953–1954	Muhammad Neguib
1954	Gamal Abdul Nasser
1954	Neguib
1954–1970	Nasser
1970–1981	Muhammad Anwar el-Sadat
1981	(acting) Sufi Abu Talib
1981–	Muhammad Hosni Mubarak

Prime Ministers

1953–1954	Muhammad Neguib
1954	Gamal Abdul Nasser
1954	Neguib
1954–1962	Nasser
1962–1965	Ali Sabri
1965–1966	Mohieddin (Muhi al-Din) Zakariya
1966–1967	Muhammad Sidki Suleiman
1967–1970	Nasser
1970–1972	Mahmud Fawzi
1971–1973	Aziz Muhammad Sidki
1973–1974	el-Sadat
1974–1975	Abd al-Aziz Higazi
1975–1978	Mamduh Muhammad Salam
1978–1980	Mustafa Khalil
1980–1981	el-Sadat
1981–1982	Mubarak
1982–1984	Ahmad Fuad Mohieddin (Muhi al-Din)
1984–1986	Kamal Hassan Ali
1986	Ali Lutfi
1986–1996	Atif Muhammad Neguib Sidki
1996–	Kamal al-Ganzouri

Foreign Ministers

1952–1970	Mahmud Fawzi (1964–1967: Deputy Prime Minister for Foreign Affairs. 1967–1970: Presidential Adviser on Foreign Affairs)
1964–1972	Mahmud Riad
1972	Muhammad Murad Galib
1972–1973	Muhammad Hasan al-Zayyat
1973–1977	Ismail Fahmi
1977	(acting) Pierre Boutros Ghali
1977–1978	Muhammad Ibrahim Kamel

1978–1979	(acting) Ghali
1979–1980	Mustafa Halil
1980–1985	Kamal Hassan Ali
1985–1991	Ahmad Esmat Abdul Meguid
1991–	Amr Muhammad Moussa

Political Parties and Movements

Arab Socialist Party of Egypt: founded 1976; a centre party; at a time of opposition to the peace overtures to Egypt supplanted by Sadat by a party of his own, and in August 1978, under threat of corporal punishment, its parliamentary members joined the National Democratic Party

Liberal Socialist Party: founded 1976; supports private enterprise and 'open door' economic policies

Muslim Brotherhood (Ikhwan): founded 1928; mainstream Islamic; officially illegal but tolerated

Nasserite Arab Democratic Party: a major opposition party

National Democratic Party: founded 1978; government party established by Anwar el-Sadat; has absorbed Arab Socialist Party

National Progressive Unionist Party (Tagammu): founded 1976; small and left-wing

New Wafd Party (originally Wafd Party): founded 1919; banned 1952; reformed as New Wafd Party in February 1978 but disbanded in June 1978; reformed August 1983; centre-left

Socialist Labour Party: founded 1978; official opposition party

Umma (National) Party: Islamic fundamentalist group

Young Egypt Party: founded 1990

Iran

Pahlavi Dynasty (1925–1979)

1925–1941	Reza Shah
1941–1979	Muhammad Reza Shah
1979	Regency Council. Chairman: Shapour Bakhtiar

Prime Ministers

1925–1926	Muhammad Ali Furughi
1926–1927	Mirza Hasan Khan
1927–1933	Mahdi Quli Hidayat
1933–1935	Muhammad Ali Furughi
1935–1939	Mahmud Jam
1939–1940	A. Matin-Daftari
1940–1941	Ali Mansur
1941–1942	Furughi
1942	Ali Zuhayli
1942–1943	Ahmad Qavam al-Saltana
1943–1944	Ali Zuhayli
1944	Muhammad Said Maragha
1944–1945	Mustafa Murtada Quli Bayat
1945	Ibrahim Hakimi
1945	(acting) Muhammad Sadr
1945–1946	Hakimi
1946–1947	Ahmad Qavam al-Saltana
1947	Sardar Fahir Hikmat
1947–1948	Hakimi
1948	Abd al-Hussein Hazhir
1948–1950	Said Maragha
1950	Hassan Ali Mansur
1950–1951	Ali Razmara
1951	Hussein Ala
1951–1952	Muhammad Mossadeq
1952	Ahmad Qavam al-Saltana
1952–1953	Mossadeq
1953–1955	Fazullah Zahedi
1955–1957	Hussein Ala
1957–1960	Manushir Iqbal
1960–1961	Jafar Sharif-Imami
1961–1962	Ali Amini
1962–1964	Asadullah Alam
1964–1965	Mansur
1965–1977	Emir Abbas Hoveida (Huvayda)
1977–1978	Janshid Amuzagar
1978	Sharif-Imami
1978–1978	Ghulam Riza Azhari
1979	Shapour Bakhtiar

Foreign Ministers

1926	(acting) Mirza Daud Miftah
1926	Hasan Taqizadah
1926	Mirza Hasan Khan
1926–1928	Ali Quli Ansari
1928	(acting) Murza Fatullah Pakrawan
1929	(acting) Abul-Qasim Amid
1929	Muhammad Ali Farzin
1929	Mirza Muhammad Ali Furughi
1930–1932	Mirza Fatullah Pakrawan
1932–1933	Furughi
1933–1934	Mirza Muhsin Rais
1935–1936	Baqir Kazimi
1936–1937	Inayatullah Sami
1937	Mustafa Adil
1938	Mirza Muhsin Rais
1938–1939	Ali Zuhayli
1939–1940	Muzaffar Alam
1940	Ibrahim Alam
1940–1941	(acting) Amari Jawad
1941–1942	Zuhayli
1942–1944	Muhammad Said Maragha
1944	Mirza Muhsin Rais
1944–1945	Nasrullah Intizam
1945	Anushiravan Sepahbodi
1945–1946	Abul-Qasim Najm
1946	Ahmad Qavam al-Saltana
1947	Sepahbodi
1947	Muhammad Qawam
1947–1948	Musa Nuri Isfandiyari
1948–1950	Ali Asghar Hikmat
1950	Ali Akhbar Siyassi
1950	Hussein Ala
1950–1951	Hussein Ala
1951	Abdullah Intizam
1951–1952	Baqir Kazimi
1952	Hussein Nawab
1952–1953	Hussein Fatimi
1953	Fazlullah Zahedi
1953	Abd al-Hussein Miftah
1953–1955	Abdullah Intizam
1955–1958	Ali Quli Ardalan

1958–1959	Hikmat
1959	Jalal al-Din Abdu
1959–1960	Yadullah Azudi
1961–1962	Hussein Quds Nahai
1962–1967	Aram
1967–1971	Ardasir Zahidi
1971–1978	Abbas Ali Khalatbari
1978–1979	Emir Husru Qasimlu
1979	Ahmad Mir-Fendereski

Islamic Republic from 1979

Heads of State

1979–1989	(de facto) Ayatollah Ruhollah Khomeini
1989–	Ayatollah Ali Khamenei

Presidents

1980–1981	Abul Hussan Bani-Sadr
1981–1989	Ali Khamenei
1989–1997	Ali Akbar Hashemi-Rafsanjani
1997–	Seyyed Muhammad Khatami

Prime Ministers

1979	Mehdi Bazargan
1980–1981	Muhammad Ali Rajai
1981–1989	Mir Hussein Moussavi

(office abolished in 1989)

Foreign Ministers

1979	Karim Sangabi
1979	(acting) Ahmad Salamatian
1979	(acting) Mehdi Bazargan
1979	Ibrahim Yazdi
1970	(acting) Abolhasan Bani-Sadr
1979–1980	(acting) Sadeq Ghotbzadeh
1981	Mir Hossein Mussavi
1981–	Ali Akbar Velayati

Political parties and movements

There are no officially recognized parties.

Islamic Republican Party: founded in 1978; ruling party until disbanded by Ayatollah Khomeini in June 1987 at request of party leaders who said that the party had achieved its purpose and might bring discord and factionalism if allowed to continue

In 1991 the parties listed below remained illegal. The Nelzat-Azadi, however, did enjoy official recognition for a while and was allowed to participate in elections

Association for the Defence of the Liberty and Sovereignty of the Iranian People: liberal

Democratic Party of Iranian Kurdistan: founded in 1945; wants autonomy for the Kurdish area; belongs to the National Council of Resistance

Democratic Party of the Iranian People: founded by dissident members of the Tudeh Party in Paris in February 1988; social democrat

Fedayin-e-Khalq (Warriors of the People): urban Marxist guerrillas

Flag of Freedom Organization for the Liberty of Iran: monarchist; liberal

Hezb-e-Komunist (Communist Party of Iran): founded in 1979 in response to the Tudeh Party being controlled by Moscow

Komala: founded in 1969; Marxist–Leninist; Kurdish wing of the Communist Party of Iran

Mujahidin-e-Khalq (People's Holy Warriors): Islamic guerrilla group; since June 1987 has included members of the National Liberation Army, between 10–15,000 strong, formed by Masud Rajavi on 20 June 1987 as a military wing; and also members of the National Council of Resistance, originally formed in Paris in 1981 under Abolhasan Bani-Sadr who left the council in 1984

Muslim People's Republican Party: though based in Tabriz has extensive membership in Azerbaijan

National Democratic Front: founded in March 1979 and leadership based in Paris from January 1982

National Movement of Iranian Resistance: led by former Prime Minister, Dr Shapour Bakhtiar (assassinated August 1991)

National Front (Union of National Front Forces): made up of Iran Nationalist Party, Iranian Party and Society of Iranian Students

Nationalist Republican Party: conservative

Nelzat-Azadi (Liberation Movement of Iran): founded 1961; led by Dr Mehdi Bazargan emphasizes human rights as defined by Islam

Pan-Iranist Party: on the far right; demands a Greater Persia

Sazmane Peykar dar Rahe Azadieh Tabaqe Kargar (Organization Struggling for the Freedom of the Working Class): Marxist–Leninist

Tudeh Party: founded 1941; declared illegal in 1949; emerged into open in 1979 but banned in April 1983; Marxist–Leninist and supported Moscow

Iraq

British Supremacy and Monarchy, 1919–58

British Military and Mandate Administration
1919–1920	Sir Arnold Talbot Wilson (Administrator)
1920–1923	Sir Percy Zachariah Cox (High Commissioner)
1923–1928	Sir Henry Robert Conway Dobbs (High Commissioner)
1928–1929	Sir Gilbert Falkingham Clayton (High Commissioner)
1929–1935	Sir Francis Humphrys (High Commissioner)

Heads of State
1921–1933	Feisal I
1933–1939	Ghazi
1939–1958	Feisal II

Prime Ministers
1920–1922	Abd al-Rahman al-Haydari al-Gaylani
1922–1923	Abd al-Muhsin al-Sadun
1923–1924	Jafar al-Askari
1924–1925	Yasin al-Hashimi
1925–1926	al-Sadun
1926–1928	al-Askari
1928–1929	al-Sadun

1929	Suleiman Tawfiq al-Suwaydi
1929	al-Sadun
1929–1930	Ibrahim Naji al-Suwaydi
1930–1932	Nuri al-Said
1932–1933	Naji Shawkat
1933	Rashid Ali al-Gaylani
1933–1934	Jamil al-Midfai
1934–1935	Ali Jawdat al-Ayyubi
1935	al-Midfai
1935–1936	al-Hashimi
1936–1937	Hikmat Suleiman
1937–1938	al-Midfai
1938–1940	Nuri al-Said
1940–1941	al-Gaylani
1941	Taha al-Hashimi
1941	al-Gaylani
1941	al-Midfai
1941–1944	Nuri al-Said
1944–1946	Hamdi al-Pachachi (Bajaji)
1946	Suleiman Tawfiq al-Suwaydi
1946	Arshad al-Umari
1946–1947	Nuri al-Said
1947–1948	Salih Jabr
1948	Muhammad al-Sadr
1948–1949	Muzahim al-Pachachi (Bajaji)
1949	Nuri al-Said
1949–1950	al-Ayyubi
1950	Al-Suwaydi
1950–1952	Nuri al-Said
1952	Mustafa Mahmud al-Umari
1952	Nur al-Din Mahmud
1953	al-Midfai
1953–1954	Muhammad Fadil al-Jamali
1954	Arshad al-Umari
1954–1957	Nuri al-Said
1957	al-Ayyubi
1957–1958	Abd al-Wahhab Mirjan
1958	Nuri al-Said

Foreign Ministers

1930–1931	Abd Allah al-Damluji
1931–1932	al-Askari

1932–1933	Abd al-Qadir Rashid
1933–1934	Nuri al-Said
1934	al-Damluji
1934	Suleiman Tawfiq al-Suwaydi
1934–1936	Nuri al-Said
1936–1937	Naji al-Asil
1937–1938	al-Suwaydi
1938–1938	Nuri al-Said
1939–1940	al-Ayyubi
1940–1941	Nuri al-Said
1941	Ali Mahmuud
1941	al-Hashimi
1941	al-Suwaydi
1941	Musa al-Shahbandari
1941	al-Ayyubi
1941–1942	Jabr
1942	al-Damluji
1942	Nuri al-Said
1942–1943	Abd al-Ilah al-Hafiz
1943	Nasrat al-Farisi
1943	al-Hafiz
1943	Tahsin al-Askari (in exile)
1943–1944	Mahmud Subhi al-Daftari
1944–1945	Arshad al-Umari
1945–1946	Hamdi al-Pachachi (Bajaji)
1946	al-Suwaydi
1946	Ali Mumtaz
1946–1948	al-Jamali
1948	Hamdi al-Pachachi (Bajaji)
1948	al-Farisi
1948	Muzahim al-Pachachi (Bajaji)
1948–1949	al-Ayyubi
1949	al-Hafiz
1949	al-Jamali
1949	Shakir al-Wadi
1949–1950	Muzahim al-Pachachi (Bajaji)
1950	al-Suwaydi
1950–1951	al-Wadi
1951	al-Suwaydi
1951–1952	al-Wadi
1952	al-Jamali
1953	al-Suwaydi

1953–1954	Abd Allah Bakr
1954	al-Shahbandari
1954	al-Jamali
1954–1955	al-Shahbandari
1955–1957	Burhan al-Din Bashayan
1957	(acting) Ali Mumtaz
1957	al-Ayyubi
1957–1958	Bashayan
1958	al-Jamali
1958	al-Suwaydi

Republic from 1958

Heads of State

1958–1963	Sovereignty Council
1963–1966	Abd al-Salim Muhammad Arif (President)
1966	(acting) Abd al-Rahman al-Bazzaz
1966–1968	al-Rahman Muhammad Arif
1968–1979	Ahmad Hasan al-Bakr
1979–	Saddam Hussein (al-Takriti)

Prime Ministers

1958–1963	Abd al-Karim Kassem (Qasim)
1963	Ahmad Hasan al-Bakr
1963–1965	Tahir Yahya
1965	Arif Abd al-Razzaq
1965–1966	Abd al-Rahman al-Bazzaz
1966–1967	Naji Talib
1967	Abd al-Rahman Muhammad Arif
1967–1968	Yahya
1968	Abd al-Razzaq al-Nayif
1968–1979	al-Bakr
1979–1991	Saddam Hussein
1991	Saadun Hamadi
1991–1993	Muhammad Hamzah al-Zubaydi
1993–1994	Ahmad Husein Khudayyir
1994–	Saddam Hussein

Foreign Ministers

1958–1959	Abd al-Jabbar al-Jumard
1959–1963	Hashim Jawwad
1963	Talib Hussein al-Shabib
1963	(acting) Salih Mahdi Ammash

267

1963	Subhi Abd al-Hamid
1964–1965	Major General Naji Talib
1965	al-Bazzaz
1965–1967	Adnan Muzahim al-Pachachi (Bajaji)
1967–1968	Ismail Khairallah
1968	Nasser al-Hani
1968–1971	Abd al-Karim Abd al-Sattar al-Shaykhli
1971	Rashid al-Rifai
1971–1974	Murtada Said Abd al-Baki al-Hadithi
1974	Sadil Yasin Taqah
1974	(acting) Hisham al-Shawi
1974–1983	Sadun Hamadi
1983–1991	Tariq Aziz
1991	Ahmad Hussein al-Samarei
1991–1992	Ahmad Husein Khudayyir
1992–	Muhammad Said Kazim al-Sahhaf

Political parties and movements

National Progressive Patriotic Front: formed in 1973 as the National Progressive Front made up of the Arab Baath Socialist Party and the Iraqi Communist Party. The Communist Party left in 1979. The other two principal members are now the Kurdistan Democratic Party and the Kurdistan Revolutionary Party

Arab Baath Socialist Party: founded in Damascus in 1947 as a revolutionary Arab socialist movement and has ruled Iraq since July 1968

Kurdistan Democratic Party: founded in 1946

Kurdistan Revolutionary Party: succeeded the Democratic Kurdistan Party and founded in 1972

Arab opposition groups:
Hizb al-Dawa al-Islamiyya (Islamic Call Party): a Shiite opposition group founded in 1968

Iraqi Communist Party: founded in 1934; was legally recognized in 1973 when it joined in the National Progressive Front; left the National Progressive Front in March 1979 and banned for its support of Iran during the Gulf War

Supreme Council of the Islamic Revolution of Iraq: a guerrilla group and the main Shiite opposition movement. Led by exiled Iraqi Shiite leader, Hojatolislam Muhammad Bakr al-Hakim, from Tehran

Umma (Nation) Party: founded in 1982 and opposes Saddam Hussein

Kurdish opposition groups:
Democratic Party of Kurdistan: founded in 1946 in opposition to the Iraqi government; led by Masud Barzani; one of the two principal Kurdish opposition groups

Kurdish Hezbollah (Party of God): a splinter group from the Democratic Party of Kurdistan and a member of the Supreme Council of the Islamic Revolution

Patriotic Union of Kurdistan: founded in 1975; one of the two principal Kurdish opposition groups

Socialist Party of Kurdistan: founded 1975

United Socialist Party of Kurdistan: a splinter group from the Patriotic Union of Kurdistan

London based:
Iraqi National Congress: has rotating leadership

Israel

Presidents
1948–1952	Chaim Weizmann
1952–1963	Isaak Ben Zwi (Isaak Simselevic)
1963	(acting) Kadish Luz
1963–1973	Zalman Shazar (Shneor Rubacov)
1973–1978	Efraim Katzir (Betcalski)
1978–1983	Yitzhak Navon
1983–1993	Chaim Herzog
1993–	Ezer Weizmann

Prime Ministers
1948–1953	David Ben-Gurion (Grien)
1953–1955	Moshe Sharett (Shertok)
1955–1963	Ben-Gurion
1963–1969	Levi Eshkol (Shkolnik)
1969	(acting) Yigal Allon
1969–1974	Golda Meir (Myerson)
1974–1977	Yitzhak Rabin

1977	(acting) Shimon Peres
1977–1983	Menachem Begin
1983–1984	Yitzhak Shamir (Jazernicki/Jagermutzen)
1984–1986	Peres
1986–1992	Shamir
1992–1995	Rabin
1995–1996	(acting) Peres
1996–	Benjamin Netanyahu

Foreign Ministers

1948–1949	David Ben-Gurion
1949–1956	Moshe Sharett
1956–1966	Golda Meir
1966–1974	Abba Eban (Aubrey Solomon)
1974–1977	Yigal Allon
1977–1979	Moshe Dayan
1979–1980	Menachem Begin
1980–1986	Yitzhak Shamir
1986–1988	(acting) Shimon Peres
1988–1990	Moshe Arens
1990–1993	David Levy
1993–1995	Peres
1995–1996	Ehud Barak
1996–	Levy

Political Parties and Movements

Agudat Israel: ultra-orthodox Jewish party

Agudat Israel World Organization: founded 1912; world-wide membership

Arab Democratic Party: founded 1988; aims to unify Arab political forces

Centre Party (Shinui): founded 1988; mainly dissidents from Labour Alignment and Likud blocs

Council for Peace and Security: founded 1988; aims at Israeli withdrawal from occupied territories in return for peace with Arabs

Degal Hatora: founded 1988; orthodox Western Jews

Gush Emunim (Community of Believers): founded 1967; establishes unauthorized Jewish settlements in occupied territories

Hadash (Democratic Front for Peace and Equality): descended

from Socialist Workers' Party and Communist Party, aims at a socialist system in Israel and peace with the Arab states

Israel Labour Party: founded in 1968 by the merger of three Labour groups, Mapai, Rafi and Achdur Ha'avoda; advocates peace settlement with the Palestinians

Kach: founded in 1977; wants a state in Israel based on the Torah and the expulsion of all Arabs from Israel and the occupied territories. Banned from the 1988 elections as a racist party. Leader Meir Kahane assassinated in 1990

Likud: founded in 1973; a parliamentary bloc of Herut, the Liberal Party of Israel, Laam, Ahdur and Tami. Likud and the Liberal Party merged in August 1988 to form the Likud National Liberal Movement. Advocates the retention of all the territories of the Palestine mandate.

Meretz: an alliance of Mapam and Shuinui and Ratz formed after the 1988 general election; policy includes separation of religion and state, the cessation of Jewish settlement in the occupied territories, and self-determination for the Palestinians; in 1992 joined the coalition government under Labour

Moledet (Homeland): founded 1988; aims at the expulsion of the Palestinians from the West Bank

Morasha (Heritage): merged with the National Religious Party in the Knesset in 1986

National Religious Party: founded 1956; aims to apply religious precepts of Judaism to everyday life

New Liberal Party: founded 1974; 1987 merger; centrist

Poale Agudat Israel: founded 1924; Orthodox Jewish party with working class support

Political Zionist Opposition (Ometz): founded 1982; one-man party

Progressive List for Peace: founded 1984; Jewish Arab; favours establishment of a Palestinian state

Ratz (Civil Rights and Peace Movement): founded 1973; a human rights party advocating a peace settlement with the Palestinians

Religious Zionism Party (Matzad): founded 1983 as a breakaway from the National Religious Party

Shas (Sephardic Torah Guardians): founded 1984; an ultra-orthodox Jewish party

Tami: founded 1981; Sephardic Jewish party

Tehiya-Zionist Revival Movement: founded 1979; opposes Camp David accords and aims at Israeli sovereignty over the occupied territories

Telem-State Renewal Movement: founded 1981 by Dayan; favours Palestinian autonomy, supports Likud

Tzomet Party: founded 1988; nationalist party

United Arab List: Arabs affliliated to the Labour Party

United Tora Judaism: formed in 1988 by the merging of Agudat Israel, Paole Agudat Israel and two small religious groups, Moria and Degel HaTorah; in 1990 joined the Likud government

United Workers' Party (Mapam): founded 1948; socialist

Yahad (Together): founded 1984; advocates a peace settlement with the Palestinians

Jordan (Transjordan until 1949)

British Residents in Transjordan
1921–1924	Harry St John Bridger Philby
1924–1939	Charles Henry Fortnum Cox
1939–1946	Alec Seath Kirkbride

Kings
1921–1951	Abdullah (Emir until 1946)
1951	(regent) Nayif for King Talal
1952–1953	Regency Council
1953–	Hussein ibn Talal

Prime Ministers
1921	Rashid Tali
1921	(acting) Mazhar al-Raslan
1921	Ali Rida al-Rikabi
1923	(acting) al-Raslan

1923–1924	Hasan Khalid al-Hussein Abul-Huda al-Sayyadi
1924–1926	al-Rikabi
1926–1931	Abul-Huda al-Sayyadi
1931–1933	Abdullah al-Sarraj
1933–1938	Ibrahim Hashim
1938–1944	Tawfig Abul-Huda
1944–1945	Samir al-Rifai
1945–1947	Hashim
1947	al-Rifai
1947–1950	Abul-Huda
1950	Said al-Mufti
1950–1951	al-Rifai
1951–1953	Abul-Huda
1953–1954	Fawzi al-Mulqi
1954–1955	Abul-Huda
1955	al-Mufti
1955	Hazza al-Majali
1955–1956	(acting Hashim)
1956	al-Rifai
1956	al-Mufti
1956	Hashim
1956–1957	Suleiman al-Nabulsi
1957	Abd al-Halim al-Nimr
1957	Hussein Fakhri al-Khalidi
1957–1958	Hashim
1958–1959	al-Rifai
1959–60	al-Majali
1960–1962	Bahjat al-Talhuni
1962–1963	Wasfi Mustafa al-Tall
1963	al-Rifai
1963–1964	Sherif Hussein ibn Nasser
1964–1965	al-Talhuni
1965–1967	al-Tall
1967	Hussein
1967	Saad Jumaa ibn Muhammad
1967–1969	al-Talhuni
1969	Abd al-Munim al-Rifai
1969–1970	al-Talhuni
1970	Abd al-Munim al-Rifai
1970	Muhammad Daud
1970	Mohammad Ahmad Tuqan
1970–1971	al-Tall

1971–1973	Ahmad Abd al-Karim al-Lawzi
1973–1976	Zayid Samir al-Rifai
1976–1979	Mudar Muhammad Badran
1979–1980	Abd al-Hamid Sharaf
1980	Qasim al-Rimawi
1980–1984	Badran
1984–1985	Ahmad Obaidat
1986–1988	Rifai
1989	Zayd ibn Shakir
1989–1991	Badran
1991	Tahir al-Nashat al-Masri
1991–1993	Shakir
1993–1995	Abd al-Salam al-Majali
1995–1996	Shakir
1996–1997	Abdul al-Karim al-Karabiti
1997–	Majali

Foreign Ministers

1939–1944	Tawfig Abul-Huda
1944–1945	Muhammad al-Shurayqi
1945–1946	Abul-Huda
1946–1947	al-Shurayqi
1947	Samir al-Rifai
1947–1949	Fawzi al-Mulqi
1949	Ruhi Abd al-Hadi
1949–1950	al-Rifai
1950	al-Shurayqi
1950	Abd al-Hadi
1950–1951	al-Rifai
1951	Mohammad Ahmad Tuqan
1951	Anastas Hananiyah
1951–1952	Abul-Huda
1952–1953	al-Mulqi
1953–1954	Hussein Fakhri al-Khalidi
1954	Jamal Tuqan
1954	Abul-Huda
1954–1955	Walid Salah
1955	Said al-Mufti
1955	Hazza al-Majali
1955–1956	al-Rifai
1956	Fakhri al-Khalidi
1956	al-Rifai

1956	Suleiman al-Nabulsi
1956	al-Mulqi
1956	Awni Abd al-Hadi
1956–1957	al-Nabulsi; State Minister, Abd Allah al-Rimawi
1957–1958	al-Rifai
1958–1959	State Minister, Khulusi al-Khayri
1959	al-Majali
1959–1961	Musa Nasir
1961	Bahjat al-Talhuni
1961–1962	Rafi al-Husseini
1962–1963	Hazim Nusaybah
1963	(acting) Amin Yunus al-Husseini
1963	Sherif Hussein ibn Nasser
1963–1964	Antun Ata Allah (Ataullah)
1964	(acting) Amin Yunus al-Husseini
1964–1965	Qadri Tuqan
1965–1966	Nusaybah
1966	Akram Zuwaytar
1966–1967	Abd Allah Sallah
1967	Muhammad Ahmad Tuqan
1967	Muhammad Adib al-Amiri
1967–1968	al-Talhuni
1968–1969	Abd al-Munim al-Rifai
1969	Tuqan
1969–1970	Abd al-Munim al-Rifai
1970	Ata Allah
1970	Muhammad Daud
1970–1972	Sallah
1972–1973	Salah Abu Zayid
1973–1976	Zayid Samir al-Rifai (State Minister: 1973–1974, Zuhayr al-Mufti: 1974–1976, Sadiq al-Shara)
1976–1979	Mudar Badran
1979–1980	Abd al-Hamid Sharaf
1980–1984	Marwan al-Qassim
1984–1988	Tahir al-Nashat al-Masri
1988–1991	al-Qassim
1991	al-Masri
1991–1993	Kamil Abu Jabir
1993–1995	Abdel-Salam al-Majali
1995–1997	Abdul al-Karim al-Kabariti
1997–	Fayez Tarawneh

Political parties and movements

Arab Baath Socialist Party: evolved in 1948 secretly out of the Arab Baath Party and emerged as a leading parliamentary group in 1956 election; largely an urban party for the educated; in the 1960s supported by the Baath in Syria, but lost popularity after the Six-Day War

Islamic Action Front: the political wing of the Muslim Brotherhood in Jordan; emerged as the single largest group in the 1989 and November 1993 parliamentary elections; opposed the Jordanian–Israeli Peace Treaty signed in October 1994

Jordan National Alliance: a coalition of central and Bedouin tribes, allowed to exist as a party following legislation of July 1992 and represented in the general election of November 1993

Jordanian Communist Party: derived support from Palestinian refugees in Jordan; legalized in 1993, but has only small following

Jordanian National Union: formed 1971; renamed Arab National Union in 1972, and abolished in 1976

Jordanian People's Democratic Party (JPDP): established in July 1989 by supporters of the Democratic Front for the Liberation of Palestine

Jordanian Popular Democratic Unity Party (JPDUP): formed November 1990 by supporters of the Popular Front for the Liberation of Palestine (PFLP)

Parliamentary Arab–Islamic Coalition Front: formed in October 1990; consists of Muslim Brotherhood, independent Islamists, the nationalists and the liberals

Pledge Party (al-Ahd): a right wing organisation, allowed to exist as a party following legislation of July 1992

Popular Union Party: a pan-Arab and centrist organisation allowed to exist as a party following legislation of July 1992

Kuwait

British Protectorate 1914–1961

Heads of State
1896–1915   Mubarak Al Sabah
1916–1917   Jabir (II) Al Sabah
1917–1921   Salim Al Sabah
1921–1950   Ahmad Al Sabah
1950–1965   Abdullah (III) Al Sabah
Independent state from 1961

Rulers
1950–1965   Abdullah (III) Al Sabah
1965–1977   Sabah (III) Al Sabah
1978–   Jabir (III) Al Sabah

Prime Ministers
1962–1963   (acting) Jabir al-Ahmad al-Jabir Al Sabah
1963–1965   Sabah al-Salim Al Sabah
1965–1978   Jabir al-Ahmad al-Jabir
1978–   Saad al-Abdullah al-Salim al-Jabir Al Sabah

Foreign Ministers
1962–1963   Sabah al-Salim Al Sabah
1963–1971   Sabah Ahmad al-Jabir Al Sabah
1971–1978   Jabir al-Ahmad
1978–   Sabah al-Ahmad al-Jabir Al Sabah

Lebanon

French Mandate 1920–1926

Military Governors
1918   Colonel P. de Piepape
1920–1923   Captain Georges Trabaud
1923–1924   Antoine Privat-Aubouard
1924–1925   General Charles Alexis Vandenberg
1925–1926   Léon Henri Charles Cayla
1926–1941   High Commissioners in Syria

Administrative Commission
1920–1922   Daud Ammun
1922   Habib al-Saad

1922–1923	al-Saad
1923–1924	Naum al-Labaki
1924–1925	Emile Eddé
1925–1926	Musa Nammur

Declared a republic in 1926; became independent in 1941

Presidents

1926–1934	Charles Dabbas
1934	(acting) Privat-Aubouard
1934–1936	Habib al-Saad
1936–1941	Emile Eddé
1941–1943	Alfred Georges Naqqash (Naccache)
1943	(acting) Ayyub Thabit
1943	(acting) Habib Abu Sahla
1943	Bishara al-Khuri
1943	Eddé
1943–1952	al-Khuri
1952	(acting) Fuad Chehab (Shihab)
1952–1958	Camille Nimir Chamoun
1958–1964	Fuad Chehab
1964–1970	Charles Alexandre Hélou (Hilu)
1970–1976	Suleiman Franjiya (Frangieh)
1976–1982	Elias Sarkis
1982–1988	Amin Pierre Gemayel
1988–1989	Interim military government
1989	René Mouawad
1989–	Elias Hrawi

Prime Ministers

1926–1927	Auguste Adib
1927–1928	Bishara al-Khuri
1928–1929	Habib al-Saad
1929	al-Khuri
1929–1930	Emile Eddé
1930–1932	Adib
1932–1943	Charles Dabbas
1934–1936	(acting) Abdullah Bayhum
1936–1937	(acting) Ayyub Thabit
1937–1938	Khayr al-Din al-Ahdab
1938	Khalid Shihab
1938–1939	Abdullah al-Yafi
1939–1941	Bayhum

1941	Alfred Georges Naqqash
1941–1942	Ahmad al-Dauq
1942–1943	Sami al-Sulh
1943	(acting) Thabit
1943	Three Directors
1943–1945	Riyad al-Sulh
1945	Abd al-Hamid
1945–1946	Sami al-Hamid Karami
1945–1946	Sami al-Sulh
1946	al-Saadi al-Munla
1946–1951	Riyad al-Sulh
1951	Hussein al-Uwayni (Oweini)
1951–1952	al-Yafi
1952	Sami al-Sulh
1952	Nazim al-Akkari
1952	Saib Sallam (Saeb Salam)
1952	(acting) Khalid Chehab (Shihab)
1952	al-Yafi
1952–1953	Khalid Chehab
1953	Sallam (Salam)
1953–1954	al-Yafi
1954–1955	Sami al-Sulh
1955–1956	Rashid Karami
1956	al-Yafi
1956–1958	Sami al-Sulh
1958	(acting) Khalil al-Hibri
1958–1960	Karami
1960	Dauq
1960–1961	Sallam (Salam)
1961–1964	Karami
1964–1965	al-Uwayni (Oweini)
1965–1966	Karami
1966	al-Yafi
1966–1968	Karami
1968–1969	al-Yafi
1969–1970	Karami
1970–1973	Sallam (Sallam)
1973	Amin al-Hafiz (Amin Hafez)
1973–1974	Munah Taqi al-Din al-Sulh (Taki al-Din Solh)
1974–1975	Rashid al-Sulh (Solh)
1975	Nur al-Din Rifai
1975–1976	Karami

279

1976–1980	Salim Hoss (al-Hus) (Selim (al-))
1980	Munah Taqi al-Din al-Sulh (Taki al-Din Solh)
1980–1984	Shafiq Wazzan (Chafic al-Wazzan)
1984–1987	Karami
1987–1990	(acting) Hoss (al-Hus) (al-Hoss); Christian claimant, Michel Aoun (Awn) (1988–1990)
1990–1992	Umar Karami
1992–1992	Rashid Solh
1992–	Rafik Hariri

Foreign Ministers

1937	Georges Thabit
1937	Khalid Abu al-Lam
1937–1938	Khayr al-Din al-Ahdab
1938	Salim Taqla (Takla)
1938	Hamid Franjiya (Frangieh)
1939	Habib Abu Sahia
1939–1941	French High Commissioners in Syria
1941–1942	Franjiya
1942–1943	Philippe Najib Boulos
1943	Jawad Boulos
1943–1945	Taqla
1945	Henri Philippe Farun
1945–1946	Franjiya
1946	Abu Sahia
1946–1947	Farun
1947–1949	Franjiya
1949–1951	Philippe Habib Taqla
1951	Hussein al-Uwayni
1951–1952	Emile Lahud
1952	Taqla
1952	Nazim Akkari
1952	Saib Salam
1952	Akkari
1952–1953	Musa Mubarak
1953	Georges Hakim
1953–1955	Alfred Naqqas
1955	Franjiya
1955–1956	Salim Lahud
1956–1958	Charles Malik
1958	Taqla
1958–1960	al-Uwayni

1960–1964	Taqla
1964	Fuad Scandar Ammun
1964–1965	Taqla
1965	al-Uwayni
1965–1966	Hakim
1966	Taqla
1966–1968	Hakim
1968	Fuad Boutros
1968	(acting) Ali Arab
1968–1969	al-Uwayni
1969	Karami
1969	Yusuf Salam
1969–1970	Nasim Majdalani
1970–1973	Khalil Abu Hamad
1973–1974	Fuad Georges Naffah
1974–1975	Taqla
1975	Lucien Dahdah
1975–1976	Taqla
1976	(acting) Camille Nimir Chamoun (Shamun)
1976	Karami
1976–1982	Boutros
1982–1984	Elie Adib Salam
1984–1987	Karami
1987–1990	Salim Hoss (al-Hus)
1990–	Faris Buwayz

Political parties and movements

Arab Democratic Party (Red Knights, Alawites): based in Tripoli; pro-Syrian

Armenian Revolutionary Federation: founded 1890; principal Armenian party

Al-Baath: founded in Syria in 1940s

Al-Baath: pro-Iraqi wing

Amal (Hope): Shiite organization

Bloc National: founded 1943; right-wing Maronite party

Al-Dustur (Constitutional Party): founded 1943; party of business élite

Harakat al-Qawmiyyin al-Arab (Arab Nationalist Movement):

281

founded in 1948 by Georges Habash and others; Marxist Arab nationalist party

Al-Hayat al-Wataniya (National Committee): founded in 1964

Hezbollah (Party of God): militant Shiite faction founded in early 1980s

Al-Hizb al-Dumuqratiya al-Ishtiraqi al-mashi (Christian Social Democrat Party): founded in 1988

Independent Nasserite Movement (also known as al-Murabitun): Sunni Muslim militia

Islamic Amal: breakaway group from Amal

Islamic Jihad: fundamentalist Islamic terrorist group and pro-Iranian

Al-Jabha al-Damuqratiya al-Barlamaniya (Parliamentary Democratic Front): advocates power-sharing

Al-Kataeb (Phalangist Party): founded in 1936; largest Maronite party

Lebanese Front: founded 1976; group of right-wing Christian parties

Mouvement de l'Action Nationale: founded 1965

Al-Najjada (The Helpers): founded 1936; Arab socialist party

Nasserite Popular Organization: merged with Arab Socialist Union in January 1987 and kept name of Nasserite Popular Organization

National Front: founded 1969; group of mainly left-wing Muslim parties
Al-Nida al-Qawmi (National Struggle): founded 1945

Parti Communiste Libanais (Lebanese Communist Party): founded 1924

Parti Démocrate: founded 1969; favours a secular democratic state

Parti National Libéral: founded 1958

Parti Populaire Syrien (PPS) or Syrian Social Nationalist Party (SSNP): founded 1932; advocates Greater Syria

Parti Socialiste Progressiste: founded in 1949 by the Druze leader Kamal Jumblatt; favours constitutional road to socialism

Parti Socialiste Révolutionnaire: founded 1964

Parti Tachnag (Armenian)

Popular Liberation Army: Sunni Muslim group active in the south

Tawhid Islami (the Islamic Unification Movement): founded in 1982; based in Tripoli; Sunni Muslim group

Oman

Formerly Muscat and Oman, and under British protection until 1970

Sultan
1970–	Qabus (Qaboos) ibn Said Al Bu Said

Prime Ministers
1970	(acting) Barayq ibn Hamud
1970–1971	Tariq ibn Taimur Al Bu Said
1971–1972	(acting) Asim Jamali
1972–	Sultan Qabus

Foreign Ministers
1970–1971	Tariq ibn Taimur
1971	Sultan Qabus
1972–1973	(acting) Fahd ibn Mahmoud Al Bu Said
1973–1982	Qais ibn Abd al-Munim al-Zawawi
1982–1990	Yusuf ibn al-Alawi ibn Abdullah
1990–	Sultan Qabus

Palestine

British Mandate 1920–1948

High Commissioners
1920–1925	Sir Herbert Louis Samuel
1925–1928	Herbert Charles Onslow Plumer
1928	(acting) Sir Harry Luke
1928–1931	Sir John Robert Chancellor

1931–1932	(acting) Mark Aitchison Young
1932–1937	Sir Arthur Grenfell Wauchope
1937–1938	(acting) Sir Eilliam Denis Battershill
1938–1944	Sir Harold Alfred MacMichael
1944–1945	John Standish Surtees Prendergast (Vereker) Gort
1945–1948	Sir Alan Gordon Cunningham

Palestinian Authority

Chairman
1994–	Yasser Arafat

Organizations and movements

Alliance of Palestinian Forces: formed in January 1994 and made up of ten 'rejectionist Palestinian factions who opposed the peace agreement with Israel: the Popular Front for the Liberation of Palestine; Palestinian Liberation Front (Talat Yaqub faction); Palestine Popular Struggle Front; Palestine Revolutionary Communist Party; Popular Front for the Liberation of Palestine–General Command; Fatah Uprising; Al-Saiqa; Hamas; Islamic Jihad; Democratic Front for the Liberation of Palestine.

Arab Liberation Front: member of the PLO and supporter of peace agreement with Israel

Democratic Front for the Liberation of Palestine (*Hawetmeh* faction): member of the PLO and supporter of peace agreement with Israel

Democratic Front for the Liberation of Palestine (dissident faction): member of the PLO and supporter of peace agreement with Israel

Al-Fatah: mainstream faction from Palestine Liberation Organization (PLO); principal mover of peace agreement with Israel

Palestinian Liberation Front: member of the PLO and supporter of peace agreement with Israel

Palestinian People's Front: member of the PLO and supporter of peace agreement with Israel

Qatar

British Protectorate 1916–1971

Sultans

1913–1945	Abdullah ibn Qasim Al Thani
1945–1947	Hamad Al Thani
1947–1949	Abdullah Al Thani
1949–1960	Ali Al Thani
1960–1972	Ahmad ibn Ali Al Thani

Independent from 1971

Emirs and Prime Ministers

1960–1972	Ahmad ibn Ali Al Thani
1972–1995	Khalifa ibn Hamad Al Thani
1995–	Hamad ibn Jasim ibn Jabr Al Thani

Foreign Ministers

1969–1972	Khalifa ibn Hamad Al Thani
1972–1985	Suhaym ibn Al Thani
1985–1989	Ahmad ibn Saif Al Thani
1989–1990	Abdullah ibn Khalifa al-Attiya
1990–1992	Mubarak Ali al-Khatir
1992–	Hamad ibn Jasim ibn Jabr Al Thani

Saudi Arabia

Kings

1926–1953	Abd al-Aziz ibn Abd al-Rahman Al Saud (Ibn Saud)
1953–1964	Saud ibn Abd al-Aziz Al Saud
1964–1975	Feisal ibn Abd al-Aziz Al Saud
1975–1982	Khalid ibn Abd al-Aziz Al Saud
1982–	Fahd ibn Abd al-Aziz Al Saud

Prime Ministers

1931–1953	Feisal ibn Abd al-Aziz Al Saud
1953–1954	Saud ibn Abd al-Aziz Al Saud
1954–1960	Feisal ibn Abd al-Aziz Al Saud
1960–1962	Saud ibn Abd al-Aziz Al Saud
1962–1975	Feisal ibn Abd al-Aziz Al Saud

1975–1982	Khalid ibn Abd al-Aziz Al Saud
1982–	Fahd ibn Abd al-Aziz Al Saud

Foreign Ministers:

1926–1928	Adullah Bey al-Damlaji
1928–1930	Fuad Bey Hamza
1930–1960	Feisal ibn Abd al-Aziz Al Saud
1960–1962	Ibrahim ibn Abdullah al-Suwayl
1962–1975	Feisal ibn Abd al-Aziz Al Saud
1975	Khalid ibn Abd al-Aziz Al Saud
1975–	Saud al-Feisal ibn Abd al-Aziz

Sudan

Anglo–Egyptian Condominium 1899–1955

Governors-General

1891–1899	Sir Horatio Herbert Kitchener
1899–1916	Sir Francis Reginald Wingate
1917–1924	Sir Lee Oliver Fitzmaurice Stack
1924–1925	(acting) Wasey Sterry
1925–1926	Sir Geoffrey Francis Archer
1926–1934	Sir John Loader Maffey
1934–1940	George Stewart Symes
1940–1947	Sir Hubert Jervoise Huddleston
1947–1954	Sir Robert George Howe
1955	Sir Alexander Knox Helm

Republic of Sudan declared in 1956

1956–1958	Sovereignty Council
1958–1964	Supreme Council of the Armed Forces
1964	President Ibrahim Abboud
1964–1965	National Defence Council
1965–1969	Supreme Council of State
1969–1971	Revolutionary Council
1971–1985	President Gaafar Muhammad al-Nimieri
1985–	Revolutionary Command Council

Syria

Under French mandate until 1941

High Commissioners
1926–1931	Henri Ponsot
1931–1938	Damien, Comte de Martel
1939–1940	Gabriel Puaux
1940	Jean Chiappe
1940–1941	Henri Dentz

Free French Delegates General
1941–1943	Georges Catroux
1943	Jean Helleu
1943–1944	Yves Chataigneau
1944–1946	General Beynet

Presidents
1932–1936	Muhammad Ali al-Abid
1936–1939	Hashim al-Atasi
1939–1941	vacant
1941	(acting) Khalid al-Azm
1941–1943	Muhammad Taj al-Din al-Hasani
1943	(acting) Ata al-Ayyubi
1943–1949	Shukri al-Quwwatli (al-Kuwatli)
1949	Husni al-Zaim
1949–1951	al-Atasi
1951–1953	Fawzi al-Salu
1953–1954	Adib Shishakli (al-Sisaqli)
1954	(acting) Mamun al-Kuzbari
1954–1955	al-Atasi
1955–1958	al-Quwwatli (Kuwatli)
1958–1961	part of United Arab Republic
1961	Military Junta
1961–1962	Nazim al-Qudsi (al-Kudsi)
1962	Military Junta
1962–1963	al-Qudsi
1963–1964	National Revolutionary Council
1964–1966	Presidential Council
1966–1970	Nur al-Din Mustafa al-Atassi
1970–1971	Ahmad al-Khatib
1971–	Hafiz al-Asad (al-Assad)

Prime Ministers

1932–1934	Haqqi al-Azm
1934–1936	Muhammad Taj al-Din al-Hasani
1936	Ata al-Ayyubi
1936–1939	Jamil Mardam
1939	Lutfi al-Haffar
1939	Nasuhi al-Bukhari
1939–1941	French High Commissioner
1941	Khalid al-Azm
1941–1942	Hasan al-Hakim
1942–1943	Husni al-Barazi
1943	Jamil al-Ulshi
1943	al-Ayyubi
1943–1944	Sadallah al-Jabiri
1944–1945	Faris al-Khuri
1945–1946	al-Jabiri
1946	(acting) al-Azm
1946–1948	Mardam
1948–1949	al-Azm
1949	Husni al-Zaim (military dictator)
1949	Muhsin al-Barazi
1949	Hashim al-Atasi
1949	Nazim al-Qudsi
1949–1950	al-Azm
1950–1951	al-Qudsi
1951	al-Azm
1951	al-Hakim
1951	(acting) Zaki al-Khatib
1951	Maruf al-Dawalibi
1951–1953	Fawzi al-Salu
1953–1954	Adib al-Shishakli
1954	Shawkat Shuqayr
1954	Sabri al-Asali
1954	Said al-Ghazzi
1954–1955	al-Khuri
1955	al-Asali
1955–1956	al-Ghazzi
1956–1958	al-Asali
1958–1961	Executive Council for the Syrian Region of the United Arab Republic
1961	Mamun al-Kuzbari
1961	Izzat al-Nuss

1961–1962	al-Dawalibi
1962	Military Junta
1962	Ahmad Bashir al-Azma
1962–1963	al-Azm
1963	Salah al-Din al-Bitar
1963	(acting) Sami al-Jundi
1963	al-Bitar
1963–1964	Amin al-Hafiz
1964	al-Bitar
1964–1965	al-Hafiz
1965	Yusuf Zuayyin
1966	al-Bitar
1966–1968	Zuayyin
1968–1970	Nur al-Din Mustafa al-Atasi
1970–1971	Hafiz al-Asad (al-Assad)
1971–1972	Abd al-Rahman Khulayfawi
1972–1976	Mahmud al-Ayyubi
1976–1978	Khulayfawi
1978–1980	Muhammad Ali al-Halabi
1980–1987	Abd al-Rauf al-Qasim
1987–	Mahmud al-Zubi

Foreign Ministers

1936–1939	Sadallah al-Jabiri
1939	Faiz Yaqub al-Khuri
1939	Khalid al-Azm
1939–1941	French Administration
1941–1943	al-Khuri
1943	Naim al-Antaki
1943–1945	Jamal Mardam
1945	Mikhail Liyan
1945	Faris al-Khuri
1945–1946	al-Jabiri
1946–1947	al-Antaki
1947–1948	Khalid Mardam
1948	Muhsin al-Barazi
1948–1949	al-Azm
1949	Adil Arslan
1949	al-Barazi
1949	Nazim al-Qudsi
1949–1950	al-Azm
1950–1951	al-Qudsi

1951	al-Azm
1951	Faydi al-Atasi
1951	Shakir al-As
1951–1952	Military Admininstration
1952–1953	Zafir al-Rifai
1953–1954	Khalil Mardam
1954	al-Atasi
1954	Izzat al-Saqqa
1954–1955	al-Atasi
1955	al-Azm
1955–1956	Said al-Ghazzi
1956–1958	Salah al-Din al-Bitar
1958–1961	United Arab Republic
1961	Mamun al-Kuzbari
1961	Izzat al-Nuss
1961–1962	Maruf al-Dawalibi
1962	Military Administration
1962	Adnan al-Azhari
1962	Jamal al-Farra
1962–1963	Asad Said Mahasin
1963	al-Bitar
1963–1965	Hasan Muraywad
1965	Ibrahim Makhus
1966	al-Bitar
1966–1968	Makhus
1968–1969	Muhammad Ayd Asawi
1969–1970	Mustafa al-Sayyid
1970–1984	Abd al-Halim Khaddam
1984–	Faruq al-Shara

Political parties and movements

National Progressive Front: founded in 1972; grouped together the
Arab Socialist Party, the Arab Socialist Unionist Party, the Baath
Arab Socialist Party, the Communist Party of Syria, and the Syrian
Arab Socialist Union Party. Dominant party is the Baath Arab So-
cialist Party

United Arab Emirates

President
1971–   Zayid ibn Sultan Nahayyan (also known as Al Bu Falah)

Prime Ministers
1971–1979   Maktum ibn Rashid Al Maktum
1979–1990   Rashid ibn Said Al Maktum
1990–   Maktum ibn Rashid Al Maktum

Foreign Ministers
1971–1980   Ahmad Khalifa al-Suwaydi
1980–1997   (acting) Rashid ibn Abdullah al-Nuaymi
1997–   Hamdan ibn Zayed al-Nahyari

Yemen Arab Republic (North Yemen)

Imamate 1904–1926; Kingdom 1926–1962

Imams
1904–1948   al-Mutawakkil al-Allah Yahya Hamid al-Din (Imam)
1948   al-Hadi Abdullah ibn Ahmad al-Wazir (usurper)
1948–1962   Ahmad al-Nasser li-din Allah
1962   Muhammad al-Mansur al-Badr (1962–1968, pretender in northern region)

Chiefs of Government
1925–1927   Ahmad al-Qusaiy
1927–1948   Abdullah ibn Hussein al-Amri (Umari)
1948   (acting) Hussein al-Kibsi
1948   Ibrahim ibn Abdullah
1948   Abdullah ibn Yahya
1948–1955   Hasan ibn Yahya
1955–1962   Ahmad
1962   Muhammad al-Badr
In exile:
1962–1967   Hasan ibn Yahya
1967–1968   Abd al-Rahman ibn Yahya

1968	(acting) Hasan ibn Yahya
1968–1970	Muhammad al-Badr

Foreign Ministers

1927–1948	Muhammad Raghib ibn Rafiq
1948	(acting) Hussein al-Kibsi
1948–195?	Muhammad ibn Abdullah al-Amri
195?–1955	Abdullah ibn Yahya
1955–1962	Hasan ibn Ali ibn Ibrahim in exile:
1962–1966	Ahmad ibn Muhammad al-Sami
1966–1967	Muhammad Abd al-Qaddus al-Wazir
1967–1970	al-Sami

Republic from 1962

Heads of State

1962–1967	Abdullah al-Sallal (President)
1967–1974	Presidential Council
1974–1975	Armed Forces Commanding Council
1975–1977	Ibrahim al-Hamadi
1977–1978	al-Qasmi
1978	Presidential Council
1978–1990	Ali Abdullah Saleh

Prime Ministers

1962–1963	Abdullah al-Sallal
1963	Abd al-Latif Dayfallah
1963–1964	Abd al-Rahman al-Iryani
1964	Hassan al-Amri
1964–1965	Hamud al-Jaifi
1965	al-Amri
1965	Ahmad ibn Muhammad Numan
1965	al-Sallal
1965–1966	al-Amri
1966–1967	al-Sallal
1967	Muhsin ibn Ahmad al-Ayni
1967–1969	al-Amri
1969	(acting) Abd al-Salam Sabrah
1969	al-Ayni
1969–1970	Abdullah ibn Hussein al-Qursumi
1970–1971	al-Ayni
1971	(acting) Sabrah
1971	Numan

1971	al-Amri
1971	(acting) Sabrah
1971–1972	al-Ayni
1972–1974	Abdullah ibn Ahmad al-Hajari
1974	Hasan ibn Muhammad Makki
1974–1975	al-Ayni
1975	(acting) Dayfallah
1975–1980	Abd al-Aziz ibn Abd al-Ghani
1980–1983	Abd al-Karim al-Iryani
1983–1990	al-Ghani

Foreign Ministers

1962	Muhsin ibn Ahmad al-Ayni
1962–1963	Abd al-Rahman al-Baydani
1963	Abdullah al-Sallal
1964	Mustafa ibn Yaqub
1964	Hasan ibn Muhammad Makki
1964–1965	Abd al-Rahman al-Iryani
1965	Abd al-Qawi Hamim
1965	al-Ayni
1965–1966	Mustafa ibn Yaqub
1966	Makki
1966–1967	Muhammad ibn Abd al-Aziz Salam
1967	al-Sallal
1967–1968	Makki
1968–1969	Yahya Jaghman
1969	Hussein ibn Ali al-Hubaysi
1969–1970	Jaghman
1970–1971	al-Ayni
1971	Ahmad ibn Muhammad Numan
1971	Abdullah ibn Abd al-Majid al-Asnaj
1971–1972	al-Ayni
1972–1973	Muhammad ibn Ahmad Numan
1974	al-Asnaj
1974	al-Ayni
1974–1975	Jaghman
1975–1979	al-Asnaj
1979	Makki
1979	Hussein ibn Abdullah al-Amri
1979–1980	Makki
1980–1984	Ali Lutfi al-Thawr
1984–1990	Abd al-Karim al-Iryani

People's Democratic Republic of Yemen (Southern Yemen)

British Rule in Aden 1839–1967

Residents
1910–1919	Major General James Alexander Bell
1919–1921	Major General James Marshall Stewart
1921–1925	Lieutenant General Thomas Scott
1925–1928	Major General John Henry Keith Stewart
1928–1931	George Stewart Symes
1931–1932/7	Lieutenant Colonel Bernard Rawdon Reilly

Chief Commissioner
1932–1937	Lieutenant Colonel Bernard Rawdon Reilly

Governors
1937–1940	Sir Bernard Rawdon Reilly
1940–1944	Sir John Hathorn Hall
1945–1950	Sir Reginald Stuart Champion
1950–1951	(acting) William Good
1951–1956	Sir Tim Hickinbotham
1956–1960	Sir William Henry Tucker Luce
1960–1963	Sir Charles Hepburn Johnston

High Commissioners
1963	Sir Charles Hepburn Johnston
1963–1964	Sir Gerald Kennedy Nicholas Trevaskis
1964–1967	Sir Richard Gordon Turnbull
1967	Sir Humphrey Trevelyan

Independence declared in 1967

Heads of State
1967–1969	Qahtan ibn Muhammad al-Shaabi
1969–1980	Supreme People's Council
1980–1986	Ali ibn Nasser ibn Muhammad
1986–1990	Haydar Abu Bakr al-Attas

Prime Ministers
1967–1969	Qahtan ibn Muhammad al-Shaabi
1969	Feisal ibn Abd al-Latif al-Shaabi
1969–1971	Muhammad ibn Ali Haytham
1971–1989	Ali ibn Nasser ibn Muhammad

1989–1990   Yasin Said Numan

Foreign Ministers
1967–1969   Ahmad al-Dali
1969   Feisal ibn Abd al-Latif al-Shaabi
1969–1971   Abu Salim al-Bayda
1971   Muhammad ibn Ali Haytham
1971–1973   Muhammad ibn Salih al-Awlaqi
1973–1979   Muhammad ibn Salih Abdullah Muti
1979–1982   Salim ibn Salih ibn Muhammad
1982–1990   Abd al-Aziz al-Dali

Political parties and movements
Yemen Socialist Party: founded 1978; successor to United Political
Organization-National Front (UPONF); Marxist-Leninist

Yemen Republic

Formed on 22 May 1990 by union of North and South Yemen

President
1990–   Ali Abdullah Saleh

Prime Minister
1990–1997   Haydar Abu Bakr al-Attas
1997–   Said Ben Ghanem

Foreign Minister
1990–   Abd al-Karim al-Iryani

Political parties and movements
Arab Socialist Baath Party: contested the 1993 general election

Democratic Unionist Party: supporters of exiled former President
of South Yemen, Ali ibn Nasser ibn Muhammad

Nasserite Correction Organization: contested the 1993 general
election

Nasserite Popular Unionist Organization: contested the 1993
general election

National Democratic Front: the main opposition group in the north based in Aden

Truth Party: contested the 1993 general election

Yemen Socialist Party: formerly dominant political force in South Yemen

Yemen Reform Group: founded September 1990; supports adherence to Islamic law

Glossary of terms

Abadan Site of important oil refinery in Iran.

Abu Musa Disputed island in Gulf. Sharjah's possession has been challenged by Iran and the Trucial Coast Sheikhdom of Umm al-Qaiwain.

Abu Musa Faction A terrorist group also known as al-Intifada (Uprising) that broke away from al-Fatah after the agreement signed by Arafat and King Hussein of Jordan on 11 February 1985. Led by Said Musa Muragha. Formed a joint rebel Fatah command with 'Abu Nidal' between February 1985 and June 1987.

Abu Nidal Organization A terrorist group, also known as the Fatah Revolutionary Council, operating on the international level, headed by the dissident Fatah leader, Sabri al-Banna. Operates principally from Iraq. Split from al-Fatah in 1973, and between February 1985 and June 1987 formed a joint rebel Fatah command with 'Abu Musa' operating out of Damascus. Apparently disintegrated in 1989. In June 1990 forces loyal to Abu Nidal surrendered to al-Fatah forces near Tyre in Lebanon.

adhan The summoning to prayer by the muezzin of the Muslim faithful.

Agudat Israel An orthodox Jewish party operating in Israel, and standing for the strict observance of Jewish law.

Agudat Israel World Organization Established in 1912 at the Congress of Orthodox Jewry held at Kattowitz in Germany (now Katowice, Poland) to assist Jewish people all over the world. At present has over 500,000 members in twenty-five countries.

Al-Ahram The most significant newspaper published in Egypt in recent decades. Established by immigrant brothers from Lebanon, Salim and Bishara Taqla, in Alexandria in 1875–6, it transferred to Cairo. In the 1950s and 1960s under the editorship of Muhammad Heikal, a confidant of Nasser, it achieved a pre-eminent position.

Alexandretta A district *sanjaq*, and port, at the top of the bay of Alexandretta in the Eastern Mediterranean, referred to in the Hussein–McMahon correspondence. Included in Syria under the French mandate, it was handed over to Turkey in 1939, and today is known as Iskenderun. It is still an area of dispute between Syria and Turkey.

Aliyah Immigration to Israel. 'First Aliyah' refers to the first main waves of Jewish immigration to Palestine during 1882 and 1884 and

1890–1 (mainly from Russia and Eastern Europe). The 'Second Aliyah' followed the failure of the October Revolution in Russia of 1905. The 'Third Aliyah' followed the Russian Revolution of 1917 and stretched into the 1920s. The 'Fourth Aliyah' refers to the influx of Polish Jews between 1924 and 1928, but also includes around 8,000 Jews from the Caucasus and the Middle East: with the Fourth Aliyah the Jewish population of Palestine rose from 84,000 in 1922 to 154,000 in 1929. The 'Fifth Aliyah' refers to the 1930s, and includes the immigration that was a consequence of the rise of Nazism in Germany.

Amal (Groups of the Lebanese Resistance) Formed in 1974 by Imam Musa al-Sadr. Gave spurt to militant Shiite Islam in Lebanon. After Syria allowed 1,200 Iranian Revolutionary Guards to settle in Baalbek area in Bekaa valley (June 1982), the Islamic faction of Amal propagated Khomeini's ideas. This developed into Hezbollah, the Party of God. The Shiite movement in Lebanon divided between Hezbollah supported by Iran, and Amal supported by Syria. In 1990 Amal was estimated to have an active strength of 5,000.

American Christian Palestine Committee Formed in 1946 by the merging of the American Palestine Committee and the Christian Council on Palestine. Led by Robert Wagner, the Democratic senator for New York, its membership included most Congressmen. A significant pressure group that helped to determine United States policy towards Palestine, and in particular managed to secure the rejection by Truman of the Morrison–Grady plan in 1946 using tactics of electoral 'blackmail'.

American–Israel Public Affairs Committee Influential pro-Israeli pressure group in the United States, particularly active after the mid-1970s.

American Palestine Committee Formed in 1943, it proved to be the most effective pressure group in the United States on the Palestine issue. Almost all members of Congress belonged. Dominated by Robert Wagner and Robert A. Taft, it was bipartisan. Worked for a congressional resolution favouring the establishment of a Jewish Commonwealth in Palestine. Roosevelt's endorsement of this idea was sent to Wagner on 15 October 1944.

anti-Semitism A word which appeared in Europe around 1860. With it, the attack on Jews was no longer based on grounds of creed but of race. Assimilation was no longer possible: according to the new doctrine, racial characteristics were unchangeable and a Jew could not, for instance, become a German through baptism and a rejection of his or her heritage. Led to the pogroms in Russia and the immigration of over 2 million Jews from Europe to the United States, Australia, South Africa and Canada, as well as stimulating the birth of Zionism. The worst manifestation of anti-Semitism in the 20th century was the systematic elimination of almost 6 million Jews by the Nazis between 1939 and 1945. Widely used as a justification for the State of Israel and its continuation. Zionist writers have challenged the notion that Arabs cannot be anti-Semitic as they are Semites themselves, and also the evidence given by Arab representatives to the Anglo–American commission of enquiry in 1946 that, as the one race with no anti-Semitic tradition they should not be made to pay for the sins of Christian Europe. Zionist leaders have often identified anti-Semitism with anti-Zionism. After efforts to do this in the United States in 1946, the British government deliberately distinguished between Zionists and Jews. In August 1990 Yitzhak Shamir stated explicitly: 'To be anti-semitic and anti-Israel go together. To be anti-Israel is a cover for it. For people who are already anti-Jewish, to be against the politics of the State of Israel is easy.'

Arab, Arabs In the 2nd century BC Arab tribes moved out of Arabia and settled in modern Syria and Iraq. But it was really only with the rise of Islam in the 7th century that the Arab culture and language spread, as Arabs conquered Syria, Iraq, Persia, Egypt, the North Africa coast and finally Spain. With this flowering of civilization, the meaning of 'Arab' changed from that of Bedouin, or nomadic tribesmen of Arabia to refer to all those peoples who spoke the Arabic language and had intermixed their blood with Arabs. In some circles the old meaning lasted. 'Arab' is not necessarily co-extensive with Islam, the Muslim religion, and there are examples of Christian Arabs as well as non-Arabic Muslims.

Arab Higher Committee In 1936 it was made up of the six Arab political parties active in Palestine and chaired by Hajj al-Husseini. Banned on 1 October 1937 for its part in the Arab rebellion, it went into exile. Reformed under Arab League auspices in 1945 it divided into two rival committees. In 1946 the Arab League appointed a new Arab Higher Committee with Hajj al-Husseini as the absent chairman, and Jamal al-Husseini as Vice Chairman and acting leader. It did not succeed in leading the Palestinians in the war against the emerging state of Israel.

Arab League The League of Arab States (Arab League) was set up by Egypt, Lebanon, Iraq, Syria, Transjordan, Yemen and Saudi Arabia in March 1945. It encouraged Arab co-operation and unity. Since then other Arab states have joined: Algeria, Bahrain, Djibouti, Kuwait, Lebanon, Libya, Mauritius, Morocco, Oman, Qatar, Somalia, Sudan, Tunisia, United Arab Emirates, and the People's Democratic Republic of Yemen. Palestine is classed as a separate state and is represented at League meetings by the Palestine Liberation Organization. Each member state has one vote in the Council, which is the Arab League's supreme authority. The Council has sixteen committees dealing with political and social affairs as well as health and communications. The League's headquarters were established in Cairo, and Egypt dominated the body, supplying the Secretary Generals until 1979 when, following the Israel–Egypt Peace Treaty, Egypt was suspended from the League. Its headquarters were moved to Tunis, and other agencies relocated in Amman and Iraq. Egypt was re-admitted to the League in May 1989.

Arab Legion The military force established in Transjordan by British officers and administered especially by John Glubb from 1920–1. Became the army of Jordan. Played an active role during the First Arab–Israeli War.

Arab rebellion The Arab uprising in Palestine between 1936 and 1939.

Arab revolt The uprising by the Sherif of Mecca and his sons against the Turks in June 1916 is also sometimes known as 'The Revolt in the Desert', after the book by T.E. Lawrence. With British finance and experts, including T.E. Lawrence, the desert army took Mecca and Aqaba. Later the Arab guerrillas sabotaged the Hejaz railway, the Turkish supply route; in 1917–18 they advanced with Allenby into Palestine and Syria, and set up an Arab government in Damascus. The revolt's leaders became the Arabs' spokesmen at the peace settlement and were later set up in control by the British: Abdullah in Jordan, and Feisal in Iraq.

Arabian–American Oil Company (ARAMCO) Formed in 1944 by Texas Oil Company, Standard Oil of New Jersey, Socony–Vacuum and Standard Oil of California. After protracted negotiations ARAMCO was acquired by Saudi Arabia and is now known as Saudi Aramco.

Arabic Originally a Semitic language from Arabia, Arabic has spread across the Middle East and North Africa. The alphabet has maintained its distinctive ancient form but the syntax, structure and vocabulary have adapted to modern needs. The written language, *Fusha* (the pure), or *Nahawi* (grammatical), is different from spoken Arabic which consists of different dialects, and means that Arabs from one area cannot understand the language spoken by those in another.

Ardahan A small town and district in north-eastern Turkey near the Russian border, ceded to Russia in 1878, recaptured by Turkey during the First World War. During 1945–6 the Soviet Union tried to reclaim it, but this was resisted, and after Stalin's death in 1953 the claim was renounced.

Armenia An area south-east of the Black Sea divided today between the Republic of Armenia, the Republic of Azerbaijan, Turkey and Iran. Of unknown ethnic origin, the people have a distinctive Indo-European language, and a religion that centres on the Armenian Catholic Church. Many lived in the Ottoman Empire. The peace treaty of Sèvres signed on 10 August 1920 between Turkey and the allies recognized the independent state of Armenia, but it ceased to exist when Turkey reconquered its Armenian provinces and the Soviet Union took over the rest.

Ashkenazi Literally means 'German'. Originally referred to Jews who lived in medieval Germany, and those who, as a result of persecution, spread from there to other parts of Europe. They had a distinctive culture based on the Yiddish language. In the 19th and early 20th centuries many of these Jews immigrated to North and South America, South Africa, Australia and New Zealand. Today the word is widely taken to mean reference to Jews of German and East European descent. It also has overtones of class domination in Israel.

Aswan dam Nasser's scheme to harness the waters of the Nile to provide the energy to move Egypt into the modern age. Built with Soviet financial assistance. Construction started in January 1960 and was completed in July 1970. The dam was officially inaugurated in January 1971. Its existence had confirmed the earlier British feasibility studies which predicted that the dam would ruin the Egyptian ecology and economy.

Azerbaijan An area situated in the north-west of Iran, on the border of the Republic of Azerbaijan. It was occupied by Soviet troops in 1941 and at the end of war the Iranian Communist Tudeh Party, with Soviet support, established two independent republics.

After the West's stand against the Soviet Union in the United Nations in March 1946, Soviet troops crushed the separatist regimes in December 1946.

Baath The Arabic word means renaissance and it has been given to a pan-Arabic socialist party which originated in Syria. Its first congress was held in Damascus in 1947. It merged with the Arab Socialist Party to become the Arab Renaissance Party in 1953 and played a part in the overthrow of Adib Shishakli's dictatorship in February 1954. Socialist in orientation, and pan-Arabist, its influence spread to Jordan, Lebanon and Iraq. During 1957 and 1958 it supported union with Egypt, but later opposed it and encouraged Syria's secession, although Baath parties in Syria and Iraq encouraged a federal union with Egypt in 1963, which came to nothing. Divisions between the Baath parties in Syria and Iraq grew in the 1960s. The Baath in Syria became more radical, while the party in Iraq (which seized power in a coup in July 1968) supported national leadership.

Bab al-Mandeb Straits joining the Indian Ocean and the Red Sea, divided by Perim Island, bordered by the Yemen on the Arabian side and Somalia and Ethiopia on the African. Of strategic importance for the Suez Canal passage.

Baghdad Railway A scheme of the Ottoman government to extend the Anatolian railway to Baghdad and the Gulf. The concession was given to a German company in 1899. Britain, France and Russia feared this extension of German interest, and there were minor international fracas over the issue. The first train from Istanbul to Baghdad did not run until July 1940.

Bar-Lev line Name given to the Israeli fortresses built at the Suez Canal between October 1968 and March 1969, during the War of Attrition.

Bedouin Mainly Arab nomads, who traditionally roamed around the desert raising sheep, goats and camels. In recent decades many have become more permanently settled.

Bekaa Valley A flat plain in Lebanon with an average east–west width of about 10 miles (15 kms), from the northern edge of which rises the Anti-Lebanon mountain range, whose ridge forms the eastern border with Syria. Scene of fighting during the Lebanese civil war.

Betar A Zionist youth movement. While travelling in Latvia and Lithuania Jabotinsky came across groups of militant Zionist youth who had organized themselves into a society, Betar (Brith Trumpeldor). Jabotinsky and his Revisionist movement expanded the influence of Betar. Betar became the youth movement of the Revisionist Party in Israel. Inherited by the Herut Party.

'**Black Letter**' Name given by Arabs to letter from Ramsay Mac-Donald to Weizmann on 13 February 1931, in which the Prime Minister reaffirmed Britain's intention to stand by the Palestine mandate, viewed as an obligation to world Jewry, to uphold the policy of the Jewish national home by further land settlement and immigration; and to condone the Zionist insistence on Jewish labour for work on Jewish enterprises.

'**Black Saturday**' Riots in Egypt on 22 January 1952 in which the Muslim Brotherhood, socialists and students, probably assisted by the police angered over the sacrifice of their fellows by the government at Ismailia, attacked the European quarter of Cairo with cries of 'Allah akbar' and 'We want arms to fight for the Canal'. The symbols of the British in Egypt – Shepheard's Hotel, Thomas Cook's and BOAC – were ravaged, together with 400 other buildings, and seventeen British subjects killed.

Black September A terrorist organization created by al-Fatah following the events of September 1970 in Jordan. Responsible for the assassination of the Jordanian Prime Minister in September 1971. Responsible for murder of eleven Israeli athletes at Munich Olympics in September 1972.

'**Black September**' Name given to the events (including civil war) in Jordan in 1970 which led to the expulsion of the PLO from that country to Lebanon.

Bosphorous The only outlet from the Black Sea to the Mediterranean, these straits are 16 miles long bounded on one side by European Turkey and on the other by Asian Turkey. After running past Istanbul the outlet goes on to the Dardanelles and the Aegean.

Buraimi Oasis Bordering Abu Dhabi, Muscat and Oman, an area disputed between Britain, representing the Gulf states, and Saudi Arabia. If the area belonged to Saudi Arabia, the oil exploration rights would belong to the American-dominated ARAMCO; if it belonged to the Gulf states, the Iraq Petroleum Company would control the oil. In 1952 Saudi Arabia sent a force to the area. Arbitration was attempted in 1954. In 1955 military forces for

Muscat and Oman and Abu Dhabi, under British military command, occupied the oasis.

caliphate The office of the successor to the Prophet Muhammad in his political and social functions. The Ottoman Sultan held this office during the First World War. Atatürk abolished the sultanate in November 1922, and the caliphate in March 1924. Islamic Congresses at Mecca in 1924, Cairo in 1926, and Jerusalem in 1931 failed to agree on a new candidate for the caliphate.

CENTCOM (Central Command) United States successor to Rapid Deployment Force scheme of 1980. Makes up part of the United States's military presence in the Middle East. Based on a capability to deploy military forces from the United States.

Committee of Union and Progress Name that a group of Young Turks in Constantinople gave themselves in 1895. Later significant in Young Turk Revolution.

condominium Description of the joint Anglo–Egyptian administration of the Sudan from 1899 to 1955. In effect, Britain ruled the Sudan. The Sudan issue led to the breakdown of the Anglo–Egyptian negotiations in 1946, as Britain insisted that the Sudan had the right to exercise self-determination and resisted the claims of the Egyptian crown. In October 1951 Egypt unilaterally abrogated the agreement of 1899 and proclaimed Farouk as King of the Sudan. Britain did not recognize this, and the rise of the Young Officers in Egypt made a settlement of the issue possible, the condominium being terminated in December 1955.

Confessional System (Lebanon) Based on a French colonial administration census of 1932, provided for a Maronite Christian President, a Sunni Muslim Prime Minister, and a Shiite speaker of Parliament.

Cyrenaica The eastern section of Libya. Conquered by Italy from the Turks in 1911–12. Resistance led by a Sanussi chief, but colonized by Italy in the 1930s. Britain supported its declaration of independence in May 1949, but it became part of the federation of Libya in 1951.

Dai al-Dua Chief missionary of the Tayyibi Ismailis (the Borahs).

Damour massacre In 1976 the Palestinian Liberation Front, assisted by Syrian artillery, attacked the Christian town of Damour just outside Beirut. The Palestinian Liberation Front cut off food and water supplies and refused to allow the Red Cross to take out the wounded. Infants and children died of dehydration. Damour was transformed into a PFLP (Popular Front for the Liberation of Palestine) stronghold.

Dar al Islam Islamic territory.

Dardanelles Straits 37 miles long, lying between the Gallipoli peninsula and Asia Minor. Linking the Mediterranean with Istanbul, and together with the Bosphorous making up the Black Sea's outlet to the Mediterranean.

Day of Atonement (Yom Kippur) The most solemn fast of the Jewish religion. Takes place eight days after the Jewish New Year.

Deir Yassin On 9 April 1948, contingents of the Irgun and the Stern Gang, under Haganah command, encountered strong Arab resistance in the village of Deir Yassin, and slaughtered 245 men, women and children, most of the inhabitants of the town. Thought by the Arabs to have been perpetrated with the approval of Ben-Gurion and the Haganah leadership to terrorize the Arab population into fleeing from their land. Begin later spoke of the 'heroic' acts of his men at Deir Yassin, and attributed the Arab flight from the new state of Israel to this incident.

Diaspora The dispersion of the Jews among the Gentiles mainly in the 8th–6th centuries BC. Usually refers to the Diaspora of the Jews around the world after the destruction of Jerusalem in 135. Since 1948 Diaspora has also described the dispersion of the Palestinian Arabs after the United Nations resolution in November 1947 for the partition of Palestine.

Eichmann trial The trial of the Nazi leader, Adolf Eichmann, described by Israeli Prime Minister David Ben-Gurion as being one of those 'responsible for what was termed "the Final Solution to the Jewish problem", that is, the destruction of six million European Jews', took place in Israel between April 1961 and May 1962. Eichmann had been kidnapped by Israeli agents in Argentina and taken to Israel. Many of the sessions of Eichmann's trial were broadcast and it was also extensively covered in Israeli newspapers and the world press. Research by Israeli university and government sociologists showed the extent of the impact of the trial on Israeli youth. The lesson was drawn that there needed to be an 'ingathering of Jews' from all parts of the world in a homeland of their own. It was also seen to be inherently dangerous for a Jewish minority to live among non-Jewish majorities. The lesson was extended to others: those countries who had allowed the Nazi extermination to take place had incurred a moral obligation to ensure Israel's survival. It has been suggested that the Eichmann trial meant that the memory of the holocaust was to the forefront of Israeli consciousness on the eve of the Six-Day War.

Eisenhower Doctrine for the Middle East Enunciated by President Eisenhower in his State of the Union address to Congress on 5 January 1957. He asked for congressional authorization for military and economic assistance to the countries of the Middle East, and for permission to use United States armed forces to protect the independence and territorial integrity of any country in the region against aggression from international Communism. The Zionist lobby delayed congressional approval until Israel had secured its position in the Sinai and the Straits of Tiran, and the doctrine was only authorized on 9 March 1957. The Eisenhower Doctrine was applied in Jordan in April 1957 to stabilize the position of King Hussein: the United States sent its Sixth Fleet to the eastern Mediterranean and gave Jordan economic assistance. After the coup in Iraq in the middle of 1958, President Chamoun of the Lebanon requested assistance in terms of the doctrine: 14,000 American Marines landed in Lebanon and Britain sent paratroopers into Jordan. The doctrine was later linked to American co-operation with CENTO.

Eretz Israel Hebrew for the 'land of Israel'. During the period of the British mandate, there were demands that the term should be used in official publications, but the indigenous Jews scorned it, and it never became popular.

***Exodus* incident** The *President Warfield*, a ship renamed *Exodus*, arrived in Palestine in the middle of 1947 with 4,493 illegal immigrants. These were returned to their French port of embarkation. But the French declined to force the refugees to land. The fate of these immigrants was determined by Begin's Irgun which hanged two British sergeants and booby-trapped their bodies. The remains were found on 31 July, and resulted in widespread outbreaks of anti-Semitism in Britain, with even synagogues being daubed with swastikas. With opinion like this in Britain, any landing of the refugees from *Exodus* was out of the question. Bevin explained that Britain had no alternative other than to send them back to Germany. The immigrants were shipped back to Hamburg, giving the Zionists their most notable propaganda success of the time. A fictitious account of the incident by Leon Uris, later made into a film by Otto Preminger, created a myth of the incident that was so widely believed that it came to be perceived as reality.

'Al Fahd' Close-knit group in government of near relations of King Fahd of Saudi Arabia.

Falashas Ethiopian Jews, many of whom were airlifted to Israel during the war in the Horn of Africa in the 1980s and 1990s. Christian converts, known in Ethiopia as 'Feres Mora', have been described as 'not converted Jews, they are Jews who left Judaism'. Under a 1962 Israeli supreme court ruling a Jew who converts to another religion loses his right to Israeli citizenship and the right to emigrate to Israel.

al-Fatah (the Palestine National Liberation Movement) Led by Yasser Arafat, established in 1957, it is the largest Palestinian movement. In 1968 it joined the Palestine National Council. There was an unsuccessful revolt against Arafat in 1983.

Faw (Fao) An Iraqi city providing access to the Gulf. Devastated during Iran–Iraq War. Rebuilt in ninety days in 1989 as a symbol of Iraq's belief in the need for peace with Iran.

fedayeen Of Arabic derivation, meaning suicide squad, associated with the Ismaili 'Assassins' in medieval Persia. From the 1950s the term has been used to describe the small Arab guerrilla groups making sabotage and terrorist raids into Israel.

'Al Feisal' Group within the Al Saud family of Saudi Arabia made up of descendants and relations by marriage of King Feisal.

Fertile Crescent A geographical term referring to the countries in the north of Arabia, usually covering what became Iraq, Syria, Lebanon, Palestine (later Israel), and Jordan. Given political connotations by schemes of Abdullah, the King of Jordan, to form a Greater Syria, and also Nuri al-Said of Iraq for a federation of the states.

Front for the Liberation of Occupied South Yemen (FLOSY) Formed in 1966 by the merger of several underground resistance groups in Aden and South Yemen to force Britain out of the area and create a union with the Yemen. During the war in Yemen, Egypt supported FLOSY, but the organization was ousted by the National Liberation Front in 1967.

Fujairah A Trucial Coast principality, part of the United Arab Emirates.

Gahal An Israeli electoral alliance of the Herut and Liberal parties. Established in 1965, it joined the National Unity Government on the eve of the Six-Day War, but it left in July 1970 over the acceptance of the Rogers plan. It advocated a strong line on security issues, and based its policies on the historic Jewish right to Palestine.

Gallipoli A peninsula on the northern side of the Dardanelles in Turkey, the scene of a failed allied campaign in 1915–16.

ghetto Name often given to the Jewish quarter in cities. Usually segregated, and sometimes considered a slum.

Gidi passes Strategic area in Sinai, of significance during Arab–Israeli Wars.

Golan Heights A plateau of strategic significance commanding the lake of Galilee and the northern Jordan valley. Extending across two Syrian provinces and formerly inhabited mainly by the Druze, it was occupied by Israel during the Six-Day War and annexed by a bill Begin pushed through the Knesset on 14 December 1981. The Israeli annexation was unanimously condemned by the Security Council, but the United States vetoed punitive action.

Greater Land of Israel (Movement) A movement which advocated the annexation of territories captured in the Six-Day War.

Greater Syria A term usually associated with Abdullah of Jordan's dreams of uniting Syria, Lebanon and Palestine under his crown, including an autonomous Jewish state.

Green Line The armistice lines between Israel and the neighbouring Arab states fixed in 1949. Also a line dividing the Christian and Arab sections of Beirut.

Gulf Co-operation Council (GCC) Established on 25 May 1981 by Bahrain, Kuwait, Oman, Qatar, Saudi Arabia, and the United Arab Emirates to provide co-operation among its members in economics, industry, agriculture, transport and communications, energy, defence and external relations. The Supreme Council is made up of the heads of member states. In 1983 the Gulf Co-operation Council set up the Gulf Investment Corporation.

Gush Emunim (Community of Believers) Formed in February 1974 by young Israeli activists who broke away from the National Religious Party. Membership open to religious and non-religious. Aimed to settle the historic site of the biblical land of Israel. In 1974 and 1975 pioneered unauthorized new settlements in 'Judea', an area populated by Arabs. In the 1980s, with some of its members being tried for terrorist offences against Arabs, it became widely regarded as a militant messianic movement.

hadith The Traditions collected by witnesses to the Prophet Muhammad's life at Medina, handed down by oral tradition and collected and edited by Bukhari (died 807) and Muslim (died 875). These numbered around 7,000.

Haganah The defence force of the Jewish colonists in Palestine, founded in the 1920s. After the assassination of Lord Moyne in November 1944, it handed over a number of Irgun and Stern Gang members to the British authorities. But by March 1945 had started to work with the Irgun and the Stern Gang to secure the British withdrawal from Palestine. Involved with the planning for the blowing up of the King David Hotel, though subsequently denounced the operation. The units of the Irgun and Stern Gang that carried out the massacre at Deir Yassin were under Haganah command. Became the Israeli Defence Force in 1948.

hajj The pilgrimage which each Muslim able to afford it is supposed to make to Mecca once in a lifetime.

Halabja Site of use of chemical weapons by Iraq on Kurdish civilians in March 1988.

Hamas (Harakat al-Muqawama al-Islamiyya) (Movement of the Islamic Resistance) A fundamentalist Islamic movement that emerged during the early months of the intifada first in Gaza and then on the West Bank. Considers itself a link in the 'chain of *jihad*' that started with Qassam's rebellion in Palestine in the 1930s, the holy war declared following the United Nations partition resolution of November 1947, and the activities of the Muslim Brotherhood after 1968.

haram An Islamic sacred enclave. Mecca is an example. Muhammad also declared Yathrib a sacred enclave and renamed it Medina, the City of the Prophet. Mecca and Medina are known as *al-Haramain* and form the holy land of Islam.

Hashemites Refers to the family of the Sherifs of Mecca, who trace their descent to the prophet Muhammad. The honorary title 'Sherif of Mecca' is handed down from father to son. Family includes the ruling houses of Iraq from 1921 to 1958, and of Jordan from 1921 to the present.

311

Hebron Site of the Cave of Patriarchs. The Mosque of Abraham is built over the tomb of Abraham which also contains the tombs of Sarah, Isaac, Rebecca, Jacob and Leah. A holy place for Muslims and Jews.

hegira (hijra) Muhammad's flight from Mecca to Medina in 622. Marks the start of the Islamic era.

Hejaz An area of Western Arabia in present day Saudi Arabia, extending from the Red Sea coast to the Gulf of Aqaba and the mountains of Midian. It includes Mecca, Medina and the port of Jedda.

Hejaz Railway Built between 1900 and 1908, it runs from Damascus to Medina, and was intended ostensibly to carry pilgrims to Mecca but also to help the Ottoman Sultan prevent rebellion in the Arabian peninsula. It was sabotaged during the Arab revolt of 1916–17.

Herut Party The heir to the Revisionist Party. Founded in June 1948 and led by Menachem Begin. In 1973 became the leading party in the Likud bloc. Advocated settlement in all parts of Eretz Israel. Although the traditional upholder of the Greater Israel ideal, it lacked a significant settlement movement.

Hezbollah (Party of God) Lebanese Shiite fundamentalist group in opposition to rival Shiite movement Amal. Estimated strength in 1990 was 5,000.

High Commissioner A title used in the Middle East for the chief British representative in Egypt, 1914–36; Aden, 1963–7. In the British and French mandated territories for the chief of the administration (Palestine, Transjordan, Iraq, Syria and Lebanon).

Histradut General Federation of Labour in Israel. Established in 1920. Affiliated with the trade unions, it negotiates labour agreements and wages. It also provides social services, education, and medical care. Until the 1960s Arab and Jewish workers belonged to autonomous national units. But Arab workers objected to this separation, and by the early 1970s about half of Israel's Arab population belonged. The Histradut refused, however, to admit workers from the occupied territories on the grounds that to do so would constitute a step towards annexation.

holocaust The mass murder of Jews by Nazis between 1939 and 1945. Also used in a wider sense to include the elimination of racial minorities and groups such as homosexuals, gypsies and the mentally retarded by the Nazis.

Holy Places A name used in the Middle East to describe sites revered by particular religions. The Jews regard all of Eretz Israel as holy, but of particular significance is the Temple Mount in Jerusalem. The Western (or Wailing) Wall bordering the mount is all that remains of the Sacred Temple. Jewish tradition holds that Divine Immanence is there. To the Muslims, Jerusalem is the third most holy site. Muslims call the Temple Mount area al-Haram al-Sherif, meaning Noble Sanctuary. Muhammad ascended to heaven from here and this is marked by the mosque of al-Aqsa, the farthest mosque. Nearby is the Dome of the Rock, which is also (but misleadingly) known as the mosque of Omar. Muhammad's horse was tied to the Western Wall. The Tomb of the Patriarchs in Hebron is sacred to both Jews and Muslims. Mecca, the birthplace of Muhammad, is the holiest city of Islam: the venerated black stone is enshrined in the Kaaba. Medina, where Muhammad took refuge, is the second holiest city. The Christian holy places include: the Church of the Holy Sepulchre, the supposed site of Christ's crucifixion; the Via Dolorosa; and the Church of Ascension in Jerusalem; the Church of the Nativity in Bethlehem; sites in Nazareth and around the Lake of Galilee.

Imam Head of mosque and prayer leader in the practice of Sunni Islam. Head of the community and ruler, in theory, in Shiite Islam.

imamate The temporal and spiritual leadership of Islam.

International Commission of Jurists (Geneva) On 5 January 1978 criticized Israeli settlement in Sinai as illegal.

intifada The Palestinian uprising, sparked off in December 1987, in the Israeli-occupied territories of Gaza and the West Bank. An Arabic word referring to the shivering of someone in fever, or the shaking of a dog with fleas.

Iraq Petroleum Company Formed in 1929 between the British owners of the Turkish Petroleum Company, the French Compagnie des Pétroles, and two American companies, Standard Oil of New Jersey and Socony–Vacuum.

Irgun (Irgun Zvai Leumi) (IZL) (Etzel) National Military Organization. Founded by a militant Zionist, David Raziel, in 1937 with the aim of wresting a Jewish state from the British authorities. Initially conducted a terrorist campaign against the Arabs. Led by Menachem

Begin from 1941, and under his leadership worked with both the Haganah and the Stern Gang. Its terrorist activities included the blowing up of the King David Hotel in July 1946, the flogging of the British army officers, and the hanging of the two British sergeants and the booby-trapping of their bodies in July 1947. Successfully wore down British morale in the mandate. When Britain stopped using corporal punishment in the mandate after the flogging incident, it gave the first indication that it would give in to terrorism. According to Bevin, no British government was able to contemplate staying on in the mandate after the hanging of the two sergeants and the subsequent reaction in Britain. Irgun units participated in Deir Yassin and Begin subsequently praised his men for helping to precipitate the Arab flight. Played a major role in securing the birth of the State of Israel by wearing down British morale, tying down British troops, and, in the view of its leader, helping to precipitate the Arab flight. After the *Altalena* incident – in which the Irgun apparently defied the authority of the Israeli government and tried to bring in arms openly from the ship, and then withdrew on 21 June 1948 after a short engagement with the official force led by Moshe Dayan – most members joined the Israeli Defence Force. Begin was admitted to the United States later in 1948, on presidential instructions, which conferred a legitimacy on the terrorist activities. The Herut Party was established by supporters of the Irgun.

Islamic Jihad Khomeini's Islamic Revolutionary Movement sent men into the Bekaa Valley and joined with Lebanese Shiite extremists in creating a secret joint command called the Council of Lebanon. This council sponsored terrorist acts perpetrated under the name of Islamic Jihad, as well as Hezbollah and Islamic Amal. Also a name of a terrorist organization that provided the immediate background for the intifada. The call of Islamic Jihad was not only to use arms against Israel but to make that fight part of the Islamic revival, with its return to religious values.

Jebalya Largest Palestinian refugee camp in Gaza Strip. In 1988 had around 60,000 inhabitants. Site of riots on 9 December 1987 in early stages of intifada.

Jewish Agency for Palestine Established in 1929 to assist Jewish immigration to Palestine, buy land for Jews in Palestine through the Jewish National Fund, develop settlements with Jewish labour, further the use of Hebrew, and fulfil Jewish religious needs in Palestine. In dealings with the British government and the League of Nations, it represented the Zionist Organization. After 1948 the

Israeli government took over many of the Agency's activities. In 1971 the Jewish Agency, made up equally of representatives of Jews of the Diaspora and the World Zionist Organization, was established as the representative of world Jewry.

Jewish National Fund Established in December 1901, it was the Land and Development fund of the Zionist Organization. Supported by contributions from Jews throughout the world, it started buying land in Palestine in 1904 which became the inalienable property of the Jewish people and was usually leased for settlement. The White Paper of 1939 stopped purchases in most of Palestine. Holding around 250,000 acres in 1948, it acquired an additional 600,000 acres with the Arab flight.

Jibalis Hill tribes of Dhofar in Oman.

jihad (holy war; literally 'struggle') A fundamental tenet of Islam, which is usually taken to mean the obligation of Muslims to fight those countries or peoples who are unbelievers until they either convert or accept the status of protected people. In practice, the pronouncement of jihad by Muslims in one country does not commit Muslims in another country. Muslims believe fighting constitutes 'the lesser jihad', whereas stirring generally against evil and for the good is 'the greater jihad'.

Kaaba The focal point of all Muslim worship, a square stone structure in the precinct of the Great Mosque in Mecca. Said to have been founded by Abraham, it houses the revered Black Stone, which pilgrims circumambulate.

Kach Party A messianic party founded in Israel in 1977 by Rabbi Meir Kahane. 'Kach' means 'Thus' in Hebrew. The party's symbol was a clenched fist. Kach proclaimed: 'Judaism was always an exclusive group and it doesn't integrate with other people. I'm a Jew, not a democrat.' Kahane was elected to the Knesset in 1984 on the platform of his Kach Party which stood for the expulsion of the 700,000 Palestinians who were Israeli citizens as well as the 1.3 million Palestinians living in the occupied territories. In 1988 the Israeli High Court upheld legislation banning Kahane from running for the Knesset in 1988 as his party was racist and anti-democratic. In the run up to the 1988 elections in Israel pollsters indicated that the Kach Party could win as many as six seats in the Knesset and become the third largest party in the parliament. After the Temple Mount killings of 1990 Kach, writing in a Brooklyn-based Orthodox Jewish newspaper, compared the Palestinians to the ancient Canaanites whose extermination, he insisted, is mandated in the Bible. Following Kahane's assassination in New York, many demonstrators in Israel wore T-shirts carrying the clenched fist symbol of the Kach Party. Commentators have suggested that against the background of the intifada some of the principles of the Kach Party have attained respectability in Israel.

Kahan Commission Established to investigate the massacres in the Sabra and Shatila camps. Reported in February 1983 criticizing Begin, Shamir, Sharon and Eitan. Sharon resigned as Minister of Defence but stayed on in the Cabinet.

Kahaneism The philosophy of Meir Kahane embracing a hatred of Arabs, liberal Jews, and Western culture.

Kharg Island The site of the main Iranian oil export terminals at the entrance to the Gulf, bombed by Iran in the Iran–Iraq War.

Khuzestan A province of Iran.

kibbutz Collective settlements in Palestine, later Israel, usually agricultural but also including some industry. First kibbutz founded in 1909 alongside the Sea of Galilee. Usually reflected socialist principles: collective ownership, shared responsibility and common education. Often regarded as a pioneering élite, the kibbitzim played an important role in organizing the illegal Jewish immigration into Palestine, as well as in the Haganah and the Palmach. Helped to halt the Arab advance in 1948. In the 1970s and 1980s their economic validity was increasingly questioned and the lifestyle eased.

Knesset The parliament of modern Israel.

Koran (Qur'an) The sacred book of Islam. Muslims regard it as the Word of God as revealed to Muhammad by the Archangel Gabriel. It emphasizes the oneness of God. As the Creator of everything, He has absolute power over His creation. The account of the creation in the Koran resembles that in the Bible, as does the succession of prophets. Jesus Christ is considered a prophet; the virgin birth is acknowledged but not the crucifixion. In moral terms the Koran calls for generosity and care for the poor. It lays down principles for fairness in trading as well as rules on marriage, divorce, inheritance and religious duties.

Kurdistan A province of Iraq.

Kurds A people speaking Kurdish who live in an area described as Kurdistan, which straddles modern Turkey, Iraq, Iran, Syria and Soviet

Transcaucasia. Largely a pastoral people who lived within tribal communities. Name 'Kurd' first used around the 7th century, when most converted to Islam. Estimates of the number of Kurds varies between 14 and 28 million. Most Kurds are Sunni Muslims and speak Kurdish, an Iranian language related to Farsi. Before the First World War the Kurds lived in both the Ottoman and Persian (Iranian) empires. In the Treaty of Sèvres (10 August 1920), the Allies agreed to create a unified independent Kurdish homeland, but the treaty was never ratified. A Kurdish nationalist movement developed in the 1920s. In 1925 the Kurds rose against the government of Turkey but were crushed. The Soviet Union at the end of the Second World War supported a Kurdish republic called Mahabad in Iran, but the republic was overthrown by Iranian troops when the Soviets withdrew in 1946. Led by Mustafa Barzani, the Kurds in 1961 started armed resistance against Iraq. In 1970 the Baath Party in Iraq offered the Kurds autonomy, but the agreement collapsed. Supported by the Shah of Iran, the Kurds in 1974–5 were so successful in their struggle against the Iraqi government that Iraq was forced to reach an agreement with Iran over sovereignty in the Shatt al-Arab waterway with its access to the Gulf, and the Kurds were then abandoned by the Shah. From 1975 four out of every five Kurdish villages in the north had been destroyed, and the inhabitants moved into the southern deserts. In 1988 Saddam Hussein used poison gas against the Kurdish town of Halabja, killing 5,000, in revenge for the Kurdish support of Iran during the Iran–Iraq War of 1980–8. After the end of the Gulf War, hundreds of thousands of Kurdish refugees returned to the north of Iraq to reclaim their ancestral homelands. Saddam Hussein attacked the Kurds again. Around 250,000 fled into Turkey, and, it is estimated, 1 million crossed into Iran. Allied troops returned to establish 'safe havens' for the Kurds in some areas of the north of Iraq, and were later partly replaced by United Nations personnel. Many Kurdish refugees came back, and there were talks with Saddam Hussein on the matter of Kurdish autonomy. Kurds have also been consistently subjected to harassment in Iran and Turkey.

Labour Alignment The alliance of the Labour Party in Israel (formed from the Mapai), and the socialist Mapam, formed in 1969. Dissolved in 1984.

Land of Israel Movement An inter-party group in Israel which opposes withdrawal from territories occupied during the Six-Day War.

Lavon affair In July 1954, possibly at the instigation of Ben-Gurion, a group of rather amateur Israeli agents tried to sabotage British and American property in Egypt in the hope of giving the impression that violent elements in Egypt opposed its *rapprochement* with Britain and the United States, and that the Egyptian government could not control these dissident elements. The operation failed. The Egyptians later released details of the ring, and hanged two members on 31 January 1955. The Israeli Defence Minister, Pinchas Lavon, was seen by some as responsible, but he tried to blame the affair on Shimon Peres, the Director-General of the Ministry of Defence, Moshe Dayan, and General Benjamin Givly, the Chief of Intelligence. Lavon was forced to resign. A committee of seven members determined that Lavon had not given the order to Givli; this led to Ben-Gurion's resignation as Prime Minister in 1963 and new elections. In 1964 Eshkol refused Ben-Gurion's request for a Board of Enquiry into the decision of the committee of seven.

Law of Return Passed by the Israeli Knesset in July 1950: gave Jews everywhere the legal right of immigration to Israel. Did not define the term 'Jew' in its national (ethnic) sense. In 1958 the Israeli supreme court ruled that the national term 'Jew', while it applied to many who did not practise Judaism, could not be applied to anyone who voluntarily adopted another faith. After a supreme court ruling in 1970 that a Jewish husband and his Gentile wife could register their children as Jews by nationality rather than religion, the Knesset amended the Law of Return to mean, in effect, one either born to Jewish mother or formally converted to Judaism. In 1981, although the Law of Return was not amended again by the Knesset, the practice developed that the ministry of religions (the deciding body under previous amendments) chose not to recognize as Jews those spouses or children who had been converted abroad under non-Orthodox auspices.

Levant Meaning lands of the rising (sun), the term used to cover the area of the Eastern coast of the Mediterranean extending from Greece to Egypt. Later usage included Syria, Lebanon, Palestine and the coastal areas of Asia Minor. The term was later taken to mean just Syria and Lebanon.

Likud A parliamentary bloc in Israel formed in September 1973, principally from the Herut and Liberal parties. Likud and the Liberal Party merged in August 1988 to form the Likud-National Liberal Movement. This right-wing bloc, which increasingly received the support of Sephardic Jews during the 1970s and 1980s, stands for the retention of all the territories of mandatory Palestine. It also emphasizes the need to absorb new immigrants and a social order based on freedom and justice. Led by Begin, then Shamir, it was the party of government from June 1977 to September 1984, and then formed the National Unity government.

Litani The principal river of Lebanon.

Maghreb Meaning 'West' in Arabic, the term is used to describe the countries of North Africa, Morocco, Algeria and Tunisia which use Arabic. It also covered the western part of Libya, Tripolitania, and since Libyan independence in 1951, has often included Libya.

Mahdi An Islamic messiah (guided one) who will restore justice and peace, and who has received his authority directly from Muhammad in a vision.

Majlis Meaning 'assembly' in Arabic and Persian. The term used for the parliaments of various North African and Middle Eastern countries, but especially that of Iran.

Majnoon oilfield An Iraqi oilfield on the borders of Iran in the Hawizah swamps, occupied during the Iran–Iraq War.

mandate A system of administration of former German colonies and Asian areas of the Ottoman Empire, largely inspired by General Jan Christian Smuts of South Africa, which under Article 22 of the Covenant entrusted the tutelage of peoples not yet able to look after themselves to advanced nations on behalf of the League. Palestine, Transjordan, Iraq (Mesopotamia) and Syria (including Lebanon) were classed as 'A' mandates: civilized but not yet ready for independence. The terms of the mandate for Palestine specifically excluded that country from the principle of self-determination. Britain was given the mandate for Palestine, Transjordan and Iraq; France for Syria and Lebanon.

Mapai A Zionist-socialist political party established in Palestine in 1930. Its leaders were the Prime Minsters of Israel from 1948–65. In 1965 it formed the 'Alignment' and in January 1968 merged with two other factions to form the Israel Labour Party. In 1969 formed an alliance with the left-wing Mapam known as the 'Labour Alignment'.

Mapam The United Workers' Party in Israel. Established in 1948 on the principles of pioneering Zionism and revolutionary socialism. Initially Moscow-orientated, but attachment weakened by

Czechoslovakian arms deal with Egypt in 1955. Formed the 'Labour Alignment' with the Israel Labour Party in 1969. Remained part of that alignment until 1984, when Mapai agreed to form a National Unity government with the Likud.

Masada The site west of the Dead Sea where the Jewish rebels made their last stand against the Roman legions in AD 73, and committed suicide to avoid capture. Excavated by Yigael Yadin from 1964. Israeli Defence Force helped in excavations. Gave rise to a secular cult which, with the annexation of East Jerusalem in 1967, seemed to merge 2,000 years of Jewish history. 'Masada complex' often compared to the 'laager mentality' of the Afrikaners in South Africa, as it developed at the same time as Israel's close relationship with South Africa. Similarities seen in embattlement by outside forces, and a resolution to die rather than give in or compromise.

Mecca As the birthplace of Muhammad, it is the holiest city of Islam. At one time capital of the Hejaz, it is now part of Saudi Arabia. A place of Muslim pilgrimage, it is the site of the Black Stone of the Kaaba.

Medina The burial place of Muhammad and his immediate successors, Medina is the second most holy city in Islam. In 622 Muhammad left Mecca for Medina (the move known as the hegira or hijra). In the Hejaz; now part of Saudi Arabia.

Mehran A major battle area in Iran during the Iran–Iraq War.

Middle East Prior to the Second World War the term Near East was more usual, and that often included the Balkans, Greece, Anatolia, and the eastern coast of the Mediterranean. By 1949 the term Middle East had replaced 'Near East' in British official documents. But in practice the term has no accepted area limitations. Usually it covers the Arab countries of Asia, Egypt and Iran, Israel and Turkey. Sometimes it includes also Cyprus, Sudan and Libya, and even Afghanistan, Pakistan, Ethiopia and Somalia.

Mitla pass Strategic area in Sinai of significance during Arab–Israeli Wars.

Morasha (Heritage) An extremist offshoot of the National Religious Party in Israel.

Mossad The Israeli intelligence organization. Has worked in close collaboration with the United States Central Intelligence Agency.

Shamir played a leading role in the body, especially between 1965 and 1975, and for a while was its chief.

Mosul An area rich in oil in modern Iraq, initially designated as a French zone of influence in the Sykes–Picot Agreement of 1916, but transferred to the British zone in the Lloyd George–Clemenceau Agreement of 1918.

Mount Scopus A ridge running to the Mount of Olives that in 1925 became the site of the Hebrew University of Jerusalem and a hospital. On 13 April 1948 the site of an Arab attack on a Jewish convoy of doctors, nurses and academics which killed sixty-eight, in retaliation for Deir Yassin. The armistice agreement at Rhodes of 1949 allowed for Mount Scopus to be a demilitarized zone. Occupied by the Israelis in the Six-Day War, the university was re-opened in 1969.

Mufti A Muslim religious official who pronounces when questioned, usually on spiritual and social matters. Normally appointed by the government but, with the exception of the Mufti of Jerusalem (1921–37), has no officially defined political role.

mullah A follower of Islam in the Shiite tradition, who is learned in theology and the shariah.

Multi-national force and observers in the Sinai (MFO) Sent into the Sinai after the October War to maintain peace in the area. Stayed until 1981.

Nablus Town in Samaria on the West Bank, absorbed into Jordan in 1948, but administered by Israel since the Six-Day War. A principal area of unrest during the intifada.

Nashashibis A prominent Palestinian family who had acquired considerable lands early in the 20th century. Principal rivals of the Husseinis, another prominent family, and this rivalry helped to shape Palestinian politics during the period of the British mandate.

Nasserism A generalized view, largely held among a new generation of Arab nationalists, that Nasser represented the forces of social progress and Arab identity, as distinct from what they regarded as hierarchical and even imperial views of some of the old ruling houses. The Western powers tended to use the term in connection with the ideas expressed in *The Philosophy of the Revolution*, which saw Egypt as the centre of the African, Arab, and Islamic circles and a challenge to Western interests.

National Liberation Front for Occupied South Yemen (NLF) An extremist Arab nationalist underground organization which operated in Aden and South Arabia, later South Yemen. Established by Qahtan al-Shaabi in June 1963 in Aden as a nationalist front to take over from the traditional authority of the sheikhs. Attacked British military installations and officials from August 1964. It led the rebellion in the area, joining briefly with the Front for the Liberation of Occupied South Yemen (FLOSY) in 1966 and at times was supported by Egypt. The British government handed over power to the NLF in Aden in 1967, and in 1970 the movement formally established the People's Democratic Republic of Yemen. After independence, the movement developed a Marxist–Leninist orientation.

National Religious Party Formed in 1955 in Israel with the merger of two Zionist religious parties. Aims to establish a society in Israel based on the law of Moses (the Torah), and campaigns on issues such as the observance of the sabbath and the observance of religious law. Insists on the Jews' right to the whole of historical Palestine and supports Jewish settlement on the West Bank. Though small, the party has usually exercised a considerable influence in the coalition governments from the 1960s onwards. Left the coalition government formed by Labour in 1976. Supported Likud coalition in the 1984 general election.

Negev The desert southern half of the Palestine mandate, extending from the Mediterranean to the top of the Gulf of Aqaba. Partly as a result of Weizmann's intervention with Truman, the United Nations allotted the area to the Zionists in the partition vote of November 1947.

Nejd The central desert area of Saudi Arabia, including the capital Riyadh, disputed between the houses of Rashid and Saud between 1880 and 1922.

Neutral Zone (Saudi Arabia–Iraq) The Nejd (later Saudi Arabian) frontier with Iraq was defined in the Treaty of Mohammara in May 1922. An agreement signed in December 1922 between Sir Percy Cox, the British High Commissioner in Iraq, and Ibn Saud, established two zones of 'neutral and common ground'. One was established on the western tip of the frontier with Kuwait (7,044 sq km in area). It was agreed that nomads could have access and that there should be no military or permanent buildings. Iraq and Saudi Arabia signed an agreement about the administration of this zone in May 1938. In July 1975 they agreed to divide the zone between their two countries, the border being a straight line through the diamond shape.

Neutral Zone (Saudi Arabia–Kuwait) The agreement of 1922 between Ibn Saud and Sir Percy Cox established the boundary between Nejd (later Saudi Arabia) and Kuwait. It also set up a Neutral Zone south of Kuwait (5,770 sq km) in which Saudi Arabia and Kuwait had equal rights. In 1963 the two countries signed a final agreement on this. From 1966 each country administered its own half of the Partitioned Zone, as it also became known. There was no agreement about the petroleum rights, and production from the onshore oil concessions was shared between Aminoil and Getty who held the concessions in Saudi Arabia and Kuwait.

al-Nizam al-Islami The ideal Islamic order to which the Muslim Brotherhood aspired.

al-Nizam al-Jahili The prevailing order in the Muslim world as described by Hasan al-Banna, the founder of the Muslim Brotherhood. Corresponding to the 'period of ignorance' before the coming of Islam.

Northern Tier A concept developed in the early 1950s against the background of the Cold War, particularly by the American State Department and John Foster Dulles, embracing the idea of a defence alliance with northern Middle East states bordering on the Soviet Union, particularly Turkey and Iran.

occupied territories The areas occupied by Israel during the 1967 Six-Day War: the Golan Heights conquered from Syria and annexed by Israel in December 1981; the West Bank conquered from Jordan; the Gaza Strip conquered from Egypt; and the Sinai Peninsula, the last third of which was handed back to Egypt in April 1982.

Operation Desert Shield The code-name for the allied coalition operation to reinforce Saudi Arabia and the Gulf area after Saddam Hussein's invasion of Kuwait in August 1990.

Operation Desert Storm The code-name for the air offensive mounted by the allied coalition against Iraq and occupied Kuwait in January and February 1991.

Operation Peace for Galilee The code-name for the Israeli invasion of Lebanon in 1982.

Organization of Arab Petroleum Exporting Countries (OAPEC) Founded in 1968 by Kuwait, Libya and Saudi Arabia. Membership confined to Arab states in which oil production a major part of the economy.

Organization of Petroleum Exporting Countries (OPEC) Established at Baghdad in 1960. Founder members were Iran, Iraq, Kuwait, Saudi Arabia and Venezuela. Qatar joined in 1961; Libya and Indonesia in 1962; Abu Dhabi in 1967; Algeria in 1969; Nigeria in 1971; Ecuador in 1973; Gabon in 1975. Membership of Abu Dhabi transferred to United Arab Emirates in 1974. OPEC aims to stabilize world oil prices, ensure fair profits for oil companies, ensure oil supplies to consumers, and arrange boycotts of companies that do not co-operate.

Orontes Main river in Syria which rises in the Bekaa Valley in Lebanon and enters the Mediterranean near Antioch in Turkey.

Pahlavi The Persian language spoken during the Parthian dynasty. Chosen as the name for the dynasty in Iran by Reza Shah in 1925. The dynasty was exiled in 1979 by Islamic fundamentalists.

Palestine Liberation Front (PLF) Originally a splinter from the Popular Front for the Liberation of Palestine–General Command in April 1977, it divided into two separate factions in 1983. One located in Tunis was loyal to Arafat. The other belonged to the Syrian-based National Salvation Front. The two factions were re-united under Abu Abbas in June 1987.

Palestine Liberation Organization (PLO) Both the PLO and its military wing, the Palestine Liberation Army, were founded in 1964. The Palestine National Council is the supreme body of the PLO. The Palestine Executive Committee deals with everyday affairs. Fatah joined the Palestine National Council in 1968, and the other terrorist and guerrilla organizations in 1969. The PLO is supported by taxes and contributions levied on Palestinians. At the same time as sheltering terrorist organizations, it has acted on a wide diplomatic front and has achieved international recognition of a Palestinian state. By July 1989 ninety-six states had given Palestinian representatives diplomatic recognition. The PLO Central Council nominated Yasser Arafat as President of the state of Palestine in April 1989. With the ending of Jordan's administrative and legal links with the West Bank in July 1988, the PLO has attempted to assert sovereignty over the occupied territories.

Palestine National Council (PNC) Made up of 379 members, this Palestinian parliament represents the guerilla groups, trade and student unions, and Palestinians throughout the world.

Palestinian Authority (often referred to by Palestinians as the Palestinian National Authority) Established under the terms of the Israeli–Palestine Liberation Organization Accord, it is the legislative and executive body responsible for exercising the powers devolved by Israel to the autonomous Palestinian areas. It is made up of a maximum of twenty-four members and is to continue until elections have been held in the West Bank and Gaza to the Palestinian Council. Yasser Arafat is the Chairman.

Palestinians The descendants of the nomads, villagers and townspeople who since antiquity have lived in the area on the eastern shores of the Mediterranean roughly covered by the Roman province of Syria Palestina. In modern times, usually refers to the Arab inhabitants of the area of the British mandate of Palestine. They include a large minority of Christians, but the majority practise Islam and speak Arabic. Until the partition of Palestine in 1948, the majority of the Palestinians were peasant farmers (*fellahin*) who lived in hundreds of scattered villages. A minority were Bedouin who moved around the Galilee hills and the southern Negev desert. A large minority of Palestinians were town-dwellers, practising professions and trades and relatively well off. With partition, around half of the 800 Arab villages – mainly in the coastal plain – were destroyed, and the Palestinian population was dispersed in refugee camps in surrounding Arab countries. By 1990 there were around 5 million Palestinians scattered across the world. 1.3 million Palestinians live in Jordan and have Jordanian citizenship. Those in Lebanon, Syria and Kuwait do not have the same rights as citizens of those states. Between 650,000 and 700,000 Palestinians are citizens of Israel and live within its pre-1967 borders; 125,000 live in East Jerusalem. Just over 800,000 Palestinians live on the rest of the West Bank, and around 15 per cent of these are refugees. There are 550,000 Palestinians in the Gaza Strip, and almost 70 per cent of these live in refugee camps. Since 1949 about 70 per cent of the inhabitants of the Gaza Strip have lived in refugee camps. Israel estimates are that the number of Palestinians living on the West Bank and Gaza Strip will reach 2 million within the next fifteen years.

Palmach The 'striking force' of the Haganah established in 1941. In 1944 a naval company and air platoon were set up within the

Palmach. In the early stages of the First Arab–Israeli War, it formed the élite fighting units, but was disbanded in October 1948 by Ben-Gurion.

Pan-Arabism The movement for Arab unity, manifestations of which have been the Fertile Crescent and Greater Syria schemes, as well as Nasser's attempt at Egyptian hegemony, and attempted unions of Egypt, Libya and Syria.

Passover A Jewish festival, held in spring, to commemorate the freeing of the Israelites from Egypt.

patriarch The title of the chief bishop in certain Orthodox churches, as well as those presiding at Antioch and Alexandria.

Peace Now A movement in Israel which arose out of popular support for a letter sent to Begin in the spring of 1978 from 350 soldiers and officers, criticizing the Prime Minister's annexation policy and arguing that it prevented Israel from establishing normal relations with its neighbours. The letter stated that security could only come though peace. Supported by writers and academics, as well as Nahum Goldmann, the former President of the World Jewish Congress, it organized mass demonstrations. The one in 1982 in Tel Aviv against Israeli involvement in Lebanon drew around 400,000 people.

Persia Deriving from Parsa, the ancient capital of the Archaemenid dynasty, a name for Iran banned in 1925 by Reza Shah, who preferred the term referring to the land of the Aryans. In 1949 Muhammad Reza Shah allowed both names to be used.

Persian Gulf That part of the Indian Ocean separating the Arabian peninsula and the coast of Iran. Now usually referred to as the 'Gulf'.

peshmerga A group of Kurdish guerrillas in Iraq; word means 'those who confront death'.

Phalange (Lebanese Phalangist Party or Kata'ib) Founded in the 1930s with the attempt by Maronite Christians to preserve Lebanon from Syrian expansion. Developed into a right-wing military movement which clashed in April 1975 with the PLO. Leadership dominated by members of the Gemayel clan. Welcomed Israeli invasion of Lebanon in 1982. Estimated strength in 1990 was 10,000.

pogrom Name given to an organized massacre of Jews in Russia, particularly in the 1880s, following the claim after the assassination of Tsar Alexander II that Russia's difficulties could be attributed to

Jewish corruption. The Russian government either acquiesced or connived in these attacks. Term also used to describe massacres of Jews elsewhere, particularly in Central Europe.

Popular Front for the Liberation of Palestine (PFLP) Founded in 1967. Led by Dr George Habash, it is Marxist–Leninist in approach and is based in Damascus. Hijacked Air France plane in June 1976 to Entebbe airport.

Popular Front for the Liberation of Palestine–General Command (PFLP–GC) A splinter from the Popular Front for the Liberation of Palestine, it is pro-Syrian. Led by Ahmad Jibril, it is based in Damascus.

'posted price' The base from which the profits of crude oil are calculated.

Progressive List for Peace A combined list of Arab and Jewish candidates who stood in the 1984 election in Israel on the platform of establishing a Palestinian state in the West Bank and the Gaza Strip.

Protocols of the Learned Elders of Zion Record of alleged meetings of Jews and freemasons towards the end of the 19th century about a plot to overthrow capitalism and Christianity, and to set up a world state under their joint rule. Published originally in a Russian newspaper in 1903, and in a book in 1905, they were supposed to have been discovered by Sergei Nilus, a Tsarist official. Attracted little attention until the Bolshevik Revolution of 1917, when comparisons were drawn between the Communist doctrine of Bolshevik Jewish leaders and the Protocols. In 1920 used to explain revolts against British rule in the East. In 1921 Philip Graves, Constantinople correspondent of *The Times*, revealed them as a forgery organized by the Tsarist secret police, and a plagiarism of a satire on Napoleon III written by a French lawyer and published in 1864. Despite these revelations, the Protocols have been widely used by Arab publicists.

Rafi Party A political party founded in 1965 in Israel by Ben-Gurion, Dayan and Peres, to represent the younger generation and modernization. On 12 December 1967 a convention of the Rafi Party decided to unite with the Mapai and Adhut Avodah parties to form the Labour Party. Ben-Gurion opposed the merger and headed a one-man party in the Knesset. On 21 January 1968 the union of the parties was formally established.

Ramadan The eighth month of the Islamic lunar year, during which, according to the Koran, all Muslims must fast. During that month between dawn and dusk Muslims should not eat, drink, smoke or have sex, but remain in a state of ritual purity. According to the Traditions, Ramadan is the month in which Muhammad received his first revelation.

Ramadan, War of The Arab name for the October War of 1973.

Ramallah A major town on the West Bank, which has a considerable Palestinian refugee population.

Rapid Deployment Force Scheme of Carter administration to move forces quickly, principally to the Middle East. Replaced by CENTCOM.

Rashid The family of sheikhs that rivalled the house of Saud in the northern Nejd desert from around 1880 to 1922.

Republican Guard The élite corps within the Iraqi army which made possible the Baath takeover in Iraq in 1968. Became the personal bodyguard of Saddam Hussein who changed the social composition of the Republican Guard, ensuring that it consisted mainly of conscripts from his area around Tikrit. Apparently routed when the coalition forces invaded Kuwait in February 1991, but some commentators have suggested that it has largely remained intact.

Revisionists (Zionist) Party established by Jabotinsky in 1925 in Palestine. Wanted a Zionist state on both sides of the Jordan. Approved of a militant and nationalist education for youth. Opposed the World Zionist Organization and in dispute with the Histradut. In 1935 left the Zionist Organization and established the New Zionist Organization. Members helped to found the Irgun and the Stern Gang. Rejoined the Zionist Organization in 1946 and after the creation of the State of Israel merged with Begin's Herut Party.

riba Usury or interest which is banned as exploitation in Islam. Banks and insurance companies are considered to earn profit (*ribh*) which is lawful for a Muslim.

Saadist Party An Egyptian political party established in 1937 by young men disillusioned with the Wafd leadership of the time. Saw themselves as the successors of Saad Zaghlul and named party after him. Supporters of Farouk, their leaders were members of the non-Wafd governments.

Sabah, Al The ruling dynasty in Kuwait.

Sabra A refugee camp in West Beirut. In September 1982 Phalangist militia, with the assistance of Israeli troops, entered the camp, ostensibly to destroy Palestinian terrorists, and massacred hundreds of the inhabitants.

Saiqa, al- A Palestinian fighting organization established in Syria in 1967–8 by the Baath party, directed by the Syrian army.

salat The formal prayer that the Muslim should perform five times a day.

Samaria A central area of the Palestine mandate containing Nablus. A term widely used by Begin, together with Judea, to describe the West Bank.

sanjak A county or subdivision of a province in the Ottoman Empire. Some countries in the Ottoman Empire were also created as separate administrative units known as independent *sanjak.*

Satanic Verses, The A novel by British author, Salman Rushdie, regarded as blasphemous by many Muslims. Published in Britain in September 1988. As Rushdie had been born a Muslim, he was considered guilty of apostasy under Islamic law. On 14 February 1989 Ayatollah Khomeini issued an edict pronouncing a death sentence on Rushdie. Rushdie apologized, but the edict was reiterated and led to a breach in diplomatic relations between Britain and Iran, as well as exacerbating race relations in Britain where fundamentalist Muslims in Bradford were regarded as having been the instigators of the affair in an attempt to secure an official position for Islam in Britain. (British laws of blasphemy apply to Islam as well as Christianity.) There were also demonstrations elsewhere in the world, particularly in the Indian subcontinent where Rushdie had been born.

Saud, house of Ruling dynasty of Saudi Arabia.

Sayyid A Muslim leader claiming descent from Ali's second son, al-Hussein.

Second multi-national force in Beirut (MNF 2) Attempted to establish authority of Lebanese government, but left in in a weakened state. In Beirut September from 1983 to March 1984.

Sephardi Means Spanish. Originally referred to the Jews expelled from Spain in 1492. Some settled in the Netherlands and still maintain a distinct community there. The majority spread throughout the Mediterranean basin and also into the Balkans dominated by the Ottoman Empire. Sephardi culture is distinct and based on a special language, Ladino, which is a mixture of medieval Spanish and Hebrew. Later 'Sephardi' was also used to describe most of the Jewish communities in the Muslim world. These communities had their own culture and had their own Arabic dialects, which they mixed with Hebrew. Those in North Africa were influenced by French culture. Sephardi use their own prayer book, which is different from the Ashkenazi version. Today the term is used to refer to Jews in Israel of North African and Middle Eastern backgrounds.

shahada The Muslim testimony: 'There is no god but Allah and Muhammad is His Prophet.'

shariah Islamic law. The sacred law of Islam covers all aspects of life and not just religious practices. For the Muslim it is the path to heaven.

Sharjah A principality on the Trucial Coast which became part of the United Arab Emirates when it was formed in 1971.

Sharm el-Sheikh A cove on the Sinai peninsula that controls the Straits of Tiran. Used by Egypt to blockade Israeli shipping in 1954. Captured by Israel in 1956 and controlled by United Nations Emergency Force, 1957–67. Captured by Israel in the Six-Day War. Returned to Egypt on 25 April 1982 in terms of Israeli–Egyptian Peace Treaty of 26 March 1979.

Shas Oriental religious party founded in 1984 in Israel.

Shatila A refugee camp in West Beirut. In September 1982 Phalangist militia, with the assistance of Israeli troops, entered the camp, ostensibly to destroy Palestinian terrorists, and massacred hundreds of the inhabitants.

Shatt al-Arab Waterway formed by the joining of the Euphrates and Tigris rivers in southern Iraq: Iraq's entry into the Gulf.

Sherif (Sharif) A Muslim leader tracing descent from Muhammad through his daughter Fatima. Often Shiite, but many are also Sunnis.

Shin Bet The Israeli Military Intelligence Agency, primarily responsible for 'internal' security matters.

Shma Yisrael The basic prayer of Judaism: 'Hear O Israel, the Lord our God is one.' Recited by the faithful each morning and evening.

Shouf mountains A range of hills in Lebanon south of the road joining Beirut and Damascus. Occupied by Israelis in 1982.

Sinai Peninsula Desert triangle in Arabia between the Suez Canal and the Gulf of Suez, and the Gulf of Aqaba.

Stern Gang (Lehi) (Fighters for the Freedom of Israel) Zionist terrorist organization founded in 1939 by Abraham Stern, a former Irgun leader, who died in 1942. After that operated under the leadership of David Yelland Friedman and then Yitzhak Shamir. Responsible for the assassination of Lord Moyne, the British Minister resident in the Middle East in November 1944. In 1945 entered into a pact with the Haganah and the Irgun to drive the British out of Palestine. Responsible for the assassination of Bernadotte, the United Nations mediator in Palestine in 1948. Always relatively small in numbers. Regarded as extreme. Disbanded by Israeli government in 1948.

Strait of Hormuz An important passage for shipping on the Gulf coast.

Supreme Muslim Council Created in 1922 to administer Muslim community affairs in Palestine. With the Mufti of Jerusalem as President, there were divisions between the two factions supporting either the Husseini family or the Nashashibi family. Dissolved at the time of the Arab rebellion on 1 October 1937. After that its members were appointed by the mandatory government.

sunna The practice laid down by Muhammad and established by the Traditions.

tahara The form of ritual purity a Muslim achieves by washing before making the *salat.*

Talmud The body of Jewish law.

Tami Oriental offshoot of the National Religious Party in Israel.

tawhid The Islamic Unitarian belief that God is one being (monotheism). This vehement opposition to polytheism is reflected in the first half of the basic tenet of Islam: 'There is no god but Allah and Muhammad is His Prophet.'

Tehiya An Israeli party, founded by nationalists in 1979, dedicated to establishing Jewish settlements on the whole of the West Bank.

Also known as the 'National Renaissance Party'.

Temple Mount The Christian name for the site in the Old City of Jerusalem known as al-Haram al-Sherif to Muslims and Har Habait to Jews. Includes the al-Aqsa Mosque, the Dome of the Rock, and the Wailing Wall, the outer Western Wall of the Second Temple.

Temple Mount killings On 8 October 1990, twenty-one Palestinians were killed on Temple Mount in Jerusalem by Israeli forces following a stoning incident involving Jewish worshippers.

Third Universal Theory Cultural revolution in Libya announced by Gadaffi in 1973. Aimed at purging both capitalism and communism from Libyan society.

Thalweg line Basis for the international frontier established in the Shatt al-Arab between Iran and Iraq in the Algiers Agreement of 1975. The Thalweg line is the middle of the deepest shipping channel in the Shatt al-Arab.

Tiran, Straits of A narrow passage, including a number of islands, which joins the Red Sea and the Gulf of Aqaba. Commands access to Eilat and Aqaba and has been controlled and used for blockade by both Egypt and Israel.

Torah (also known as Pentateuch) First five books of the Old Testament. Records God's revelation to Moses and the Jewish people made on Mount Sinai around 1000 BC. The Torah contains 613 commandments, including prohibition of murder and idolatry, and regulates all aspects of daily life, from sexual relations to matters of hygiene. Also used to refer to the scroll read in synagogue containing the body of Jewish teaching.

Transjordan An area on the East Bank of the Jordan River. Abdullah established as Emir by Britain in 1921 and Transjordan held by Britain under mandate until 1946. With the incorporation of the West Bank became the Kingdom of Jordan in 1948.

Tripolitania North-west region of Libya.

Trucial Coast Seven principalities or sheikdoms along the Arabian coast of the Gulf – Abu Dhabi, Umm al-Qaiwain, Dubai, Ajman, Fujairah, Ras al-Khaimah and Sharjah – in treaty relationship with Britain from the 19th century to 1971. Then formed into United Arab Emirates.

Tudeh A communist party in Iran. Founded in 1941 in north Iran, it aimed at social and economic reforms. In 1945, in collaboration with the Soviet Union, tried to take over Azerbaijan, at that time separated from Iran. Suppressed after the Iranian armies in December 1946 occupied the two independent republics that had been proclaimed in Azerbaijan and Kurdistan. Banned in 1949 after a member attempted to assassinate the Shah. It supported Mossadeq and the nationalization of oil, but was banned again with the return of the Shah.

turuq (**singular** *tariqa*) Sufi mystical orders of Islam.

ulema (singular ulim) Followers of Islam who are learned in theology and the shariah.

umma Community of Islam.

Unified National Leadership of the Uprising (UNLU) Formed in 1988. Included representatives of both the PLO and Islamic Jihad. Helped to institutionalize the intifada.

United Arab Republic The union of Syria and Egypt, formed in February 1958 and dissolved in September 1961 with Syrian secession. Egypt continued to use the name into the 1970s.

United Nations Disengagement and Observer Force (UNDOF) Established by agreement of 31 May 1974 to supervise and inspect the separation of forces in the Golan Heights.

United Nations Emergency Force (UNEF) Established in 1956 to supervise the cessation of hostilities in the Suez–Sinai War. Stationed on Egyptian soil until May 1967, it helped to ensure free passage of shipping in the Straits of Tiran and to prevent armed clashes between Egypt and Israel.

United Nations Interim Force in Lebanon (UNIFIL) Established in 1978 to prevent Palestinian terrorist attacks from Lebanon into northern Israel.

United Nations Relief and Works Agency for Palestinian Refugees in the Near East (UNRWA) Established by the General Assembly in December 1949 to assist the Arabs dispossessed by the creation of the State of Israel and the First Arab–Israeli War. The Arab states opposed efforts to resettle and rehabilitate the refugees, and demanded their return to what had become Israel. UNRWA concentrated on providing housing, food and education in the refugee camps.

Va'ad Leumi The National Council of the Jews of Palestine, established in 1920. Concerned with local government, administration, and taxation of the Jewish community in Palestine. Recognized by the British in 1926, it usually followed the lead of the Jewish Agency. Represented the Jewish community to the mandatory government and to the commissions of enquiry. In 1948 its activities were taken over by the provisional government of Israel.

Vanunu affair In October 1986 Mordechai Vanunu, who worked at the Dimona plant in the Negev, claimed in an interview in the London *Sunday Times* that Israel had developed thermo-nuclear weapons and was stockpiling them. Captured by the Mossad in Rome, Vanunu was imprisoned for treason in Israel.

vilayet The Ottoman Empire in the last quarter of the 19th century was divided into *vilayet* or provinces.

Wafd A leading nationalist party in Egypt, 1919–53. Initially led by Zaghlul and then Nahas, it opposed attempts by Farouk to restrict parliamentary power. Though suspicious of Britain, it was considered by the British as representative of Egyptian nationalism, and it was under British direction that Farouk appointed a Wafd Prime Minister in 1942. In government, 1924, 1928, 1930, 1931–7, 1942–4, 1950–2. The Wafd was revived in the Mubarak period and allowed to contest the elections of May 1984; it won fifty-seven seats in the National Assembly.

Wailing Wall (Western Wall) The lower courses of the outer wall of Herod's Temple (destroyed by the Romans in AD 70) in Jerusalem and the only remaining part. The most hallowed site of Jewish pilgrimage. The Arabs regard it as part of al-Haram al-Sherif, where Muhammad had tethered his horse after his journey from Mecca to Jerusalem while he ascended to the seventh heaven. The removal by police on 28 September 1928 of a screen illegally placed near the 'Wailing Wall' to separate Jewish men and women at prayer led to disputes between Jews and Muslims and riots in Jerusalem in August 1929, resulting in the British commission of enquiry under Sir Walter Shaw. Between 1948 and 1967 Jordan denied Jews access to the 'Wailing Wall'. Captured by Israel in the Six-Day War. In October 1990, twenty-one Arabs were killed by Israeli forces following a stoning incident at the 'Wailing Wall'. The Security Council condemned the Israeli action.

War of Attrition Formally announced by Nasser on 8 March 1969. He aimed to destroy the Bar Lev line fortifications that the Israelis had constructed on the east side of the Suez Canal. By the middle of 1970 it was evident that Egypt was having to sustain considerable losses.

War of Independence The Israeli name for the First Arab–Israeli War, 1947–9.

West Bank The name given to the area west of the Jordan river by the Jordan government after its incorporation into Jordan in 1948. Occupied by Israel in 1967.

Wheelus Field A large United States Air Force base in Libya, taken over from the Italians during the Second World War and evacuated in June 1970.

White Revolution Mounted in 1963 by the Shah of Iran to modernize and Westernize his state: included land distribution, literacy campaigns and emancipation of women.

wilayat-e-faqih A doctrine outlined by Khomeini according to which the government should be entrusted to the ulema (Islamic scholars). This was a departure from the acceptance of State authority, and the implied recognition of the separation of religion and politics.

Yamit A town in Sinai developed by Israel, and evacuated in April 1982 under the 1979 Egyptian–Israeli Peace Treaty.

Yarmuk river A tributary of the Jordan river which is the boundary between Syria and Jordan.

yeshiva A Jewish theological school.

Yiddish A language that is a mixture of Hebrew, medieval German and some Slav words spoken by the Ashkenazim. Written in Hebrew characters.

Yishuv The Jewish community in Palestine.

Young Turks The Young Turk movement was formed around 1889 as a result of growing dissatisfaction with the despotism of Abdul Hamid II. It recruited supporters from students at military colleges. In 1895 a group of Young Turks in Constantinople called themselves the Committee of Union and Progress. Some serving officers in 1906 began to form themselves into revolutionary cells, and in 1908 there was mutiny in the Turkish armed forces. Apart from a period of six months, the Young Turks ruled the Ottoman Empire from 1908 until 1918. Initially the Young Turks established a constitution, parliamentary government and liberal reforms. Later they ruled by military dictatorship.

Zionism The word Zionism was probably first used by Nathan Birnbaum in a series of articles published between 1886 and 1891. It has come to be understood as meaning a movement for the re-establishment of a Jewish nation in Palestine. Followers of Zionism emphasize the historic links between the Jews and Palestine. Herzl is commonly regarded as the father of political Zionism, but similar ideas had been expressed earlier by Benjamin Disraeli, George Eliot, Moses Hess and Leon Pinsker. Herzl's *Der Judenstaat* appeared in Vienna in February 1896. In his preface Herzl stated that his idea was an old one: the establishment of a state for the Jews. Anti-Semitic fervour made that an urgent necessity: that force had shown that the Jews could not assimilate and had made them into one people. Herzl asked that the Jews be granted sovereignty over territory adequate for their national requirements. They would see to the rest. Many Jews rejected Zionism. Non-Jews have described themselves as Zionists: Winston Churchill and Jan Christian Smuts are leading examples. In 1975 the United Nations General Assembly denounced Zionism as 'a form of racism and racial discrimination'. This met with international outcry. The Israeli government moved towards using the term 'pro-Israel' instead of Zionist. On 23 September 1991 President Bush asked the General Assembly to repeal its denunciation of Zionism: 'Zionism is not a policy; it is the idea that led to the creation of a home for the Jewish people, to the state of Israel. And to equate Zionism with the intolerable sin of racism is to twist history and forget the terrible plight of Jews in World War II and, indeed, throughout history. To equate Zionism with racism is to reject Israel itself – a member of good standing of the United Nations.' The General Assembly of the United Nations on 16 December 1991 repealed its resolution that proclaimed Zionism as a form of racism. The Arab states opposed this and argued that the repeal would encourage Israel to continue settlements in the occupied territories.

Topic bibliography

1. The emergence of modern nation states in the Middle East

Histories of the Arabs and the Middle East
Lucid and scholarly overviews include: Albert Hourani, *A History of the Arab Peoples* (1991); Peter Mansfield, *A History of the Middle East* (1991); M.E. Yapp, *The Near East since the First World War* (1991); Bernard Lewis, *The Shaping of the Modern Middle East* (1994). For analyses of the rise of Arab nationalism, see George Antonius, *The Arab Awakening. The Story of the Arab National Movement* (1938); a summary of critiques of Antonius can be found in George E. Kirk, *A Short History of the Middle East from the Rise of Islam to Modern Times* (7th edn, 1964). See also William Yale, *The Near East. A Modern History* (1958); Sydney Nettleton Fisher and William Ochsenwald, *The Middle East. A History* (4th edn, 1990); M.E. Yapp, *The Making of the Modern Near East 1792–1923* (1987); Peter Mansfield, *The Ottoman Empire and its Successors* (1973); John Bagot Glubb, *Britain and the Arabs. A Study of Fifty Years, 1908 to 1958* (1959); Jon Kimche, *The Second Arab Awakening* (1970); Albert Hourani, *Great Britain and the Arab World* (n.d.); Zeine N. Zeine, *Arab–Turkish Relations and the Emergence of Arab Nationalism* (1958), *The Struggle for Arab Independence* (1960), *The Emergence of Arab Nationalism* (1966); Sylvia G. Haim, *Arab Nationalism: An Anthology* (1962); Albert Hourani, *Arabic Thought in the Liberal Age, 1789–1939* (1962).

Imperial interests of Great Powers
For the imperial interests of the Great Powers see: Fritz Fischer, *Germany's Aims in the First World War* (1967); *War of Illusions: German policies from 1911 to 1914* (1975); William I. Shorrock, *French Imperialism in the Middle East, the Failure of Policy in Syria and Lebanon 1900–1914* (1976); Briton Cooper Busch, *Britain and the Persian Gulf 1894–1914* (1967); F. Hinsley (ed.), *British Foreign Policy under Sir Edward Grey* (1977); John C. Wilkinson, *Arabia's Frontiers: The Story of Britain's Boundary Drawing in the Desert* (1991).

Western diplomacy and the making of the modern Middle East
For contradictory accounts of the Hussein–McMahon correspondence, the Sykes–Picot Agreement and the subsequent diplomacy leading to the creation of the modern Middle East see: A.L. Tibawi, *Anglo–Arab Relations and the Question of Palestine 1914–1921* (1977) which is interesting on the Arabic translations; Elie Kedourie, *In the Anglo–Arab Labyrinth* (1976) quotes extensively from Foreign and

India Office minutes. A recent non-specialist account is David Fromkin, *A Peace to End All Peace. Creating the Modern Middle East 1914–1922* (1989). Marian Kent, *Oil and Empire, British Policy and Mesopotamian Oil 1900–1920* (1976); *Moguls and Mandarins. Oil, Imperialism and the Middle East in British Foreign Policy, 1900–1940* (1993); and Jukka Nevakivi, *Britain, France and the Arab Middle East 1914–1920* (1969) consider the significance of oil. See also William J. Olson, *Anglo–Iranian Relations during World War I* (1984); Jacob Goldberg, *The Foreign Policy of Saudi Arabia: The Formative Years, 1902–1918* (1986); Gary Troeller, *The Birth of Saudi Arabia: Britain and the Rise of the House of Sa'ud* (1976). Specific monograph studies include: Zeine N. Zeine, *The Struggle for Arab Independence. Western Diplomacy and the Rise and Fall of Feisal's Kingdom in Syria* (1960); Bruce Westrate, *The Arab Bureau. British Policy in the Middle East, 1916–1920* (1992); H.N. Howard, *The King–Crane Commission* (1963); Aaron S. Kleiman, *Foundations of British Policy in the Arab World. The Cairo Conference of 1921* (1970); John Darwin, *Britain, Egypt and the Middle East Imperial Policy in the Aftermath of War 1918–1922* (1981); Yehoshua Porath, *The Emergence of the Palestinian–Arab National Movement, 1918–1929* (1974) and *The Palestinian Arab National Movement 1929–1939. From Riots to Rebellion* (1978); Kenneth W. Stein, *The Land Question in Palestine, 1917–1939* (1984); Yehoshua Porath, *In Search of Arab Unity, 1930–1945* (1986).

T.E. Lawrence (Lawrence of Arabia)

The disputed significance of T.E. Lawrence is covered in the official biography by Jeremy Wilson, *Lawrence of Arabia. The Authorised Biography of T.E. Lawrence* (1989). See also Desmond Stewart, *T.E. Lawrence* (1977); Philip Knightley and Colin Simpson, *The Secret Lives of Lawrence of Arabia* (1976); John E. Mack, *A Prince of Our Disorder. The Life of T.E. Lawrence* (1976); Michael Yardley, *Backing into the Limelight. A Biography of T.E. Lawrence* (1985); J.N. Lockman, *Scattered Tracks on the Lawrence Trail. Twelve Essays on T.E. Lawrence* (1996).

British Empire in the Middle East

Accounts of the British Empire in the Middle East include: Elizabeth Monroe, *Britain's Moment in the Middle East* (2nd edn, 1981); Howard M. Sachar, *Europe Leaves the Middle East* (1972); Wm. Roger Louis, *The British Empire in the Middle East 1945–1951* (1984); Brian Lapping, *End of Empire* (1985); Ritchie Ovendale, *Britain, the United States, and the Transfer of Power in the Middle East, 1945–1962* (1996). See also Daniel Silverfarb, *The Twilight of British Ascendancy in the*

Middle East. A Case Study of Iraq (1994). Glen Balfour-Paul, *The End of Empire in the Middle East. Britain's Relinquishment of Power in her Last Three Arab Dependencies* (1991) is an account of Britain's withdrawal from the Sudan in 1956, South-west Arabia in 1967, and the Gulf in 1971, based on both first-hand experience and research. Frank Brenchley, *Britain and the Middle East. An Economic History 1945–87* (1989) is an analysis by a former ambassador and specialist on Middle East affairs in the Foreign Office, which highlights the factors important to economic relations between Britain and the Middle East. See also Paul W.T. Kingston, *Britain and the Politics of Modernization in the Middle East, 1945–1958* (1996).

Syria and Lebanon

Histories of the emergence of different states include: John P. Spagnolo, *France and Ottoman Lebanon: 1861–1914* (1977); Stephen Hemsley Longrigg, *Syria and Lebanon under French Mandate* (1959); Meir Zamir, *The Formation of Modern Lebanon* (1985); A.L. Tibawi, *A Modern History of Syria including Lebanon and Palestine* (1969); A.B. Gaunson, *The Anglo–French Clash in Lebanon and Syria, 1940–1945* (1987); David Roberts, *The Ba'th and the Creation of Modern Syria* (1987); Moshe Ma'oz and Avner Yaniv (eds), *Syria under Assad: Domestic Constraints and Regional Risks* (1986); Patrick Seale, *The Struggle for Syria; A Study of Post-War Arab Politics, 1945–1958* (1986) and *Asad of Syria. The Struggle for the Middle East* (1988); Moshe Ma'oz, *Asad. The Sphinx of Damascus* (1988); Gordon H. Torrey, *Syrian Politics and the Military, 1945–1958* (1964); Nikolaos Van Dam, *The Struggle for Syria: Sectarianism, Regionalism, and Tribalism in Politics, 1961–1980* (2nd edn, 1981); Eberhard Kienle, *Ba'th v. Ba'th: The conflict between Syria and Iraq 1968–1989* (1990); Eliezer Tauber, *The Formation of Modern Syria and Iraq* (1995); Bonnie F. Saunders, *The United States and Arab Nationalism. The Syrian Case, 1953–1960* (1996).

Jordan

Nasser H. Aruri, *Jordan: A Study in Political Development (1921–1965)* (1972); P.J. Vatikiotis, *Politics and the Military in Jordan. A Study of the Arab Legion 1927–1957* (1967); Philip P. Graves (ed.), *Memoirs of King Abdullah of Transjordan* (1950); H. St. J.B. Philby, *Arabian Jubilee* (1952); Elizabeth Monroe, *Philby of Arabia* (1973); Trevor Royle, *Glubb Pasha* (1992).

Egypt and Sudan

L.A. Fabunmi, *The Sudan in Anglo–Egyptian Relations. A Case Study in Power Politics 1800–1956* (1960); Muddathir Abdel Rahim, *Imperialism & Nationalism in the Sudan; A Study in Constitutional & Political Development 1899–1956* (1986); M.W. Daly, *Empire on the Nile. The Anglo–Egyptian Sudan, 1898–1934* (1986); *Imperial Sudan. The Anglo–Egyptian Condominium, 1934–56* (1991); Peter Woodward, *Condominium and Sudanese Nationalism* (1979); Hoda Gamal Abdel Nasser, *Britain and the Egyptian Nationalist Movement 1936–1952* (1994); John Marlowe, *Anglo–Egyptian Relations 1800–1953* (1954); P.J. Vatikiotis, *The Modern History of Egypt* (1969); Israel Gershoni and James P. Jankowski, *Egypt, Islam, and the Arabs: The Search for Egyptian Nationhood, 1900–1930* (1986); Trefor E. Evans (ed.), *The Killearn Diaries 1934–1946* (1972) (Lord Killearn was the British High Commissioner and then Ambassador in Egypt, 1934–46, entry on p. 172).

Iraq

Majid Khadduri, *Independent Iraq 1932–1958* (2nd edn, 1960); *Republican Iraq: A Study of Iraqi politics since the Revolution of 1958* (1969); Stephen Hemsley Longrigg, *Iraq 1900 to 1950. A Political, Social and Economic History* (1953); Reva S. Simon, *Iraq between the Two World Wars. The Creation and Implementation of a Nationalist Ideology* (1986); Lord Birdwood, *Nuri As-Said. A Study in Arab Leadership* (1959); Waldemar J. Gallman, *Iraq under General Nuri. My Recollections of Nuri al-Said, 1954–1958* (1964); Robert A. Fernea and Wm. Roger Louis (eds), *The Iraqi Revolution of 1958. The Old Social Classes Revisited* (1991); Abid A. Al-Marayati, *A Diplomatic History of Modern Iraq* (1961); Henry C. Sanderson, *Ten Thousand and One Nights. Memories of Iraq's Sherifan Dynasty* (1973); Philip Willard Ireland, *Iraq. A Study in Political Development* (1970); Uriel Dann, *Iraq under Qassem. A Political History, 1958–1963* (1969); Lorenzo Kent Kimball, *The Changing Pattern of Political Power in Iraq, 1958 to 1971* (1972); Sa'ad Jawad, *Iraq & the Kurdish Question 1958–1970* (1981); Kamel S. Abu Jaber, *The Arab Ba'th Socialist Party: History, Ideology, and Organization* (1966); Marion Farouk-Sluglett and Peter Sluglett, *Iraq since 1958: From Revolution to Dictatorship* (1987); Majid Khadduri, *Arab Contemporaries: The Role of Personalities in Politics* (1973); John F. Devlin, *The Ba'th Party; A History from its Origins to 1966* (1976); Yitzhak Nakash, *The Shi'is of Iraq* (1994).

Iran

Rouhollah K. Ramazani, *The Foreign Policy of Iran 1500–1941* (1966),

Iran's Foreign Policy 1941–1973. A Study of Foreign Policy in Modernizing Nations (1975), and *Revolutionary Iran. Challenge and Response in the Middle East* (1986); Shahram Chubin and Sepehr Zabih, *The Foreign Relations of Iran. A Developing State in a Zone of Great-Power Conflict* (1974); Ervand Abrahamian, *Iran between Two Revolutions* (1982); Richard W. Cottan, *Nationalism in Iran* (2nd edn, 1979); Nikki R. Keddie and Mark J. Gasiorowski (eds), *Neither East nor West. Iran, the Soviet Union, and the United States* (1990).

Saudi Arabia
David Holden and Richard Johns, *The House of Saud* (1981); Robert Lacey, *The Kingdom* (1981); William B. Quandt, *Saudi Arabia in the 1980s. Foreign Policy, Security, and Oil* (1981); Anthony H. Cordesman, *Western Strategic Interests in Saudi Arabia* (1987); Fouad Al-Farsy, *Modernity and Tradition. The Saudi Equation* (1990); David E. Long, *The Kingdom of Saudi Arabia* (1997).

The Yemens
Histories of the Yemens include: Manfred W. Wenner, *Modern Yemen 1918–1966* (1967); Harold Ingrams, *The Yemen. Imams, Rulers & Revolutions* (1963); Dana Adams Schmidt, *Yemen: The Unknown War* (1968); Edgar O'Ballance, *The War in the Yemen* (1971); S.H. Amin, *Law and Justice in Contemporary Yemen: The People's Democratic Republic of Yemen and the Yemen Arab Republic* (1987); Robin Bidwell, *The Two Yemens* (1983); Robert D. Burrowes, *The Yemen Arab Republic: The Politics of Development 1962–1987* (1987); Tareq Y. Ismael and Jacqueline S. Ismael, *The People's Democratic Republic of Yemen: Politics, Economics and Society* (1986); J.E. Peterson, *Yemen: The Search for a Modern State* (1982); Saeed M. Badeeb, *The Saudi–Egyptian Conflict over North Yemen, 1962–1970* (1986); Robert W. Stookey, *South Yemen: A Marxist Republic in Arabia* (1982); Fred Halliday, *Revolution and Foreign Policy. The Case of South Yemen 1967–1987* (1990).

The Gulf
Sir Charles Belgrave, *The Pirate Coast* (1966) concentrates on the early history of the Gulf up to 1821; Donald Hawley, *The Trucial States* (1970); J.B. Kelly, *Eastern Arabian Frontiers* (1964); John Duke Anthony, *Arab States of the Lower Gulf: People, Politics, Petroleum* (1975); J. Alvin Cotrell (ed.), *The Persian Gulf States: A General Survey* (1980); Jill Crystal, *Oil and Politics in the Gulf: Rulers and Merchants in Kuwait and Qatar* (1990); Mustafa M. Alani, *Operation Vantage: British Military Intervention in Kuwait 1961* (1990); J.E. Peterson, *The Arab*

Gulf States: Steps toward Political Participation (1988); J.B. Kelly, *Arabia, the Gulf and the West* (1980); B.R. Pridham, *The Arab Gulf and the Arab World* (1988); Ian Richard Netton *Arabia and the Gulf; From Traditional Society to Modern States* (1986); Rosemarie Said Zahlan, *The Making of the Modern Gulf States: Kuwait, Bahrain, Qatar, the United Arab Emirates and Oman* (1989); John A. Sandwick (ed.), *The Gulf Cooperation Council. Moderation and Stability in an Interdependent World* (1987); Calvin H. Allen Jr, *Oman. The Modernization of the Sultanate* (1987); Ian Skeet, *Muscat and Oman: The End of an Era* (1974); F.A. Clements, *Oman. The Reborn Land* (1980); John C. Wilkinson, *The Imamate Tradition of Oman* (1987); Donald Hawley, *Oman and its Renaissance* (4th edn, 1987); Robert Geran Landen, *Oman since 1856: Disruptive Modernization in a Traditional Arab Society* (1967); J.E. Peterson, *Oman in the Twentieth Century: Political Foundations of an Emerging State* (1978); Gulf Public Relations, *Glimpses of Qatar 1985* (1985) (an official work useful for basic information); Ahmad Mustafa Abu-Hakima, *The Modern History of Kuwait 1750– 1965* (1983); Fuad I. Khuri, *Tribe and State in Bahrain* (1980); Muhammad Morsy Abdullah, *The United Arab Emirates. A Modern History* (1978); Ali Mohammed Khalifa, *The United Arab Emirates: Unity in Fragmentation* (1979); Malcolm C. Peck, *The United Arab Emirates: A Venture in Unity* (1986); Abdullah Omran Taryam, *The Establishment of the United Arab Emirates, 1950–85* (1987).

Security concerns in the Gulf are covered in: M.E. Ahari, *The Gulf and International Security. The 1980s and Beyond* (1989); Paul Jabber et al, *Great Power Interests in the Persian Gulf* (1989); Hossein Amirsadeghi, *The Security of the Persian Gulf* (1981); Hussein Sirriyeh, *US Policy in the Gulf, 1968–1977* (1984).

Camp David accords and peace treaty between Egypt and Israel

See: Jimmy Carter, *Keeping Faith* (1982); Zbigniew Brzezinski, *Power and Principle* (1983); William B. Quandt, *Camp David. Peacemaking and Politics* (1986); Mohamed Ibrahim Kamel, *The Camp David Accords* (1986); Ezer Weizman, *Battle for Peace* (1981); Moshe Dayan, *Breakthrough: A Personal Account of the Egypt–Israel Peace Negotiations* (1981).

2. The birth of the State of Israel

Anti-Semitism

Histories of anti-Semitism include: Leon Poliakov, *The History of Anti-Semitism* (3 vols, 1975); Ernest L. Abel, *The Roots of Anti-Semitism* (1975); Leonard Schroeder, *The Last Exodus* (1979); James Parkes, *The Jew in the Medieval Community* (1938); Jacob Katz, *Out of the Ghetto. The Social Background of Jewish Emancipation, 1770–1870* (1973). For specialized studies see: Peter G.J. Pulzer, *The Rise of Political Anti-Semitism in Germany and Austria* (1964); Colin Holmes, *Anti-Semitism in British Society, 1876–1939* (1979); Paul Lendvai, *Anti-Semitism in Eastern Europe* (1971); Shmuel Almog (ed.), *Antisemitism through the Ages* (1988); Barnet Litvinoff, *The Burning Bush. Antisemitism and World History* (1988).

Origins of Zionism

Standard histories on the origins of Zionism, by Zionists, include: Walter Laquer, *A History of Zionism* (1972); David Vital, *The Origins of Zionism* (1975); *Zionism: The Formative Years* (1982); *Zionism: The Crucial Phase* (1987). See also Harold Fisch, *The Zionist Revolution. A New Perspective* (1978). For the case made by some Arab writers that the roots of Zionism can be found in the designs of imperialism in early nineteenth-century Europe, see A.W. Kayyali (ed.), *Zionism, Imperialism and Racism* (1979).

Founders of modern Zionism

Theodor Herzl's diaries are available: see, Raphael Patai (ed.), trans. Harry Zohn, *The Complete Diaries of Theodor Herzl* (5 vols, 1960). Biographies include: Desmond Stewart, *Theodor Herzl* (1974); Alex Bein, *Theodor Herzl, A Biography* (1957); Israel Cohen, *Theodor Herzl, Founder of Political Zionism* (1959); Jacob de Haas, *Theodor Herzl, A Biographical Study* (2 vols, 1927); Josef Fraenkel, *Theodor Herzl, A Biography* (1946); Josef Patai, trans. Francis Magyar, *Star over Jordan, the Life of Theodore Herzl* (1946); Amos Elon, *Herzl* (1975). For an account of Ahad Ha-Am, see Leon Simon, *Ahad Ha-am. Asher Ginzberg; A Biography* (1960). For an account of Weizmann's early life, see Chaim Weizmann, *Trial and Error* (1940); Paul Goodman (ed.), *Chaim Weizmann, A Tribute on his Seventieth Birthday* (1945); Dan Leon and Yehuda Adin, *Chaim Weizmann, Statesman of the Jewish Renaissance* (1974); Meyer W. Weisgal and Joel Carmichael, *Chaim Weizmann – A Biography by Several Hands* (1962); Meyer W. Weisgal, *Chaim Weizmann – Scientist Builder of the Jewish Commonwealth* (1944);

Jehuda Reinharz, *Chaim Weizmann. The Making of a Zionist Leader* (1985). For an account of the Manchester School based on information from Lord Sieff, see Jon Kimche, *Palestine or Israel* (1973). See also Isaiah Friedman, *Germany, Turkey, and Zionism 1897–1918* (1977).

Zionism in Britain during the First World War

On the Samuel memorandum see: Viscount Samuel, *Memoirs* (1945); John Bowle, *Viscount Samuel* (1957). On the role of Mark Sykes see: Roger Adelson, *Mark Sykes, Portrait of an Amateur* (1975); Christopher Sykes, *Two Studies in Virtue* (1953).

Balfour Declaration

On the background to the Balfour Declaration see: Leonard Stein, *The Balfour Declaration* (1961); Isaiah Friedman, *The Question of Palestine, 1914–1918* (1973); Jon Kimche, *The Unromantics. The Great Powers and the Balfour Declaration* (1968); John Marlowe, *Milner, Apostle of Empire* (1976); Doreen Ingrams (ed.), *Palestine Papers 1917–1922, Seeds of Conflict* (1972).

Establishment of Palestine mandate

For the establishment of the mandate see: Michael L. Dockrill and J. Douglas Goold, *Peace without Promise, Britain and the Peace Conference, 1919–23* (1981); Richard Meinertzhagen, *Middle East Diary 1917–1956* (1959). Bernard Wasserstein, *The British in Palestine. The Mandatory Government and the Arab–Jewish Conflict 1917–1929* (1978) (revised edn, 1991); see also Neil Caplan, *Palestine Jewry and the Arab Question 1917–1925* (1978).

Zionism in Britain and Palestine in the 1930s

For accounts of the influence of the Zionist lobby on British government policy in the early 1930s see: Norman Rose, *Lewis Namier and Zionism* (1980); N.A. Rose, *The Gentile Zionists. A Study in Anglo–Zionist Diplomacy 1929–1939* (1973); Alan R. Taylor, *Prelude to Israel. An Analysis of Zionist Diplomacy 1897–1947* (1961); Martin Kolinsky, *Law, Order and Riots in Mandatory Palestine, 1928–35* (1993). Zionist reaction to the Arab rebellion is covered in Nicholas Bethell, *The Palestine Triangle. The Struggle between the British, the Jews and the Arabs 1935–48* (1979); Michael J. Cohen, *Palestine: Retreat from the Mandate. The Making of British Policy, 1936–45* (1978). Yehoyada Haim, *Abandonment of Illusions: Zionist Political Attitudes towards Palestinian Arab Nationalism, 1936–1939* (1983) offers a detailed analysis of Zionist opinion.

Zionist lobby in the United States
For the significance of the Zionist lobby in the United States see: Joseph B. Schechtman, *The United States and the Jewish State Movement* (1966); Naomi W. Cohen, *American Jews and the Zionist Idea* (1975); Philip J. Barum, *The Department of State in the Middle East 1919–1945* (1978); Zvi Ganin, *Truman, American Jewry and Israel 1945–8* (1979); John Snetsinger, *Truman, the Jewish Vote and the Creation of Israel* (1974); Samuel Halperin, *The Political World of American Zionism* (1961); Michael J. Cohen, *Truman and Israel* (1990).

Last years of Palestine mandate
For accounts of the last years of the mandate see: Ritchie Ovendale, *Britain, the United States, and the End of the Palestine Mandate, 1942–1948* (1989); Martin Jones, *Failure in Palestine. British and United States Policy after the Second World War* (1986); Michael J. Cohen, *Palestine and the Great Powers 1945–1948* (1982); Alan Bullock, *The Life and Times of Ernest Bevin* (vol. 3, 1983).

Foundation of the State of Israel
For the immediate foundation of the State of Israel see: Bernard Postal and Henry W. Levy, *And the Hills Shouted for Joy* (1973); Zeev Sharef, *Three Days* (1972); Simha Flapan, *The Birth of Israel: Myths and Realities* (1987). Tom Segev, *1949. The First Israelis* (1986) is an account of Israel's first year as a state.

General histories
General accounts can be found in Ritchie Ovendale, *The Origins of the Arab–Israeli Wars* (1984; 2nd edn, 1992); and Charles D. Smith, *Palestine and the Arab–Israeli Conflict* (1988). Martin Gilbert, *Exile and Return. The Emergence of Jewish Statehood* (1978), and Harold Wilson, *The Chariot of Israel, Britain, America, and the State of Israel* (1981), are Zionist texts. A detailed history is offered by Howard M. Sachar, *A History of Israel* (2 vols, 1976–87). See also Don Peretz and Gideon Doron, *The Government and Politics of Israel* (3rd edn, 1997).

3. The significance of oil

Histories of oil in Middle East
The history of British oil interests in the Middle East is recounted in Marian Kent, *Oil and Empire. British Policy and Mesopotamian Oil*

1900–1920 (1976); see also Geoffrey Jones, *The State and the Emergence of the British Oil Industry* (1981); Michael J. Hogan, *Informal Entente. The Private Structure of Cooperation in Anglo–American Economic Diplomacy 1818–1928* (1977). George W. Stocking, *Middle East Oil. A Study in Political and Economic Controversy* (1970) is an overall history up to 1970; see also Stephen H. Longrigg, *Oil in the Middle East; Its Discovery and Development* (3rd edn, 1968).

United States involvement

The American involvement is analysed in: Irvine H. Anderson, *Aramco, the United States and Saudi Arabia; A Study of the Dynamics of Foreign Oil Policy, 1933–1950* (1981).

OPEC and OAPEC

The Arab perspective on OPEC is given in Fadhil J. al-Chalabi, *OPEC and the International Oil Industry: A Changing Structure* (1980); for the development of OPEC and OAPEC see Zuhayr Mikdashi, *The Community of Oil Exporting Countries: A Study in Governmental Co-operation* (1972).

Significance of Saudi Arabia

On the significance of Saudi Arabia see: Mordechai Abir, *Saudi Arabia in the Oil Era* (1988); and the account of its longest-serving minister, Jeffrey Robinson, *Yamani; The Inside Story* (1988).

Oil weapon

Yusif A. Sayigh, *Arab Oil Policies in the 1970s: Opportunity and Responsibility* (1982); Benjamin Shwadran, *Middle Eastern Oil Crises since 1973* (1986); Sheikh R. Ali, *Oil and Power: Political Dynamics in the Middle East* (1987); and Roy Licklider, *Political Power and the Arab Oil Weapon: The Experience of Five Industrial Nations* (1988) cover the use of the oil weapon by the Arabs.

Oil production policies

M.S. El Azhary (ed.), *The Impact of Oil Revenues on Arab Gulf Development* (1984) contains an essay on oil production policies; see also Atif A. Kubursi, *Oil, Industrialization & Development in the Arab Gulf States* (1984). Gad G. Gilbar, *The Middle East Oil Decade and Beyond. Essays in Political Economy* (1997) examines the influence the production, export and revenues of oil exerted on domestic, regional and international relations, 1973–1982.

4. Terrorism

Zionist terrorism

The most revealing first-hand account of Zionist terrorism is that by the leader of the Irgun: Menachem Begin, *The Revolt. Story of the Irgun* (1951). See also the following biographies and studies of Begin: Eitan Haber, *Menahem Begin. The Legend and the Man* (1978); Gertrude Hirschler and Lester S. Eckman, *Menahem Begin. From Freedom Fighter to Statesman* (1979); Eric Silver, *Begin. A Biography* (1984); Sasson Sofer, *Begin. An Anatomy of Leadership* (1988). Other works specifically on the Irgun include: Yaacor Meridor, *Long is the Road to Freedom* (1955); and Samuel Katz, *Days of Fire. The Secret History of the IZL* (1968). For an investigation of the blowing-up of the King David Hotel see Thurston Clarke, *By Blood and Fire. The Attack on the King David Hotel* (1981). Accounts of Haganah include: Munya Mardor, *Haganah* (1966); Ephraim Dekel, *Shai: Historical Exploits of Haganah Intelligence* (1959); Leonard Slater, *The Pledge* (1970). A study of the ideological and political development of the Stern Gang can be found in Joseph Heller, *The Stern Gang. Ideology, Politics and Terror, 1940–1949* (1995). There is an account of Lord Moyne's assassination by the Stern Gang in Gerald Frank, *The Deed* (1963); and of Bernadotte's assassination in Amitzur Ilan, *Bernadotte in Palestine, 1948* (1989). The British army's campaign against Zionist terrorism is described in David A. Charters, *The British Army and Jewish Insurgency in Palestine, 1945–47* (1989). General accounts assessing the significance of Zionist terrorism include: Arthur Koestler, *Promise and Fulfillment: Palestine 1917–1949* (1983); Christopher Sykes, *Cross Roads to Israel* (1965); David Hirst, *The Gun and the Olive Branch* (1977); Michael J. Cohen, *Palestine and the Great Powers 1945–1948* (1982); Ritchie Ovendale, *Britain, the United States, and the End of the Palestine Mandate, 1942–1948* (1989). For the significance of Deir Yassin and the Arab flight see Benny Morris, *The Birth of the Palestinian Refugee Problem, 1947–1949* (1988). For accounts of terrorism in the occupied territories see Geoffrey Aronson, *Israel, Palestinians and the Intifada. Creating Facts on the West Bank* (1990); David Newman (ed.), *The Impact of Gush Emunim: Politics and Settlement in the West Bank* (1985); Robert I. Friedman, *The False Prophet; Rabbi Meir Kahane from FBI Informant to Knesset Membership* (1990).

Palestine Liberation Organization

Histories of the Palestine Liberation Organization include: Alain Gresh, *The PLO. The Struggle Within. Towards an Independent*

Palestinian State (rev. edn, 1988), which is based on the organization's own papers; Helena Cobban, *The Palestine Liberation Organization. People, Power and Politics* (1984); Shaul Mishal, *The PLO under Arafat. Between Gun and Olive Branch* (1986) was sponsored by the Tel Aviv University Research Project on Peace; Aryeh Y. Yodfat and Yuval Arnon-Ohanna, *PLO Strategy and Politics* (1981) is an Israeli account based on Arab sources. Alan Hart, *Arafat. Terrorist or Peacemaker?* (3rd edn, 1987) is a journalist's account based on personal interviews. Kemal Kirisci, *The PLO and World Politics. A Study of the Mobilization of Support for the Palestinian Cause* (1986) examines the PLO's attempts to establish itself as a pressure group in the United Nations and on the world scene. See also Hazem Zaki Nuseibeh, *Palestine and the United Nations* (1982); and Augustus Richard Norton and Martin H. Greenberg (eds), *The International Relations of the Palestine Liberation Organization* (1989) which looks at the period up to *c.* 1987. Zeev Schiff and Raphael Rothstein, *Fedayeen. Guerrillas against Israel* (1972) is a journalists' account; John Laffin, *Fedayeen. The Arab–Israeli Dilemma* (1973) inclines towards pro-Israeli sentiments; see also Edgar O'Ballance, *Arab Guerilla Power 1967–1972* (1974). Aaron David Miller, *The Arab States and the Palestine Question. Between Ideology and Self-Interest* (1986) is a brief and useful account of Arab states' attitude to the PLO. Aaron David Miller, *The PLO and the Politics of Survival* (1983) offers a brief analysis of the various factions within the PLO and the role played by the organization in the politics of the Middle East. Rashid Khalidi, *Under Siege: PLO Decisionmaking during the 1982 War* (1986) is an important source, written by a Palestinian born in Beirut; see also Raphael Israeli, *PLO in Lebanon. Selected Documents* (1983). Yonah Alexander and Joshua Sinai, *Terrorism; The PLO Connection* (1989) claims to be an historical record of the PLO written by two Israelis; it has been criticized as unreliable.

Accounts of Arab terrorist incidents

Contemporary journalists' accounts of Arab terrorist incidents include: the *Christian Science Monitor* correspondent, John Cooley, *Green March, Black September* (1973); the *Daily Telegraph* reporter, Christopher Dobson, *Black September* (1974). The 1972 Olympic Games outrage is covered in Serge Groussard, *The Blood of Israel: The Massacre of the Israeli Athletes* (1975). The Israeli retaliation is described in David Tinnan *Hit Team* (1976). See also Peter Snow and David Phillips, *Leila's Hijack War* (1970) and Leila Khaled, *My People Shall Live* (1973). The Entebbe raid is covered in: Yehuda Ofer,

Operation Thunder: The Entebbe Raid (1976); Yeshayahu Ben Porat et al, *Entebbe Rescue* (1977); Tony Williamson, *Counter Strike Entebbe* (1976); and Max Hastings, *Yoni, Hero of Entebbe* (1979). The Vienna OPEC kidnappings are described in Colin Smith, *Carlos; Portrait of a Terrorist* (1976). Islamic terrorism in a wider context is considered in Amir Taheri, *Holy Terror. The Inside Story of Islamic Terrorism* (1987).

5. The Mossadeq crisis in Iran, 1950–4

Participants' accounts

Accounts by participants include: Anthony Eden, *Full Circle* (1960); Dwight D. Eisenhower, *Mandate for Change* (1963). On the intelligence side there is that by C.M. Woodhouse, *Something Ventured* (1982), who planned the operation for MI6; Kermit Roosevelt, *Countercoup; The Struggle for the Control of Iran* (1979), and *Nationalism in Iran* (1979) by Richard W. Cottam, who served in the Central Intelligence Agency in 1953 in Iran alongside Kermit Roosevelt.

Monographs

See also Christopher Andrew, *Secret Service: The Making of the British Intelligence Community* (1985); and Brian Lapping, *End of Empire* (1985). An account of the role of the Labour Foreign Secretary is given by Bernard Donoghue and G.W. Jones, *Herbert Morrison* (1973); and of the Anglo–Iranian Oil Company, Henry Longhurst, *Adventure in Oil* (1959). An outstanding collection of essays examining the themes of the Anglo–American relationship, nationalism, religion and oil is: James A. Bill and Wm. Roger Louis (eds), *Musaddiq, Iranian Nationalism, and Oil* (1988). See also Homa Katouzian, *Mussadiq and the Struggle for Power in Iran* (1990).

6. The rise of Nasser and the attempts to export his philosophy of the revolution

Biographies of Nasser

A critical biography of Nasser is that by Anthony Nutting, *Nasser* (1970). See also Robert Stephens, *Nasser. A Political Biography*

(1971); Peter Woodward, *Nasser* (1991). Jean Lacouture, *Nasser: A Biography* (1973) is an account by a French journalist.

Nasser's philosophy and Egyptian politics
For Nasser's philosophy, see Gamal Abdel Nasser, *The Philosophy of the Revolution* (1959). For a first-hand account of the rise of Nasser, see Mohammed Neguib, *Egypt's Destiny* (1955). Studies of Egyptian politics include R. Hriar Dekmejian, *Egypt under Nasser. A Study in Political Dynamics* (1972).

Egypt's relations with the Soviet Union
The relations with the Soviet Union are covered by: Mohamed H. Heikal, *Sphinx and Commissar. The Rise and Fall of Soviet Influence in the Arab World* (1978); Oles M. Smolansky, *The Soviet Union and the Arab East under Khrushchev* (1974); Aryeh Yodfat, *Arab Politics in the Soviet Mirror* (1973).

Nasser's attempts to export his philosophy of the revolution
Probably the most incisive and subtle analysis is by the assassinated former president of the American University of Beirut, Malcolm H. Kerr, *The Arab Cold War. Gamal 'Abd Al-Nasir and his Rivals 1958–1970* (3rd edn, 1971). An account of the background to the formation of the United Arab Republic from the Syrian perspective is Patrick Seale, *The Struggle for Syria. A Study of Post-War Arab Politics 1945–1958* (1987).

7. The Suez Crisis of 1956

Background of Anglo–Egyptian relations
For the background of Anglo–Egyptian relations and the Middle East Command see Ritchie Ovendale, *The English-Speaking Alliance. Britain, the United States, the Dominions and the Cold War 1945–51* (1985); for the re-negotiation of the Anglo–Egyptian Treaty of 1936 see Ritchie Ovendale, 'Egypt and the Suez Base Agreement', in John W. Young (ed.), *The Foreign Policy of Churchill's Peacetime Administration 1951–1955* (1988); and Evelyn Shuckburgh, *Descent to Suez. Diaries 1951–56* (1986). (Shuckburgh was Private Secretary to Anthony Eden from 1951 to 1954, and in charge of Middle Eastern Affairs in the Foreign Office from 1954 to 1956).

British accounts, including those of officials involved
Accounts by British officials involved in the Suez Crisis include: Anthony Eden, *Full Circle* (1960); Selwyn Lloyd, *Suez 1956* (1978); Earl of Kilmuir, *Political Adventure. The Memoirs of the Earl of Kilmuir* (1964); Harold Macmillan, *Riding the Storm* (1971); Anthony Nutting, *No End of a Lesson. The Story of Suez* (1967); R.A. Butler, *The Art of the Possible* (1971). Significant biographical accounts using British Cabinet papers include: Robert Rhodes James, *Anthony Eden* (1986); Alistair Horne, *Macmillan 1894–1956* (1988); see also Philip M. Williams, *Hugh Gaitskell. A Political Biography* (1979). More general works on the British side include: Roy Fullick and Geofrey Powell, *Suez: The Double War* (1979); Terence Robertson, *Crisis: The Inside Story of the Suez Conspiracy.* (1964). For accounts of the reaction of British public opinion see: L. Epstein, *British Politics in the Suez Crisis* (1964); Russell Braddon, *Suez: Splitting of a Nation* (1973). Military planning is covered in Robert Jackson, *Suez 1956: Operation Musketeer* (1980).

The role of the United States
American autobiographical accounts include: Dwight D. Eisenhower, *Waging Peace* (1966); and Robert Murphy, *Diplomat among Warriors* (1964). Leonard Mosley, *Dulles: A Biography of Eleanor, Allen and John Foster Dulles and their Family Network* (1978), is an important work about the head of the CIA and the Secretary of State, based on oral history material. The traditional analysis of Dulles as a strong Secretary of State is in Herman Finer, *Dulles over Suez* (1964). This interpretation is examined in Townsend Hoopes, *The Devil and John Foster Dulles* (1973); Stephen Ambrose, *Eisenhower the President* (vol. 2, 1984). A significant account of the role of the CIA is in Chester Cooper, *The Lion's Last Roar: Suez 1956* (1978).

Commonwealth and Suez
The role of the Commonwealth is covered in James Eayrs, *The Commonwealth and Suez. A Documentary Survey* (1964); and the account by the Australian Prime Minister of his mission to Nasser, Robert Menzies, *Afternoon Light* (1967).

France
Principal works by French participants are: Jacques Georges-Picot, *The Real Suez Crisis. The End of a Great Nineteenth Century Work* (1975); Andre Beaufré, *The Suez Expedition 1956* (1969); Christian Pineau, *1956 Suez* (1976). See also Robert Henriques, *One Hundred Hours to*

Suez (1957). Sylvia Crosbie, *A Tacit Alliance. France and Israel from Suez to the Six Day War* (1974) describes the evolving Franco–Israeli alliance.

Israeli preparations
The Israeli preparations are covered in: Shimon Peres, *David's Sling. The Arming of Israel* (1970); Moshe Dayan, *The Story of My Life* (1976); Shabtai Teveth, *Moshe Dayan* (1972); Abba Eban, *An Autobiography* (1977); Michael Bar-Zohar, *Ben-Gurion* (1978); Yigal Allon, *The Making of Israel's Army* (1970); David Ben-Gurion, *Israel: A Personal History* (1971).

Egyptian accounts
The most useful first-hand Egyptian account is Mohamed H. Heikal, *Cutting the Lion's Tail. Suez through Egyptian Eyes* (1986); Kennett Love, *Suez. The Twice-Fought War* (1970) is the classic analysis sympathetic to the Egyptian position.

Retrospective
A retrospective examination of the Suez Crisis from all of these perspectives and also one which offers important material on Operation Alpha is: Wm. Roger Louis and Roger Owen (eds), *Suez 1956. The Crisis and its Consequences* (1989). See also Keith Kyle, *Suez* (1991); Ritchie Ovendale, *Britain, the United States, and the Transfer of Power in the Middle East , 1945–1962* (1996).

Eisenhower Doctrine for the Middle East
Accounts of the Eisenhower Doctrine for the Middle East include: Donald Neff, *Warriors at Suez; Eisenhower Takes America into the Middle East* (1971); Harold Macmillan, *Riding the Storm* (1971); Alistair Horne, *Macmillan 1957–1986* (1989); Stephen Ambrose, *Eisenhower the President* (vol. 2, 1984); Michael Ionides, *Divide and Lose. The Arab Revolt of 1955–1958* (1960), *United States Policy in the Middle East September 1956–June 1957 Documents* (1968); M.S. Agwani (ed.), *The Lebanese Crisis, 1958. A Documentary Study* (1965).

8. The Arab–Israeli wars and the peace process

Diplomatic histories
Diplomatic histories narrating the wars in the context of Great

Power politics and local rivalries include: Ritchie Ovendale, *The Origins of the Arab–Israeli Wars* (1984 2nd edn, 1992); Charles D. Smith, *Palestine and the Arab–Israeli Conflict* (1988). Maxime Rodinson, *Israel and the Arabs* (2nd edn, 1982) concentrates on the Palestinian aspect. An Israeli perspective can be found in Howard M. Sachar, *A History of Israel. From the Rise of Zionism to our Time* (1977). See also T.G. Fraser, *The Arab–Israeli Conflict* (1995).

Strategy
Colonel Trevor N. Dupuy, *Elusive Victory. The Arab–Israeli Wars, 1947–1974* (1978); and a work by the President of Israel, Chaim Herzog, *The Arab–Israeli Wars: War and Peace in the Middle East* (1982) offer accounts of the strategies employed.

Politics of Great Powers leading to First Arab–Israeli War
The role of the politics of the Great Powers in the events leading to the outbreak of the First Arab–Israeli War are covered in: Ritchie Ovendale, *Britain, the United States, and the end of the Palestine Mandate, 1942–1948* (1989); Martin Jones, *Failure in Palestine: British and United States Policy after the Second World War* (1986); and Michael J. Cohen, *Palestine and the Great Powers* (1982). Wm. Roger Louis and Robert W. Stookey (eds), *The End of the Palestine Mandate* is an important collection of essays, including one on the Arab perspective by Walid Khalidi.

British military predicament 1945–1947
The British military predicament is comprehensively analysed in David A. Charters, *The British Army and Jewish Insurgency in Palestine, 1945–47* (1989).

Birth of the State of Israel and First Arab–Israeli War
Simla Flapan, *The Birth of Israel: Myths and Realities* (1987) is based on Israeli archive material. John Bagot Glubb, *A Soldier with the Arabs* (1957) is an essential account of the First Arab–Israeli War by the head of the Arab Legion; Larry Collins and Dominique Lapierre, *O Jerusalem* (1972) tells the story largely from the Israeli perspective; see also Yigal Allon, *The Making of Israel's Army* (1970) for a history by one of the architects of Israel's defence force; Jon Kimche, *Seven Fallen Pillars* (1953); Dan Kurzman, *Genesis 1948: The First Arab–Israeli War* (1972); Amitzur Ilan, *The Origin of the Arab–Israeli Arms Race. Arms, Embargo, Military Power and Decision in the 1948 Palestine War* (1996); see also Benny Morris, *Israel's Border Wars 1949–*

1956. Arab infiltration, Israeli Retaliation, and the Countdown to the Suez War (1993). Uri Bialer, *Between East and West: Israel's Foreign Policy Orientation 1948–1956* (1990) describes the extent to which Israel pursued a non-aligned foreign policy before allying itself to the West. Peter Y. Medding, *The Founding of Israeli Democracy 1948–1967* (1990) is an explanation of why a democratic system, established in Israel in difficult circumstances, developed and thrived until at least 1967. See also S. Ilan Troen and Noah Lucas (eds), *Israel. The First Decade of Independence* (1995).

Franco–Israeli alliance and the Suez Crisis

The alliance between Israel and France leading to the Suez–Sinai War is analysed by Sylvia Crosbie, *A Tacit Alliance. France and Israel from Suez to the Six Day War* (1974). Material on the Israeli side can be found in: Moshe Dayan, *The Story of My Life* (1976); Shimon Peres, *David's Sling. The Arming of Israel* (1970); Abba Eban, *An Autobiography* (1977); David Ben-Gurion, *Years of Challenge* (1963); Shabtai Teveth, *Moshe Dayan* (1972); Michael Bar-Zohar, *Ben-Gurion* (1978). Most of these works also contain significant material on the background to the Six-Day War. Mohamed H. Heikal, *Cutting the Lion's Tail: Suez through Egyptian Eyes* (1986) is an inside account by Nasser's confidant; see also Kennett Love, *Suez. The Twice-Fought War* (1970), for the classic analysis sympathetic to Nasser.

Six-Day War

A valuable collection of essays by Arab scholars on the Six-Day War is Ibrahim Abu-Lugod (ed.), *The Arab–Israeli Confrontation of June 1967: An Arab Perspective* (1970); for an account based on Jordanian military records, see Samir A. Mutawi, *Jordan in the 1967 War* (1987). The significance of the Israeli airforce is assessed in Robert Jackson, *The Israeli Air Force Story. The Struggle for Middle East Aircraft Supremacy since 1948* (1970). General accounts include: Walter Laquer, *The Road to War 1967. The Origins of the Arab–Israel Conflict* (1968); John Bulloch, *The Making of a War. The Middle East from 1967 to 1973* (1974). Stephen J. Roth (ed.), *The Impact of the Six-Day War. A Twenty-Year Assessment* (1988) is an a long-term perspective offered by the institute of Jewish Affairs. Abba Eban, *Personal Witness. Israel through My Eyes* (1993) contains the account of Israel's emissary abroad.

War of Attrition
For an Israeli account of the War of Attrition see Yaacov Bar-Siman-Tov, *The Israeli–Egyptian War of Attrition 1969–1970* (1980).

October War
Perhaps the most significant work on the Arab side offering personal insight into the planning for the October War, is Mohamed Heikal, *The Road to Ramadan* (1975); see also Anwar el-Sadat, *In Search of Identity* (1978); Mahmoud Riad, *The Struggle for Peace in the Middle East* (1981); David Hirst and Irene Beeson, *Sadat* (1981); Raymond A. Hinnebusch Jr, *Egyptian Politics under Sadat. The post-populist Development of an Authoritarian-Modernizing State* (1985). For an Israeli perspective see: Golda Meir, *My Life* (1975); Shlomo Aronson, *Conflict and Bargaining in the Middle East. An Israeli Perspective* (1978); Chaim Herzog, *The War of Atonement* (1975). The international perspective is described in Robert Owen Freedman, *Soviet Policy towards the Middle East since 1970* (1975); William B. Quandt, *Decade of Decisions. American Policy towards the Arab–Israeli Conflict, 1967–1976* (1977); see also, Walter Laquer, *Confrontation. The Middle East War and World Politics* (1974). Frank Aker, *October 1973. The Arab–Israeli War* (1985) is a military analysis.

Shuttle diplomacy, Camp David, and the Egyptian–Israeli Peace Treaty
Accounts of the shuttle diplomacy can be found in: Henry Kissinger, *Years of Upheaval* (1982); Howard M. Sachar, *Egypt and Israel* (1981); Anwar el-Sadat, *In Search of Identity* (1978); Gerald Ford, *A Time to Heal* (1979); Yitzhak Rabin, *The Rabin Memoirs* (1979); Ismail Fahmy, *Negotiating for Peace in the Middle East* (1983); George Lenczowski, *American Presidents and the Middle East* (1990). For the negotiations at Camp David see: Jimmy Carter, *Keeping Faith* (1982); Zbigniew Brzezinski, *Power and Principle* (1983); Cyrus Vance, *Hard Choices: Critical Years in American Foreign Policy* (1983); William B. Quandt, *Camp David. Peace Making and Politics* (1986); Gertrude Hirschler and Lester S. Eckman, *Menachem Begin: From Freedom Fighter to Statesman* (1979); Ilan Peleg, *Begin's Foreign Policy, 1977–1983* (1987); Sasson Sofer, *Begin. An Anatomy of Leadership* (1988); Matti Golan, *Shimon Peres* (1982); Moshe Dayan, *Break-through: A Personal Account of the Egypt–Israel Peace Negotiations* (1981); Robert Slater, *Warrior Statesman. The Life of Moshe Dayan* (1992); Ezer Weizmann, *Battle for Peace* (1981); Mohamed Ibrahim Kamel, *The Camp David Accords* (1986).

Rise of Messianic Zionism in Israel and the peace movement

For accounts of the rise of 'political messianism' see: Adam Keller, *Terrible Day. Social Divisions and Political Paradoxes in Israel* (1987); Michael Jansen, *Dissonance in Zion* (1987); Bernard Avishai, *The Tragedy of Zionism. Revolution and Democracy in the Land of Israel* (1985). David Hall-Cathala, *The Peace Movement in Israel 1967–87* (1990) is an account by a social anthropologist. See also Mordechai Bar-On, *In Pursuit of Peace. A History of the Israeli Peace Movement* (1996). For discussions of the role of nationalism and religious fundamentalism in the shaping of Israeli identity see Robert Wistrich and David Ohana (eds), *The Shaping of Israeli Identity. Myth, Memory and Trauma* (1995).

Likud and its attitude to a Palestinian state

An overall account can be found in Howard M. Sachar, *A History of Israel*, Vol. II: *From the Aftermath of the Yom Kippur War* (1987). See also Benjamin Netanyahu, *A Place Among the Nations. Israel and the World* (1993).

United States support for Israel

George Lenczowski, *American Presidents and the Middle East* (1990) offers an historical overview. See also Stephen Green, *Living by the Sword, America and Israel in the Middle East 1968–87* (1988); Coral Bell, *The Reagan Paradox* (1989). American first-hand accounts include: Alexander M. Haig, *Caveat. Realism, Reagan, and Foreign Policy* (1984); Caspar Weinberger, *Fighting for Peace* (1990); Alan R. Taylor, *The Superpowers and the Middle East* (1991); H.W. Brands, *Into the Labyrinth. The United States and the Middle East* (1994); Bernard Reich, *United States–Israel Relations after the Cold War* (1995).

Immigration of Soviet Jews to Israel

For a detailed analysis of the Israeli government's handling of the émigrés from the Soviet Union see Clive Jones, *Soviet Jewish Aliyah 1989–1992. Impact and Implications for Israel and the Middle East* (1992).

The peace process

A narrative account of the early stages can be found in John King, *Handshake in Washington. The Beginning of Middle East Peace?* (1994). Ziva Flamhaft, *Israel on the Road to Peace. Accepting the Unacceptable* (1996) and David Makovsky *Making Peace with the PLO. The Rabin Government's Road to the Oslo Accord* (1996) analyse the Israeli perspective.

9. The rise of revolutionary Islam and the Khomeini Revolution in Iran

Islam

Malise Ruthven, *Islam in the World* (1984) is an informative introduction for a novice reader. Bernard Lewis, *The Political Language of Islam* (1988) covers the origins and developments of most of the important concepts of Islam, though little cognizance is taken of modern evolutions of the terms. A fairly comprehensive survey of the rise of Islam and its contemporary significance in Middle Eastern countries is offered by John L. Esposito, *Islam and Politics* (1984). Accounts of the social significance of Islam today include: Edward Mortimer, *Faith and Power: The Politics of Islam* (1982); Michael Gilsenan, *Recognizing Islam: An Anthropologist's Introduction* (1982); Henry Munson Jr, *Islam and Revolution in the Middle East* (1988); Nikki R. Keddie, *Iran: Religion, Politics and Society; Collected Essays* (1980); and Elie Kedourie, *Islam in the Modern World: And Other Studies* (1980), which also offers a critique of Western policies in the Middle East. Albert Hourani, *Islam in European Thought* (1991) focuses on relations between European and Islamic thought. Perceptive analyses of the significance of modern Islam in the Middle East can be found in: James P. Piscatori, *Islam in a World of Nation States* (1986); James P. Piscatori (ed.), *Islam in the Political Process* (1983); James P. Piscatori and George S. Harris (eds), *Law, Personalities, and Politics of the Middle East. Essays in Honor of Majid Khadduri* (1987).

Fundamentalist Islam

The links between Islam and Egyptian nationalism are examined in Israel Gershoni and James P. Jankowski, *Egypt, Islam and the Arabs: The Search for Egyptian Nationhood, 1900–1930* (1987). Emmanuel Sivan, *Radical Islam: Medieval Theology and Modern Politics* (1985) is a study of Sunni fundamentalism in Egypt, Syria and Lebanon from 1954. Shireen T. Hunter (ed.), *The Politics of Islamic Revivalism: Diversity and Unity* (1988) is a collection of papers on revivalist movements in Islamic societies in Saudi Arabia, Iraq, Egypt, Morocco and other countries; Dilip Hiro, *Islamic Fundamentalism* (1988) offers a concise guide to the subject. See also Youssef M. Choueiri, *Islamic Fundamentalism* (1990). Recent specialist studies of Shiite Islam include: Moojan Momen, *An Introduction to Shi'i Islam: The History and Doctrines of Twelver Shi'ism* (1985); R. Hrair Dekmeijan, *Islam in Revolution: Fundamentalism in the Arab World* (1985) which has been criticized for 'naïve typologizing'; Juan R.I. Cole and Nikki

R. Keddie (eds), *Shi'ism and Social Protest* (1986); and Martin Kramer (ed.), *Shi'ism, Resistance and Revolution* (1987). For developments during the Gulf War see James Piscatori (ed.), *Islamic Fundamentalism and the Gulf Crisis* (1991). See also R. Hrair Dekmeijian, *Islam in Revolution. Fundamentalism in the Arab World* (2nd edn, 1995); Dale F. Eickelman and James Piscatori, *Muslim Politics* (1996).

Rise of revolutionary Islam in Iran

Analyses of the reasons for the rise of revolutionary Islam in Iran include: Sepehr Zahib, *Iran since the Revolution* (1982); Ervand Abrahamian, *Iran between Two Revolutions* (1982); a first-hand account by the United States Ambassador, William H. Sullivan, *Mission to Iran* (1981); and by the British Ambassador, Anthony Parsons, *The Pride and the Fall: Iran 1974–1979* (1984). Phil Marshall, *Revolution and Counter-Revolution in Iran* (1988) offers a brief analysis in the context of the positive role of the Iranian working class, while the account in Hossein Bashiriyeh, *The State and Revolution in Iran, 1962–82* (1984), attempts to integrate a Marxist approach with that of more conventional political scientists. Said Amir Arjomand, *The Turban for the Crown: The Islamic Revolution in Iran* (1988) argues that it was neither the work of the peasants nor the industrial working class. Mehran Kamrava *Revolution in Iran. The Roots of Turmoil* (1990) looks particularly at the structure of the Pahlavi state and the organizations opposing it, and examines the interplay between culture, economics and enforced Westernization. Shaul Bakhash, *The Reign of the Ayatollahs. Iran and the Islamic Revolution* (1986) is a balanced narrative account. Dilip Hiro, *Iran under the Ayatollahs* (1985), using Western newspapers, periodicals and interviews, offers some insight into the personalities. A work offering the Islamic approach and uncritical of Khomeini is Asaf Hussein, *Islamic Iran; Revolution and Counter-Revolution* (1985). Marvin Zonis and Daniel Brumberg, *Khomeini, the Islamic Republic of Iran, and the Arab World* (1987) looks at the Arab reaction to Khomeini. Specialist analyses of different aspects include Sepehr Zabih, *The Iranian Military in Revolution and War* (1988); and Ervand Abrahamian, *Radical Islam: The Iranian Mojahedin* (1989). The significance of the Rushdie affair is analysed by James P. Piscatori, 'The Rushdie affair and the politics of ambiguity', *International Affairs* 66 (1990). Martin Wright (ed.), *Iran: The Khomeini Revolution* (1989) is a valuable collection of articles written from different perspectives.

10. The Palestinian refugee issue and the uprising in the occupied territories

Growth of Palestinian nationalism

Muhammad Y. Muslih, *The Origins of Palestinian Nationalism* (1988) argues that by 1920 Palestinian nationalism had become a movement encompassing all the Arabs of Palestine. For an Israeli account of the growth of Palestinian nationalism, see Yeshoshua Porath, *The Emergence of the Palestinian-Arab National Movement 1918–1929* (1974) and *The Palestinian Arab National Movement 1929–1939* (1977). Yosef Gorny, *Zionism and the Arabs, 1881–1948* (1987) argues that the Zionists did not appear to have had long-term plans for the expulsion of the Arabs, but assumed that the Arabs would accept their position as a national minority.

King Abdullah's collusion with the Zionists

A number of recent works have concentrated on Abdullah's 'collusion' with the Zionists over the annexation of the West Bank: Mary C. Wilson, *King Abdullah, Britain and the Making of Jordan* (1987); Uri Bar-Joseph, *The Best of Enemies: Israel and Transjordan in the War of 1948* (1987). Avi Shlaim, *Collusion across the Jordan. King Abdullah, the Zionist Movement, and the Partition of Palestine* (1988) argues that by secretly endorsing Abdullah's plan to enlarge his kingdom, Britain became an accomplice to this 'collusion' to prevent the establishment of a Palestinian Arab state.

Birth of Palestinian refugee problem

Benny Morris, *The Birth of the Palestinian Refugee Problem, 1947–1949* (1987) is a work by an author who has been described as remaining 'within the boundaries of Zionist discourse'. It has been criticized in Shabtai Teveth, 'The Palestinian refugee problem and its origins (Review Article)', *Middle Eastern Studies* XXVI (1990), pp. 214–49.

Palestinians and the Palestinian diaspora

Laurie A. Brand, *Palestinians in the Arab World: Institution Building and the Search for Peace* (1988) examines the experience of the Palestinian communities in the Palestinian diaspora, particularly in Egypt, Kuwait and Jordan. The situation of Palestinians within the boundaries of the old mandate is discussed in Alexander Scholch (ed.), *Palestinians over the Green Line: Studies on the Relations between Palestinians on Both Sides of the 1949 Armistice Line since 1967* (1983). The impact of Israeli settlement on the West Bank is covered in

David Newman (ed.), *The Impact of Gush Emunim: Politics and Settlement in the West Bank* (1985); see also Robert I. Friedman, *The False Prophet: Rabbi Meir Kahane from FBI Informant to Knesset Membership* (1990).

The Palestinian uprising (intifada)

The background to the intifada is discussed in David McDowall, *Palestine and Israel: The Uprising and Beyond* (1988); Geoffrey Aronson, *Israel, Palestinians and the Intifada: Creating Facts on the West Bank* (1990). Ze'ev Schiff and Ehud Ya'ari, *Intifada: The Palestinian Uprising – Israel's Third Front* (1990) is an account by Israeli journalists. Don Peretz, *Intifada: The Palestinian Uprising* (1990) examines the impact of the uprising not only in the occupied territories but on Israeli life. Zachary Lockman and Joel Beinin (eds), *Intifada. The Palestinian Uprising against Israeli Occupation* (1990) is a wide-ranging collection of essays including one by Edward W. Said, as well as eyewitness accounts and overall analyses of the perspectives in which the intifada can be considered. Michael C. Hudson (ed.), *The Palestinians. New Directions* (1990) is a collection of essays on the implications of the intifada for the Palestinian people. See also Martin Wright (ed.), *Israel and the Palestinians* (1989); *Middle East Report*, 20 (1990); Helena Cobban, 'The PLO and the *Intifada*', *The Middle East Journal* 44 (1990), pp. 207–33; Don Peretz, 'The *intifada* and Middle East Peace', *Survival* XXXII (1990), pp. 387–401.

11. War in Lebanon

Background history

H. Cobban, *The Making of Modern Lebanon* (1985) is a lucid and readable account of Lebanon's development and unravels the intricacies of the country's religious and sectarian groups.

Lebanese civil war

Analyses of the civil war in Lebanon, 1975–6, and its immediate aftermath include: Harald Vocke, *The Lebanese War. Its Origins and Political Dimensions* (1978); Walid Khalidi, *Conflict and Violence in Lebanon: Confrontation in the Middle East* (1979); John Bullock, *Death of a Country. The Civil War in Lebanon* (1977); Marius Deeb, *The Lebanese Civil War* (1980); P. Edward Haley and Lewis W. Snider (eds), *Lebanon in Crisis. Participants and Issues* (1979); David Gilmour, *Leba-*

non. The Fractured Country (1983). The significance of the disappearance of Musa al-Sadr, a Shiite community leader, while on a visit to Libya in 1978 is discussed in Fouad Ajami, *The Vanished Imam: Musa al Sadr and the Shia of Lebanon* (1986). Rex Brynen, *Sanctuary and Survival. The PLO in Lebanon* (1990) focuses on the PLO's efforts to maintain a political and military base of operations in Lebanon, and covers the period from 1969 to after the 1982 war.

Israeli invasion in 1982

Jonathan Randal, *The Tragedy of Lebanon. Christian Warlords, Israeli Adventurers and American Bunglers* (1983) is a contemporary account by a journalist of the Israeli invasion of Lebanon in 1982, based on interview material. Itamar Rabinovich, *The War for Lebanon, 1975– 1983* (1984) is, in effect, an Israeli account which assesses the role of Syria and Israel in the conflict, while the book by two Israeli journalists, Ze'ev Schiff and Ehud Ya'ari, *Israel's Lebanon War* (1985) exposes the role of Sharon and other Israeli leaders. Revealing material on Sharon's position can be found in Uzi Benziman, *Sharon – An Israeli Caesar* (1986), and Stephen Green, *Living by the Sword. America and Israel in the Middle East 1968–87* (1988). See also: *The Beirut Massacre: The Complete Kahan Commission Report* (1983).

A devastating critique of American and Israeli policy is offered by George W. Ball, *Error and Betrayal in Lebanon* (1984). First-hand accounts of the role of American officials can be found in Caspar Weinberger, *Fighting for Peace* (1990) and Alexander M. Haig, *Caveat. Realism, Reagan, and Foreign Policy* (1984).

Richard A. Gabriel, *Operation Peace for Galilee* (1984) is a contemporary account of the Israeli invasion; the consequences for Israeli society are discussed in Adam Keller, *Terrible Days. Social Divisions and Political Paradoxes in Israel* (1987), and Michael Jansen, *Dissonance in Zion* (1987). There is also a report by the non-governmental commission of international lawyers and human rights activists: *Israel in Lebanon: The Report of the International Commission to enquire into Reported Violations of International Law by Israel during its Invasion of Lebanon* (1983).

An overall account of Israel's involvement in Lebanon is offered in Yair Evron, *War and Intervention in Lebanon: The Israeli–Syrian Deterrence Dialogue* (1987).

Shiite politics

Augustus Richard Norton, *Amal and the Shi'a. Struggle for the Soul of Lebanon* (1987) tells the story of Shiite politics from the point of view of an American military observer in the United Nations Truce Supervision Organization in south Lebanon.

Social and regional factors

Recent collections of papers which also cover social and regional factors include: Naddim Shehadi and Dana Haffar Mills (eds), *Lebanon; A History of Conflict and Consensus* (1988); and Halim Barakat, *Toward a Viable Lebanon* (1988).

Peacekeeping operations

Peacekeeping operations are covered in: Istvan Pogany, *The Arab League and Peacekeeping in the Lebanon* (1987); John Mackinlay, *The Peacekeepers: An Assessment of Peacekeeping Operations at the Arab–Israel Interface* (1989); Bjorn Skogmo, *UNIFIL: International Peacekeeping in Lebanon, 1978–1988* (1988).

12. The Iran–Iraq War

Background to conflict

Tareq Y. Ismael (ed.), *Iraq and Iran. Roots of Conflict* (1982) is a useful collection of documents and maps covering the legal and historical background to the conflict, while Jasim M. Abdulghani, *Iraq & Iran: The Years of Crisis* (1984) is a narrative historical account of the relationship up to the outbreak of the war, with a bias towards the Iraqi side. The disputed border and the 'Algiers Agreement' of 1975 is covered in Kaiyan Homi Kaikobad, *The Shatt-al-Arab Boundary Question. A Legal Reappraisal* (1988). An early collection of apposite essays on the background to the conflict, as well as accounts of the implications for the oil industry and minorities, is Shirin Tahir-Kheli and Shaheen Ayubi (eds), *The Iran–Iraq War. New Weapons, Old Conflicts* (1983). Another early collection, based on the proceedings of a conference at Exeter in July 1982, offers background contributions mainly from the Iraqi perspective and some accounts of the war, 1980–2: M.S. El Azhary (ed.), *The Iran–Iraq War. An Historical, Economic and Political Analysis* (1984).

Accounts of war and role of Gulf states

The relationship between Iraq and the six Gulf states, an analysis of the financial aid to Iraq from Arab states (particularly Saudi Arabia and Kuwait), as well as an assessment of cultural relations can in found in the competently researched volume by Gerd Nonneman, *Iraq, and the Gulf States & the War: A Changing Relationship, 1980–1986 and Beyond* (1986). Majid Khadduri, *The Gulf War. The Origins and Implications of the Iraq–Iran Conflict* (1988) offers an overall perspective, including an analysis of the significance of the role of the Gulf states, mainly from the Iraqi viewpoint, while John Bullock and Harvey Morris, *The Gulf War: Its Origins, History and Consequences* (1989) lean towards sympathies with the Iranian side in what is more a political account than a description of military battles.

Military dimension
The military dimension is emphasized in Edgar O'Ballance, *The Gulf War* (1988).

International and regional dimensions
Works emphasizing the international and regional dimensions of the war include: M.E. Ahari (ed.), *The Gulf and International Security: The 1980s and Beyond* (1989); and Hanns W. Maull and Otto Pick (eds), *The Gulf War: Regional and International Dimensions* (1989).

Postwar accounts
Postwar accounts include the readable overview (without references) by Dilip Hiro, *The Longest War. The Iran–Iraq Military Conflict* (1989); and a collection of essays assessing the domestic, regional and international implications, Efraim Karsh (ed.), *The Iran–Iraq War. Impact and Implications* (1989).

13. The Gulf War

An account of the rise of Saddam Hussein, written against the background of the Gulf crisis of 1990, can be found in Judith Miller and Laurie Mylroie, *Saddam Hussein and the Crisis in the Gulf* (1990); see also Efraim Karsh and Inari Rautsi, *Saddam Hussein. A Political Biography* (1991). For collections of documents on the background to the war, see Cambridge International Documents Series, Vol. I, *The Kuwait Crisis: Basic Documents* (1991); Vol. 2, *The Kuwait Crisis: Sanctions and their Economic Consequences* (1991). Pierre Salinger with Eric Laurent, *Secret Dossier. The Hidden Agenda behind the Gulf War* (1991) is an account by the former press secretary of President John F. Kennedy. An Arab journalist's insider account can be found in Adel

Darwish and Gregory Alexander, *Unholy Babylon. The Secret History of Saddam's War* (1991). For a collection of articles on the response of fundamentalist movements to the Gulf War see James Piscatori (ed.), *Islamic Fundamentalism and the Gulf Crisis* (1991). See also Mohamed Heikal, *Illusions of Triumph. An Arab View of the Gulf War* (1992); Amatzia Baram and Barry Rubin (eds), *Iraq's Road to War* (London, 1993). Aharin Levran, *Israeli Strategy after Desert Storm. Lessons of the Second Gulf War* (1997) offers an Israeli perspective. Narrative accounts include: John Bulloch and Harvey Morris, *Saddam's War. The Origins of the Kuwait Conflict and the International Response* (1991); Dilip Hiro, *Desert Shield to Desert Storm. The Second Gulf War* (1992); Lawrence Freedman and Efraim Karsh, *The Gulf Conflict 1990–1991. Diplomacy and War in the New World Order* (1993); Rick Atkinson, *Crusade. The Untold Story of the Gulf War* (1994). International perspectives of the Gulf War are analysed in Ken Matthews, *The Gulf Conflict and International Relations* (1993); Alex Danchev and Dan Keohane, *International Perspectives on the Gulf Conflict 1990–91* (1994).

The conflict between Iraq and Kuwait which culminated in the Gulf War of 1990–1 has produced a spate of works inclined to characterise Saddam Hussein as a villainous dictator and the coalition that fought him as an heroic alliance. This literature has often had a hidden agenda: its implicit concern has been the continued existence of the State of Israel at the time of the ending of the Cold War, and it has done little to explain why Saddam Hussein became a hero to so many ordinary Arabs and why the United Nations was prepared to enforce resolutions against Iraq but not against Israel. *War in the Gulf, 1990–91: The Iraq–Kuwait Conflict and Its Implications* (1997) by Majid Khadduri and Edmund Ghareeb offers an alternative explanation, and continues the earlier attempt by Heikal to challenge the conventional Western view. Unlike many of the previous tomes, the concentration here is not on military strategy, but on the political and legal aspects. There is a detailed analysis of Iraq's historical claims to Kuwait considered in the context of imperial history.

Short list of reference works consulted

Adams, Michael (ed.), *Handbooks to the Modern World. The Middle East* (1988)
Allen, R.E. (ed.), *The Concise Oxford Dictionary of Current English* (1990) for adoption of Arabic words.
The Annual Obituary, 9 vols (1980–8), (1981–9)
BBC Monitoring. Summary of World Broadcasts
BP Statistical Review of World Energy (June 1997)
The Christian Science Monitor
Current History
The Economist
The Guardian (London)
Hiro, Dilip, *Dictionary of the Middle East* (1996)
The Independent (London)
The Independent on Sunday (London)
Information Please Almanac, Atlas & Yearbook 1990 (1990)
The International Who's Who 1990–91 (1990)
Israeli Mirror
Janke, Peter with Richard Sim, *Guerrilla and Terrorist Organizations: A World Directory and Bibliography* (1983)
Keesing's Record of World Events
Laffin, John, *Know the Middle East* (1985)
Mansfield, Peter (ed.), *The Middle East. A Political and Economic Survey* (5th edn, 1980)
The Middle East and North Africa 1997, Europa Publications (1996)
Middle East International
Middle East Journal
Monthly Bulletin of Statistics, United Nations Department of International Economic and Social Affairs (September 1990)
Mostyn, Trevor and Albert Hourani (eds), *The Cambridge Encyclopedia of the Middle East and North Africa* (1988)
New York Times International
Obituaries from The Times 1951–75, 3 vols (1975–9)
The Observer (London)
Paxton, John (ed.), *The Statesman's Year Book*
Shimoni, Yaacov and Evyatar Levine (eds), *Political Dictionary of the*

Middle East in the Twentieth Century (1972)

Spuler, Bertold, *Rulers and Governments of the World*, vols 2 and 3 (1977)

Time

The Times (London)

Truhart, Peter, *International Directory of Foreign Ministers 1589–1989* (1989)

Truhart, Peter, *Regents of Nations. Systematic Chronology of States and Their Political Representatives in Past and Present*, parts I and II (1984–5)

Vronskaya, Jeanne, *A Biographical Dictionary of the Soviet Union 1917–1988* (1989)

Who Was Who 1897–1980, 7 vols (1920–81)

Who Was Who in America, 7 vols (1943–85)

Who's Who 1997 (1997)

Who's Who in the Arab World 1990–1991 (1991)

Who's Who in France 1979–80 (1979)

Who's Who in Israel and Jewish Personalities from all over the World (1985)

Who's Who in Lebanon 1988–89 (1988)

Economic and social statistics

1. Proved oil reserves at end of 1996

Reserve Production (R/P) ratio. If the reserves remaining at the end of any year are divided by the production in that year, the result is the length of time that those remaining reserves would last if production were to continue at the current level.

	Thousand million tonnes	Thousand million barrels	Share of total	R/P ratio
North America				
USA	3.7	29.8	2.9%	9.7
Canada	0.8	6.9	0.7%	9.4
Mexico	7.0	48.8	4.7%	42.7
Total North America	***11.5***	***85.5***	***8.3%***	***18.1***
S. & Cent. America				
Argentina	0.3	2.4	0.2%	8.2
Brazil	0.7	4.8	0.4%	16.5
Colombia	0.4	2.8	0.3%	12.1
Ecuador	0.3	2.1	0.2%	14.8
Peru	0.1	0.8	0.1%	18.3
Trinidad & Tobago	0.1	0.6	0.1%	11.3
Venezuela	9.3	64.9	6.2%	57.5
Others	0.1	0.8	0.1%	22.9
Total S. & Cent. America	***11.3***	***79.2***	***7.6%***	***36.1***
Europe				
Denmark	0.1	1.0	0.1%	12.3
Italy	0.1	0.7	0.1%	18.0
Norway	1.5	11.2	1.1%	9.3
Romania	0.2	1.6	0.2%	32.2
United Kingdom	0.6	4.5	0.4%	4.6
Others	0.2	1.5	0.1%	10.1
Total Europe	***2.7***	***20.5***	***2.0%***	***8.2***
Former Soviet Union				
Azerbaijan	1.0	7.0	0.7%	*
Kazakhstan	1.1	8.0	0.8%	47.7
Russian Federation	6.7	48.7	4.7%	22.1
Uzbekistan	0.1	0.6	0.1%	10.9
Others	0.2	1.2	0.1%	14.2
Total Former Soviet Union	***9.1***	***65.5***	***6.4%***	***25.5***

Table continued

	Thousand million tonnes	Thousand million barrels	Share of total	R/P ratio
Middle East				
Iran	12.7	93.0	9.0%	69.1
Iraq	15.1	112.0	10.8%	*
Kuwait	13.3	96.5	9.3%	*
Oman	0.7	5.1	0.5%	15.8
Qatar	0.5	3.7	0.4%	22.5
Saudi Arabia	35.8	261.5	25.2%	83.4
Syria	0.4	2.5	0.2%	11.3
United Arab Emirates	12.6	97.8	9.4%	*
Yemen	0.5	4.0	0.4%	30.0
Others	†	0.2	†	12.1
Total Middle East	**91.6**	**676.3**	**65.2%**	**93.1**
Africa				
Algeria	1.2	9.2	0.9%	19.4
Angola	0.7	5.4	0.5%	20.9
Cameroon	0.1	0.4	†	10.8
Congo	0.2	1.5	0.1%	17.9
Egypt	0.5	3.7	0.4%	11.4
Gabon	0.2	1.3	0.1%	10.2
Libya	3.9	29.5	2.8%	56.4
Nigeria	2.1	15.5	1.5%	19.9
Tunisia	†	0.3	†	9.5
Others	0.1	0.7	0.1%	17.2
Total Africa	**9.0**	**67.5**	**6.4%**	**25.0**
Asia Pacific				
Australia	0.2	1.8	0.2%	8.5
Brunei	0.2	1.4	0.1%	23.0
China	3.3	24.0	2.3%	20.7
India	0.6	4.3	0.4%	16.5
Indonesia	0.7	5.0	0.5%	8.6
Malaysia	0.5	4.0	0.4%	15.4
Papua New Guinea	†	0.3	†	7.1
Vietnam	0.1	0.6	0.1%	9.7
Other Asia Pacific	0.1	1.0	0.1%	13.1
Total Asia Pacific	**5.7**	**42.4**	**4.1%**	**15.7**
TOTAL WORLD	**140.9**	**1036.9**	**100.0%**	**42.2**
Of which OECD	14.2	105.8	10.2%	14.5
Of which OPEC	107.2	788.6	76.1%	78.6
Of which non-OPEC ◊	24.7	182.7	17.6%	15.2

*Over 100 years
†Less than 0.05
◊ Excludes Former Soviet Union
Source: *BP Statistical Review of World Energy*, June 1997.

2. World oil production (thousand barrels daily), 1986, 1991, 1996*

	1986	1991	1996	Change 1996 over 1995	1996 share of total
North America					
USA	10230	9075	**8300**	− 0.3%	11.4%
Canada	1805	1980	**2460**	+ 2.4%	3.4%
Mexico	2760	3125	**3280**	+ 8.1%	4.9%
Total North America	*14795*	*14180*	*14040*	*+ 2.1%*	*19.7%*
S. & Cent. America					
Argentina	465	525	**805**	+ 7.4%	1.2%
Brazil	590	645	**800**	+ 13.5%	1.2%
Colombia	305	430	**635**	+ 7.4%	1.0%
Ecuador	300	305	**395**	− 0.2%	0.6%
Peru	180	115	**120**	− 1.4%	0.2%
Trinidad & Tobago	170	150	**140**	− 1.3%	0.2%
Venezuela	1885	2500	**3145**	+ 6.6%	4.8%
Others	90	80	**100**	+ 5.9%	0.1%
Total S. & Cent. America	*3985*	*4750*	*6140*	*+ 6.8%*	*9.3%*
Europe					
Denmark	75	145	**215**	+ 12.0%	0.3%
Italy	50	85	**105**	+ 3.6%	0.2%
Norway	905	1985	**3315**	+ 12.2%	4.6%
Romania	220	145	**140**	− 2.0%	0.2%
United Kingdom	2665	1915	**2735**	− 0.3%	3.9%
Others	570	505	**415**	− 5.8%	0.6%
Total Europe	*4485*	*4780*	*6925*	*+ 5.3%*	*9.8%*
Former Soviet Union					
Azerbaijan	270	240	**185**	− 0.7%	0.3%
Kazakhstan	485	570	**480**	+ 11.3%	0.7%
Russian Federation	11295	9320	**6075**	− 1.9%	9.0%
Uzbekistan	60	70	**165**	—	0.2%
Others	325	270	**255**	+ 15.1%	0.3%
Total Former Soviet Union	*12435*	*10470*	*7160*	*− 0.5%*	*10.5%*

Table continued

	1986	1991	1996	Change 1996 over 1995	1996 share of total
Middle East					
Iran	2060	3500	**3715**	+ 0.3%	5.5%
Iraq	1895	280	**590**	+ 9.6%	0.8%
Kuwait	1365	200	**2155**	+ 2.7%	3.2%
Oman	565	715	**895**	+ 3.8%	1.3%
Qatar	355	420	**475**	+ 2.4%	0.6%
Saudi Arabia	5210	8820	**8920**	+0.5%	12.8%
Syria	200	470	**605**	+ 1.0%	0.9%
United Arab Emirates	1595	2640	**2600**	+ 3.2%	3.5%
Yemen	10	105	**370**	+ 5.0%	0.5%
Others	50	55	**50**	+ 0.3%	0.1%
Total Middle East	*1305*	*17295*	*20375*	*+ 1.5%*	*29.2%*
Africa					
Algeria	1195	1345	**1395**	+ 5.6%	1.8%
Angola	280	500	**710**	+15.3%	1.0%
Cameroon	175	145	**100**	− 4.3%	0.2%
Congo	120	160	**230**	+23.2%	0.3%
Egypt	810	900	**900**	− 3.0%	1.3%
Gabon	165	295	**360**	+ 1.7%	0.5%
Libya	1065	1540	**1440**	+ 0.3%	2.1%
Nigeria	1465	1890	**2150**	+ 8.0%	3.2%
Tunisia	110	110	**90**	− 1.5%	0.1%
Others	60	35	**110**	+92.7%	0.2%
Total Africa	*5445*	*6920*	*7485*	*+ 5.6%*	*10.7%*
Asia Pacific					
Australia	580	605	**615**	+ 6.1%	0.8%
Brunei	165	165	**165**	− 5.3%	0.2%
China	2620	2830	**3170**	+ 6.4%	4.7%
India	660	700	**745**	− 5.9%	1.0%
Indonesia	1430	1670	**1640**	+ 4.5%	2.3%
Malaysia	510	660	**725**	+ 0.3%	1.0%
Papua New Guinea	—	—	**105**	+ 6.3%	0.2%
Vietnam	—	80	**170**	+12.7%	0.3%
Others	170	220	**225**	+ 2.5%	0.3%
Total Asia Pacific	*6135*	*6930*	*7560*	*+ 3.8%*	*10.8%*
TOTAL WORLD	*60585*	*65325*	*69685*	*+ 2.9%*	*100.0%*
Of which OECD	19505	19350	**21375**	+ 3.3%	29.9%
Of which OPEC	19515	24800	**28225**	+ 2.8%	40.5%
Of which Non-OPEC †	28635	30045	**34295**	+ 3.8%	49.0%

* Includes crude oil, shale oil, oil sands and NGLs (natural gas liquids – the liquid content of natural gas where this is recovered separately)
Excludes liquid fuels from other sources such as coal derivatives.
† Excludes Former Soviet Union
Note: Annual changes and shares of total are on a weight basis

Source: *BP Statistical Review of World Energy,* June 1997.

3. World oil consumption (thousand barrels daily), 1986, 1991, 1996*

	1986	1991	1996	Change 1996 over 1995	1996 share of total
North America					
USA ♦	15665	16000	**17400**	+ 3.1%	25.2%
Canada	1540	1630	**1735**	+ 4.1%	2.4%
Mexico	1230	1520	**1605**	+ 3.3%	2.2%
Total North America	*18435*	*19150*	*20740*	*+ 3.2%*	*29.8%*
S. & Cent. America					
Argentina	430,9	410	**445**	+ 4.9%	0.6%
Brazil	1210	1290	**1600**	+ 7.1%	2.2%
Chile	100	150	**225**	+ 8.6%	0.3%
Colombia	175	215	**275**	+ 3.7%	0.4%
Venezuela	390	405	**425**	− 5.3%	0.6%
Others	1010	1145	**1365**	+ 4.0%	2.0%
Total S. & Cent. America	*3315*	*3615*	*4335*	*+ 4.4%*	*6.1%*
Europe					
Austria	215	240	**240**	+ 1.6%	0.3%
Belgium & Luxembourg	485	545	**595**	+ 8.6%	0.9%
Bulgaria	220	120	**1135**	+ 7.7%	0.2%
Czech Republic	210	145	**155**	+ 1.6%	0.2%
Denmark	215	185	**235**	+ 8.7%	0.3%
Finland	230	220	**215**	+ 3.4%	0.3%
France	1830	2020	**1930**	+ 2.1%	2.8%
Germany	2810	2835	**2920**	+ 1.6%	4.2%
Greece	250	325	**375**	+ 4.8%	0.6%
Hungary	200	170	**145**	− 8.0%	0.2%
Iceland	10	15	**15**	+ 2.5%	†
Republic of Ireland	100	100	**120**	+ 3.4%	0.2%
Italy	1770	1920	**1955**	− 0.8%	2.8%
Netherlands	700	765	**810**	− 1.6%	1.1%
Norway	200	195	**230**	+ 8.9%	0.3%
Poland	350	315	**360**	+10.2%	0.5%
Portugal	195	240	**255**	− 6.3%	0.4%
Romania	320	310	**280**	+ 2.7%	0.4%
Slovakia	120	85	**80**	+ 0.7%	0.1%
Spain	925	1055	**1220**	+ 4.2%	1.8%
Sweden	385	325	**360**	+ 8.3%	0.5%
Switzerland	280	275	**260**	+ 3.5%	0.4%
Turkey	375	470	**615**	+ 1.4%	0.9%
United Kingdom	1645	765	**1790**	+ 2.5%	2.5%
Others	360	350	**285**	+ 0.6%	0.4%
Total Europe	*14400*	*14990*	*15580*	*+ 2.2%*	*22.3%*
Former Soviet Union					
Azerbaijan	175	165	**170**	—	0.3%
Belarus	600	480	**245**	+ 0.1%	0.4%
Kazakhstan	375	435	**225**	−6.1%	0.3%
Russian Federation	4970	4890	**2565**	−12.4%	3.9%
Turkmenistan	70	100	**80**	+ 0.3%	0.1%

Table continued

	1986	1991	1996	Change 1996 over 1995	1996 share of total
Ukraine	1270	1155	345	− 8.5%	0.5%
Uzbekistan	235	220	130	− 2.1%	0.2%
Others	705	550	175	+ 1.2%	0.3%
Total Former Soviet Union	*8400*	*7995*	*3935*	*− 9.4%*	*6.0%*
Middle East					
Iran	865	995	1170	− 3.9%	1.7%
Saudi Arabia	975	1175	1160	+ 3.7%	1.6%
United Arab Emirates	175	320	335	+ 0.8%	0.5%
Others	1005	990	1295	+ 2.8%	1.9%
Total Middle East	*3020*	*3480*	*3960*	*+ 0.7%*	*5.7%*
Africa					
Algeria	180	205	215	—	0.3%
Egypt	420	470	500	+ 5.6%	0.7%
South Africa	290	360	435	+ 2.6%	0.6%
Others	805	975	1170	+ 3.9%	1.7%
Total Africa	*1695*	*2010*	*2320*	*+ 3.7%*	*3.3%*
Asia Pacific					
Australia	610	675	785	+ 1.1%	1.1%
Bangladesh	35	35	50	+ 3.9%	0.1%
China	2010	2410	3615	+ 7.3%	5.2%
India	935	1220	1630	+ 7.9%	2.4%
Indonesia	465	675	900	+ 9.4%	1.3%
Japan	4495	5410	5830	+ 0.5%	8.1%
Malaysia	195	290	395	+ 3.4%	0.6%
New Zealand	85	110	125	+ 2.5%	0.2%
Pakistan	165	230	340	+13.6%	0.5%
Philippines	160	225	360	+ 4.4%	0.5%
Singapore	265	380	510	− 1.1%	0.8%
South Korea	590	1255	2145	+ 6.9%	3.1%
Taiwan	395	570	725	− 0.3%	1.1%
Thailand	240	445	785	+ 9.4%	1.1%
Others	325	345	480	+ 7.1%	0.7%
Total Asia Pacific	*10970*	*14275*	*18675*	*+ 4.4%*	*26.8%*
TOTAL WORLD	*60235*	*65515*	*69545*	*+ 2.4%*	*100.0%*
Of which OECD	36455	38985	41775	+ 2.4%	59.6%
Of which European Union 15	11755	12540	13020	+ 2.0%	18.7%
Of which Other EMEs ◊	13810	17185	22550	+ 4.8%	32.6%

*   Inland demand plus international aviation and marine bunkers and refinery fuel and loss
♦   US processing gain (834,000 b/d in 1996) has been deducted
†   Less than 0.05
◊   Excludes Central Europe and Former Soviet Union
Note: •
Differences between world production and consumption figures are accounted for by stock changes, consumption of non-petroleum additives and substitute fuels, and unavoidable disparities in the definition, measurement or conversion of oil supply and demand data. Annual changes and shares of total are on a weight basis

Source: *BP Statistical Review of World Energy,* June 1997.

4. Oil imports and exports, 1996*

	Million tonnes				Thousand barrels daily			
	Crude imports	Product imports	Crude exports	Product exports	Crude imports	Product imports	Crude exports	Product exports
USA	373.6	92.0	4.9	42.2	7482	1918	98	880
Canada	34.1	6.8	55.8	17.6	683	142	1118	367
Mexico	–	8.3	77.4	5.1	–	173	1550	106
S. & Cent. America	54.3	15.8	102.9	45.6	1087	329	2061	951
Western Europe	389.8	83.1	49.5	36.2	7807	1732	991	755
Former Soviet Union & Cent. Europe	19.6	12.6	76.6	55.9	393	263	1534	1165
Middle East	4.5	3.7	741.8	111.0	90	77	14856	2314
North Africa	7.1	5.2	104.6	31.7	142	108	2095	661
West Africa	2.0	6.5	142.8	2.7	40	136	2860	56
East & Southern Africa	22.4	4.0	–	–	449	83	–	–
China	22.6	15.8	20.9	3.3	453	325	419	69
Other Asia Pacific	259.6	94.4	49.3	49.6	5199	1968	987	1034
Japan	226.1	55.5	–	6.2	4528	1157	–	129
Australasia	22.9	3.8	9.2	4.7	459	79	184	98
Destination not known*	10.0	23.0	12.9	18.7	200	479	258	390
TOTAL WORLD	1448.6	430.5	1448.6	430.5	29012	8975	29012	8975

* Includes changes in the quantity of oil in transit, movements not otherwise shown, unidentified military use, etc

Notes:

Bunkers are not included as exports

Intra-area movements (for example between individual countries in Western Europe) are excluded

Source: *BP Statistical Review of World Energy*, June 1997.

5. Population estimates (thousands)

	1937	1950	1955	1960	1965	1970	1976	1980	1985	1989	1995
Bahrain	82	110	128	147	185	198	266	344	422	499	600
Egypt	16,008	20,393	23,063	25,948	29,600	33,330	38,228	42,133	48,500	53,080	62,900
Iran	16,200	16,276	18,325	20,182	23,428	29,260	33,592	39,300	47,820	54,200	67,300
Iraq	3,940	5,278	6,152	7,085	7,160	9,440	11,505	13,240	15,580	18,280	20,400
Israel	386[1]	1,258	1,748	2,114	2,563	2,910	3,591	3,880	4,230	4,510	5,600
Jordan	442[2]	1,269	1,437	1,695	1,976	2,320	2,779	2,920	3,510	4,100	5,400
Kuwait	n.a.	n.a.	n.a.	223	475	710	1,066	1,370	1,710	2,050	1,500
Lebanon	925	1,257	1,466	1,646	2,330	2,790	2,961	2,670	2,670	2,900	3,000
Oman	500	550	550	565	565	750	n.a.	980	1,190	1,420	2,200
Palestinian Affairs (West Bank & Gaza Strip)	–	–	–	–	–	–	–	–	–	564[3]	860
Qatar	16	20[4]	35	45	70	80	190	230	300	420	600
Saudi Arabia	6,130	n.a.	6,036[6]	n.a.	6,750	7,740	7,013[5]	9,370	11,590	14,430	17,900
Sudan	6,880	n.a.	10,263[6]	11,770	13,540	15,700	16,126	18,680	21,820	24,480	28,100
Syria	2,628	3,215	3,681	4,555	5,300	6,250	7,595	8,700	10,270	11,720	14,700
United Arab Emirates	76	80	80	86	111	200	656[7]	1,010	1,350	1,550	1,900
Yemen (Aden)	650	100[8]	139[8]	1,155	1,240	1,440	1,749	n.a.	2,100	2,200	–
Yemen (Sanaa)	3,990	4,500	n.a.	5,000	5,000	5,700	6,400	n.a.	8,710	9,300	–
Yemen	–	–	–	–	–	–	–	–	–	–	14,500

[1] Jewish population of Palestine only. Palestine 1,383,000. [2] Excluding West Jordan. [3] Figure is a 1988 estimate. [4] 1949. [5] 1974 census. [6] 1950. [7] 1975 census. [8] Aden Colony only.

Sources: Peter Mansfield (ed.), The Middle East. A Political and Economic Survey (5th edn, 1980); Monthly Bulletin of Statistics (United Nations Department of International Economic and Social Affairs), XLIV (9) September 1990, pp. 1–5; Keesing's Record of World Events (Catermill Publishing), Vol. 42, Reference Supplement 1996.

6. Economic and social summary

	Life expectancy (years)		Adult literacy (% of adult population)		Infant mortality (per 1,000 live births)		Urban population (% of population)		Government spending (% of GDP)			GNP per capita 1993
	1960	1993	1970	1995	1960	1992	1960	1992	Education 1990	Health 1990	Defence 1993	
Algeria	47	67	25	62	270	55	30	53	9.1	5.4	2.5	1,650
Bahrain	–	72	–	85	17	21	75	83	4.8	6	5.5	7,870
Egypt	46	64	35	51	300	57	38	44	3.8	1	4.8	660
Iran	50	66	29	72	254	65	34	58	4.6[1991]	1.5	4.3	2,190[1992]
Iraq	48	66	34	58[1992]	222	58	43	73	3.7[1989]	–	15.3	1,940[1989]
Israel	69	77	89	95[1992]	40	9	76	92	8.9	4.2[1991]	9.8	13,760
Jordan	47	70	47	87	218	28	43	69	3.9[1991]	1.8	9.4	1,190
Kuwait	60	75	54	79	128	14	78	96	5.0	–	12.1	23,350
Lebanon	60	69	69	92	92	34	41	85	–	–	4.4	690[1985]
Libya	47	64	37	76	268	68	22	84	9.6[1986]	–	6.3	5,410[1988]
Morocco	47	64	22	44	265	57	29	47	5.2[1991]	0.9	3.8	1,030
Oman	40	70	–	44[1992]	378	20	4	11	3.6[1991]	2.1	15.3	5,600
Palestine	–	71	–	–	36[1993]	–	–	–	–	–	–	3,485[1991]
Qatar	–	72	–	79	36	26	73	79	3.4	3.1	4.4	15,140
Saudi Arabia	44	70	9	63	292	28	30	74	6.2	3.1	13.1	7,940[1992]
Sudan	39	53	17	46	292	99	10	23	4.8[1980]	1.0	11.6	400[1990]
Syria	50	68	40	71	218	36	37	51	4.3[1991]	0.4	8.6	1,170[1991]
UAE	53	74	16	79	239	20	44	82	2.1[1991]	9.0	5.7	22,470
Yemen	–	51	8	41[1992]	–	106	9	31	6.1[1986]	1.5	12.5	520[1991]

Source: Keesing's Record of World Events (Keesing's Worldwide LLC), Vol. 42, Reference Supplement 1996, pp. R156, R159.

Maps

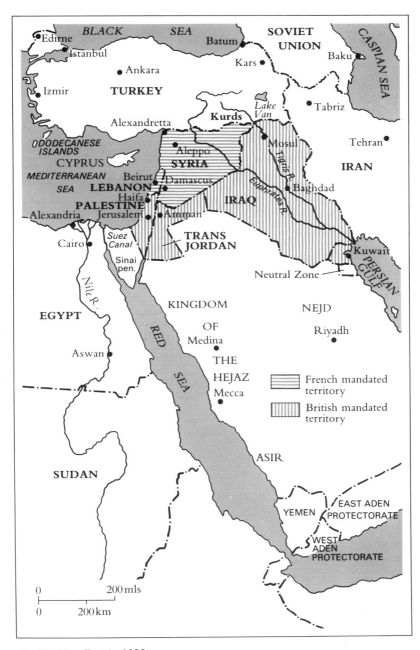

1. *The Near East in 1923*

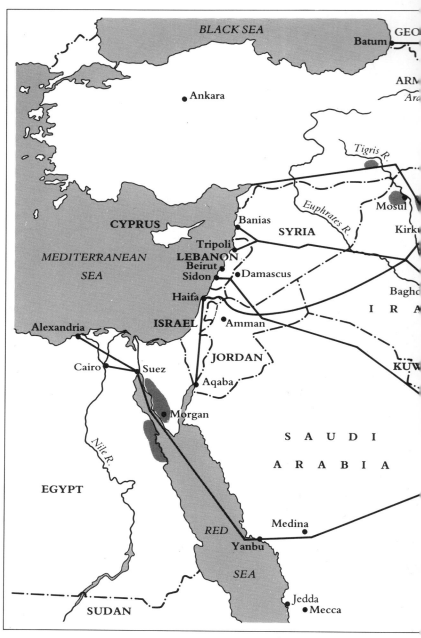

2. *Major oilfields and pipelines in the Near East*

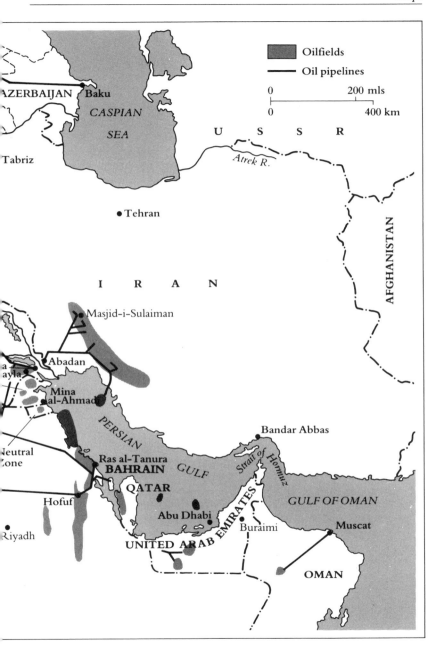

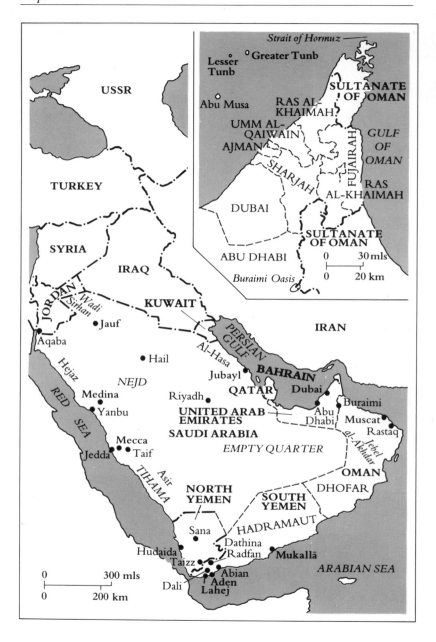

3. Arabia

384

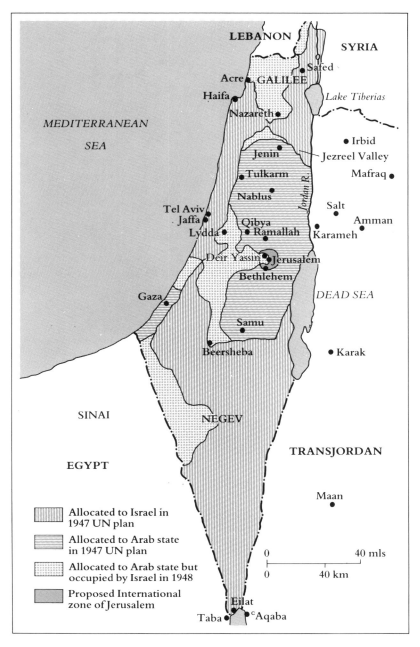

4. Palestine and Transjordan, 1947–8

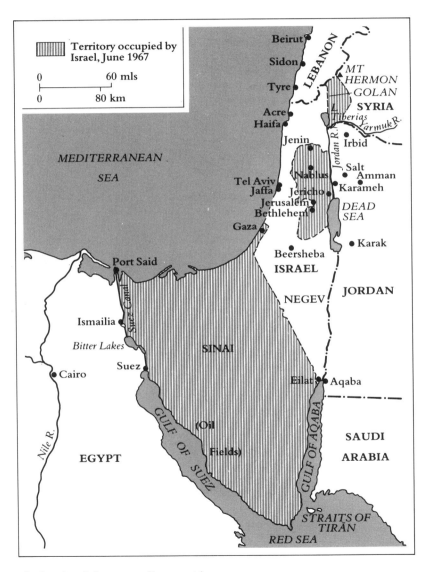

5. *Israel and the surrounding countries*

387

6. *Iran and Iraq*

Index

Note: Page references in **bold** indicate major entries